FOR THE CAUSE OF

LIBERTY

A THOUSAND YEARS
OF IRELAND'S
HEROES

TERRY GOLWAY

SIMON & SCHUSTER

NEW YORK   LONDON   TORONTO   SYDNEY   SINGAPORE

SIMON & SCHUSTER
Rockefeller Center
1230 Avenue of the Americas
New York, NY 10020

SIMON & SCHUSTER and colophon are registered trademarks of
Simon & Schuster, Inc.

Designed by Maura Fadden Rosenthal

Manufactured in the United States of America

10 9 8 7 6 5 4 3 2 1

Library of Congress Cataloging-in-Publication Data

Golway, Terry–
    For the cause of liberty : a thousand years of Ireland's
heroes / Terry Golway.
        p.   cm.
    Includes bibliographical references and index.
    1. Ireland—History.   2. Nationalism—Ireland—
History.   3. Revolutionaries—Ireland—Biography.
4. Nationalists—Ireland—Biography.   5. Heroes—
Ireland—Biography.   I. Title.

DA911   .G57 2000
941.5—dc21   99-058497

ISBN 0-684-85556-9

PHOTO CREDITS

Modern Ireland by R. F. Foster (used by permission of
    Penguin Books Ltd.): p. 8
Drawn by Jeff Ward: p. 12
National Gallery of Ireland: pp. 30, 40, 49, 56, 67, 98
National Museum of Ireland: pp. 16, 57, 62, 91, 103, 112, 124,
    130, 135, 156, 230, 234, 242, 247
National Library of Ireland: pp. 110, 127, 152, 159, 166, 184,
    185, 193, 196, 200, 211, 215, 225, 250, 258, 263
Kelvin Boyes: pp. 285, 288
Courtesy of Linen Hall Library, Victor Patterson Archive,
    Belfast: p. 291
Pacemaker Press International: p. 303
Eamonn Farrell/Photocall: p. 319
Courtesy of *Irish Echo*: pp. 325, 327

FOR KATE AND CONOR

CONTENTS

CHAPTER ONE

CONQUEST

THE FIRST KING of England to dispatch troops to Ireland did so with the blessing of the Pope. The King was Henry II; the Pope was Adrian IV—the only Englishman to sit on the throne of Saint Peter.

Adrian gave his assent in 1155, long before the Reformation, long before religious differences were introduced to Ireland as a means of distinguishing friend from foe. Henry II and Adrian considered themselves modernizers, and Ireland, they decided, required modernizing. The native people who populated the island, the Gaels, were descendants of Celtic tribes who had conquered Ireland and the rest of Europe centuries before the birth of Christ. The Romans never made it to Ireland, and so the Gaelic Irish developed a flourishing civilization and language that bore few traces of Roman influence. But the Irish had enthusiastically embraced the Church of Rome. Patrick, a native of Britain who was kidnapped and sold into slavery in Ireland, converted the island to Christianity without a struggle in the fifth century.

Detached not only from the Continent but from the neighboring island to the east, the Gaels were different, different in their practice of Christianity, different in their law and customs. Religious irregularities such as divorce and the active leadership of women in religious life were permitted in Gaelic Christianity, while little heed was paid to the Papacy. Ireland had a vibrant, distinctive literature, filled with heroic tales of pagan warriors, when the rest of Europe was thrashing through the dark ages. The most famous of these legendary warriors was Cuchulain, a great champion who was slain in defense of his homeland.

In its political life, Ireland, unlike England, had yet to develop a strong, centralized monarchy, although there was no shortage of kings. Indeed, there were dozens, scores, of them scattered throughout the island, ruling over communities called *rí túathe*. While there was a High King, or *ard rí*, he did not rule as Henry ruled in England. The High King's position was mostly ceremonial, although one of them, Brian Boru, gained fame when he united the island's disparate communities and then defeated the Vikings at the Battle of Clontarf in 1014.

The island's customs certainly puzzled its powerful English neighbors, who saw in such cultural difference evidence of ignorance and barbarism. Gaelic Ireland was rural and socially mobile. Land was not enclosed, and property rights were unclear. The family, not the individual, was the basic unit of Gaelic society. When a king died, all male descendants were eligible to succeed him. The eventual successor was chosen in an election and given a Gaelic title—for example, the head of one of Ireland's most prominent families, the O'Neills (or Ui Neills), held the title of The O'Neill. A hereditary class of lawgivers, called Brehons, presided over a complex regulatory system that baffled outsiders. People who considered themselves wronged fasted until their antagonist agreed to submit the dispute to arbitration. Poets were accorded special places in a king's court as well as in society, for they were regarded as the keepers of cultural memory, a unifying force in an island of many small and often fractious kingdoms. Harpers, too, were important members of society's elite—the harp began appearing on Irish coats of arms in the thirteenth century, and it serves as modern Ireland's state emblem.

Pope Adrian made his view of the Gaels clear in giving his blessing to Henry's proposed incursion. "You have expressed to us your desire to enter the island of Ireland in order to subject its people to law and to root out from them the weeds of vice," Adrian wrote to Henry. "We, therefore . . . do hereby declare our will and pleasure that . . . you shall enter that island and execute whatever may tend to the honour of God and the welfare of the land."

These people thought to be trapped in the weeds of vice were, in fact, the keepers of Europe's cultural memory. Just as the Romans hadn't made it to Ireland—a land they called Hibernia because of what seemed to them to be a cold, winterlike climate—neither had the Vandals, Visigoths, and other warriors whose victories over Rome ushered in the dark ages. During the last centuries of the first millennium, Irish monks patiently copied the great works of Western literature, while scholars traveled to devastated Europe to reintroduce the very idea of civilization.

Still, Henry and Adrian believed that the Irish themselves required an introduction to civilization. But Henry didn't act immediately on the Pope's blessing. In the meantime, one of Ireland's many kings, Dermot MacMurrough, was looking for outside help to further his political ambitions on the island. So, in 1167, he invited troops from England—they were French-speaking Normans who had settled in England after William the Conqueror's invasion—to help him. Three years later, the Earl of Pembroke, also known as Strongbow, traveled from England to Ireland to fight alongside MacMurrough. He eventually married MacMurrough's daughter, and when MacMurrough died, Strongbow succeeded him as king of the region known as Leinster, one of Ireland's four provinces. The others became known as Ulster, Munster, and Connaught. Eventually, each province was subdivided into counties, for a total of thirty-two.

Henry II found Strongbow just a bit too ambitious, a possible threat to England's ambitions in Ireland. So, sixteen years after receiving Adrian's approval, he led an expedition to Ireland in 1171 to put Strongbow in his place. The cost of making his point was high: the troops he led into Ireland in 1171 have, in a sense, never left.

From the very beginning of the English presence in Ireland, the invaders regarded the natives as aliens and savages, and themselves as the keepers of civilization. "The Irish live like beasts," complained an English visitor, who insisted that the Irish were "more uncivil, more uncleanly, more barbarous . . . than in any part of the world that is known." Later visitors would complain about a variety of local customs, from drinking the blood of living cattle to the communal ownership of land. Indeed, the more the English saw of Ireland, the more they found reason to be appalled: they didn't like the Irish diet, the overt sexuality of many Irish women (and the fact that married Irish women kept their family names instead of adopting their husband's), even Irish hairstyles and clothing. (Or the lack thereof. One observer remarked that the poor rural Irish "show their shameful parts without any shame.") Pope Adrian's successor, Alexander III, shared this distaste for Gaelic ways. He wrote to Henry II of the "enormities of vice with which the people of Ireland are infected." Alexander said it was up to "the noble king of the English" to bring order to "this barbarous and uncouth race."

But many of the Normans who had marched with Strongbow and some who arrived later with Henry were of a different view. They remained in Ireland, formed settlement communities mostly along the island's east coast, intermarried with the native Gaels, and assimilated into Gaelic Ireland. They were considered, in the phrase of that day,

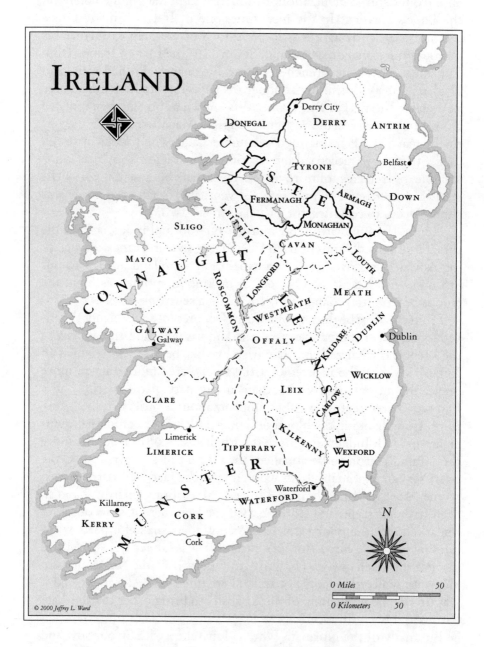

IRELAND

Derry City

DONEGAL   DERRY   ANTRIM

ULSTER

TYRONE   Belfast

FERMANAGH   ARMAGH   DOWN

MONAGHAN

LEITRIM   CAVAN

SLIGO   LOUTH

MAYO   CONNAUGHT   ROSCOMMON   LONGFORD   MEATH

LEINSTER

WESTMEATH

GALWAY   OFFALY   KILDARE   DUBLIN

Galway   Dublin

WICKLOW

CLARE   LEIX   CARLOW

Limerick   KILKENNY

LIMERICK   TIPPERARY   WEXFORD

Waterford

Killarney   MUNSTER   WATERFORD

KERRY   CORK

Cork

N

0 Miles   50

0 Kilometers   50

© 2000 Jeffrey L. Ward

hiberniores hibernis ipsos, or "more Irish than the Irish." Eventually, they would become known as Old English, as opposed to new English settlers who arrived in later centuries.

Henry II did not press his expedition in Ireland, and for centuries there was no systematic attempt to spread the small English settlement. Some Irish chieftains accepted Henry as their lord (but not their king), but some didn't. The Normans established an Irish Parliament in 1297 in an attempt to centralize administration around the old Viking city of Dublin, but its jurisdiction reached only a small portion of the east coast. That area, a few hundred square miles of some of Ireland's most fertile land, was known as the Pale. Outside its borders, Gaelic Ireland made its own laws, lived by its own customs. The people there were said to be "beyond the Pale."

When new English influences began to replace the fading Normans, the Irish Parliament set out to make sure those within the Pale remained apart from those beyond. In 1366, Parliament passed a series of laws, called the Statutes of Kilkenny, designed to prevent the Norman-like assimilation of English settlers into Gaelic Irish society. Among other restrictions, the laws forbade the English living in Ireland from marrying the natives, speaking the Irish language, and playing native Irish sports such as hurling. In addition, Irish "babblers, rhymers [and] harpers" were barred from mixing with the English.

Still unvanquished, Gaelic Ireland remained a threat to the English settlement centered in and around Dublin. Small military engagements were common through the thirteenth and fourteenth centuries, with the Irish often using their knowledge of the terrain to good advantage over the better-equipped English. English political disputes, too, were having an effect on Ireland, as they would for the remainder of the millennium. England's civil conflict, the Wars of the Roses, ended with the ascension of Henry VII, founder of the Tudor dynasty, but portions of the English settlement in Ireland remained loyal to the cause of the defeated Richard III. In an attempt to gain greater control over the country and to tighten England's loose administrative ties to Ireland, the Crown packed the Irish Parliament with Tudor supporters. And, in 1494, the Irish Parliament was persuaded to pass a law subordinating itself to the English Crown. The legislation was called Poyning's Law, named after England's top administrator in Ireland at the time, and it was a milestone in Anglo-Irish relations. Until Poyning's Law, the English settlement could claim to be a self-governing entity under the Crown. The new statute, however, rendered the Irish Parliament meaningless, and the legislature would become a symbol of Ireland's political degradation for nearly four hundred years. The Irish Parliament could pass bills only after the Crown had given its sanction, and could meet only with the monarch's approval. A viceroy, or Lord Lieutenant, was dispatched as the Crown's chief representative in Ireland. An administrative nerve center called Dublin Castle became the seat of English administration for Ireland, and it would continue to serve the Crown until 1922.

Still, the English in Ireland nervously watched as their influence, and indeed the Pale itself, shrank while Gaelic Ireland not only seemed to prosper, but became downright emboldened. The Gaelic leaders recruited well-armed mercenaries from Scotland called gallowglasses. Conflicts between settlers and natives continued to erupt, and the English colonists asked for help from the Pope, who, they hoped, would call for a crusade "against the . . . Irish enemies."

Henry VIII came to the English throne in 1509, and soon there would be no more appeals to the Pope. Rather, the Pope—and those who remained loyal to him—would be considered among the King's enemies. Henry's secession from Rome and his claim to be the spiritual head of the new, state-supported Church of England was a decisive moment in Irish history, changing forever the relationship between the two countries. The Gaelic Irish and the Old English did not abandon Catholicism and refused to accept the King's claim to be a spiritual as well as a political leader. The English already regarded the Gaelic Irish as backward aliens, and Ireland's refusal to disown the Pope was interpreted not only as evidence of Irish ignorance, but also as proof of their disloyalty to the Crown. The Gaelic Irish in turn defensively embraced their Catholicism as a badge of nationality. But it was England, not Ireland, that made political and even racial distinctions between Catholic and Protestant in Ireland, and those distinctions, brutally enforced, would define Irish society for the next five hundred years.

In 1534—the year after he annulled his marriage, married Anne Boleyn, and was excommunicated from the Catholic Church— Henry put down a rebellion led by the son of one of Ireland's most powerful families, Thomas FitzGerald. Members of the FitzGerald family were descendants of Norman settlers and had served both Henry VII and Henry VIII as the Crown's top administrators in Ireland, holding the title of Earl of Kildare. The FitzGeralds moved in two worlds, for they had the respect of Gaelic Ireland even while they served the English Crown. Thomas FitzGerald held the formal, Crown-granted title of Lord Offaly and the informal nickname of Silken Thomas, for he and his allies wore silk fringes on their jackets. Silken Thomas cared little about the politics of religion. But he did care about his family's place as one of Ireland's leading families, and he feared that the FitzGeralds were losing their coveted influence with the King. Silken Thomas was determined to show that London could not take the family for granted. An armed challenge was a rather dramatic way of making his point, and an ineffective one. An English army attacked FitzGerald's forces in Maynooth, County Kildare. The rebels were forced to surrender, and they were promptly given what was called the "pardon of Maynooth." They were executed. Silken Thomas was hanged, and his family's lands confiscated.

Land, Henry decided, could make believers out of dissenters. He demanded that all privately held property in Ireland be surrendered to him so he could regrant the holdings. Landowners therefore would hold their property at the Crown's pleasure, subject to their continued loyalty. Control over the island was made even tighter in 1541, when the Irish Parliament declared Henry VIII to be the King of Ireland instead of merely being its lord. Ireland, Parliament said, was to be "knit forever to the imperial crown of the realm of England." This was a sign of England's new determination to Anglicize its neighbor, politically as well as culturally. Many of Ireland's chieftains and nobles swore their allegiance, with some of them promising to give up their Irish customs and clothes. Henry VIII also was proclaimed head of the new state religion in Ireland, the Church of England, later to become known as the Church of Ireland.

Queen Elizabeth, who succeeded to the throne in 1558, was determined to see that the process of Anglicizing Ireland continued. The Crown organized the provinces of Munster in the south and Connaught in the west, with each supervised by a Crown-appointed president, to bring local government in line with English law and customs. Elizabeth said she wished to direct "that rude and barbarous nation to civility" through "discreet handling rather than by force and the shedding of blood." If, however, force became necessary, she authorized her administrators to "oppose yourself and your forces to those whom reason cannot bridle."

Reason, at least Elizabeth's interpretation of it, indeed was having a hard time in Ireland. As the Queen pushed, the Gaelic Irish pushed back, aware that a struggle for land and power was taking shape. Sporadic but strictly local rebellions were constant and costly, beginning with an uprising in 1559 in Ulster, the northern province and the least penetrated by English influence. Other rebellions broke out in the late 1560s and again ten years later. Gaelic chieftains attempted to link up with England's rivals in Europe, specifically Catholic Spain, and Spanish and Italian troops landed in 1580—eight years before the

Spanish Armada set sail—to help foment rebellion. Elizabeth was forced to garrison Ireland with thousands of troops, an expense that left her nearly bankrupt. The native Irish in the province of Munster found themselves pushed aside to make way for Protestant settlers from England. It was the beginning of the plantation system of colonization, a model that would be followed in other parts of Ireland and in America. If the Irish insisted on disloyalty, then Ireland would have loyalty imposed upon it.

Hugh O'Neill was the Elizabethan ideal of what the Irish ought to become. He was born in 1550 in Dungannon, County Tyrone, the scion of a family that ruled large portions of Ulster. Henry VIII had given Hugh's grandfather Conn Bacach O'Neill the royal title of Earl of Tyrone, and when succession to the earldom was in question, Queen Elizabeth stepped in to bestow young, redheaded Hugh with the title of Baron of Dungannon, heir to Conn Bacach O'Neill. Pa-

Hugh O'Neill

tronage, it was thought, would keep this promising young man in check.

Hugh was educated in Ireland in the style of a young English nobleman. He became a ward of the Crown when his father was murdered by a half-brother, Shane O'Neill, during a feud over control of the family's titles and power. Elizabeth's representatives watched over him closely. One of the Crown's most important advisers, Sir Henry Sidney, invited Hugh to live with him in his castle in Kent. There, Hugh met members of England's most powerful families and lived the life of a sophisticated Elizabethan, dining with diplomats and conversing with literary figures. He was becoming very much the civilized Englishman.

Elizabeth would not say the same of young Hugh's Uncle Shane, an ambitious and unpredictable man who claimed the ancient Gaelic title of The O'Neill, thus asserting leadership of the O'Neill family. He was a drinker who treated his frequent hangovers by burying himself from the neck down in moist sand. There is no record indicating the effectiveness of this remedy, but it is worth noting that Shane kept drinking throughout his short and violent life.

Shane O'Neill resented stepped-up incursions of English administration in Ulster and the military strongholds that were being built to keep people like himself in check. He organized a rebellion in 1559, a year after Elizabeth's coronation, but soon threw himself at the Queen's mercy, prostrating himself in court in 1562 and bemoaning his lack of education and civility. After pledging his loyalty, he was allowed to return to Ulster in peace.

But Shane was soon back on the march, attempting to assert his authority and, at the same time, undermining his nephew Hugh's position as heir to the title of Earl of Tyrone. "My ancestors were Kings of Ulster, Ulster was theirs, and shall be mine," he wrote. He would fight anyone, English or Irish, who threatened his domain.

He rampaged through counties Fermanagh and Armagh in Ulster, but his army finally was defeated not by the Queen's forces, but by his Irish enemies—the O'Donnells, another prominent Ulster family. He was killed after fleeing from the O'Donnells, and his head dispatched to Dublin, where it was mounted on a pike and put on display for four years.

By the the time of Shane's death, Hugh O'Neill was an assimilated, Anglicized Irishman. He spoke English at a time when his countrymen spoke Irish, he was well mannered, and he looked the part of a leader, with his red beard, broad shoulders, and fine dress. He complained of Ireland's refusal to adopt English ways, sentiments that further endeared him to the Crown and inspired hope that here, at last, was an Irish leader who might quell the island's rebelliousness. He returned to his family's castle in Tyrone, joined the Queen's army, and helped put down one of the several rebellions that broke out as Elizabeth attempted to extend her control in Ulster. He served in the Irish Parliament and supported a plan to bring more English colonists into Ireland. And later in life, he married (it was his third wedding) Mabel Bagenal, the young daughter of a former marshal of the English army and the sister of the incumbent marshal.

But the English polish did nothing to diminish O'Neill's interest in family politics. He regarded Shane O'Neill's sons as rivals, and one of them was found in chains, hanging from a tree, after telling the English that Hugh was secretly negotiating with archrival Spain. There was no doubt who committed the murder. Hugh O'Neill was summoned to London to explain himself to Elizabeth's Privy Council. He delivered a long, dissembling treatise on "the ancient form of government among us in Ulster," and got off with a warning.

O'Neill's loyalty was rewarded in 1587, when the Crown gave him the coveted title of Earl of Tyrone, which gave him control over a vast region of Ulster, covering much of what would become the six counties of Northern Ireland. He traveled again to London, and while there he visited local shops in search of furniture and other accessories. He also ordered a supply of lead. It was for the roof of his castle, he explained.

On Christmas Day 1591, a young man escaped from his cell in Dublin Castle after more than three years of harsh imprisonment. He was known as Red Hugh O'Donnell, the eighteen-year-old son of a family whose anti-English sentiments had caused his imprisonment. The government had held Red Hugh in chains to guarantee the family would be peaceful.

The O'Donnells had made peace with their rivals the O'Neills, and Red Hugh himself was Hugh O'Neill's son-in-law. With help from his father-in-law's allies, Red Hugh made his way through bitter cold to his home in Ulster. He suffered terribly from frostbite, and when he finally arrived both big toes had to be amputated. He was determined to exact revenge, but Hugh O'Neill told the English that they needn't worry. In a letter to the Queen, O'Neill promised to "do my best to persuade" Red Hugh to remain loyal to the Crown. "And if he shall not be directed by my counsel . . . I will be as ready to serve against him and scourge him as any man shall be in this kingdom."

Hugh O'Neill served Her Majesty's forces yet again in 1593, when he rode with his brother-in-law Sir Henry Bagenal to oppose a small rebellion led by another of his sons-in-law, Hugh Maguire, who feared losing his lands in County Fermanagh to the English. O'Neill was wounded in one engagement, and complained that Bagenal didn't appreciate his efforts. Meanwhile, Maguire enlisted the help of Red Hugh, who eagerly joined the fledgling rebellion. Two of O'Neill's sons-in-law were on the rebel side.

O'Neill found himself caught between his English training and his Gaelic blood, between loyalty and ambition, between the old order, which still might be preserved, and the new, which threatened everything. In the meantime, he was invested with the title of The O'Neill in a traditional Gaelic ceremony in the town of Tullaghoge. He now held two titles—he was the royal Earl of Tyrone and the Gaelic The O'Neill. England and Ireland waited to see which he held dearer.

Finally, in February 1595, he committed himself. His Gaelic blood prevailed over his English training. He joined forces with Red Hugh O'Donnell and united the often divided factions of Ulster under his command, putting together a well-trained, well-equipped army of some six thousand men. In June, he ambushed forces under the command of his brother-in-law Bagenal. The Irish won a spectacular victory in Clontibret, County Monaghan, fighting not only with ferocity but with skill and discipline, attributes that were not always associated with Irish insurgents. The Queen was warned of the consequences of O'Neill's decision: "He is worthily reputed the best man of war of his nation," a report noted. "Many of his followers are well-trained soldiers . . . and he is the greatest man of territory and revenue within that kingdom."

The Queen proclaimed him a traitor to the Crown. Privately, she spoke bitterly of O'Neill as "my monster of the North." O'Neill ordered his own castle in Dungannon destroyed, expecting that the English might do it themselves. Its contents, including the lead he had bought in London but never used for the castle's roof, were shipped to safer locations.

After the Battle of Clontibret, the rebellion became more an exercise in shadow boxing than outright war. O'Neill and O'Donnell agreed to a short truce, enabling them to buy time and to appeal to Catholic Spain for support. In a letter to the son of Spain's King Philip II, O'Neill and O'Donnell stated that they were intent upon "freeing the country from the rod of tyrannical evil." Philip, who had seen his great armada broken up and defeated in 1588, dispatched a new fleet to Ireland in 1596. Bad weather, however, prevented a landing. Philip, a persistent man, was undeterred. A 136-ship fleet with nearly thirteen thousand men aboard was dispatched in 1597. Yet again storms intervened, and the fleet was broken up.

Both sides were preparing for war in earnest when O'Neill agreed to a conference with the lord general of the English army in Ireland, the Earl of Ormond. Speaking to each other from opposite banks of a stream, O'Neill urged the Englishman to withdraw his troops from Ulster, suggesting that if he did so, the rebellion would cease. A member of Ormond's party demanded that O'Neill offer two of his sons, who were standing beside him, as hostages to guarantee the peace. O'Neill refused: "You do not know the North as I know it," he shouted across the stream. "If my sons were out of this country the people would despise them. And if they were not here in Ulster how would you treat them?" When his listeners reminded him of Elizabeth's generosity, he sneered: "Her Majesty never gave me anything but what belonged to me."

No one had ever heard Hugh O'Neill speak this way.

Sir Henry Bagenal was determined to put an end to the rebellion and to his hated brother-in-law. The early death of his sister Mabel, O'Neill's third wife, after just four years of marriage, only inflamed his desire for revenge. Mabel Bagenal had died in Sir Henry's home, having walked out on her philandering husband. So when O'Neill beseiged an English garrison at Blackwater Fort near a place called Yellow Ford in County Tyrone, Bagenal seized the opportunity. He insisted on leading a massive relief column of four thousand men to attack the rebels.

O'Neill had five thousand men under his command, and he was ready for the attack when it came on August 14, 1598. His troops were supplied with ammunition made from the supply of lead that had never found its way to the roof of Dungannon Castle.

Bagenal's men marched in a mile-long column across open ground, skirting bogs and woods. O'Neill placed skirmishers out of sight, beyond the trees on either side of Bagenal's column. The Irish attacked in guerrilla-like fashion, harassing and then disappearing into the countryside. Bagenal's cavalry couldn't give pursuit through the woods and bogs. Through it all, Bagenal kept marching toward O'Neill's main force, even as his column began to fall apart. O'Neill had had plenty of time to reinforce his position, setting traps for enemy cavalry and building a long trench filled with water and other obstacles. O'Neill's trench was so long, perhaps a mile, that Bagenal couldn't outflank him.

The Irish opened fire on the already exhausted English as they approached the rebel fortress from the surrounding hills. O'Neill's pikemen then advanced, and O'Donnell attacked from the flank. The English were stunned and confused. Bagenal, wearing a helmet as he moved closer to the fighting, tried to regroup for a new advance. A bullet struck him in his face as he raised his visor. He was killed instantly.

The battle became a rout, and when it was over, more than half of Bagenal's four thousand men were dead, wounded, or missing. It was the worst defeat the English ever suffered in Ireland. The Battle of Yellow Ford made Hugh O'Neill famous throughout Europe. Both King Philip and the Pope wrote to congratulate him. Despite England's efforts and expenditures, Hugh O'Neill, and not Queen Elizabeth, was in command in Ireland.

The war spread from Ulster to Munster. Elizabeth's advisers in Dublin put out a peace feeler to O'Neill, but when she heard of it, the Queen noted icily that there would be no compromise with a traitor. She informed her administrators in Dublin that they ought to be "ashamed" of their "absurdities." Elizabeth put out a call for the thousands of reinforcements it would take to keep Ireland and Hugh O'Neill from humiliating the Crown and establishing a hostile kingdom on England's western flank. A new commander was dispatched to Ireland—Charles Blount, Lord Mountjoy, a determined and clever man who was one of Elizabeth's top soldiers. The urgency of the moment was not lost on the Queen. Hugh O'Neill wrote to the King of Spain yet again, saying that with the help of some six thousand or seven thousand Spanish soldiers, "we shall be masters of this kingdom."

During one of several truces that interrupted the fighting, O'Neill put into writing a declaration of principles for which he and his troops were fighting. O'Neill demanded that the Catholic religion be allowed to be "openly preached and taught," that all top administrators be Irish rather than English, that lands taken from rebellious Gaelic chieftains be returned, and that the Irish be allowed to travel and trade with all the same rights as Englishmen. When one of Elizabeth's advisers saw O'Neill's demands, he told her: "He means to be head and monarch of Ireland." Those closer to the situation saw it a bit differently; they understood that he was creating something Ireland had not seen before: a well-trained, disciplined army organized around a set of national principles. "This island of Ireland shall be at our direction and counsel as Irishmen," O'Neill said. He was, in effect, making an argument for what later generations would call Home

Rule—an Ireland that ruled its own affairs but was loyal to the Crown of England.

In late September 1601, a fleet of twenty-four Spanish warships sailed unopposed into the harbor of Kinsale, a port town thirteen miles south of the major city of Cork. The commander had nearly four thousand soldiers at his disposal. Hugh O'Neill, however, was three hundred miles to the north, in his home province of Ulster. The English commander, Mountjoy, was in Kilkenny when he heard the news, and he immediately went to Cork to prepare a march against the invaders.

O'Neill, who always preferred patient waiting to rash fighting, tried to assess the risk to his army. He and O'Donnell knew they had a worthy foe in Mountjoy, and it long ago had become clear that they couldn't win without the support of Spain. But now the Spanish had landed in Munster.

Mountjoy redeployed troops from other parts of the country, building a force of more than six thousand to face the Spaniards. He understood just how close he, and the English, were to the brink: "If the Spaniards should prevail at first, all Ireland will follow," he wrote. Finally, O'Neill began his long march from Dungannon in early November. Red Hugh O'Donnell already was marching south to join the Spanish. Irish rebels had made common cause with England's most formidable enemy, and now were fighting not just an Irish battle, but a European war.

With admirable skill and discipline, O'Neill evaded the English attempt to intercept and destroy him. He and O'Donnell took up positions outside Kinsale; the combined strength of the Ulster army was about 6,500, not counting the Spanish. The English had about 7,500 battle-ready troops. The two sides faced each other for three weeks, waiting.

O'Neill ordered an attack in the predawn hours of a stormy Christmas eve. It seemed an uncharacteristically bold move, leading to speculation afterward that Red Hugh O'Donnell, still burning to avenge his years in prison, persuaded him to abandon his usual caution. Whatever the case, three Irish divisions moved forward toward the English line as thunder rattled overhead and streaks of lightning traced a brightening sky. Men armed with muskets opened fire. An English officer ordered a cavalry charge at the center of the Irish attack. O'Neill's disciplined army, which had made war on the Queen for six years, suddenly, inexplicably, broke down. Infantrymen fled, and were chased down and hacked to death. What had figured to be a hotly contested battle turned into a lopsided rout. One of Mountjoy's subordinates marveled: "No man can yield reasons for this miraculous victory."

The Battle of Kinsale was over in an hour. Hugh O'Neill took the shattered remainder of his army back to Ulster. Red Hugh O'Donnell, who had lost his way before the attack began but then tried valiantly to halt the chaotic retreat, was dispatched to Spain to plead for reinforcements. The Spanish invaders withdrew and returned home. In a letter to the new Spanish King, Philip III, O'Neill tried to engender a case of royal guilt. He noted that "the help which Your Majesty sent us . . . came to land in the province of Munster, so far from our own lands that we had to march one hundred leagues in the depth of winter, through enemy country." This time, however, there would be no more help from Spain. And Red Hugh O'Donnell was dead before the year was out, very likely poisoned by an English agent in Spain.

Hugh O'Neill believed he would fight again, but with O'Donnell's death he realized that all was lost. His army was shattered, and, in a gesture that symbolized the new order, Lord Mountjoy's men invaded Ulster and destroyed the ancient stone chair where generations of O'Neills had been inaugurated as The O'Neill. Gaelic Ireland was shattered, too.

Hugh O'Neill surrendered, and submitted to the authority of the Crown in March 1603. Elizabeth pardoned O'Neill and offered a generous settlement just before she died. When O'Neill learned of Elizabeth's death, he burst into tears.

Ulster was a defeated and famished land, and O'Neill was exhausted and broken. He could no longer bear to live in the province where his ancestors had once been kings. And so, on September 14, 1607, Hugh O'Neill, the Earl of Tyrone, joined Red Hugh O'Donnell's brother, the Earl of Tyrconnell, and along with family members, they set sail for France, never to return to Ireland. The "flight of the earls" marked the end of old Gaelic Ireland. Hugh O'Neill died ten years later in Italy, after trying vainly to interest Spain in another invasion.

By sailing to exile, O'Neill and his allies inadvertently handed England an opportunity to change the course of history in Ulster and indeed all of Ireland. The consequences of their decision would last for hundreds of years. The English confiscated the O'Neill and O'Donnell holdings, and Ulster would be transformed from the most stubbornly Gaelic province to the most devoutly loyal. Colonists were transported from Scotland and England to stock Ulster with dependable Protestants whose devotion to the Crown was unquestioned.

The colonizing of Ulster was more systematic than what had been attempted in Munster decades before. In 1600, about 2 percent of Ireland's one million people were descended from English or Scots settlers, some of them already settled in Ulster. Over the next one hundred years, that percentage would increase to nearly 30. The gentry who were granted parcels of land in Ulster were required to bring over ten Protestant families for each one thousand acres of land they received. About half these settlers would be Scots, whose native shores were just thirteen miles from Ulster's northeast corner. The Scots were not members of the Church of England, they were Dissenters—Presbyterians. Although they were subject to some forms of legal discrimination, the Scots Presbyterians at least were Protestant, and they could be expected to be loyal to English rule. In fact the new King of England, James I, was a Scot—James Stuart, formerly James VI of Scotland.

The new settlers were expected to improve the land they lived on, generally for low rents. And so, remote Gaelic Ulster began to be transformed into an English outpost. The settlers built towns, developed trades, and founded new industries, such as timber export.

The native Irish were supposed to be segregated from the settler population, but that notion never worked. The remnants of Gaelic Ulster instead remained, working lands that had once belonged to them—if not individually, then collectively. The newcomers knew that they were living on and improving property that had been taken from the native Irish. One English official wrote to London that many settlers feared that the native Irish would rise up and cut the throats of the "poore dispersed Brittish." The Irish, however, remained quiet for the time being.

By 1622, some thirteen thousand settlers were living in Ulster, and by 1640, about 100,000 English and Scots natives had crossed the Irish Sea to new homes on confiscated lands. They dominated trade in the new towns springing up in the plantations. Merchants in London undertook the responsibility of rebuilding the city of Derry, which was renamed Londonderry. (The native Irish, however, continued to call the city Derry.) Ireland was becoming a country of two separate societies, suspicious of and hostile toward one another. The Irish would not accept the settlers, the authority they represented, or the privileges they were accorded based on their religion and their loyalty to England.

The plantation of Ulster seemed to the English to be such a success that London contemplated another, this one in the westernmost province of Connaught. Accordingly, a quarter century after Hugh

O'Neill's flight, the government began confiscating lands held by Catholics, and this time, no distinction was made between Gaelic Catholics and Old English Catholics. The Old English, descendants of Norman settlers, were outraged, for many of them had tried mightily to prove that they could be loyal to the Crown of England as well as to the Church of Rome. Their rage turned to fear as they saw their influence in the Irish Parliament begin to fade when Protestant members from Ulster and elsewhere took control of the legislature with the blessing of England's Lord Lieutenant, Thomas Wentworth. And in London, an increasingly aggressive and rabidly anti-Catholic Parliament began taking steps that would lead to the English Civil War. In 1641, the Puritan-dominated Parliament passed legislation calling for the suppression of Catholicism in Ireland, declaring that all Catholics were to be considered "recusants," which meant that they were subject to civil penalties because they did not believe in the English monarch's religious authority. England began to govern Ireland on the principle that to be Catholic was to be of suspect loyalty. In doing so, the English alienated Gaelic Irish and Old English alike.

Though divided by class—the Old English generally were members of the gentry—Ireland's Catholics were united as recusants. Their hold on two thirds of Ireland's land suddenly seemed weak. So the Gaelic Irish and Old English formed an alliance that would become known as the Confederation of Kilkenny, named for the city in which the alliance was founded.

With the English distracted by conflict between the Puritan Parliament and King Charles I, James's successor, the Irish saw an opportunity to head off further persecution and to reverse the Anglicization of their country. Confederate leaders developed a plan to seize Dublin Castle and present the King and Parliament with a fait accompli. A drunken conspirator, however, betrayed what might have been a stunning Irish victory. Despite the setback, the Irish in Ulster rose again on October 23, 1641, doing so in the name of "God, King, and Ireland." Gentry and peasant alike joined forces; the gentry striking what they hoped would be a preemptive move against further confiscation, the peasants responding to past grievances. The rebels did not have the disciplined army of Hugh O'Neill (although one of the rebellion's leaders was Sir Phelim O'Neill, a relative of Hugh's), but they surely had Red Hugh O'Donnell's passion for vengeance. They turned on the settlers, particularly those in the Ulster plantation. In the town of Portadown, County Armagh, about one thousand Protestant men, women, and children were rounded up, led to a bridge, and thrown into the water below. Those who didn't drown were killed after swimming to shore. One woman said the insurgents took her five children from her and threw them off the bridge. A Protestant clergyman said that "the rebels buried many of the British Protestants alive."

Horrific as the slaughter was, it was exaggerated in supposed eye-witness accounts given to a government commission. Some Protestants gave casualty figures that exceeded the Protestant population of Ireland at the time. But it is impossible to exaggerate the significance of the 1641 massacre in the Irish Protestant mind. In parts of modern Northern Ireland, the murders in Portadown are remembered as if they took place a generation ago. Though Catholics would suffer an even worse slaughter at the hands of Scots settlers in Ulster several months later—Catholic children were murdered with special zeal—Portadown came to represent Protestant conviction of Irish barbarism, and confirmed fears of Catholic Irish skulking through the night to retrieve what had once been theirs.

In early 1642, the rebel army came under the command of yet another O'Neill, Owen Roe O'Neill, a nephew of Hugh O'Neill. The rebels continued to insist that they were loyal to the English Crown, but, ironically enough, their assurances meant little to those who controlled England. King Charles I would be executed in 1649 and for more than a decade, the English Crown would cease to exist.

The aristocratic Owen Roe O'Neill had just returned to Ireland after an absence of four decades. He was about sixty years old—his year of birth is uncertain, but he was probably born about 1580—and had spent thirty-five years in the service of Spain. Like his uncle Hugh, Owen Roe never gave up hope that Spain would once again come to the assistance of an Irish rebellion.

The rebel Irish army was unlike the troops he had commanded on the Continent. They were poorly armed and virtually untrained. "I am killing myself bringing them to some order and discipline, so as to be able to withstand the enemy," he wrote. Complicating his assignment was the division within his confederation. The Old English and Gaelic Irish may have had their Catholicism in common, but not a great deal more. The Old English landowners were reluctant to press the rebellion, for they had much to lose, and they hoped for a pardon. The Gaelic Irish, with nothing to lose, pressed for continued conflict. O'Neill agreed with the Gaels, but he would have to fight without the full support of the Old English.

Owen Roe O'Neill won a measure of revenge for his uncle's defeat at Kinsale with a startling victory in 1646 at Bunburb in the heart of the old O'Neill country, County Tyrone. He inflicted enemy losses comparable to those at Yellow Ford, but he could not follow up on the victory, and he died under mysterious circumstances in 1649, when the man who had won the English Civil War came to Ireland to subdue the rebels.

Oliver Cromwell was a fanatic Protestant who was determined to avenge the Catholic atrocities of 1641, and to put down (ironically enough) Irish loyalty to the deposed and beheaded Charles I. Parliament commissioned Cromwell to settle Ireland's Catholic problem and to quell permanently Ireland's rebellion. He surely was the man for the job, believing as he did that the Irish Catholics were "barbarous wretches."

Cromwell went straight to what he saw as God's work. He believed the Irish, aside from practicing a despised and corrupt religion, were a race of savages. "You, unprovoked, put the English to the most unheard of and most barbarous massacre . . . that ever the sun beheld," he wrote of the Irish. The Irish, he said, were better off for the English presence, in part because of "the example of English industry [and] commerce." He landed in Dublin on August 15, 1649, and with an army of more than twenty thousand infantry and cavalry, he beseiged the town of Drogheda in County Louth on September 10. The town was an outpost of English soldiers still loyal to King Charles, but the citizenry was mostly Catholic. Cromwell's first attempt to breach the town's walls ended in failure, which did nothing for the already impassioned temperament of his Puritan army. He attacked again, and this time, "being in the heat of the action, I forbade [the soldiers] to spare any that were in arms in the town." That order was interpreted broadly, and the soldiers slaughtered anybody they found. About 3,500 people were killed. Those who tried to surrender were executed. In an unmistakable sign of what Cromwell's expedition sought to achieve, every Catholic priest in the town was murdered.

Cromwell was modest about his achievement in Drogheda; he would accept no credit for the slaughter: "It is right that God alone should have all the glory," he wrote.

There was more "glory" to come. Cromwell's men marched south and rampaged through the port town of Wexford, slaughtering two thousand people, including at least 250 women. Terrified Irish towns began surrendering as soon as Cromwell's men drew near. The rebellion that had begun in 1641 was put down in a matter of months. Thousands of Catholics, even those who played no part in the rebellion, were rounded up under Cromwell's orders and transported to the West Indies as slaves. Priests were targeted for murder, and a £5 reward was offered for their capture. The celebration of Catholic Mass was prohibited.

Cromwell was now free to impose his solution to England's Irish problem, which was summed up in a phrase: "Hell or Connaught." Catholic landowners in Ulster, Munster, and Leinster were stripped of their property and dispatched to Ireland's fourth province, the remote, stony land of Connaught west of the River Shannon. Among the nearly fifty thousand people sent to what amounted to internal exile were the Sarsfields, who held large tracts of land in County Kildare. Patrick Sarsfield had been a member of the Irish Parliament and the descendant of soldiers who had come to Ireland with Henry II. He was a member of the small Catholic gentry—English-speaking, loyal to the Crown, and well assimilated into Anglo-Irish culture. Nevertheless, he was a Catholic, and he and his wife and their five children were forced to leave behind their manor house for the famished west. Sarsfield estimated that the land he was given in Connaught was worth about one-twentieth the value of his confiscated holdings.

Before Cromwell, Catholics owned about 60 percent of the country's land; by the time Cromwell redistributed land to his soldiers, allies, and other reliable Protestants, Catholics owned just about 20 percent. Connaught became, in essence, a reservation populated by Catholic gentry. Catholics who were not landowners were allowed to remain where they were. The new Protestant landowners, after all, would require laborers, farmers, and other workers.

Cromwell's campaign lasted nine months and left Ireland dazed and embittered. He returned to England in May 1650. An English administrator, Colonel Richard Lawrence, noted that "plague and famine had so swept away whole counties that a man might travel twenty or thirty miles and not see a living creature, either man, beast or bird."

For centuries afterward, the Irish would speak of the curse of Cromwell.

The Crown was restored in 1660 with Charles II. Hostage to England's religious-based politics, Ireland's Catholics saw reason for hope in 1685 when a Catholic, James II, became King. The Irish expected the appointment of Catholic administrators in Ireland and even the election of a Catholic-dominated Parliament in Dublin. Although still subordinate to the Crown, the Irish Parliament could, with the Crown's cooperation, pass legislation rescinding Cromwell's confiscation of Catholic land. The Protestant settlers from England and Scotland, never secure as a minority on the island, always bearing in mind the massacre of 1641, feared a legal reversal of decades of English policy. But James II's Queen, Mary of Modena, bore a son, ensuring the unthinkable—that a Catholic would succeed James and reestablish a Catholic dynasty in Protestant England. In the so-called Glorious Revolution of 1688, England's nobility invited Prince William of Orange, a Dutch Protestant, to assume the Crown with his wife, Mary, who was the daughter of James II. With no popular support, James II could do nothing to resist his son-in-law's usurpation. He fled to France and prepared to fight for his crown on more hospitable terrain—Ireland. With him was Patrick Sarsfield, the son of the Member of Parliament whose lands Cromwell had confiscated forty years earlier.

Like Owen Roe O'Neill and others before him, Patrick Sarsfield had left Ireland to become a soldier on the Continent. In 1675, when he was about twenty, the tall, powerful, and hotheaded young man joined an English brigade attached to the French army—in that way he would not have to take an oath required of English officers renouncing Catholic doctrine. He left his posting in France in 1678 and traveled to England at the very moment when the country was in the thrall of what was called the Popish plot, which consisted of rumors that Jesuits were planning to overthrow the King. When a judge who was taking evidence, such as it was, about the reports was found beaten to death, authorities were panic-stricken. Catholics were prohibited from London and its outskirts, and Patrick Sarsfield was arrested because of his religion. Authorities were outraged when they learned that a Catholic was serving as an officer in the King's army. Sarsfield eventually was released, but others arrested in the Popish plot panic were executed, including, in Ireland, the Archbishop of Armagh, Oliver Plunkett.

Sarsfield's family successfully petitioned the Crown to get some of its land back, although it took years of legal action to rid the property of the Protestant who had taken it over. When the Catholic James II ascended to the throne in 1685, he almost immediately faced a minor internal rebellion. Sarsfield volunteered to serve in His Majesty's army. He was given a commission and rose to the rank of lieutenant colonel. When the English nobility invited William of Orange to take the throne of England, Sarsfield fought for James's lost cause, and accompanied him to exile in France.

Now, the battle for the Crown of England would be fought in Ireland.

On March 12, 1689, James landed in Kinsale, the scene of Hugh O'Neill's defeat. Sarsfield joined him and was given the challenging

Patrick Sarsfield

assignment of whipping the Irish army into shape. Some troops had no shoes, no weapons, and hardly any food. Because of its geography, Ulster once again loomed as a flashpoint. Its proximity to Scotland suggested a route by which James might return to London. Shortly after James and Sarsfield landed in Kinsale, Irish troops loyal to James besieged the Protestant stronghold of Derry, which was supporting William. The city's thirty thousand civilians were reduced to eating rats, but when the city's commander, Robert Lundy, seemed ready to surrender, the populace turned on him. The cry of the besieged city was "No surrender!" It would become the Protestant motto.

Once again, war in Ireland took on an international dimension when France landed six thousand troops to fight alongside James. It was a circular strategy: the English occupied Ireland because they feared it would be a staging area for England's enemies; the Irish, in seeking to throw off English rule, invited England's enemies to assist their rebellions; the English saw their fears realized and became even more determined to crush the Irish. The siege of Derry was lifted in July 1689, and Prince William of Orange, now King William III of England, landed in Ireland the following June to take personal command of the army. Two kings, then, were in the field in Ireland, fighting over the throne of England. History would record the coming battle as a fight between the orange (for William) and the green (the national color of Ireland).

The two armies met on a field outside Drogheda, along the banks of the River Boyne. Patrick Sarsfield already had shown himself to be the Irish army's boldest commander, having won a series of significant victories in the west that cleared William's troops out of Connaught. He gained a reputation for moving quickly—while marching toward Sligo in the fall of 1689, his cavalry had covered thirty-four miles in a single day—and for seizing the opportunities given him. He also had won a reputation as a humane commander. After capturing Sligo and discovering that the town's garrison was starving, he invited his opponent's officers to dine with him.

On the bright, warm morning of July 1, 1690, Sarsfield commanded a cavalry brigade more accustomed to irregular tactics than open-field battles. But here, along the banks of the Boyne, there would be little opportunity for maneuver.

The fighting began at about eight o'clock, when some six thousand Williamites attacked not the main body of Irish troops, but its poorly manned left flank. James mistakenly concluded that William was attempting to outflank him, and he hurriedly split his army, dispatching Sarsfield's cavalry, among other units, to the west. In effect, Sarsfield was taken out of action, for the battle did not take place on the flank. William sent fifteen thousand troops, double what was left of the main Irish army after James split it, in a direct frontal assault. After hours of hotly contested fighting, with William prominent at the head of the English columns, a defeated James left the field in the company of Sarsfield's cavalry. He retreated all the way to Dublin, and from there sailed to France, never to return to Ireland or England.

Although it did not seem so at the time, the Battle of the Boyne was one of the pivotal events in Irish history. Protestant Ireland, particularly in Ulster, adopted the orange of King William as their counter to the green of Irish nationalists, and King William himself was deified as a Protestant hero. Every year on July 12 (the change in the calendar about fifty years later moved the anniversary by eleven days) Protestants parade through the cities and towns of Northern Ireland to celebrate the anniversary of the Battle of the Boyne. Banners carry such mottos as: "Remember 1690!" and "No Surrender!" When possible, the parades are routed through Catholic neighborhoods, to remind residents which side won on that hot July day.

For Patrick Sarsfield and thousands of his soldiers, the war went on. After the Battle of the Boyne, Sarsfield was at his most audacious, moving quickly when least expected, striking hard with his cavalry and then disappearing into the countryside. His most famous victory came in August, about a month after the Irish army had retreated to the walled city of Limerick, with William following quickly—too quickly, as Sarsfield learned. William's ammunition and heavy artillery, the guns he would need if he were to besiege the Irish in Limerick, were lumbering well behind his main force.

Sarsfield ordered five hundred cavalry into action, then rode hard for two days through enemy territory, just barely evading enemy patrols, before reaching the English artillery encampment. As the Irish closed in, they managed to discover the enemy's password: "Sarsfield." The man himself moved toward the camp and was challenged by an English sentry, who asked him for the password.

He replied: "Sarsfield is the word. And Sarsfield is the man!" With that, the Irish swarmed into the camp, overpowering it and then disabling the powerful guns. When William later tried to storm Limerick's walls without the guns and extra ammunition, he suffered an appalling defeat, losing five thousand men. One of William's aides noted that "the ill success at Limerick was well known to be owing to the want of ammunition occasioned by Sarsfield falling upon the artillery." Sarsfield's ride became the stuff of legend and not a little myth, a dashing tale of heroism at a time of despair. Before the war was over, some of Sarsfield's men were calling him "the father of his country."

The war's last pitched battle came at Aughrim, County Galway, in July 1691. There Sarsfield found himself under heavy attack early in the fighting as he protected the army's vulnerable right wing. The battle appeared to be tilting in favor of the Irish until the army's French commander, the Marquis de Saint-Ruth, ordered what he thought would be a climactic cavalry charge. "They are beaten," he shouted to his men, just before an English cannonball took off his head. Leaderless, the Irish collapsed in a heap. Sarsfield, paralyzed by Saint-Ruth's order to protect the right wing, watched as the tide of battle turned. He could no longer affect the outcome; the battle was lost. From his position, however, he saw that the rout would become a slaughter unless somebody stood and fought. He ordered his cavalry to charge the onrushing English in hopes of keeping the enemy cavalry at bay while the Irish infantry retreated. An English observer noted that Sarsfield had "performed miracles, and if he was not killed or taken it was not for any fault of his." The Irish had entered the battle with about twenty thousand men, about the size of the Williamite army they opposed. Estimates of Irish killed in action at Aughrim range from three thousand to seven thousand.

The Irish again retreated to the walled city of Limerick, but this time there would be no dashing raid behind enemy lines, no disciplined defense. Sarsfield was in command now, and he surprised friend and foe alike when he decided to sue for peace. The war in Ireland, he decided, was over, but the war against William and England would be carried on elsewhere. He understood that the battle for Ireland was part of a larger great power rivalry between England and its continental enemies. If he could no longer fight for Ireland on Irish soil, he would negotiate a peace, flee, and resume the fight in France. Ever the optimist, he thought he would be crossing the English Channel to invade England within a year.

Negotiations soon were underway, and during the course of the talks, Sarsfield asked the English officers on hand if they had changed their opinion of the Irish after such a long and difficult war. They conceded nothing. Sarsfield, however, acknowledged one difference between the two armies: the quality of their leaders. William won admiration for his bravery in battle, while James skulked away to France after the Boyne. "As low as we now are," he told the English, "change but kings with us and we will fight it over again with you."

The document Sarsfield signed in 1691, the Treaty of Limerick, was generous. Sarsfield and his men and their families, some twelve thousand people, were allowed to leave Ireland for France. They would become known to Irish history as "the Wild Geese" who flew from Ireland to join the armies of Europe. Sarsfield immediately joined the French army, which was fighting the English on the Continent. Two years after leaving Ireland, and just three months after the birth of his son, Patrick Sarsfield found himself once again battling forces under the command of King William, this time near

Flanders. A bullet hit him in the chest; he lingered for days as the wound grew worse. "Would it were for Ireland!" he said. And then he died.

The Treaty of Limerick was loosely worded, but it hardly seemed punitive. The English confiscated the lands of those who accompanied Sarsfield to France, further reducing Catholic ownership, from about 20 percent of the country to 15 percent. But Catholics were granted limited freedom of worship, and rebels who swore allegiance to King William were allowed to keep their property and their professions, a startling contrast to the terms imposed by Cromwell. The Protestants in the Irish Parliament, however, did not share William's generosity. They had had enough of Catholic Ireland's rebellions. They wanted revenge. The spirit if not the vague letter of the Treaty of Limerick was soon dispensed with as the Irish Parliament passed highly punitive legislation designed to further oppress Catholics in a country they still dominated in numbers.

Population figures would no longer mean anything. Ireland was to be ruled by and for its Protestant minority.

CHAPTER TWO

PROTESTANT NATION

A DEPRESSED JONATHAN SWIFT, one of England's most powerful clergymen, packed his belongings and left London on June 1, 1713. He was headed for the land of his birth, Ireland, and was none too pleased about it, for he was being sent into exile, and an ignominious exile at that. Not even a year before, he had been at the center of power and politics in London, a man whose counsel and pen made and broke reputations. His widely circulated pamphlet *The Conduct of the Allies* contained a fierce denunciation of England's involvement in the War of the Spanish Succession, and the cost of the war to England: "It will no doubt be a mighty comfort to our grandchildren, when they see a few rags hung up in Westminster Hall which cost a hundred millions, whereof they are paying the arrears, to boast as beggars do that their grandfathers were rich and great," he wrote, with the savage scarcasm that made him a feared man. At forty-six, he was at the height of his power, destined, or so he thought, for promotion to Bishop in his beloved Church of England.

It was an illusion all along, for even when his friends and allies were in power, Jonathan Swift was a man who did not command trust among England's power elite. He was, after all, a man of wit and irony, of suspect independence, a man not entirely comfortable with himself and with the roles he should have been expected to play. He was determined to "vex the world." Bishoprics went to other sorts of clergymen, dependable men, men who did not question the power arrangements of the time. His peers would receive the rewards of office. For Jonathan Swift, there was a consolation prize: Dean of Saint Patrick's Cathedral in Dublin, the premier Church of Ireland congregation in the Irish capital. The archbishop who sent Swift to Ireland admitted: "I thought a Dean could do less mischief than a Bishop."

Swift understood why he had been posted to Ireland, and he was incapable of pretending to be happy about it. During the sonorous rituals that marked his official installation at Saint Patrick's, he was overcome with depression and loneliness. Some one hundred visitors called on him the following day to offer their welcome; Swift remained in his bedroom, receiving none of the well-wishers. He was ill for the next two weeks—learning that he would have to pay £1,000 for repairs to the Dean's residence certainly didn't help his already dyspeptic disposition.

The Ireland to which Swift returned was settling into the new arrangements brought about after the defeat of James II and Patrick Sarsfield. Those arrangements, however, bore little resemblance to the liberal conditions outlined in the Treaty of Limerick. Confiscation of Catholic land was only the first step in a systematic degradation of the native population, who made up 75 percent of Ireland's 2.5 million people at the beginning of the eighteenth century. The Irish Parliament, under the control of a privileged class of Protestant landlords, was determined to prevent future rebellions. Many Irish Catholics still supported the cause of the vanquished James II. And so in 1704, the Irish Parliament, with the approval of the Crown, passed the Act to Prevent the Further Growth of Popery. It was the first of what became known as the Penal Laws, and the combined effect was to turn Catholics in Ireland into outlaws, or worse. Ireland's highest ranking judge said that English law in Ireland "does not presume any such person to exist as an Irish Roman Catholic." Irish Catholics were banished from every aspect of civic life. Catholic education was banned. Catholics could not join the armed services. They could not buy land, nor could they inherit it in the traditional manner—when a Catholic landowner died, the estate was split up among the surviving sons rather than passed down whole to the oldest son. If the oldest son became Protestant, however, he inherited his father's land intact. Bit by bit, large Catholic holdings were reduced to small plots. Catholics could not vote, nor could they sit in Parliament. A Catholic who owned a horse valued at more than £5 could be whipped on sight; a Protestant could seize the horse. Catholics (and Presbyterians, concentrated in the northeast corner of Ulster) were required to pay a tithe to support the state-established Church of Ireland, the equivalent of the Church of England. Catholic priests were ordered to leave the country under pain of death, and bounties of £20 were offered to those who turned in a priest to authorities. Nevertheless, the priests remained, sharing their flock's suffering and strengthening the bond between the people and their church.

The laws were never fully enforced, but their effect made the simple act of going to Mass an exercise in rebellion, and such defiance was commonplace. Catholics continued to worship in fields, and they sent their children to the many ad hoc schools that sprang up in reaction to the ban on Catholic education. Itinerant schoolmasters wandered the countryside, offering instruction literally in hedges, far from the prying eyes of the authorities. The schoolmasters often were fluent in Latin and Greek, and the dispossessed Catholics, most of whom still spoke Irish, eagerly grasped the chance for an education. A landlord's agent complained that "as to school masters, we have too many, and too many mere scholars, for we abound with schools and schoolboys, and it would be better that our youth should be hammering at the anvil than at bog Latin."

Barred from formal education and alienated from the political, cultural, and economic life of the country, Ireland's Catholics were consigned to lives of horrendous poverty, some of the worst in Europe. A Protestant clergyman in Ulster traveled through parts of rural, Catholic Ireland and was appalled. He wrote that he had never seen "such dismal marks of hunger and want as appeared in the countenances of the poor creatures I met on the road." Travelers throughout the 1700s commented on the atrocious living conditions of Ireland's majority population. Those who had the strength to better their lot were punished for their efforts, because any improvement to the land they rented inevitably led to an increase in rent. But scowling English observers complained that the Catholic Irish were lazy, content to live in squalor, without any of the work ethic that characterized the Protestant settlement.

Increasingly, the poor tenants relied on a single crop, the potato, for themselves, using their other crops to pay the rent. The potato required little effort to grow and was nutritious enough to feed a family. It became not just the staple of Ireland's poor. It became, for many, their only source of food.

Meanwhile, against the odds and clearly against the wishes of the ruling minority, a small Catholic middle class sprang up in Ireland's port cities. Trade was one of the few avenues for advancement the Penal Laws allowed Catholics, in part because the Irish Parliament was filled with men who made their money from the rents they collected, and such men looked down on those forced to make a living in trade. And so some Catholics found a path to modest economic independence through the import of wine and luxury goods shipped from

Spain and France and bound for the gentry's tables. These business-men were, however, a small minority of the general Catholic popula-tion, and they had no more political power than their landless, impoverished fellow Catholics.

The Penal Laws achieved the intended effect of preventing Ireland's Catholics from threatening the political order. The Anglo-Irish statesman Edmund Burke said the Penal Laws were "as well fit-ted for the oppression, impoverishment and degradation of a people, and the debasement in them of human nature itself, as ever proceeded from the perverted ingenuity of Man." But English policy in Ireland had more utilitarian goals than the mere degradation of a people. The Irish economy, too, was to be degraded and debased in order to limit competition with England. For example, the English Parliament in 1699 banned the export of Irish wool to England. English wool man-ufacturers feared competition from Ireland and demanded that this promising industry be suppressed, and so it was. Likewise, Ireland's thriving export of cattle was brought to an end in the late 1600s after English graziers complained about competition from Ireland. The ban on cattle exports not only stunted one of Ireland's leading export industries, but hurt Irish port cities dependent on increased trade.

Under Poyning's Law, the Irish Parliament was powerless to do anything about the English Crown's restrictions on Ireland's econ-omy. The Dublin legislature was subservient to the Crown, and the Crown wished Ireland to remain politically and economically depen-dent on England. In time, members of Ireland's ruling class chafed under the restrictions on the country's economic and political growth. They believed that they were entitled to all rights and liber-ties granted to Englishmen because they were, in fact, Englishmen who happened to live in Ireland. (Some members of the ruling elite, however, spent little or no time in Ireland, choosing instead to live in England. Their large property holdings gave them enormous power despite their absence.) They were members of a class that came to be known as the Protestant Ascendancy. They made up about 10 percent of Ireland's population, and had in common English ancestry, mem-bership in the established Church of Ireland, and a common sense of privilege based on nationality and class. Usually their wealth was based in the land, but membership in the class was open to the profes-sions, particularly law. England was their cultural touchstone, and they tried to re-create in Ireland little bits of England with their clubs, their hunts, and their gardens, not to mention their absolute belief in the power and merit of aristocratic rule.

Their city was the Irish capital, Dublin, at the center of the old

English Pale. Political life revolved around the Irish Parliament, which may have been emasculated as a law-making body but nevertheless was part of an extensive system of political patronage in the capital. The Ascendancy's monuments were the ornate public buildings in Dublin that began to take shape during the reign of George I, beginning in 1714. Georgian architecture dominated Dublin, giving the capital a distinctive look that has been preserved to the present.

The Ascendancy's rule was a government of, for, and by the privileged, a provincial imitation of the tight circle of powerful landed families that ruled England. And while it ruled as Protestants, the Ascendancy did not include all Protestants in its nation within a nation. The Scots Presbyterian settlers who were colonizing large parts of Ulster were effectively barred from government service through legislation passed in 1704 requiring that officeholders receive the sacraments of the Church of Ireland. The Presbyterians, who made up about 15 percent of the island's population, were known as Dissenters, for they dissented from the established church, and thus were briefly excluded from the island's power arrangements. Once again, religious tests and distinctions were introduced to Ireland not by the native population, but by English settlers and their descendants as a means of dividing rulers from the ruled.

What Dublin was for the Ascendancy, the small town of Belfast became for the Ulster Presbyterians, a center of provincial culture and identity. Dublin was a capital of privilege; Belfast was a capital of industry and meritocracy. Dublin was home to patronage-ridden government; Belfast home to a fledgling, enterprising middle class suspicious of inherited privileges. Vital and curious, open to arguments against aristocratic rule, Belfast's tradition of religious dissent would take on a political character as new ideas of political liberty and democracy took shape in the eighteenth century. The Toleration Act in 1719 finally granted Dissenters, or Presbyterians, full citizenship, but their suspicions about Dublin and the Ascendancy remained. Some felt so unwanted that they left Ulster for the promise of greater freedom in America, beginning the long tradition of transatlantic Irish exile.

As a Dean in the Church of Ireland, Jonathan Swift's views of Catholics and Presbyterians were thoroughly conventional. He considered neither group to be a part of the Ascendancy nation. But he asserted that the Irish Ascendancy, if not the lower classes, deserved to be treated as the equals of their brethren in England, and were entitled to the same political and economic freedoms as any royal subject born in London.

Jonathan Swift

Swift was born in Dublin in 1667, was taken to England as an infant, then returned to Ireland to begin his schooling as a young boy. He would hardly have accepted the notion that he was Irish; while he spent the formative years of boyhood, adolescence, and young adulthood in Dublin, and attended Trinity College there, England defined his aspirations.

He began writing at the turn of the eighteenth century. At the same time, an Irish Protestant bureaucrat and philosopher named William Molyneux created a sensation with the publication of a tract entitled *The Case of Ireland's Being Bound by Acts of Parliament in England*

Stated. Molyneux's concerns were economic, although they inevitably received a national interpretation: he argued that Ireland ought to have equal status with England under a common crown, but his chief complaint was with English laws that restricted Irish trade and thus stunted Ireland's economy. It was an assertion of a certain sort of Irish identity, but surely only a certain sort. Referring to the native Irish, he noted that "the great Body of the present people of Ireland are the Progeny of the English . . . and there remains but a mere handful of the Ancient Irish at this day, I may say, not one in a thousand."

Molyneux's treatise had an enormous influence on Swift. In 1707, less than a decade after *The Case of Ireland* was published, Swift wrote his *Story of an Injured Lady,* which set out the case for Ireland's equality with England and for the unrestricted development of the Irish economy. *Story* wasn't published until after Swift's death. By then, his arguments surprised nobody.

Swift kept a low profile during his first few years as Dean of Saint Patrick's. In a letter to his friend Alexander Pope, Swift described his life in the deanery: "You are to understand that I live in the corner of a vast unfurnished house; my family consists of a steward, a groom, a helper in the stable, a footman and an old maid, who are all at board-wages; and when I do not dine abroad or make an entertainment (which last is very rare), I eat a mutton pie and drink half a pint of wine; my amusements are defending my small dominions against the archbishop, and endeavouring to reduce my rebellious choir."

When he roused himself from these depressing circumstances and ventured into the neighborhood surrounding Saint Patrick's, what he saw could hardly have improved his spirits. The cathedral was near a neighborhood known then, as now, as the Liberties. There, in the second decade of the eighteenth century, some six thousand people were living in poverty. The breadwinners were weavers, some 1,700 of them, and they suffered as a result of England's restrictions on Irish woolen goods. They were so poverty-stricken that they appealed to the government for charity. Officials dispatched £100.

Swift had been in Ireland for seven years when the British Parliament passed what was known as the Declaratory Act in 1720. In outlining a case "for better securing the dependency of Ireland," the Declaratory Act reduced the powers of the Irish House of Lords, further driving home the point that Ireland's Parliament was but a creature of London, and that Ireland itself was but a dependency of England. Swift was inspired to reenter the world of political argument, and published a tract entitled *A Proposal for the Universal Use of Irish*

Manufacture, Etc. Swift, writing anonymously, appealed to Catholics and Protestants alike to assert their rights as citizens of Ireland and, indeed, to refrain from buying goods made in England. "It is wonderful to observe the Biass among our People in favour of Things, Persons, and Wares of all Kinds that come from England," he wrote, anticipating the complaints of nationalists in centuries to come.

"Let a firm Resolution be taken, by Male and Female, never to appear with one single Shred that comes from England. . . . I heard the late Archbishop of Tuam mention a pleasant Observation of some Body's; that Ireland would never be happy 'till a Law were made for burning every Thing that came from England, except their people and their Coals." Nationalists later simplified Swift's prose to a powerful and provocative slogan: Burn everything English except their coal.

The pamphlet outraged authorities, but because Swift published it anonymously, there was no author to prosecute. So Swift's printer, a man named Edward Waters, was brought into court on charges of sedition. A jury returned a verdict of not guilty eight times, and eight times the presiding judge ordered the jury to reconsider. After a ninth try, the case was dropped. The government had been made to look foolish; more important, Swift had identified a cause around which all Irish people could rally, except for Irish landlords, whose indolence and greed came under attack. Swift charged that their "unmeasurable screwing and racking" of their tenants had "already reduced the miserable People to a worse condition than the Peasants in France, or the Vassals in Germany and Poland."

Four years later, the Dean seized upon another issue with which to rally the Irish and castigate their overseers. The Irish Parliament petitioned London to provide more copper coins for its growing cash economy. An English ironmonger, William Wood, paid English authorities a £10,000 bribe for a contract to produce £108,000 worth of copper coins. The Irish Parliament protested to no avail, and word had it that Wood was producing coins of inferior metal in order to enhance his profit. Swift used this obscure issue to wonderful advantage, writing a series of vehement letters under the pen name M. B. Drapier, who claimed to be a small shopkeeper. What followed, in seven letters, was later described as "the most perfect pieces of oratory ever composed since the days of Demosthenes."

In his fourth and most famous letter, published in October 1724, Swift put forward an astonishingly radical assertion: "For in reason, all government without the consent of the governed is the very definition of slavery." To his fellow Irish, Drapier announced: "You are and ought to be as free a people as your brethren in England."

The British Prime Minister, Robert Walpole, had vowed to "ram" the new coin "down the throats of the Irish." But Swift confounded the government. The Drapier was the hero of the hour, particularly in Dublin, where it was hardly a secret that the Dean of Saint Patrick's had written the letters. "He became the idol of the people of Ireland," wrote a contemporary, Lord Orrey. The people gave him a new title: Hibernian Patriot.

A new Irish tradition, constitutional agitation, was born. In the face of mass protest, the government backed down and canceled Wood's contract. A new Lord Lieutenant, Lord Carteret, was sent to Ireland to restore the government's credibility. He immediately offered a £300 reward to anyone who could identify the true author of the offending letters. It was an exercise in irony that the Dean himself no doubt appreciated. After all, Carteret knew full well that the offending party was his old friend from their days together in London, Dean Swift.

Swift's relationship with the people whose liberty he so passionately proclaimed was tortured, to say the least. In the mid-1720s, while spending a summer with his mistress in the rural countryside of County Cavan, he railed against his neighbors, calling them "a thievish race of people." And, although he championed a system of government based on "the consent of the governed," he continued to display only disdain for both Catholicism and Presbyterianism, the religions of the overwhelming majority of Ireland's population. His notion of "the governed" was restricted to members of the established Church of Ireland. He condemned the failings of Anglo-Irish landlords, but he never summoned his gift for invective against the debilitating injustice of the Penal Laws.

And yet, in his most powerful use of satire, he lampooned the Ascendancy's attitudes toward Ireland's majority population in *A Modest Proposal*. Once again, Swift wrote under a pseudonym, this time assuming the persona of an amiable bureaucrat who wished only to help resolve the problem of overpopulation among impoverished Irish Catholics. In 1729, when *A Modest Proposal* appeared, Ireland had suffered three years of famine, during which the poor suffered terribly.

"It is a melancholly Object to those, who walk through this great Town, or travel in the Country, when they see the Streets, the Roads, and Cabbin-doors crowded with Beggars of the Female Sex, followed by three, four, or six children, all in Rags." What to do with these unsightly poor children? "I have been assured by a very knowing American of my Acquaintance in London, that a young healthy Child, well nursed, at a Year old [is] a most delicious, nourishing, and wholesome Food; whether Stewed, Roasted, Baked or Boiled. . . . A Child will make two Dishes at an Entertainment for Friends; and when the Family dines alone, the fore or hind quarter will make a seasonable Dish; and seasoned with a little Pepper or Salt, would be very good Boiled on the fourth Day, especially in Winter."

By the time of *A Modest Proposal,* Swift had taken his place in the pantheon of great English-language writers. *Gulliver's Travels,* another political satire with overtones for Anglo-Irish relations, had been published in 1726, earning Swift recognition as an irascible genius.

Swift spent much of the ensuing years contemplating, in his own ironic fashion, his death. While not without the awful humor so evident in his political writing, he grew melancholy as old age descended. In one of his last letters, written in 1740 when he was seventy-three, he complained that he "cannot express the mortification I am under both in body and mind. . . . I am sure my days will be very few; few and miserable they must be."

There were more days than perhaps he had expected. He lived for five more years, dying on October 19, 1745. He was buried in Saint Patrick's, his grave marked with the epitaph he had written for himself: "Go, passer-by, and imitate, if you can, one who spent himself to the utmost in Freedom's cause."

It was a vexing claim, to say the least, for Swift had been at the height of his powers during the passage of the Penal Laws and yet spent no energy in condemning this violation of freedom's cause. The freedom he sought was narrow but, all the same, a threat to the accepted order. He demanded for a certain class, that is, the deserving members of the Church of Ireland, the rights and privileges of Englishmen. In this sense, he did spend himself to the utmost, and established a sense of Anglo-Irish identity.

As Swift approached his end, the transfer of land from Catholic to Protestant was nearly complete. Catholics by and large were now tenant farmers, called cottiers, whose plight varied from barely tolerable to outright miserable. The most impoverished among them lived along roadsides in ramshackle cabins made of sod. A British administrator in Ireland wrote to the King about "the miserable situation of the lower ranks of his subjects in this kingdom." The administrator had no doubts about the cause of Irish poverty; unlike his successors in later decades, he did not find blame in the Irish character. "What from the rapaciousness of their unfeeling landlords and the restrictions on their trade, they are amongst the most wretched people on earth," he wrote.

It was not always the rapacious landlords who demonstrated a lack of feeling, but their agents. Middlemen who leased the land directly from the landlord and in turn rented the land to tenants were the curse of Irish rural life, for they often were greedier than the landlords themselves. And they, like the landlords, made their money simply through control of the land, not by actually farming.

The restrictions on trade certainly helped keep the poor in their wretched state, but, ironically enough, they also helped build what became a signature Irish industry based in Ulster. When the Irish wool industry came under English protectionist assault, textile manufacturers turned to linen, which the crown encouraged and even subsidized, for it presented no competition to any English industries. Entire families took up the linen trade, with women and children doing the spinning and the adult males bringing the goods to market. Linen Halls were built in Belfast and other cities, including Dublin, to coordinate trade with England and the Continent. Although nearly all of Ireland's thirty-two counties developed a linen industry, it centered in northeast Ulster, which became a world capital of linen. By the late 1800s, 80 percent of the value of Ireland's exports consisted of linen or yarn.

Government support for the linen industry benefited the Scots Presbyterians of Ulster who controlled the trade, and the investment seemed to pay off in the year of Swift's death. Scotland in 1745 rose up for one last time against wholesale assimilation into what was now called Great Britain. The Act of Union in 1707 had united Scotland with England and Wales, but the Gaelic Scots in the Highlands still resisted. They were defeated at the Battle of Culloden in 1745. The Irish, including the Scots Presbyterians in Ulster, remained neutral in this dispute.

With all its inequities, Ireland at least seemed pacified. But while members of the Ascendancy were not inclined to rebellion, they were beginning to ask why they remained so dependent, politically and economically, on Britain.

Henry Flood, the son of a political family from County Kilkenny and a graduate of Oxford University, took his place in the Irish House of Commons on November 20, 1759. Irish Parliaments had no fixed tenure, which meant many years could go by without a general election. And fewer than half the three hundred members of the Irish House of Commons were selected in anything resembling a legitimate election. A hundred or so landlords approved the majority of the members.

Two days after Flood's parliamentary debut, a mob of about one thousand Dubliners gathered outside the Parliament building and hurled insults at government officials and members of the Irish House of Commons as they passed. At one point, the outraged citizenry erected a mock gallows, vowing to destroy a member of the House who, rumor had it, was about to introduce a bill that would unite Ireland and England as one country. Eventually, the Dubliners were persuaded to disperse, but two weeks later, a much larger crowd—perhaps as many as ten thousand—actually broke into Parliament and demanded that members swear that they would "never . . . consent to a union" between Ireland and England. Several officials were physically assaulted, including Henry Flood's father, who was Ireland's Attorney General. Warden Flood's coach was attacked outside the gates of Trinity College, and, after being on the wrong end of several cudgels, he appeased his assailants by swearing to "be true to his country."

The unrest was not confined to Dublin, and was broader than questions of politics. Ireland in 1759 was emerging from yet another agricultural crisis. Poor harvests in the mid-1750s caused widespread distress and hunger. In the countryside, hungry farmers and laborers took matters into their own hands, organizing themselves in bands called the Whiteboys—they wore white clothes as they stole through the fields at night—and terrorized landlords and tenants who tried to settle on farms from which poor farmers had been evicted. The Whiteboys were a secret society, a phenomenom that would reappear from time to time in rural Ireland over the next century and a half. Members pledged a solemn oath of membership and spoke nothing of what they did at night.

Hailing from a small village, Callan, far from the substantial buildings of Georgian Dublin, Henry Flood understood that life in the fields was precarious, that an Ireland dependent on grain imports and unable to feed itself because of English-imposed economic restrictions was never far from the abyss.

As the son of the Attorney General—technically, an illegitimate son, as his father and mother lived together for more than a decade and had several children before their marriage—and the grandson of a Member of Parliament, Flood was an establishment figure, one who would have been expected to work within the government. And so he did at first. But his independent temperament could abide such rote loyalty only so long. By 1763, Flood found himself in league with a rump group of reformers. He seized upon the Irish administration's extensive system of patronage, which was distributed freely among members of the House of Commons to buy their support. It was, he said, evidence of the government's corruption. He shocked his colleagues in the House by citing what he called the "real grievances" of the poor Irish, who, he reckoned, made up five sixths of Ireland's population.

He was concerned about Ireland's finances, which were in disarray because of the patronage system. If it continued, he said, Ireland would "sink into voluntary slavery by a supine timidity that will render us contemptible even to our tyrants." The harsh assessment once again shocked his listeners and led to a furious counterattack from government officials.

Flood was acquiring a taste for opposition. It certainly allowed him to exercise his talent for oratory and theatrics, which in combination inspired particularly pointed invective. His speeches helped lead to a reform of Ireland's finances, and he soon became the leader in what was fashioned the Patriot Party in the Irish Commons. He was hardly anti-English; indeed, his speeches and his political maneuvers sought to win for Ireland the freedom and liberty which the English themselves enjoyed. "We have heard of the freemen of Athens," he said. "We have heard of the freemen of Rome. We hear of those in America. Why should we not hear of the freemen of Ireland? Come then, my countrymen, let us be united."

In making such solicitations, however, Flood was hardly suggesting that Irish Protestants unite with Irish Catholics. He opposed concessions to Catholics. The nation he sought to define, to identify, was Irish, not English or British, but it was exclusively Protestant. He referred to his class as the "Protestant nation" of Ireland. His fellow members of the Patriot Party likewise saw themselves as distinctly Irish at a time when many of the gentry still regarded themselves as English people living in Ireland.

In a series of letters published in a Dublin newspaper in 1768, Flood, using the pen name of Philadelphus and adopting the tactics, if not the style, of Jonathan Swift, laid out the Patriot position: Irish Parliaments ought to be subject to fixed duration (a measure limiting Parliaments to ten years soon passed), and Irishmen should resist the English Privy Council's power over the Irish Parliament and should demand an end to English interference in Ireland's economy, especially the regulation of grain. The letters were a natural progression of

the thinking of Molyneux and Swift, fierce and certain in their assertion that Protestant Irish were the equal of Englishmen and therefore
deserved to be accorded the liberties of Englishmen.

Flood saw in almost every failure of governance the destructive influence of Ireland's political and economic dependence on England.
Even the agitation of the Whiteboys was not as threatening as the re-
pressive measures urged by England's representatives in the Irish administration. Referring to calls to crush the Whiteboys through brute
military force, Flood asked: "Can you call the country free in which
these things are done? . . . [Has] oppression become patriotism? Shall
a man be called a patriot because he can drag his chariot wheels over
the necks of miserable men, because he takes the cause of the strong
against the weak, of an oligarchy against a whole? Patriotism consists
in relief, not in oppression."

Although he gained notice and power as an effective opposition
leader, Henry Flood was, after all, a child of government service.
With a change in governments in London, Flood found himself negotiating for high office. After protracted talks, he was appointed as the
Irish administration's vice treasurer in 1775. From being an institutional critic of the Irish administration's use of patronage, Flood now
was part of the very establishment he had so convincingly criticized.
His allies were outraged. One wrote: "Flood, the champion of his
country, the bulwark of her liberties, [has] deserted the glorious cause
in which he had been for fourteen years triumphantly engaged."

The Patriots were without a leader, but not for long.

Henry Grattan was fourteen years younger than Henry Flood, born
in 1746 to a family as prominent as the Floods. His father was among
Ireland's top lawyers; his mother was the daughter of Ireland's Chief
Justice. In one of his most famous decisions, Grattan's maternal
grandfather in 1749 indicted a Dublin physician and political agitator
named Charles Lucas for his attacks on the government and the Irish
establishment. Ireland, Lucas had asserted, should not be dependent
on "a foreign parliament." The Chief Justice denounced him as an
"infamous, inconsiderable, and impudent scribbler, who . . . has dared
to attempt the utter subversion of our Constitution, and to bring us
into absolute anarchy and confusion."

Lucas fled Ireland to avoid arrest when Grattan was two years old.
When Lucas returned to Ireland in 1763 after receiving a pardon,
Grattan was a student at Trinity College, and was not nearly as con-
temptuous of Lucas's remarks as his grandfather had been.

Henry Grattan

Lucas demonstrated that he had not changed during his exile. He immediately assailed Dublin's municipal government for its corrupt patronage system. Among those holding a position with the government in question was James Grattan, Henry's father.

James Grattan could hardly contain himself on the subject of Charles Lucas. But Henry Grattan told his father that he considered Lucas to be a great Irish patriot. James Grattan threw his seventeen-year-old son out of their comfortable home in Dublin. Years later, an aging but unforgiving James Grattan would revise his will to make sure his son Henry received nothing.

Grattan returned to Trinity, earned a law degree in 1767, and went to England for five years of further studies. He allowed himself a number of distractions, including opera, poetry, and debates in the House of Commons. Each in its own way schooled him in theatrics and in rhetoric, skills he would soon put to good use.

Britain was on the verge of war in America when Grattan returned to Dublin. He saw no reason to regret his embrace of Charles Lucas, and he supported the reforms Henry Flood championed in the Irish House of Commons. Inevitably, as he began to travel in Patriot circles in Dublin, Grattan crossed paths with Flood, and the two men took to each other. Both loved oratory and argument, both had rejected the path of their fathers, and both shared a flair for the dramatic. In 1774, as Flood was negotiating for his government position, the two friends were cast together in a Dublin production of *Macbeth*. Flood played the title role; Grattan played MacDuff.

Grattan was not long in the Irish House of Commons when an issue arose that would demonstrate not only his leadership, but the tactical advantages he had as a member of the opposition over Flood, now a member of the government. The Irish, particularly the Presbyterians in Ulster, found themselves taking the side of the American colonists in their disputes with Britain. Like the Irish, the Americans were trying to establish their own identity, their own economy, and, indeed, their equality with Englishmen. And there were a great many Irish people in America. Ulster Presbyterians had been emigrating to America in great numbers since the early 1700s—by the time of the Revolution, there were some quarter-million Ulstermen in America, most of them in the backwoods. (Among them were the Jacksons, late of County Fermanagh and now living in the Carolinas. The family patriarch literally worked himself to death trying to farm the backwoods, leaving behind a widow, two children, and another on the way. The two older boys would enlist in the American rebel army and die. Their mother died of smallpox during the war, leaving thirteen-year-old Andrew Jackson, the son of Ulster immigrants, an orphan.)

Henry Grattan filled the void in Patriot leadership left by Flood in declaring his opposition to a plan to send four thousand British troops from Ireland to America. The soldiers, he said, were being "sent to butcher our brethren in America." Flood had no choice but to support the government. He called the soldiers sent to America "armed negotiators." The Patriots in the Irish House of Commons, numbering about thirty-five in a house of three hundred members and consisting of well-heeled gentry who supported free trade and legislative independence, would now rally around Grattan, not Flood.

Hostilities in America provided Grattan with more than just an opportunity to denounce the government. It quickly became clear that Britain was in for a hard time, and that challenge served to embolden Ireland's radicals and reformers, Grattan included. As Britain continued to redeploy troops from Ireland to America, there was much anxiety that a hostile nation—France, most likely—could seize the moment by landing an army in Ireland to threaten Britain's west coast. This was, of course, the strategic nightmare of British military planners. A homegrown corps of part-time militiamen was enlisted to patrol Ireland. That corps became known as the Volunteers, and by 1778 it numbered forty thousand—including, in some parts of the country, Catholics. With no other choice, Britain had taken the risky step of training and arming a group of civilians in a land where its rule was the subject of heated debate—though not, as in America, of outright rebellion.

The opposition party in Ireland had been handed a powerful card, and Henry Grattan had no qualms about playing it. In 1779, with Britain reeling from the shock of General Burgoyne's defeat at Saratoga two years earlier, Grattan introduced a bill demanding free trade for Ireland. Ireland's overwhelming rural poverty, its failure to exploit natural resources, and its subservience to English industry made the economy an important nationalist issue. Grattan's motion was approved without opposition in the Irish House of Commons. It was a stunning victory. In a display of the forces at work in Ireland, the Volunteers assembled outside Parliament to salute members for passing the long-sought legislation. Technically, of course, free trade could have been overruled in London, but with the war in America dragging on, England could hardly afford to alienate Ireland—particularly an Ireland that boasted forty thousand Volunteers, some of doubtful loyalty. In the days afterward, while the bill was being transmitted to the King for his consideration, the Volunteers continued to demonstrate in favor of it, sometimes wielding swords and shooting off muskets. Two artillery pieces were hauled out near Parliament. Adorning them were placards reading: "Free Trade or This." Several months later, the British Parliament approved the measure. British restrictions on Irish trade ended.

Grattan fully understood the magnitude of his victory, and certainly appreciated that it was not by eloquence alone that Ireland had won this battle. His colleague Hussey Burgh understood what had happened, too. Some weeks after the free trade bill passed, Burgh was arguing in favor of Grattan's proposal to limit taxation in Ireland. More genteel members suggested that such agitation was inappropriate; that it was important to keep the peace. "Peace!" Burgh thundered. "Talk not to me of peace; it is smothered war. England has sown her laws like dragon's teeth, and they have sprung up as armed men!" The Volunteers were now a force in Irish politics, and Grattan soon accepted a commission as a colonel. Along with other reformist politicians and independent-minded squires, Grattan spent his spare time drilling and training the men under his command—although he had no military experience himself. But he knew there would be more battles to come, and the Volunteers would have a role to play.

On April 19, 1780, Grattan took to the floor of the Irish House of Commons to declare that it was time for Ireland to assert its legislative independence from Britain. This was not a statement of separatism, much less of republicanism, that is, a government without a King and based on some notion of equality. Grattan was not advocating the complete independence of Ireland, as America was claiming on the battlefield. Grattan's idea of independence was an autonomous legislature, free to govern Ireland's domestic policy as it saw fit. The motion failed, but the challenge was unmistakable. "I will never be satisfied so long as the meanest cottager in Ireland has a link of the British chain clanking to his rags. . . . As anything less than liberty is inadequate to Ireland, so is it dangerous to Great Britain . . . anything less, we would be her bitterest enemies."

It was a warning that could not pass unheeded, especially as membership in the Volunteers doubled to eighty thousand by 1781, the fateful year in which Lord Cornwallis surrendered to George Washington at Yorktown. In February 1782, only months after the calamitous British defeat in America, the Volunteers assembled for a convention in Dungannon, County Tyrone, and resolved that only the King and the Parliament of Ireland could legislate for Ireland. The claims of Britain's Parliament were, the Volunteers asserted, "unconstitutional, illegal, and a grievance." Equally alarming to the British was a resolution proclaiming the Volunteers' support for a relaxation in the Penal Laws designed to keep Irish Catholics far from power. This ecumenical message was troubling, indeed, for those who counted on the continued division of Ireland by religion.

Thanks to the disaster in America, a new Whig government, more sympathetic to the Irish than the Conservatives who had been in power during the American war, took office in London. Negotiations with Grattan began at once, and by the time the Irish Parliament assembled for an opening session on April 16, 1782, it was clear that something dramatic was about to take place. Volunteers lined the streets as Members of Parliament filed by. Grattan had been ill in late winter and early spring, but he left his sickbed for the dramatic occasion. Weak and drawn, he rose to address his colleagues and a packed, apprehensive gallery: "I am now to address a free people. Ages have passed away, and this is the first moment in which you could be distinguished by the appellation." He then introduced the very same resolutions calling for legislative independence that had been defeated two years before. This time, they passed without opposition, and the Whig government in London agreed to them. The Declaratory Act of 1719, despised by Swift, deplored by Flood, and reviled by Lucas, was repealed. "Ireland is now a nation," Grattan said. "Spirit of Swift! . . . Your genius has prevailed! Ireland is now a nation!"

In his joy, however, he considered the next question: what sort of nation would Ireland be?

Grattan, unlike his mentor, Flood, believed in an inclusive Ireland—an Ireland that regarded its majority population as citizens and partners in an Irish nation. Although Flood eventually supported some measures to ease laws regulating Catholic landholding, he asked: "If the Catholic is given power, can a Protestant government continue?" He concluded that it could not.

Grattan, however, held to the radical notion that Catholics ought to be given full rights as citizens, that they ought to be emancipated from the last of the Penal Laws. "The question is now whether we shall be a Protestant settlement or an Irish nation," he said. "For so long as we exclude Catholics from natural liberty and the common rights of man we are not a people." After he had won legislative independence, Grattan expended much energy and passion in the cause of Catholic emancipation. He argued, in vain, for a bill that would relieve the impoverished Catholics of the tithe they paid to support the established church, the Church of Ireland. Even before his victory in 1782, he had supported relief acts that had allowed Catholics to buy land again and hold leases on the same terms as Protestants. Eventually, he found himself working together with members of a group called the Catholic Committee, made up of merchants and professionals, which sought once and for all to eliminate legal discrimination against Catholics. Among the more impressive committee members with whom Grattan met was a Dublin barrister, a Protestant, named Theobald Wolfe Tone.

Flood did not share Grattan's enthusiasm for Catholic emancipation, nor did he agree that the choice was between an all-Protestant settlement or an inclusive nation. Like Swift, he believed that the Irish nation was a Protestant nation. It could not be otherwise. And after 1782, he sought to reestablish himself as Ireland's preeminent voice of reform. He left his government position and resumed a place with the opposition in the Irish Parliament. There, he argued that Grattan's victory was meaningless, since it did not include a provision calling for Britain to renounce forever a right to legislate for Ireland. Flood's maneuver split the Patriot Party, regained him some popular support among the Volunteers (who were disbanded, except for a few units, after the end of the American war), and led to a violent exchange between the onetime friends on the House floor. Grattan, in a sweeping condemnation of Flood's career, especially his decision to join the government, said: "Sir, your talents are not so great as your life is infamous; you were silent for years, and you were silent for money; when affairs of consequence to the nation were debating, you might be seen passing by these doors like a guilty spirit. . . . I therefore tell you in the face of your country, before all the world—you are not an honest man."

Flood, with magnificent disdain, dismissed Grattan's attack as the work of "disappointed vanity." He challenged Grattan to meet him on what was called in those times a "field of honor." The former friends showed up at the appointed place the following morning, prepared to settle their dispute with guns. The police arrived, however, and no shots were fired. Flood soon faded from Irish politics, and was dead within a decade. He left to Grattan the thankless task of making Ireland into a nation.

And thankless it surely was. Grattan soon discovered that he had earned a hollow victory. The Irish Parliament may have won new powers, but, as Grattan learned through bitter experience, liberty, freedom, and good government did not automatically follow. Although the institution became known as Grattan's Parliament, he never joined the government (although he accepted £50,000 as a token of appreciation for past services), and he continued to hector his colleagues on everything from trade to Catholic rights to reform of Parliament's patronage system. All to no avail. Instead of granting greater freedom, Parliament passed laws strengthening the police as landlords wrung their hands about all those dispossessed Catholics nursing ancient grudges and perhaps bearing arms. "The people of this country supposed that England acceded to their liberties, and they were right; but the present ministry have sent the curse after the blessing," Grattan thundered. "You have got rid of the British Parliament, but we will buy the Irish. . . . Taxes shall be drawn from the poor by various artifices to buy the rich . . . and the old enemies of your constitution made the rulers of the realm."

By the time Grattan's Parliament marked its tenth anniversary in

1792, Grattan himself was frustrated as the promise of independence was smothered by corruption and bigotry. There were others, men and women who had cheered the revolutions in America and France, who might have told him that his exertions would come to nothing, for they were convinced that only sweeping, revolutionary change would win liberty for Ireland.

Theobald Wolfe Tone made his way through the streets of Dublin on the morning of October 10, 1791, to catch a 10:30 coach to Belfast, the bustling commercial town of eighteen thousand people that had become the center of radical politics in Ireland. The hundred-mile journey took nearly two full days, allowing Tone and his friend and traveling companion Thomas Russell ample time to prepare for their deliberations with the men of the north.

In appearance and temperament, they were an unlikely pair. Tone was a thin, delicate-looking twenty-eight-year-old with a pock-marked face. Russell, twenty-three, had a military bearing. He was tall, tan, and handsome with a muscular chest. To the chagrin of his coachmaker father, Tone dreamed of being a soldier even into adult-hood. Russell, a commissioned officer, was the son, nephew, and brother of soldiers, and he had been in battle in India. Tone was charming and outgoing, observing life and its absurdities with a be-mused smile; Russell was earnest and given to self-flagellation over his perceived moral failings. Tone was a graduate of Trinity College, where he was not the most promising of students but had proved to be an engaging and provocative writer. Russell received his education at home from his father, who instructed him in Greek and Hebrew.

They were not, however, so different as would appear. They en-joyed wine and shared an avid interest in attractive women. But Tone was happily married, and he confined his interest to flirtatious banter and candid diary entries. Russell was single and not so restrained.

Though born into the Church of Ireland, they were not from landed families. They enjoyed benefits denied Catholics and even Presbyterians, but they did not enjoy the full privileges of the Anglo-Irish Protestant Ascendancy, which emphasized bloodlines and own-ership of the land. Like the young John Adams in pre–Revolutionary War America, these striving products of Ireland's middle class dis-dained a political order based on birth and holdings.

Belfast was familiar to Russell. He had been dispatched to the city to serve as an ensign in the local artillery barracks in 1790. There, he was soon in touch with some of the city's captains of commerce, in-

Theobald Wolfe Tone

cluding two members of one of Belfast's most prominent merchant families, Henry Joy McCracken and his sister, Mary Ann Mc-Cracken. Mary Ann, twenty years old and full of independent ideas about the role of women in society, was quite taken with Russell's appearance: she described him as a "model of manly beauty . . . one of those favoured individuals whom one cannot pass in the street without being guilty of the rudeness of staring in the face while passing, and turning round to look at the receding figure."

With his charm, good looks, and skepticism of the status quo, Rus-

Thomas Russell

sell fit in well in Belfast society, where the measure of a man's worth was based on achievement and character (and, no doubt inevitably, on appearance), but not birth. Russell's new friends viewed Dublin and its political placeholders as servants of aristocratic privilege, of a class that looked down on men of commerce and trade. The publication of Thomas Paine's *Rights of Man* in February 1791 created a sensation. Tone later remarked that Paine's assault on aristocratic privilege and sectarian bigotry became the Koran of Belfast. The city's successful

Presbyterian merchants saw themselves as children of the Age of Reason, inheritors of radical new notions of democracy and liberty of the sort Paine embraced. Their material success made them staunch meritocrats, deeply suspicious of inherited privilege and economic protectionism, which they regarded as a form of tyranny.

Russell sold his military commission and plunged into Belfast's radical politics, keeping Tone informed of developments. He helped organize a grand procession to commemorate Bastille Day on July 14. An observer of the scene noted that the "French Revolution acted as a spell on the minds of Irishmen . . . such was the demonstration of public feeling in the liberal and enlightened town of Belfast, the Athens of Ireland." The proceedings culminated in a banquet during which toasts were offered to Paine and to the memory of Benjamin Franklin. Russell returned to Dublin and persuaded his friend to make the trip north to meet the men who wished to break the power of artistocratic, religious-based rule in Ireland.

It was to be Tone's first visit to Belfast, and he had reason to question the commitment of the city's radical middle class. Just four months before his visit, these same northerners had rejected resolutions Tone had submitted, through Russell's connections, calling for a "complete internal union" among all Irish reformers. It was a clear suggestion that Catholics be fully included in any reform movement. The rejection stung Tone; he said it turned him into a "red-hot Catholic," although it is hard to know how he would recognize the symptoms, for he had no Catholic friends.

Tone spent the ensuing months reflecting on the state of his country and its persistent divisions. Tone was very much a product of the Enlightenment of the late eighteenth century, a well-read, rational young man who regarded aristocratic rule as a remnant of the corrupt past, and democracy as the inevitable wave of the future. He was an earnest reformer, a younger version of Henry Grattan, until the French Revolution and the publication of Paine's *Rights of Man.* Already something of a romantic, a man who dreamed of military adventures but who was stuck in the dreary profession of law, he seized upon Paine's manifesto and the French Revolution as proof that society could be changed to a more rational, more enlightened model of democracy. "I soon formed my theory. . . . To subvert the tyranny of our execrable government, to break the connection with England, the never-failing source of all our political evils, and to assert the independence of my country—these were my objects," he wrote. "To unite the whole people of Ireland, to abolish the memory of all past dissensions, and to substitute the common name of Irishman, in place of the denomination of Protestant, Catholic and Dissenter—these were my means."

In August 1791, he published what became his most famous broadside. Entitled *An Argument on Behalf of the Catholics* and published under the name "A Northern Whig," it followed Paine's *Rights of Man* as the next literary sensation in Belfast. He wrote: "My argument is simply this: That Ireland, as deriving her government from another country, requires a strength in the people, which may enable them, if necessary, to counteract the influence of that government, should it ever be, as it indisputably has been, exerted to thwart her prosperity: That this strength may be most constitutionally acquired . . . through the medium of a Parliamentary Reform: And, finally, that no Reform is honourable, practicable, efficacious or just, which does not include as a fundamental principle, the extension of elective franchise to the Roman Catholics."

When Tone arrived in Belfast with Russell, he was astonished to discover that the same people who regarded his July resolutions as too radical had read his *Argument* and were now ready to agitate for Catholic emancipation. They were preparing to organize the likeminded into a political organization.

Tone and Russell paid calls on the city's radicals, who included some of the leading businessmen. There was much political discussion over food and drink, so much so that Tone complained after a few days that "nothing more than eating and drinking had yet gone forward." For his part, Russell apparently found the pace to his liking. He indulged himself in the very activities Tone found irritating. He smoked, took ample opportunity to socialize with Belfast's young women, and stayed up long into the early morning. And while he enjoyed himself at the moment, he often woke up to great misgivings about his character. A worried Tone noted that his friend thought he was "losing his faculties."

Finally, after a full week of socializing and discussion, Tone, Russell, and a handful of allied thinkers formally organized a new political organization that would be called the Society of United Irishmen. The group unanimously passed resolutions Tone had written declaring that "the weight of English influence in the Government of this country is so great, as to require a cordial union among all the people of Ireland, to maintain that balance which is essential to the preservation of our liberties, and the extension of our commerce." The members resolved that "the sole constitutional mode by which this influence can be opposed is by a complete and radical reform of the representation of the people in Parliament." In other words, they supported constitutional agitation, not revolutionary violence. And they declared "that no reform is practicable, effacious, or just, which shall not include Irishmen of every religious persuasion." And so was born a society based on principles in conflict with the principles of government in Ireland. The English and the Anglo-Irish imposed religious distinctions on Ireland to repress the majority population. The Society of United Irishmen declared itself opposed to those distinctions.

Tone and Russell returned south to Dublin after a memorable and wildly successful fortnight in Belfast. Within weeks, the Dublin Society of United Irishmen was founded, and this branch, unlike the Belfast society, actually included several Catholics among its members. Tone himself paid little heed to the new organization he had done so much to bring about. He was content to let others run the proceedings, for he quite suddenly had more pressing business—a delegation of Ireland's leading Catholics, impressed by his argument on their behalf, asked him to serve as assistant secretary of their Catholic Committee. With the job came an annual salary of £200, money Tone and his family desperately needed, for he was working only sporadically at the law. He threw himself into the new work, and left the United Irishmen to figure out on their own, for the time being, how to achieve their goal of an Ireland free of sectarian division.

Cracks had appeared in the monolith Henry Flood had called a "Protestant nation."

CHAPTER THREE

THE COMMON NAME OF IRISHMAN

IN THE FALL of 1792, the Duchess of Leinster received a letter from her twenty-nine-year-old son in Paris dated "1st Year of the Republic, 1792." Lord Edward Fitzgerald, scion of one of Ireland's most prominent families, had found in republican France a new society, purged of the old order of landed families and aristocratic titles—a society without the trappings of privilege that had surrounded him from birth.

Edward Fitzgerald saw in the bloodshed and chaos of the French Revolution the makings of a new and purer nation-state. That he would take such a view surprised few of the people who knew him well. One relative remarked that Lord Edward "has acted a romance all of his life." In Paris, he kept company with the Anglo-American journalist and firebrand Thomas Paine. Of the violent atmosphere in this first year of the French republic, Lord Edward wrote: "I can compare it to nothing but Rome in its days of conquest—the energy of the people is beyond belief."

Until the French Revolution, the Irish seemed content to settle for the legislative independence that Grattan championed, together with free trade and a separate Parliament that remained loyal to the Crown. With the storming of the Bastille and the publication of Paine's *Rights of Man*, the political atmosphere in Ireland, particularly in Belfast, changed dramatically. Suddenly, mere legislative independence seemed hollow. Ireland, after all, was not very different under Grattan's Parliament than it was under direct rule from London. Theobald Wolfe Tone had become a good deal more dubious about Grattan's supposed victory. "The Revolution of '82," he wrote, "was a revolution which enabled Irishmen to sell at a much higher

Lord Edward Fitzgerald

price their honour, their integrity, and the interests of their country. ... The power remained in the hands of our enemies, again to be exerted for our ruin." Fitzgerald agreed. He compared the constitution of 1782, which granted Ireland an independent Parliament, to "a young person who though improved in his outward appearance is grown worse in his heart."

In looking to France for inspiration, Ireland's radicals took their challenge to Britain to another level, because the French revolutionaries struck fear in the hearts of Europe's monarchs and aristocrats, particularly in England. And few were as intoxicated with the French spirit as Lord Edward Fitzgerald, the High Church Dubliner and the son of the old order.

On November 18, 1792, Lord Edward attended a dinner called to celebrate the new French republic's military victories over Austria and the Netherlands. The specter that had haunted Europe's governments since the fall of the Bastille had become reality. Republican France was exporting its revolution. The dinner offered a mix of British radicals and French officers, among others. Swept up in the enthusiasm, Lord Edward formally renounced his title, announcing that henceforth he would be simply Citizen Edward Fitzgerald. His fellow citizens in Paris noted that he took to wearing revolutionary fashions: close-cropped hair and simple jackets.

Fitzgerald's love affair with France and its republican ideals found further expression in his affection for a nineteen-year-old child of the Revolution, Pamela de Genlis. Fitzgerald married Pamela after a two-week courtship and brought her back to Dublin, where they proceeded to scandalize fashionable society. Of Fitzgerald, a friend complained, "he is turned a complete Frenchman, crops his hair, despises his title, walks the streets instead of riding." And while Dublin's aristocracy wore mourning clothes in honor of Louis XVI, who went to the guillotine on January 21, 1793, Pamela adorned her hair with pink ribbons.

Fitzgerald and his bride were in Ireland no more than a few weeks when Britain and France declared war on each other in February 1793. The authorities immediately cracked down on pro-French radicals and reformers, and prepared to move against an armed band of Catholic agrarian agitators called the Defenders, who were waging pitched battles against their Protestant counterparts, the Peep o' Day Boys, in parts of rural Ireland. The Defenders, like the Whiteboys of Henry Flood's time, were a secret society that threatened landlords, mutilated their cattle, and stirred up other forms of collective protest against high rents and other grievances. But unlike past secret societies, which focused on local disputes, the Defenders harbored greater ambitions than sectarian warfare and punishing local landlords. The ideas and spirit of the French Revolution had made their way to the fields of Connaught and Ulster, and the Defenders eagerly adopted broad, if vague, goals about democracy and social justice.

The Peep o' Day Boys, on the other hand, were the polar opposites of the middle-class, urban, and politically active merchants of Belfast who celebrated Bastille Day and read Thomas Paine. They lived in the countryside and were filled with the spirit of sectarian warfare that was so much a part of Ulster's legacy in the century since the Battle of the Boyne. The Protestant rural movement consolidated in 1795 in the formation of the Orange Order, which took its name from King William of Orange, victor at the Boyne. In time, the Orange Order would become the keeper and enforcer of Protestant privilege in Ulster.

War with France made it easy for the government to question the loyalties of the pro-French agitators in Ireland. In Belfast, British troops rioted in the streets, attacking a public house that displayed pictures of Benjamin Franklin and leaders of the French Revolution. Finally, the government ordered a raid on the meeting place of the Dublin Society of United Irishmen, Tailor's Hall, on May 23, 1794. The organization's papers were seized, and the society itself was suppressed, although it was kept alive in secret.

An embittered Wolfe Tone thought about giving up on revolution entirely. The Catholic Committee, to which he had devoted himself for nearly two years, had disbanded abruptly after winning a few reforms, called Relief Acts, including voting rights equal to those granted Protestants (for males holding property of at least 40 shillings in value). Parliament, however, had been unwilling to grant Catholics full emancipation. The elite positions in law and government remained exclusively Protestant. Catholics, who made up 75 percent of Ireland's four million people in the 1790s, continued to be barred from Parliament. The Catholic Committee chose not to continue the fight for full citizenship. Tone, now the father of four, resigned himself to returning to his long-neglected career as a lawyer.

Undeterred, Thomas Russell set out to keep the organization alive in rural Ulster, far from the authority of the Dublin-based government. During one of his many trips to Belfast, he met with his friends Henry Joy McCracken and Mary Ann McCracken to discuss their organizing efforts in the north. Mary Ann warned him to move cautiously, for if they failed or slipped up, the government surely would put them to death. "Of what consequence [are] our lives or the lives of a few individuals compared to the liberty and happiness of Ireland," Russell replied.

Even as the radicals tried to reorganize their suppressed organization into a series of small cells, Henry Grattan still was trying to win full Catholic emancipation and other reforms through constitutional agitation. In late 1794, a shake-up in British politics led to a change in London's attitude toward Ireland's Catholics. Or so it seemed. A liberal-minded Whig named Lord Fitzwilliam was dispatched to Dublin to represent the Crown as Lord Lieutenant, or Viceroy, and he shared Grattan's view on Catholic rights and on the need for real reform of the Irish Parliament. He saw as his mission "to purify as far as circumstances and prudence will permit, the principles of government." Grattan was elated. Fitzwilliam arrived in Dublin with much fanfare on January 4, 1795, and Grattan became his chief adviser.

Fitzwilliam immediately began sacking the patronage holders who sucked up so much of the Irish treasury, and then indicated that he would support full Catholic emancipation. Grattan prepared the necessary legislation, and it was introduced on February 12, 1795. An immensely satisfied Grattan assured ecstatic Catholics that "your emancipation will pass. Rely upon it, your emancipation will pass."

It did not. Annoyed with Fitzwilliam's mass dismissals of loyal patronage holders, British Prime Minister William Pitt fired the Lord Lieutenant on February 21 and ordered him to return to London. Dublin came to a standstill as he and his wife were driven through the streets to the River Liffey, where they boarded a boat. In Belfast, Protestant-owned shops closed down and the streets were decorated in black bunting to protest Fitzwilliam's departure. Reform was dead. So were the chances of Catholic emancipation. Henry Grattan would now give way to those with a more radicial vision of a new Ireland.

Even before Fitzwilliam's ignominious dismissal, Wolfe Tone had been in touch with an eccentric Anglican clergyman named William Jackson, whom the French revolutionaries dispatched to Dublin from Paris to serve as a liaison between the United Irishmen and the French Committee on Public Safety. After meeting with Jackson in April 1794, Tone wrote a memorandum for the clergyman to take back to Paris. The Irish, Tone wrote, were ready for revolution: "In Ireland, a conquered and oppressed and insulted country, the name of England and her power is universally odious, save with those who have an interest in maintaining it." If the French could send an expeditionary force of ten thousand troops to Ireland, Tone asserted, two great victories could be achieved: the Irish masses would throw off British rule, and the French would have humiliated their enemies in their own backyard.

Jackson was arrested two weeks later. Luckily, Tone had given the incriminating memo not to Jackson directly, but to a go-between, who made copies in his own handwriting and got rid of the original. The evidence against Tone was gone, but he quickly sought to make a deal with the government. He was granted immunity, and he prepared a document about his dealings with Jackson after extracting a promise that nothing he said would be used in the case against the clergyman. Government officials didn't consider Tone very important; they were happy to make the deal in exchange for Tone's promise to leave the country.

Tone arranged to sell his house and property in County Kildare, and his family, grieving over the loss of the fourth Tone child, Richard, who died in infancy, prepared to start a new life in America. During the the spring of 1795, after Lord Fitzwilliam departed, Tone and his friend Thomas Russell paid a visit to Thomas Addis Emmet, a son of Ireland's state physician and a brilliant attorney who defended suspects accused of membership in the banned United Irish movement. Emmet had recently astonished his colleagues when, in pleading for the life of a client convicted of administering the United Irishmen's oath—a capital offense—he read the seditious words aloud in court: "I will endeavour, so much as lies in my ability, to forward a brotherhood of affection, an identity of interest, a communion of rights, and a union of power, among Irishmen of all religious persuasions." When he completed his reading, he directed his attention to the judges: "My Lords, here, in the presence of this legal court . . . I myself, in the presence of God, declare: I take the oath!"

Emmet's clients were spared the death sentence. And Emmet, an upper-class graduate of Trinity College who had been transformed by the revolution in America, was marked as a dangerous man.

Tone and Russell joined Emmet at the lawyer's home, and as they strolled through his property, Emmet gestured toward a study under construction on the grounds. Emmet promised to "consecrate" the new room for use as a meeting place after Ireland won its freedom. Tone jokingly pleaded with Emmet to make sure he stocked the room with "a few dozen of his best old claret" because Russell no doubt would be in attendance at the meetings.

Tone, his wife Matilda, and their party then traveled to Belfast, where they were treated to dinners in their honor and a gift of £1,500 raised from Belfast's radical community. Tone and Russell joined their friend Henry Joy McCracken and several other allies on a hike to the summit of a hill high over Belfast. There, they vowed to each other that they would "never desist in our efforts until we had subverted the authority of England over our country, and asserted our independence." As a solemn formality, McCracken swore Tone into the reorganized Society of United Irishmen, which was now loosely modeled after the secret societies of rural Ireland. Wolfe Tone then set sail for America on June 13.

Government officials reckoned he would cause no more trouble.

The Ireland he left behind had not changed a great deal for all the talk of revolution and the promises of reform. The majority popula-

Henry Joy McCracken

tion, the island's Catholics, saw little practical improvement in their daily lives despite the lifting of most of the Penal Laws through the Catholic Relief Acts of 1778 and 1782. Those reforms were enough for nervous middle-class Catholics, but they did nothing to address the basic imbalance between the landed, Protestant gentry and the landless, mostly Catholic tenant farmers and laborers. Save for the continued bar on Catholics in political office and top professions, the Penal Laws were eased, but their legacy was not so easily re- pealed. The mass of Irish remained impoverished and uneducated, in-

culcated with both a resentment toward the elite usurpers and a deference to the landlords who could cast them off the land on a whim.

The social inequities and religious divisions offended the sensibilities of Henry Joy McCracken and his sister, Mary Ann. Though
reared in a deeply religious Presbyterian family, they sympathized
with the plight of Catholics and indeed with the poor in general.
Members of their mother's family built a poorhouse in Belfast to look
after the needs of the impoverished, and the McCracken children
were frequent visitors.

John McCracken, the family patriarch, was a prosperous sea captain and descendant of Scots settlers in Ulster. His wife, Ann, was the
offspring of one of Belfast's leading families, the Joys. Henry Joy Mc-
Cracken was born on August 31, 1767, Mary Ann on July 8, 1770.
The McCracken family personified the spirit of Belfast's new merchant class. John McCracken sought his fortune well beyond Ireland
and Britain, and Ann demonstrated both noteworthy independence
and business acumen in opening her own muslin business after her
marriage.

Though neither John nor Ann was active in Belfast's tempestuous
politics, current events and the city's exciting civic life were ever present in the household. The two eldest McCracken boys, Francis and
William, eagerly joined the Belfast Volunteers, and, in a singular ecumenical moment, they joined their Protestant colleagues in attending
the opening of Belfast's first Roman Catholic Church in 1784 in full
uniform.

Their parents, too, embraced the new thinking. Rejecting traditional schooling that provided only the basics for girls, the McCrackens sent their children to a progressive, meritocratic private school
that was defiantly coeducational, with girls receiving exactly the same
education as boys. Mary Ann McCracken flourished in this atmosphere, and discovered she had a talent for mathematics. The effects
of this liberating experience were evident years later, in a letter Mary
Ann wrote to her brother Henry Joy (or Harry, as she called him).
Taking a skeptical note of women's societies that served as mere auxiliaries for male-only organizations, she wondered whether the women
organizers "have any rational ideas of liberty and equality for themselves, or [are they] contented with their present abject and dependent situation, degraded by custom and education."

Henry Joy worked in the family textile business from the time he
was seventeen. He took the family's civic commitments seriously, and
helped found Belfast's first Sunday school, which catered to the
working classes. He persuaded some of his friends to serve as teach-

ers. For the McCrackens, religion was not a political badge but a deeply spiritual and moral commitment. Henry Joy asserted that "all evils . . . proceed from the want of real, vital and practical religion, for were all who profess to be Christians truly so in heart and practice . . . there would neither be slave holding in America . . . nor any of the numerous and unjust and oppressive laws with which [Britain] abounds." Chief among those injustices, in McCracken's view, was the oppressive tithe that Ireland's Catholics paid to maintain the Protestant Church of Ireland.

Given his lack of religious bias, he was well suited to the job of recruiting members from the Catholic Defenders movement into the reorganized Society of United Irishmen. McCracken won credibility with Catholics not just with words but by publicly supporting them when they came under attack by Protestant mobs in the Ulster countryside. He and a friend paid for an attorney to investigate attacks on Catholic property in County Armagh. His goodwill and determination made a deep impression on Ulster's Catholics.

All the while, however, government agents were watching. An official memo took note of McCracken's frequent visits to rural areas, where the Defenders lived: "McCracken is frequently sent out on a mission to the country. . . . I will have a watch upon him day and night," the memo read.

In the meantime, Lord Edward Fitzgerald carried on an aggressive recruiting mission in and and around Dublin. One observer noted that Fitzgerald was especially active in the rural areas near his country home in County Kildare. There, it was said, he "danced among the rustics at bonfires, and in short uniformly conducted himself among them with such uncommon . . . freedom and affability [that] he stole away the hearts of the people."

Though quite clearly committed to revolution, Fitzgerald was not yet a member of the Society of United Irishmen. He was close enough to its leaders, however, to meet with them to discuss tactics and strategy. In early 1796, he suggested that the society send representatives to Europe to begin direct negotiations with the French revolutionary government.

Fitzgerald didn't know that Theobald Wolfe Tone had left his exile in America and already was in Paris pleading for French help for Ireland.

Tone and his party had landed in Philadelphia in early August 1795. He was in touch with other Irish exiles within days of his arrival. The exiles introduced him to a French diplomat in the city, who supported Tone's idea to recross the Atlantic to present his ideas to the French government in person. Tone sailed for France on December 17, 1795, leaving Matilda behind. He didn't know it when he left, but she was pregnant again.

He arrived in France on February 1, 1796, and presented himself to the American ambassador, the future President James Monroe, who gave him a reference at the French Ministry for Foreign Affairs. He spent the next several months shuttling from meeting to meeting, writing memoranda and otherwise pleading Ireland's case to France's top political and military officials. He was alternately exhilarated and depressed, but always he was lonely. "Here I am, alone, in the midst of Paris, without a single soul to advise or consult with and nothing in fact to support me but a good intention," he wrote. "Sad! Sad!"

His good intention, however, soon proved enough for one young French military leader—General Lazare Hoche, who, at twenty-eight, had emerged as one of the country's two great military leaders. The other was his rival, Napoleon Bonaparte, who was winning glorious victories in Italy.

Tone drew up a proposal calling for an invasion force of up to twenty thousand men. French officials already were considering it when Lord Edward Fitzgerald began his negotiations with French agents in Hamburg in late May. Fitzgerald proposed a more modest landing, but the French were impressed with Tone's ambitious plans. They told Fitzgerald they recognized "the importance of the proposed operation" and were "about to put it into execution." Indeed they were. On June 19, the French Directory wrote to Hoche: "We intend, Citizen General, to restore to a people ripe for revolution the independence and liberty for which it clamours. Ireland has groaned under the hateful yoke of England for centuries."

Amazingly, Tone—the amateur soldier and untested revolutionary—had succeeded. Some time later, no less an authority than the Duke of Wellington would observe that "Wolfe Tone was a most extraordinary man. . . . With a hundred guineas in his pocket, unknown and unrecommended, he went to Paris in order to overturn the British government in Ireland. He asked for a large force, Lord Edward Fitzgerald for a small one. They listened to Tone."

Fitzgerald left Hamburg convinced that revolution was coming to Ireland, and that the French would supply troops and arms to advance the cause of republican virtue. He was back in Ireland in September. But the situation soon changed dramatically.

Ireland had come close to outright war, with or without the French, during Fitzgerald's absence. The Protestant Peep O' Day Boys were rampaging through Catholic areas, forcing the inhabitants to flee their homes and making a mockery of the founding principles of the United Irishmen. A few days before Fitzgerald's return, British authorities decided to "cut the head off the monster," in the words of Lord Castlereagh, chief aide to the Lord Lieutenant. Castlereagh was particularly concerned about the "Presbyterian element in the North," which he identified as "the real centre of genuine republican sympathy." A search party was dispatched to arrest Thomas Russell, whose activities in Ulster had stirred great anxiety among government officials. Russell surrendered peacefully. He spent the next six years in prison awaiting trial.

Knowing that soldiers would be looking for him, Henry Joy McCracken steered clear of his family home in Belfast, remaining in the countryside with the farmers and laborers he was recruiting into the United Irish movement. Finally, though, the government caught up with him. He was arrested in County Armagh on October 10 and dispatched into solitary confinement in Kilmainham jail in Dublin.

Lord Edward Fitzgerald followed events with growing apprehension. At last, he took the solemn oath of membership in the Society of United Irishmen. He would become the organization's commanding general.

In France, Theobold Wolfe Tone, who had dreamed even into adulthood of a career as a soldier, wore the colors of a French general. "Put on my regimentals for the first time, am pleased as a little boy in his first breeches," he wrote. He was ecstatic, with reason; Hoche was to be in charge of an invasion force that was assembling near Brest on the French coast. Some fifteen thousand French troops were preparing to board forty-five ships that would be loaded down with cannon and ammunition. Tone was ordered to prepare to ship out in late November. He wrote a letter to Matilda, who was making her way across the Atlantic with their children. "[S]hould the worst happen, remember you will be their only parent—I need not, indeed, I cannot say more," he wrote. But if he survived, he promised his long-suffering wife that he would "devote the remainder of my life to making you happy and educating our children."

He was ordered aboard the *Indomptable,* which carried eighty guns. Hoche boarded the *Fraternité,* a frigate, but not before disappearing for a two-night liaison with, in Tone's appreciative description, "a charming little aristocrat." They set sail on December 15.

There was trouble almost immediately. Several ships collided as they tried to manuever into the open sea in darkness. Somehow, the

Fraternité became separated from the main fleet and was eventually blown out to sea, not to be seen again until it returned to France a month later. The loss of the commander was catastrophic, but the armada regrouped and set sail for its destination: Bantry Bay, on the southwest coast of Ireland.

The last few months of 1796 found Lord Edward Fitzgerald playing the role of respected son of one of Ireland's great families. He and Lord Castlereagh, who had ordered the arrests of Lord Edward's allies, often saw each other socially and exchanged pleasantries, knowing all the while that they were pitted against each other in an unspoken but increasingly dangerous struggle. When not socializing with Dublin's elite, Fitzgerald and a friend named Arthur O'Connor set off on organizing missions in the west of Ireland, the most likely place for the French invasion they believed would come.

Winter came early to Ireland in 1796. Fitzgerald, after spending a few days with his wife, Pamela, in their County Kildare home, set out for Dublin just before Christmas for a series of meetings with the United Irish leadership. Lord Edward still was in Dublin on Christmas Day when Pamela heard startling news: a French fleet had arrived in Bantry Bay.

The ships had arrived off the Irish coast on December 21. Surprise was complete—even the United Irishmen were unprepared. The French were expecting a friendly force to greet them, but from the deck of their ships, they saw only the barren, snow-covered terrain of County Kerry.

A gale blew in on December 23, sending twenty ships out to sea, helpless in the face of the storm. The French decided to go forward, although they now had only 6,400 soldiers available and just four cannons. But Christmas Eve came and went without a landing. The French commanders, none of them as bold as Hoche, were paralyzed. The winds kicked up again on Christmas Day, dragging more ships out to sea. Tone was disconsolate: everything he had planned for had gone so well until the shore was in sight. "We have been now six days in Bantry Bay, within five hundred yards of the shore, without being able to effectuate a landing," he wrote. "Well, let me think no more about it; it is lost, and let it go. . . . If God Almighty sends me my dearest love and darling babies in safety, I will buy or rent a little spot, and have done with the world forever. I shall neither be great, nor famous, nor powerful, but I may be happy."

What was left of the fleet departed Bantry Bay on December 27 without firing a shot.

The authorities in Dublin and in London understood just how close they had come to disaster. The United Irishmen, on the other hand, understood just how close they had come to success. And they acted accordingly, in their disparate ways. The government prepared to launch a ruthless campaign against the United Irish movement. And the United Irishmen welcomed hundreds of new recruits who regarded the failed landing not as a defeat, but as a sign that the conspirators really did know their business.

Though Edward Fitzgerald knew the French were preparing an invasion, he had had no advance warning that the fleet was on its way. Still, he saw only good in the failure in Bantry Bay. His sister, Lucy, noted that she had never seen him "with such pleasure." His days were spent shuttling from Dublin to Belfast, where the northern leaders would soon become impatient with talk. He thought it wise to stay away from his family's Dublin seat, Leinster House, and indeed some of his relatives began to distance themselves from him as rumors spread of his activities. But Lucy became a convert to republicanism during the early months of 1797, and, like Edward and his wife Pamela, seemed to delight in shocking her social circle. "Went to town for a ball at Lady Clare's," Lucy wrote. "I had my hair turn'd close up, was reckon'd democratic; and was not danced with." But Pamela, who had given birth to a daughter nine months before, had become less inclined to delight in revolution. "To tell you the truth," she wrote to Lucy, "I fear to look at the future."

In early February 1797, Lord Edward, the lawyer Thomas Addis Emmet, and other top United Irish leaders met in Dublin for an emergency meeting. The situation, especially in the north, was getting near the breaking point. Arms were being stockpiled in secret; the Defenders were eager to strike. A delegate was dispatched to Paris to ask for another landing, this one of 20,000 to 25,000 soldiers and 100,000 weapons. The United Irishmen promised to deliver between 30,000 and 40,000 men of their own to the campaign.

In Belfast, seat of the unrest, the spirit of enlightenment gave way to the shadow of fear. Arrests were commonplace; men were taken away by soldiers on mere suspicion of being United Irishmen. The men and women who only months before had reveled in the spirit of the French Revolution now witnessed firsthand the effect of words put into action. The tension in Belfast horrified Mary Ann McCracken. In the early hours of Saint Patrick's Day, she poured out her feelings in a letter to her imprisoned brother Harry. She wrote of her hopes for a new Irish nation, one that would offer women a greater role in the running of the country: "I hope the present Era will produce some women of sufficient talents to inspire the rest with a genuine love of Liberty.... I think the reign of prejudice [against women] is nearly at an end, and that the truth and justice of our cause alone is sufficient to support it, as there can be no argument produced in favour of the slavery of woman that has not been used in favour of general slavery.... I therefore hope it is reserved for the Irish nation to strike out something new and to [show] an example of candour, generosity and justice."

By the time she sent her letter, Ulster was under martial law. In taking up his post as military commander of the region, Lieutenant General Gerard Lake of the British army wrote of the United Irishmen and their allies: "Nothing but terror will keep them in order." Lake not only had the regular British army under his command, but also a corps of militia known as yeomen. With officers recruited from the gentry, the yeomen eventually numbered forty thousand troops, nearly all of them Protestant, and were particularly noteworthy for their brutality.

Lake ordered cold-bloodedly efficient searches that turned up nearly six thousand firearms and thousands of freshly forged pikes. Men suspected of republican sympathies were flogged, and when Lake learned that some members of his militia were leading a double life as sworn members of the United Irishmen, he ordered four of them—men who refused to turn informer—executed as an example to the others.

Within two months, Lake was satisfied with the performance of his troops, although he cautioned authorities that there still was work to be done. "The flame is smothered," he wrote, "but not extinguished."

The winds, however, had carried embers far beyond Ulster. In the tiny town of Boolavogue in County Wexford, an agent from the Dublin executive of the United Irishmen was recruiting members door-to-door. The effort proved so encouraging that the recruiters began distributing anti-government literature after Sunday Mass in the town chapel.

When the agents from the United Irishmen took their effort a step further by handing out society propaganda calling for revolution, a local Protestant clergyman informed the government of the outrage. The minister took note of disturbing developments in Boolavogue: "A visible change took place in the temper and manner of the lower classes," he wrote. "There were surly expressions.... There were threats, whispers and hints ... of revenge upon enemies." Soon, fifteen local men were arrested and marched to the Wexford jail. All fifteen men worshipped in the same little Roman Catholic chapel. The local curate in Boolavogue was Father John Murphy, a husky, unassuming forty-four-year-old cleric who had studied under the Dominicans in Spain. He was a Wexford man himself, reared by tenant farmers in the townland of Tincurry. Father Murphy received his first formal lessons from hedge schoolmasters who roamed the Irish countryside, frustrating the intent of the ban on Catholic education.

Father Murphy's superiors took note of the presence of agitators outside of his church. Some years earlier, the local bishop, James Caufield, had made his opinions clear: "Loyalty to the gracious good King George III; submission to His Majesty's government ... obedience and observance of the laws are to be [an] indispensable duty to every Roman Catholic." Bishop Caufield summoned Father Murphy of Boolavogue for a refresher course in the duties of a Roman Catholic in Ireland.

News of increased tension and violence reached Henry Joy McCracken in Dublin's Kilmainham jail. McCracken's brother John described the deteriorating situation in Belfast and throughout Ulster. John detailed "the barbarities committed on the innocent country people by the yeomen and the Orangemen. The practice among them is to hang a man up by the heels with a rope full of twist, by which means the sufferer whirls round like a bird roasting at the fire, during which he is lashed with belts ... to make him tell where he has concealed arms. Last week, at a place near Dungannon, a young man being used in this manner called to his father for assistance, who being inflamed at the sight, struck one of the party a desperate blow with his turf spade; but, alas! his life paid the forfeit of his rashness—his entrails were torn out and exposed on a thorn bush."

General Lake believed only terror would pacify the country, and terror the country would get.

As the crisis intensified, Fitzgerald, Emmet, and other leaders of the United Irish movement were paralyzed. Indecision as well as internal conflicts exacerbated the situation. With Belfast and the rest of Ulster suffering the terror of General Lake's soldiers, Ulster leaders argued that the time had come to strike. Control of the Society of United Irishmen, however, had passed from Belfast to Dublin, and the leaders in the south hesitated in the face of sudden, all-out rebellion.

Meetings in the capital broke up amid bitter and angry words. Fitzgerald's chief ally, Arthur O'Connor, pressed for immediate action, even without the French. Fitzgerald was ready to start the war, but he still held out hope for a French-led rebellion.

Emmet, along with his closest ally, a Catholic doctor named William McNeven, argued that the country wasn't ready for rebellion, and indeed the Society's forces in and around Dublin were conspicuously unorganized. Unlike Fitzgerald, Emmet held no romantic visions of a sweeping social revolution in Ireland to replicate the insurrection in France. But he believed French help was critical, because he doubted the wisdom of sending the poor Irish against Britain's mighty armed forces. Emmet's arguments won the day, prompting O'Connor to leave Ireland, depriving Lord Edward of a valued friend and confidant.

Soon, however, Fitzgerald recruited a new ally to take O'Connor's place, a man named Thomas Reynolds. He was a stranger, but he had impeccable credentials—his sister-in-law was Wolfe Tone's wife, Matilda. Fitzgerald immediately took him into his confidence, promoted him within the Society, and invited him to his home. This made Reynolds's future work easy: he soon became a government informer, and reported details of Fitzgerald's deliberations to the government's administrative center in Dublin Castle.

On his way back to France after the disappointment in Bantry Bay, Theobald Wolfe Tone vowed that he would settle down and attend to the education of his children. But he clearly was not of a mind to make good on such a rash promise. He plunged yet again into the work of conspiracy, renewing his alliance with Hoche. He finally met the man who had done so much to bring Ireland to the brink of revolution—Thomas Paine himself. "He is vain beyond all belief," Tone wrote, "but he has reason to be vain and for my part I forgive him. He has done wonders for the cause of liberty."

By the middle of 1797, plans were drawn up for another French invasion force, and once again Hoche was to be in command. Tone set out for Germany in mid-September to confer with the young general. He found a man dying of tuberculosis. Tone was appalled. "It is terrible to see a fine handsome fellow, in the very flower of youth and strength, so reduced," he wrote. "My heart bleeds for him." He died at 4:00 A.M. on September 19 at the age of twenty-nine. Tone wrote Matilda: "Dearest Love . . . we have lost our brave general, Hoche . . . I am in a very sincere affliction."

A despondent Tone returned to Paris and to the work at hand. He cajoled his contacts in the French government. Finally, just before Christmas 1797, he won an audience with Napoleon. He presented Bonaparte with "a whole sheaf of papers relative to Ireland" and he conceded to the great general that he, Tone, was not to be considered a military leader.

"But," Bonaparte replied, "you are brave."

Tone soon received orders to prepare once again for an expedition to liberate Ireland. Bonaparte, as commander of the armies in northern France, gave orders to build a fleet that could transport fifty thousand men with artillery. Thousands of men were put to work preparing to support the invasion force. Word reached a horrified Dublin Castle: the French would soon be on the seas again.

In County Wexford, trees were being turned into shafts for pikes while blacksmith shops became the munitions factories of an aroused peasantry. A local member of the United Irishmen wrote that "every man had firearms of some sort, or a pike; the latter weapon was easily had at this time, for almost every blacksmith was a United Irishman." In November 1797, sixteen parishes in the county were threatened with martial law, which meant that authority would pass from civilians to a military whose methods had been given full display in Ulster under General Lake. Father Murphy's parish in Boolavogue was among those under the military's threat. The curate received an urgent letter from his bishop, James Caufield, demanding that Catholics "surrender to their magistrates their arms, guns, muskets, pistols, blunderbusses, swords, spears, pikes and any and every warlike . . . weapon in their possession."

The local landlord, Lord Mountmorris, began showing up at Catholic churches carrying with him a written oath of loyalty to King George III, which he requested that parishioners sign in hopes of avoiding the full brunt of martial law. He found this an easy task, until he arrived in Boolavogue to address Father Murphy's congregation. Mountmorris read the oath of loyalty aloud: "I will use every possible exertion to prevent and suppress all tumult, riot or secret conspiracy. . . . I never will take the oaths of the United Men." When he finished, not a man moved to sign the document. Murphy said nothing to encourage them. The astonished landlord sputtered for a moment, and then let loose with a tirade warning of the terrors martial law would surely bring.

The landlord's words had the intended effect. Father Murphy

signed the oath, followed, grudgingly, by the men of his parish. When he learned of Father Murphy's recalcitrant parishioners, Bishop Caufield threatened to suspend the priest from his duties if his flock continued to show such dangerous defiance.

McCracken spent the Christmas holidays of 1797 in a sickbed, but at least it was his own bed and not that of a prison hospital. He had been granted bail in early December, after serving more than a year in Kilmainham. Much had changed in the movement during his imprisonment, but he had been kept abreast of events thanks to liberal visitation rights. Edward Fitzgerald visited him during the summer to discuss the tensions in Ulster. Fitzgerald wore a disguise when he came to the prison, and he fooled everybody except the prison governor's wife, who recognized him but said nothing, for she had taken a liking to McCracken and his comrades.

Prison had changed McCracken. "Yesterday, two men were hanged in front of the jail for robbing the Mail in June last," he wrote to Mary Ann. "They died with the greatest fortitude. One of them going past our window for execution turned round and saluted us with the greatest composure. It gives me a carelessness about death to see such sights."

By February 1798, McCracken was sufficiently healthy again to resume the life of a conspirator. He became a liaison between Dublin, where the center of the movement had shifted, and Belfast. Amid rumors of an imminent French invasion, continued outbreaks of agrarian violence, and further military crackdowns, Fitzgerald called for a convention of United Irish delegates in Dublin on February 26. McCracken was there, along with Emmet and the rest of the society's top leaders. McCracken pushed for an immediate rebellion. Conditions in the north, he said, were intolerable. The sectarian yeomen corps had brought the province to the edge of rebellion. McCracken was no orator, and his education could not compare with that of some of his colleagues, but his argument was based on the terrors he had seen or heard of in Ulster. Of the would-be soldiers he had recruited into the movement, he said: "They would rather be in the field like men than hunted like wild beasts, and see their friends carried off to jail, their houses ransacked and the Orange yeomen riding roughshod over them day by day."

Other delegates, from the south as well as the north, agreed. Although they knew the French were preparing an invasion fleet, the militant delegates wanted immediate action. The British military, they argued, already were making war on the general population, so the revolutionaries couldn't wait for the French. Lord Edward was similarly inclined, but Emmet remained opposed. Though deeply suspicious of the French, he argued once again that no rising in Ireland could succeed without France's intervention. Lord Edward countered: "We have overwhelming numbers and the element of surprise." He had documents showing that there were 279,896 men sworn into the secret army, an astonishing figure. The British had about 75,000 troops, including regular army and militia, at their disposal in Ireland, and on the very day that the conspirators gathered in Dublin, General Ralph Abercromby, commander in chief of His Majesty's forces in Ireland, dispatched a letter to London containing his opinion of the men under his command. The British army, he wrote, was "in a state of licentiousness which must render it formidable to everyone but the enemy."

Fitzgerald gave his handwritten analysis of the movement's organization to his new adviser, Thomas Reynolds, who turned over the document to government authorities. They were stunned to read of the movement's strength.

Despite the wishes of McCracken and Fitzgerald, however, the United Irishmen would not be summoned to action right away. The cautions of Emmet and McNeven had an impact: the convention agreed to a resolution that "requested" the militants "to bear the shackles of tyranny a little longer."

The conspirators went their separate ways understanding that the revolution was near.

Lord Edward threw himself into the details of the coming rebellion. He concentrated much of his strategic thinking on Dublin. The United men would seize the city's important buildings while a huge army in the countryside isolated the capital and cut off troop movements. Understanding the rudimentary nature of his prospective army, Lord Edward suggested tactics that would allow men armed with ten-foot pikes to overcome the advantages held by trained soldiers with firearms. The British, he wrote, could be "attacked by an irregular Body armed with pikes or such bold Weapons. . . . Perhaps at the same Moment, they may be dreadfully galled from the Housetops, by Showers of Bricks, Coping Stones, etc., which may be at Hand." He asserted that guns "should not intimidate" men with pikes because in close quarters "powder and ball" are useless.

The Dublin conspirators scheduled a meeting for March 12 in the home of Oliver Bond, an affluent draper. Thomas Reynolds communicated this information to the government, and constables burst in on the meeting and arrested all thirteen men in attendance, including Emmet. As the Ulster leaders had been routed in 1797, now the Leinster leaders were in custody—except for Fitzgerald. Search parties were dispatched immediately to bring in the commander in chief of the United Irish army, the son of Ireland's noblest family.

As a sheriff's party demanded entrance to Leinster House, Lord Edward hustled out a back door and disappeared into the narrow, crowded streets. The sheriff and his men came upon Lord Edward's wife, Pamela, shoving papers into a fireplace. Among the documents she hadn't yet burned, and which the sheriff seized, was Lord Edward's handwritten plan for an assault on Dublin. The government had all it needed to send Fitzgerald to the gallows.

Fitzgerald spent the next two months on the run. Despite the imprisonment of his colleagues, he and the men who replaced the jailed leaders circulated a written statement to the public that left no mystery about what was afoot: "Be firm, Irishmen, but be cool and cautious . . . and above all we warn you, again and again we warn you, against doing the work of your tyrants, by premature, by partial or divided exertion."

Near the end of March, British military officials in Ireland were warning London that the countryside was filled with increasingly brazen and well-armed farmers who seemed intent on bloodshed. "The insolence of the people is astonishing," wrote one British administrator.

Such complaints hardly moved the British commander in chief, General Abercromby. His jaundiced eye saw fault not only with the soldiers under his command, but with the Irish gentry for whose benefit law and order were maintained. He viewed them as ignorant and lazy, hardly deserving of support. "The pursuit of pleasure or political intrigue," he wrote, seemed to be their main interest. It was hardly a wonder, he said, that the people were so alienated from the government.

On March 30, Britain's top civil administrator, Lord Camden, the Lord Lieutenant, declared Ireland to be in a state of rebellion and proclaimed martial law throughout the country. Abercromby resigned, and all power passed into the hands of the new commander in chief, General Lake, the man who had brought Ulster to heel in 1797.

The army fanned out into the countryside on a mission to seize arms and break the United Irishmen. Within a few weeks, the army introduced an innovative device designed to make interrogation more efficient: the triangle—a wooden, three-sided scaffolding upon which unlucky citizens could be fastened and then flogged with a cat-o'-

nine-tails until they provided soldiers with information about arms and the whereabouts of suspected members of the United Irishmen.

Another efficient technique was the pitch cap. Men with French-style cropped hair—croppies—were seized, restrained by the hands, and turned over to soldiers skilled in the art of pouring boiling tar, or pitch, into a conelike hat. The cap was then placed on a suspect's head so that the boiling tar ran down his face, into his mouth and eyes. If the soldiers were in a particularly feisty mood, they allowed the tar to cool off and harden, and then ripped the cap off the suspect's head, taking hair, scalp, and sometimes ears. One particularly ingenious soldier in Wexford added gunpowder to the mix and then set it afire, ripping off the tops of victims' heads.

On April 27, the notorious North Cork Militia moved into County Wexford to apply General Lake's methods of law and order.

In Dublin, Fitzgerald was making final preparations for the rebellion from his hiding place on Thomas Street. His mother's second husband (and his former tutor), William Ogilvie, paid him a secret visit in late April, carrying with him an offer from government officials to flee Ireland without fear of arrest. Fitzgerald refused, saying that honor required that he remain with his fellow conspirators until the end. He paid an unannounced call on his wife, Pamela, in the rooms she rented after her husband's escape from Leinster House. The sight of Lord Edward was such a surprise that Pamela, seven months pregnant, went into labor. She delivered a daughter, Lucy, later that night.

Early May brought terrible news. Napoleon had changed his mind, and there would be no French support for a rebellion in springtime. Fitzgerald was counting on some five thousand soldiers, but the French said the troops would not be available until August. Emmet's fears were about to come true. Ireland's poorly trained citizen army would have to fight the power of the British without French support.

Lord Edward nevertheless pressed forward with his preparations. The date for the rebellion was fixed for May 23. But on the night of May 19, as Lord Edward lay in bed nursing a cold and reviewing plans for the imminent rebellion, the police burst into his hiding spot on Thomas Street. An officer named Major Swann announced: "You know me, my Lord, and I know you. It will be vain to resist." Fitzgerald pulled out a dagger and stabbed Swann three times. Another officer, a Captain Ryan, came to Swann's aid. He and Lord Edward wrestled with each other, stumbling and finally falling down a flight of stairs together. Fitzgerald stabbed Ryan more than a dozen times, ripping open his stomach. Another member of the arresting party shot Lord Edward in his right shoulder. The struggle was over, and Lord Edward was taken into the government's custody and was charged with treason.

When word reached Belfast that Fitzgerald was under arrest, Henry Joy McCracken recommended a desperate course. Some of the top army officers in Ulster were due to attend a concert on May 21, two days before the rebellion was to begin. McCracken suggested the United Irishmen kidnap the officers as a dramatic gesture to inspire the rest of the country. The commander of the insurgent Ulster army, Robert Simms, turned down the plan.

Not surprisingly, very little went according to plan on May 23. Fitzgerald's plan to seize Dublin Castle and other strongpoints never came close to reality; indeed, there was hardly any rebel activity in the capital. In the countryside, however, thousands slipped away from their homes under the cover of darkness and assembled at pre-arranged meeting places. Modern weapons were few, artillery nearly nonexistent. For the most part, the rebels prepared for battle bearing pikes, scythes, and pitchforks.

In and around Father Murphy's parish of Boolavogue, there were no ragtag columns of men prepared to resist the rampaging military, and Father Murphy continued to demand that his parishioners surrender their weapons. Some terrified people who were unarmed actually made crude pikes in order to turn them in to the authorities and thus—they hoped—ensure that they and their homes would be safe.

Father Murphy met with the men of Boolavogue on May 26 and continued to urge the surrender of weapons even as word spread of horrendous atrocities throughout the county. Later that night, Father Murphy joined the men in a walking tour of an area known as the Harrow. Some carried arms despite the priest's pleas. After visiting a home rumored to be a possible target for the soldiers, Father Murphy and his men stumbled upon a patrol of yeomen led by a Lieutenant Bookey. The troops opened fire; Father Murphy's men scrambled for cover, and Bookey and one of his troops galloped toward the house Murphy had just left and set it ablaze. Their goal accomplished, the two men turned and found their comrades gone, driven off by Father Murphy's men. A shot rang out, and Bookey's comrade fell dead. Men with pikes swarmed around Bookey and hacked him to death.

The men of Boolavogue were rebels now. They turned to Father Murphy and asked what they should do next.

"It would be better for us to die like men than to be butchered like dogs in the ditches," Father Murphy said. "If I have any men to join me, I am resolved to sell my life dearly."

Father Murphy led them to the town of Oulart, where they joined other rebel columns from the area on a hill that offered a sweeping view of the countryside. There, on Sunday morning, May 27, they saw in the distance the approach of the dreaded North Cork Militia, which was joining other British units preparing for battle. The rebels from Boolavogue dug in, and Father Murphy took command of an ambush party on the rebels' flank. Hidden behind a ditch, Father Murphy's party watched the red-coated enemy infantry wheel around to face the rebel entrenchment. To Father Murphy's rear, a British cavalry unit waited to cut off the expected rebel retreat. The North Cork men began their assault, unaware of the threat on their flank. When he sensed that some of his inexperienced men might break ranks, Father Murphy moved among them. "Remain firm, together!" he said. With the North Corks committed and the battle at its peak, Father Murphy ordered his men into action. Those with muskets fired, then the pikemen charged. The disparity in equipment mattered little, for the pikemen fought with ferocious courage as they took on their tormentors. The North Corks were cut to pieces; more than a hundred were killed. Eight United men were killed. Father Murphy was hardly the hero of the battle, but he had played an important role. And he had been noticed. Afterward, word spread among the British that the cleric from Boolavogue was marching with the rebels.

The battle of Oulart Hill was a stunning Irish victory. Four days later, the United Irish movement in Wexford proclaimed a republic, to be ruled for the time being by a directory consisting of four Catholics and four Protestants. The victorious army continued to march against and defeat superior British forces, and Father Murphy led his men in a series of battles as they sought to extend rebel rule over Wexford's major towns. Lord Castlereagh, Britain's second most powerful administrator in Ireland, wrote to London of the danger in Wexford: "Rely upon it, there never was in any country so formidable an effort on the part of the people."

The question was: Would the effort spread?

So powerful were the connections between Lord Edward Fitzgerald's family and Britain's ruling aristocracy that King George III and his son, the Prince of Wales, received personal pleas for clemency. But when Captain Ryan, the officer whom Fitzgerald had stabbed, died of his wounds, the charge of murder was added to Lord Edward's indictments. There would be no clemency. As if to taunt him, a gallows was set up near his cell window.

But Fitzgerald's own wound continued to worsen, and soon blood poisoning set in. Family members were summoned to his bedside, and he died on June 4, 1798. Later, one of his well-placed relatives, his uncle the Duke of Richmond, would write: "Most will find it in their hearts to forgive, even if not to applaud, a man so gallant, generous and simple."

The commanding general of the rebel army was taken to his grave as the rebellion he dreamed of got underway.

For a time Ulster had posed the greatest threat to the British Crown's authority in Ireland. But the arrest of the northern leaders, the fracturing of bonds between Protestant and Catholic in the countryside, and General Lake's campaign of repression in 1797 had changed that. The United movement was but a shell of what it had been.

Robert Simms, the United commander for County Antrim, did not send his men into the field on the night of May 23, for he was waiting for the French. When it became clear that the French weren't coming, Simms abruptly resigned. Henry Joy McCracken was named as his replacement.

He had never been in a battle in his life.

Several local magistrates were due to assemble in Antrim town on June 7, a Thursday. McCracken seized on the idea of capturing Antrim and taking the authorities hostage. He sketched out a plan for an assault on the town as well as a series of coordinated attacks throughout Counties Antrim and Down. He figured he would have an army of some twenty thousand rebels—seven thousand of them members of the Defenders, the rural secret society. He issued his orders in a proclamation addressed to "The Army of Ulster," and he dated it—in the fashion of revolutionary France—"The First Year of Liberty, 6 June, 1798." The following morning, McCracken dressed in the uniform of the disbanded Volunteers and took his place at the head of the rebel column. He planted a green flag on a hill, and addressed his troops, who had arrived singing "la Marseillaise." "If we succeed today, there will be sufficient praise lavished on us; if we fail we may expect proportionate blame," McCracken said. "But whether we succeed or fail, let us try to deserve success."

Four rebel columns assaulted Antrim on June 7. The men under McCracken's direct command engaged British soldiers in close street fighting. The battle was tilting in favor of the rebels until one contingent mistook a British bugle call as a signal for a renewed cavalry charge. It was, in fact, a signal to the British to retreat. The untrained army panicked, officers began quarreling over tactics, and the tide of the battle shifted. British reinforcements arrived, dispatched to Antrim quickly after McCracken's battle plans wound up in the hands of the British command. McCracken left his position in a churchyard to personally reorganize the fleeing rebels, picking up a discarded pike and shouting that he would run through the next man who tried to flee. It was to no avail. McCracken was knocked over in the rush to escape. The battle was lost.

McCracken retreated to the mountains outside of Belfast as his army scattered. Meanwhile, rebellion had broken out in nearby County Down, but the rebels there were no more successful than those in Antrim. British troops defeated a rebel column in a climactic battle in the town of Ballynahinch, putting a quick end to the rebellion in Ulster.

Mary Ann McCracken left her home in Belfast to look for her beloved Harry when she heard of his retreat to the nearby countryside. After two days of searching, she came upon several local residents who took her to the cave where her brother was hiding. He was exhausted, frustrated, and bitter. They talked about the failed rebellion and its consequences long into the night, and Mary Ann returned to Belfast the next day to begin making arrangements for his escape to America. On June 18, McCracken put his bitterness into writing in a letter to his sister.

"These are the times that try men's souls," he wrote, echoing Thomas Paine. "[The] present unfortunate state is entirely owing to treachery, the rich always betray the poor." McCracken had convinced himself that the rebels in County Antrim were on the verge of victory, but were betrayed by "a few wicked men."

Despite the danger, McCracken ventured out of his hiding place and made his way to the home of his lover, Mary Bodle, who lived in the vicinity. Unknown to the McCracken family, Mary and Henry Joy had a daughter, Maria.

Mary Ann arranged to book her brother on a foreign ship out of Belfast. The plan was foiled, however, when a patrol of yeomen militia stumbled on McCracken and arrested him. The news reached Mary Ann on July 8—her twenty-eighth birthday.

In County Wexford, the stench of the dead was unbearable. Still, the rebels forged ahead under a hot son, emboldened with each small success. Lord Castlereagh, who already had warned complacant London of the dangers in the county, now confessed that even he may have underestimated the rebels' strength. "The rebellion in Wexford has disappointed all my speculations," he wrote. "I had not a conception that the insurgents could remain together and act in such numbers."

By early June, the rebels controlled most of the county, although they had suffered a critical defeat in the town of New Ross. On June 16, Father John Murphy led his division to high ground in a place called Vinegar Hill, near the River Slaney. They were joined by perhaps as many as twenty thousand rebels. Among them was Father Murphy's brother, Pat. From his position atop the hill, Father Murphy watched as an equal number of British soldiers under the command of General Lake marched toward the giant rebel encampment. A British victory would be a blow that even this resilient and determined rebel army could not survive.

The Battle of Vinegar Hill began at seven o'clock in the morning on the first day of summer, June 21. Lake's troops opened fire with cannons to prepare for wave after wave of infantry. The cannon fire was effective and deadly. Pat Murphy was among those killed in the onslaught.

The rebels were slowly driven to the summit of Vinegar Hill. Desperate men with pikes charged batteries of artillery, with horrible results. With no choice but retreat, Father Murphy led his troops off the hill in the direction of Wexford town. Behind him, General Lake's men moved among the wounded, killing them where they fell.

Father Murphy and his men from Boolavogue camped outside Wexford town, while the Irish army's commanders met to discuss an end to the rebellion. A parlay was underway among the British, too, and when it was over, the Lord Lieutenant, the Earl of Camden, was sacked and replaced by Lord Charles Cornwallis, the man who had surrendered to George Washington at Yorktown.

Father Murphy rejected talk of a negotiated surrender. Instead, he proposed carrying the rebellion to surrounding counties. "I will never advise anyone to surrender and give up arms," he said. His colleagues disagreed, so he was now in command on his own, and he marched his men forty-five miles through the dust and heat on June 22. They continued to march during the ensuing week, through parts of County Carlow, County Kilkenny, and County Laois, skirmishing with British forces along the way and hoping to inspire local residents into action. But even their successes did not rouse the people in whose name they were fighting. "We have lost," Father Murphy told his troops after days of marching. "We will go home to Wexford to meet our fate."

An early summer fog covered the hills and meadows during the long march home. Word came that a British column was marching nearby. The priest ordered an immediate attack, but he became separated from the main body, lost in the fog with hostile troops all around him.

He made his way to the town of Tullow with his bodyguard, and found refuge in a stable. On the morning of July 2, a party of local yeomen on the lookout for fugitive rebels decided to help themselves to two horses belonging to a local family. They burst into the very stable in which Father Murphy was sleeping.

They didn't know who he was, but he had the appearance of somebody who had been on the run. Murphy and his bodyguard were brought to a local military headquarters, where he was frisked. The search revealed a crucifix, some clerical vestments, and sacramental oils. An interrogator immediately went to work, mocking him and grabbing the priest's crotch. Father Murphy said nothing. More persuasive methods were called upon: the priest and his bodyguard were stripped and brought to the town square, where they were flogged. A rope was produced, and Father Murphy was summarily hanged in the square. When he was dead, the troops cut off his head, threw his body into a barrel of pitch, set it on fire, and put the priest's head on a spike near the town chapel.

With an escort of heavily armed men, Henry Joy McCracken was brought from Carrickfergus jail to his native city of Belfast on July 16. His court-martial began a day later, and Mary Ann was in the courtroom when he arrived. "The moment I set my eyes on him I was struck with the extraordinary serenity and composure of his look," she wrote. She was with their father, John, who had been ill earlier in the springtime. Though the old captain had recovered, Mary Ann now noticed that he seemed to be "sinking beneath the weight of old age and affliction." A Crown prosecutor took the elder McCracken aside and made an offer: if he could persuade his son to turn informer, his life might be spared. John McCracken told the prosecutor that his son would rather die than be dishonored.

Henry Joy himself was summoned to join the prosecutor and his father, and the offer for information was presented again. Henry Joy replied that he would do anything his father wished. "Harry, my dear,

I know nothing of this business, but you know best what you ought to do," he said.

Henry Joy replied: "Farewell, father."

Henry Joy McCracken was ordered to be hanged at 5:00 P.M. on the very day his trial started. Mary Ann hurried to his cell for a final conversation. "I wish you to write to Russell, inform him of my death, and tell him that I have done my duty," he said, referring to their imprisoned mutual friend, Thomas Russell. Mary Ann produced a pair of scissors, and snipped a lock of her brother's hair.

When the time came, she walked with him hand in hand toward the gallows, until she was prevented from walking any further. The gallows had been erected near the site of the Sunday school Henry Joy had founded. From his place on the platform, McCracken looked out at the crowd that had gathered, and he spotted his sister. He gave no last speech.

Mary Ann had one final plan. She knew of a doctor who specialized in resuscitation, and asked him to come to their house after her brother's body was cut down from the gallows and brought home. But he didn't show up, sending instead his brother, a surgeon. With Mary Ann looking on, the doctor tried to revive the corpse of Henry Joy McCracken, to no avail.

Some time later, Mary Ann learned of her brother's little daughter, and against the wishes of her family, took in four-year-old Maria and became a second mother to the child. Years later, when Maria grew up and married, she opened her home to her beloved aunt, who had never married, and it was in Maria's house that Mary Ann died in 1866, when she was ninety-six years old.

Word of the rebellion had come as a shock to Wolfe Tone, for he had assumed that his colleagues in the United Irish movement would await French help before striking. He mourned the death of Lord Edward Fitzgerald and fretted over the fate of his two imprisoned friends, Thomas Russell and Thomas Addis Emmet. And he was puzzled and disheartened when he read of the disappointing rising in Ulster, once the capital of revolutionary fervor.

Realization that rebellion was indeed underway in Ireland helped rekindle at least a spark of interest among French military leaders. Plans were quickly drawn up for an expedition of some eight thousand men to be landed in stages. The first foray would be under the command of General Jean Joseph Humbert, who set sail for Ireland in August with just over one thousand men. They landed in Killala in northern County Mayo on August 22. Hundreds of United Irishmen rallied to the French column, and Humbert went on the offensive, marching south toward Castlebar. There, as General Lake and Lord Cornwallis frantically moved to counter the invaders, the combined French and Irish army routed the town's garrison. So swift was the British retreat that it became known as the "Races of Castlebar."

Once they got their bearings, however, the British commanders put their overwhelming superiority of numbers and arms to work. Humbert surrendered on September 8. The French soldiers were treated as prisoners of war, but the Irish who marched with the French were given no such courtesies. General Lake's men slaughtered the rebels after they surrendered their arms. An exception was made for Irish officers serving on Humbert's staff. They were brought before a court-martial in Dublin, convicted, and hanged. Among them was Wolfe Tone's brother, Matthew.

Wolfe Tone himself was at sea when Humbert surrendered. He was aboard a ship named for his friend Hoche, part of an eight-ship expedition carrying three thousand French troops intended to reinforce Humbert. After several delays, the landing force reached the coast of County Donegal on October 10. But the British navy spotted the French ships and gave pursuit. As it became clear that the expedition might never reach shore, the French commander urged Tone to leave the slow, lumbering *Hoche* and transfer to a smaller ship that might have a better chance of outrunning the British. "Shall it be said of me that I fled whilst the French were fighting the battles of my country?" he replied.

The *Hoche* came under attack on October 12, and Tone took command of one of the ship's batteries. He fought with desperate and reckless courage, but the *Hoche* was doomed, and Tone was taken prisoner. He expected to be treated as a legitimate combatant. Instead, he was put into chains and transported to Dublin.

Tone wore the unform of a French officer to his court-martial. He pleaded guilty to the charges arraigned against him, but asked the court's permission to explain his actions. "I have attempted to follow the same line in which Washington succeeded . . . I have attempted to establish the independence of my country; I have failed in the attempt; my life is in consequence forfeited and I submit. . . . I have labored to abolish the infernal spirit of religious persecution by uniting the Catholics and the Dissenters; to the former I owe more than can ever be repaid . . . the Catholics did not desert me."

Only Tone's method of death remained to be decided. He wished a soldier's death by firing squad. But the court would grant him no such honor. He was sentenced to die by hanging, just like any other criminal guilty of a capital offense. He wrote a letter to his wife, Matilda: "The hour is at last come when we must part; as no words can express what I feel for you and our children, I shall not attempt it ... be assured I will die as I have lived, and that you will have no reason to blush for me."

On Sunday, November 11, he was told that he was to be hanged the following afternoon. At some point during the night, he slit his throat with a razor left by his brother, who had been imprisoned in the same cell before he was hanged. A guard found him in the morning lying in a pool of blood.

He had missed his jugular vein, but he was gravely injured. After a week of suffering, a doctor warned him that any slight movement could prove fatal. "I can yet find words to thank you, sir; it is the most welcome news you could give me," he said. And then he died, at age thirty-five. Sir George Hill, a member of one of Ireland's most prominent families, found Tone's death by his own hand most unsatisfactory. "I would have sewed up his neck and finished the business," he said.

The rebellion was over. In six months of fighting, thirty thousand people had lost their lives. By comparison, twenty-five thousand Americans had died in the six years it took for America to win its liberty.

While government officials in London and Dublin breathed easier, they could not easily erase from their minds the horror of the previous six months. Though penetrated by spies, reduced by arrest and intimidation, and hampered by inexperience and lack of arms, the rebel army of amateur soldiers had fought with courage and intelligence. They won a few battles, but they never really had a chance. And yet they had fought.

The United Irish ideal of an Ireland rid of sectarian divisions had frightened the Anglo-Irish Ascendancy in Dublin and the British establishment in London. Prime Minister William Pitt began maneuvering to establish a full political union between Britain and Ireland, which would end Ireland's claim to nationhood. In order to achieve it, the Irish Parliament would have to vote itself out of existence. This act of political suicide required certain inducements, and they were quietly offered: promises of peerages and other forms of Crown patronage. Cornwallis was among the officials making the promises. "I despise and hate myself every hour for engaging in such dirty work," he said.

It was left to Henry Grattan to raise one last objection to the plan for union: "The Constitution [of 1782] may, for a time, be lost—the character of the country cannot be so lost. The Ministers of the Crown may at length find that it is not so easy to put down for ever an ancient and respectable nation." It was his last speech on the floor of the vanishing Irish House of Commons. He would die in May 1820, at the age of seventy-four. On his deathbed, he told his son: "I die with a love of liberty in my heart."

The Act of Union took effect on January 1, 1801. The semi-independent kingdom of Ireland ceased to exist. It was now wedded to England (as well as Scotland and Wales) as a province in an entity

Robert Emmet

called the United Kingdom. The "ancient and respectable nation" had, however, produced a generation of memorable martyrs, nearly all of them Protestant. The rebellion of 1798 established an ideal from which later generations would draw inspiration: a secular republic, purged of British domination as well as sectarian division.

The era's final words were spoken two years after the Act of Union took effect, in a Dublin courtroom by Thomas Addis Emmet's younger brother, Robert. He and Thomas Russell, who had been released from prison in 1802, tried to reorganize the United Irish movement, but their efforts ended ignominiously. They launched a rebellion that lasted a few hours on the night of July 23, 1803. Thirty people were killed, including the Chief Justice of Ireland and his son-in-law, who were piked to death after their coach was attacked.

Robert Emmet was arrested on August 25. His fate was certain. He was convicted and sentenced to be hanged. But his final words, delivered extemporaneously after he learned his fate, would live far longer than he did.

"I have but one request to ask at my departure from this world," he told judge and jury. "It is the charity of its silence. Let no man write my epitaph; for as no man who knows my motives dare now vindicate them, let not prejudice or ignorance asperse them. Let them rest in obscurity and peace, my memory be left in oblivion and my tomb remain uninscribed, until other times and other men can do justice to my character. When my country takes her place among the nations of the earth, then and not till then, let my epitaph be written."

His co-conspirator Thomas Russell was arrested on September 7, 1803, and was brought to Downpatrick, County Down, for trial. Mary Ann McCracken wrote to him on October 15 and enclosed "a small supply" of cash. Russell wrote back to the McCracken family: "I have no wish to die . . . but had I a thousand lives I would willingly risk or [lose] them in it, and be assured Liberty will in the midst of these storms be established. . . . Politically I have done nothing but what I glory in."

He was hanged on October 21. Mary Ann McCracken requested of him what she had asked of her brother: a lock of hair.

Thomas Addis Emmet, freed from prison, left for America after his brother was hanged. He settled in New York City, where he was reunited with a group of former United Irishmen who had fled Ireland for America. They immediately plunged into American politics, becoming staunch Jeffersonians at a time when the new nation was debating the nature of this new system known as a republic. The Federalists, who supported John Adams, regarded Emmet and his colleagues as dangerous radicals.

Emmet became one of New York's most respected lawyers and, in 1816, was appointed state Attorney General. He died in 1827 at age sixty-three in the midst of arguing a case before a federal court. He was buried with great public ceremony in the graveyard of Saint Paul's Church in lower Manhattan. A thirty-foot obelisk marks his final resting place; on it are carved the eagle of America and the harp of Ireland.

CHAPTER FOUR

EMANCIPATION AND STARVATION

THE ACT OF UNION was meant to assimilate Ireland into Great Britain and to make civilized Englishmen out of the Irish. No longer would Ireland claim to be a separate and distinct nation. Instead, it was to be a province integrated into the world's dominant power, with one hundred members in the 658-member House of Commons in London. The position of Ireland's Catholics changed overnight, without even the pretense of consent. Once an oppressed majority within their own nation, they became an oppressed minority within the United Kingdom of Great Britain and Ireland. Irish Protestants' fears of being overrun in their own country could be put at ease, for they were now citizens of a truly Protestant nation.

With the creation of the Union, the notion of an independent, French-style Irish republic seemed ridiculously unreachable. Rather than building on Grattan's independent Parliament, Irish nationalists would have to break a political union as powerful as the one that bound together the states in America. Indeed, Ireland and England were supposed to be like New York and New Jersey: political entities within a larger union.

Government power was centered in Dublin Castle, where an Under Secretary oversaw day-to-day operations and acted as London's eyes and ears. Above the Under Secretary were the Chief Secretary, who held a government ministry and spoke for the government on Irish matters in the House of Commons, and the Lord Lieutenant, who was the monarch's top representative and who, when in Ireland for state occasions, lived in provincial splendor in the Vice Regal Lodge in Dublin's Phoenix Park.

The administrators, bureaucrats, and patronage holders were all

Protestants. Catholics were barred from the government because of the last remnant of the Penal Laws, which required that officeholders take an oath acknowledging Catholic dogma as false. Local government was run by a system of grand juries, also closed to Catholics. The rebellion of 1798 had not persuaded the Protestant Ascendancy of the dangers of an alienated majority in their midst. They chose to consolidate their monopoly on power, rather than to conciliate, and to regard dissension as a matter for the criminal justice system, which, of course, also was restricted to Protestants. Some twenty thousand regular army troops, in addition to more than thirty thousand part-time yeomen, were stationed in Ireland to enforce the law.

Not everyone was pleased with the new arrangement between the two islands, chief among them the Lord Lieutenant himself, Cornwallis, who had held his nose as he assisted in the dissolution of the Irish Parliament. Cornwallis believed that genuine assimilation of Ireland required full Catholic emancipation. Catholics, he argued, ought to be allowed to participate fully in the life of the country, accept government positions, and even take seats in the House of Commons. Prime Minister Pitt agreed, and hinted strongly that Catholic emancipation would follow the Act of Union. But King George III, a virulent anti-Catholic, refused, and emancipation was dropped. "I would rather give up my throne and beg my bread from door to door throughout Europe than consent to such a measure," the King said. Cornwallis, who had attempted to conciliate Catholic Ireland, resigned in disgust.

In a practical sense, the bars on Catholic advancement in the professions and in politics meant little to the vast majority of the Irish poor. During a visit to Ireland a quarter century after the Union, Sir Walter Scott noted of the Irish that "their poverty has not been exaggerated: it is on the extreme verge of human misery." When food prices fell, as they did in 1815 with the end of the Napoleonic Wars, landlords found grazing more economical than farming, so they evicted their tenants and turned the land over to cattle, a species less likely to complain.

Despite their misery, the Irish were remarkably fertile. The population grew from five million in 1791 to seven million in 1821 and to eight million in 1841, when some 65 percent of Irish people lived off the land and 80 percent lived in the countryside. The expanding rural population increased pressure on the land, leading to cutthroat competition, high rents, and a population at risk of starvation. The landlord, often living in Britain, became the symbol of social injustice, but he was not alone in the exploitation of the Irish Catholic peasantry. A

French visitor to Ireland at the turn of the century explained Irish society simply: "A rich man . . . lets a large tract of country to one man, who does not intend to cultivate it himself, but to let it out to three or four others; those who have large shares farm them to about a score, who again let them to about a hundred comfortably situated peasants, who give them at an exorbitant price to about a thousand poor labourers."

Those who actually did the cultivation found themselves turning over nearly everything they grew to pay the rent—everything, that is, except the potatoes they grew for themselves. The potato was something of a miracle crop. It was cheap, and it grew in great quantities in the damp Irish soil. By the 1840s, three million Irish farmers and their families ate little else.

Most Irish tenant farmers and their families, numbering about five million people by 1841, lived in tiny cabins, many built of mud walls and containing just one room and beds of straw. Their sole possession, other than a few sticks of furniture, was a pig, which often shared the family's living quarters. They had no stake in government and society, not even in the very land they tilled. If tenants improved the land, they could expect a rent increase. And, worse, the improvements were considered the property of the landlord, not the tenants who made them, except in Protestant Ulster, where tenants were allowed more rights. Some tenants were forced to work for wages in addition to cultivating the fields to pay the rent. A visitor to the west of Ireland in 1825 noted that "there are parts of Connaught where a man plants his potatoes at the proper season and shuts up his cabin and goes to England and labours; and perhaps his wife and children beg on the roads." The alienation of the farmers was evident in the continued presence of secret societies in the countryside and the growth of the brewing and distilling industries.

Even worse off than the tenant farmers were unskilled laborers. A government survey in the 1830s found that some 585,000 laborers, supporting at least double that many children, were out of work at least thirty weeks a year. There was no social welfare for them. They begged or starved.

Ireland after the Union was run as it was run during Swift's time, as a Protestant entity. Without emancipation, Catholics were barred from serving in even the lowest government offices. Their poverty grew worse as the Irish economy remained subservient to Britain's, serving as a source of cheap food and labor. Meanwhile, Protestants in Ulster were learning that loyalty had its rewards. Belfast was but a large town of twenty thousand at the turn of the century; within fifty years, its population grew to 100,000, and it was a thriving manufacturing center. It became the only major city in Ireland into which industrial capital was invested.

The British came to view Irish poverty as a sign of racial inferiority, about which, of course, the British could do nothing. Irish dependence on the potato was not a symptom of poverty, but of fecklessness and sloth. Because it was so easy to grow and maintain, the potato only encouraged Irish laziness. The potato was like Catholicism—proof that the Irish were a lower species, beyond the help of civilization. This aggressively apathetic view would find its way into public policy when Britain was confronted with the effects of Irish poverty beginning in the mid-1840s. "The English people are naturally industrious—they prefer a life of honorable labour to one of idleness," wrote a correspondent for *Fraser's Magazine,* a British publication, in 1845. "Now of all the Celtic tribes, famous everywhere for their indolence and fickleness . . . the Irish are admitted to be the most idle and most fickle. They will not work if they can exist without it." *Punch* magazine, known for its witty coverage of British politics and culture, regularly published anti-Irish diatribes blaming the people themselves for their poverty. The Irish, *Punch* asserted, were "the missing link between the gorilla and the Negro."

A lawyer named Daniel O'Connell saw in these impoverished, powerless people the makings of a mass movement that could shake Britain's ruling establishment without firing a shot. He was tall and solidly built, with a resonant voice and a gift for invective. Catholic Ireland had not produced such a leader in generations.

Daniel O'Connell was born in rural County Kerry in 1775 to a Catholic family that had held on to its power through shrewd evasion of the Penal Laws. His uncle Maurice, known as Hunting Cap, was an affluent landlord and an accomplished smuggler. But the family's success did not shield them entirely from the sanctions of Protestant Ireland—Daniel O'Connell's parents had been married in a Protestant church because the law did not recognize marriages performed by Catholic priests.

In accordance with Gaelic custom still thriving in Kerry, young Daniel spent his early years with poor, Irish-speaking foster parents who lived on his biological father's property, and he began his education at age four under the supervision of a hedge schoolmaster. Living amid the remnants of old Ireland, he grew up with a strong sense of all that had been taken away from the country's native population.

Daniel O'Connell

He was sent to France to attend college, and while there he witnessed the bloodshed of the French Revolution. He left the country the day after Louis XVI went to the guillotine. He never forgot the horror: liberty, he would say many years later, was not worth a drop of human blood. He returned to Ireland in 1796 to study law, and was in Dublin to observe the panic which the Bantry Bay expedition inspired. The very idea of French revolutionaries poised to invade Ireland had "the blood of my youth boiling in my veins," he wrote.

O'Connell quickly made a name for himself as a lawyer, but his religion barred him from the most prestigious cases. They went to lawyers admitted to the top of the profession, or the inner bar, as it was called. The inner bar was Protestant only. By age thirty, Daniel O'Connell had gone as far as he could go in his profession, with no chance at winning the large fees that came with important cases. Money already was a problem for him, for he had been cut out of Hunting Cap's will in 1802 when he secretly married a distant cousin named Mary O'Connell. He would spend a good portion of his life worrying about paying his bills.

O'Connell was a complex study in politics and identity. He loathed the rebellion of 1798, and served briefly in a loyalist lawyers' militia in 1803, but he opposed the Act of Union in 1800. He believed in emancipation for Catholics, but he declared that he was no "Papist," because he denied that the Pope had any temporal authority in Ireland. And his opposition to the Union didn't prevent him from presenting King George IV with a tribute and a garland when the King visited Ireland in 1821. "Loyalty is not the peculiar prerogative of one sect or another," he explained. He abhorred slavery, argued in favor of full rights for the Jews of Britain and Ireland, and supported a variety of measures to reform the aristocracy's domination of Ireland. And yet he was far from a revolutionary.

In this spirit, he founded in 1823 an organization called the Catholic Association, to win full citizenship, or emancipation, for Catholics. Membership was based on a single ingenious idea: he would recruit not only his fellow middle-class Catholics, but the mass of rural Catholics. Thanks to one of the reforms passed before 1798, Catholic males holding property worth 40 shillings or more were allowed to vote. The property restriction was hardly an obstacle, as even the barest amount of possessions could, with a wink, be valued at 40 shillings. The landlords were more than happy to wink away because the new voters could be counted on to vote in the landlords' interest, since they had to declare their votes publicly. Failure to vote in accordance with a landlord's wishes could, and often did, mean eviction.

O'Connell regarded the 40-shilling freeholders and their families as the key to winning emancipation. Membership in the Catholic Association would be open to all, and members were asked to subscribe a penny a month—a sum so low that even the poorest could subscribe.

By 1825, the penny-a-month scheme was bringing in £1,000 a week. For the first time in modern Western European history, landless farmers and laborers were recruited into a political organization. The Duke of Wellington, soon to be Prime Minister, immediately understood the organization's significance. "If we cannot get rid of the Catholic Association we must look to civil war in Ireland sooner or later," he wrote.

O'Connell put the association's apparatus to work in 1826, during a parliamentary election in Waterford. The seat was traditionally the property of the Beresfords, one of Ireland's most powerful families. Ten days before the election, O'Connell somewhat belatedly mobilized the association behind the candidacy of a liberal Protestant named Villiers Stuart. The scheme seemed far too ambitious, but O'Connell went to Waterford to canvass voters himself, and wrote to his wife on June 26: "We are beating those bigoted and tyrannical wretches." Indeed he was. The election was conducted over several days, and the Catholic Association, funded with all those pennies, not only hired agents and organizers, but found employment and housing for voters who were evicted or fired for voting against the Beresford interests. Incredibly, Stuart won. The *Times* of London gave voice to the anxiety in Britain: "In Ireland, where a little while ago a Protestant shoeblack would have grinned with contempt at the titled head of the most ancient Catholic family, the tables are completely turned."

Two years later, O'Connell himself decided to run for Parliament from a constituency in County Clare. No Catholic had run for Parliament in 150 years, although there was no actual legal barrier to seeking election. It was only afterward, when an elected member was required to swear an oath offensive to Catholics (it referred to their religion as "superstitious" and "idolatrous"), that there was effectively a ban on Catholics. O'Connell's opponent was a well-regarded landlord named Vesey Fitzgerald, a Protestant who supported Catholic emancipation.

One of Ireland's newest members of Parliament, a strapping twenty-four-year-old named William Smith O'Brien, followed events in Clare with great interest and some discomfort. Vesey Fitzgerald was an old friend of his father, Sir Edward O'Brien, and both older men were popular Protestant landlords. Both had opposed the Act of Union in 1800 and both were committed to Catholic emancipation, as was the young William. But William, a cautious young man, expressed some reservations about where the emancipation movement might lead. "While I trust that a Catholic constituency will never again send to Parliament any representative who is hostile to the concession of their rights, I must think that the kindly relations subsisting between landlord and tenant ought not, upon light grounds, to be torn asunder," he wrote.

William's family could trace ancestors back hundreds of years, indeed, back to Brian Boru. Intermarriage through the years produced a line that was represented in William's very name: the Anglo Smith and the Gaelic O'Brien. But he had no trouble accepting his distinctive Irish identity: "From my boyhood I have entertained a passionate affection for Ireland," he wrote. "A child of its most ancient race, I have never read the history of . . . past wrongs . . . without a deep sentiment of indignation."

Despite his sympathy for the Catholic cause, William's father, Edward, was determined to see his friend Fitzgerald prevail over O'Connell, whom he regarded as an outsider. He delivered impassioned speeches, insisting that Fitzgerald was a friend of the Catholics and, equally important, that he would wield great influence as a government insider.

He was arguing against history.

O'Connell's candidacy took on the character of a crusade, and the Catholic Association not only arranged for large demonstrations, but also provided housing and food for those who came from great distances to see the new leader. Edward O'Brien looked on helplessly as his tenants declared their votes against his expressed interest.

Daniel O'Connell won by a margin of two to one. Sixty thousand people turned out to witness the announcement of his victory. He went to Dublin and told cheering supporters: "What I now say I wish to reach England, and I ask, What is to be done with Ireland? What is to be done with the Catholics? They must either crush us or conciliate us."

Wellington, the Prime Minister, agreed, saying he had two choices: civil war in Ireland or Catholic emancipation. O'Connell's election surely would inspire a string of Catholic electoral victories. What would happen if England turned away these elected representatives of the people? He introduced a bill allowing Catholic emancipation, and it passed in February 1829. An infuriated King George IV vowed to withhold his approval, but he relented when Wellington threatened to resign.

The government, however, extracted a measure of revenge: it raised the property qualification for voters from 40 shillings to £10, virtually eliminating the rural poor who elected O'Connell. Then, in an obvious bit of spite, the Emancipation Act was not made retroactive, so

O'Connell was forced to submit himself to the voters in Clare again, because he had been elected before the Emancipation Act became law. The young MP William Smith O'Brien delivered a stinging rebuke, asserting, correctly, that the "gentry" in County Clare had been "unanimously opposed" to O'Connell's election. One of O'Connell's supporters challenged Smith O'Brien to a duel, which was arranged. The two men fired at each other and missed.

Even with a more restricted franchise, voters once again chose O'Connell as their MP from Clare, this time with no opposition. At age fifty-five, Daniel O'Connell had succeeded in his life's ambition. The last bars to Catholic citizenship had fallen. Daniel O'Connell would be known to Irish history as the Liberator.

Once installed in the House of Commons, O'Connell immediately introduced legislation calling for repeal of the Union. It went nowhere, of course. Rather than walk away with his ideological purity intact, O'Connell dropped his demand for repeal and worked with a liberal-minded Whig government in London to win a series of reforms in Ireland, including a compromise over the payment of tithes to the Church of Ireland that shifted the burden to landlords rather than the predominantly Catholic tenants.

In addition, O'Connell won government support for measures to assist the Irish poor and to reform local government. The British began an ambitious program of school construction, resulting in a network of what were called national schools. Literacy rates began to climb and would continue to do so for the rest of the century. And, thanks to O'Connell's relationship with the Whigs, a new Under Secretary, Thomas Drummond, won rare praise in Ireland for his decency and fairness. As the second in command in Dublin Castle, Drummond lectured the Anglo-Protestant gentry in words that history has remembered. "Property," he said, "has its duties as well as its rights."

At the height of his powers in the 1830s, the leader of a thirty-nine-member Irish delegation in Parliament, O'Connell offered a new model for Irish reformers. Working in alliance with British liberals, he won reforms that at least eased the plight of the Irish Catholic masses, even if they did little to advance the cause of nationalism. Shrewd and pragmatic, he worked from the inside rather than remain on the outside.

He became a hero not only to Irish Catholics, but to a group of middle-class, mostly Protestant intellectuals who became known as Young Ireland. And young they were. They could have been O'Connell's children, and in a sense, they were, for they were inspired by his democratic defiance of Britain during the struggle over emancipation. In another sense, they were the grandchildren of Wolfe Tone, for like him, they sought to substitute the common name of Irishman in place of religious distinctions.

Young Ireland became a force in Irish politics and culture in the early 1840s. It was broad enough to include conservative nationalists who wished to retain political links to the British Crown as well as avowed separatists who wanted complete independence. What all members shared, however, was a sense of identity with the land of

Thomas Davis

their birth, regardless of their religion. Through the pages of a remarkable weekly newspaper called *The Nation,* the Young Irelanders foiled the intent of the Act of Union through a vigorous reassertion of a distinct Irish identity, one that knew no sectarian qualification. Although the newspaper had Catholic contributors and in fact was edited by a Catholic, Charles Gavan Duffy, its chief political writer was an affluent Anglo-Protestant journalist named Thomas Davis, the son of a surgeon in the British army. A contemporary once described Davis as "more like a young Englishman than a young Irishman," and yet (or perhaps as a result) he asserted that no matter what the Act of Union said, the Irish were not and would never become British.

Davis was born in 1814 and was reared in the comfort of upper-middle-class Dublin. His father died before he was born, and many later noted that Davis's strong attachment to Daniel O'Connell took on the affection and tension of a father-son relationship. He studied law at Trinity College and graduated in 1834, but instead of embarking on a legal career, he traveled to Europe to study the fledgling nationalist movements on the Continent. He served a term as president of the Dublin Historical Society, and in an address to members in June 1840, he told his all-Protestant audience that they ought to learn more about the history of the land they were born in. "Gentlemen, you have a country. . . . You are Irishmen," he declared.

He took up journalism, and began his lifelong argument that the assimilation of Ireland was neither desirable nor possible. "Ask us not to copy English vice, and darkness, and misery, and impiety; give us the worst wigwam in Ireland and a dry potato than Anglicise us," he wrote. In an essay tracing the origins of feudalism in Ireland, he demanded justice for landless Irish tenant farmers. "What are the evils under which our peasantry labour?" he wrote. "Poverty. Give them land of their own to work on, they will then have motives to labour, and will soon cease to be poor. . . . Give them the education which the possession of property gives, and they will grow prudent and economical."

His articles, although unsigned, attracted notice at a time when the political stability of the 1830s was becoming undone. The Whigs were losing their grip on power in London, and the Conservatives, traditionally unsympathetic to Ireland, were prepared to form a new government with Robert Peel, a bitter political enemy of O'Connell, as Prime Minister. Irish reformers anticipated the worst, and Davis decided that he needed to act on, and not simply reflect on, his beliefs. On April 19, 1841, he joined a group called the Loyal National Repeal Association. The association's chairman was Daniel O'Connell.

O'Connell had founded the Repeal Association in 1840 in anticipation of a hostile Tory administration. He had dropped his demand
for repeal of the Act of Union while he worked with the Whigs, but
with the Whigs on their way out of power, O'Connell declared that
repeal was back on the Irish agenda. He intended to reprise the tactics
that had won Catholic emancipation in the late 1820s. This time,
however, O'Connell was marching for a much more radical measure.
Catholic emancipation at least had the support of some liberal-
minded Englishmen, but repeal of the Union had no supporters in
Parliament even among Whigs. Skeptics thought O'Connell was, at
sixty-five, too old to mount such an arduous campaign. Nevertheless,
O'Connell said he would not hold back: "My struggle has begun," he
said. "I will terminate it only in death or Repeal."

As in the days of emancipation, the masses were recruited, and
once again their small contributions gave them a stake in the organization while providing O'Connell with a campaign treasury. The
association was built village by village, and agents—called repeal war-
dens—acted as the organization's eyes and ears in the countryside,
monitoring recruitment and keeping in touch with the membership.
The group's Dublin headquarters became a laboratory of mass
democracy, introducing citizens to the rudiments of organization and
political thought.

Knowing from experience the value of a dramatic gesture, O'Connell declared himself a candidate for Lord Mayor of Dublin, a symbolic post with mostly ceremonial duties. No Catholic had held the
title for a century and a half. He won, and donned the red robes, hat,
and gold chain of office in November 1841. Cheering crowds gathered to celebrate his installation, and O'Connell shouted to them:
"Boys, do you know me now?" Months later, in the same splendid at-
tire, he led a delegation to Buckingham Palace to congratulate the
young Queen Victoria, who had just given birth. Repeal, he emphasized repeatedly, would not affect Ireland's relationship with the
British monarchy. "I want you not to violate your allegiance to the
lovely and beautiful being that fills the throne—our gracious Queen,"
he told supporters.

Thomas Davis was not as enthusiastic about the monarchy, but he
admired and liked O'Connell, so he kept his reservations to himself.

Davis, together with Charles Gavan Duffy, an Ulster Catholic, and
a mutual friend named John Dillon, founded *The Nation* in July 1842.
Davis promised that the paper would "inflame and purify" the Irish
masses "with a lofty and heroic love of country—a nationality of the
spirit . . . which may embrace Protestant, Catholic and Dissenter."

Written and edited by urban intellectuals, *The Nation* was passed from house to house and was read aloud to gatherings of illiterate country people. News of the Repeal Association was displayed prominently. Davis wrote a memorable series of letters to Irish Protestants, arguing that they ought to embrace their Irish identity. Under the pen name of "The Celt," he preached the importance of education, and asserted that Ireland's national claim required a return to the Irish language. He pleaded for a greater understanding of Irish history, and foresaw the development of distinctly Irish literature and arts. And, in tribute to the role of poetry in Irish history and culture, he tried his hand at verse. One ballad poem, "A Nation Once Again," would become the most famous anthem of Irish nationalism.

When Daniel O'Connell proclaimed that 1843 would be the year of repeal, Davis and his friends at *The Nation* were ready to take him at his word. O'Connell planned a series of demonstrations that became known as monster meetings. Hundreds of thousands turned out to hear O'Connell, who occasionally whipped up the crowd with ambiguous statements about violence, keeping Prime Minister Peel guessing about his intentions. He declared that his audience "may soon have the alternative to live as slaves or die as free men." At another meeting, he said that he hoped to recruit up to three million people for the Repeal Association. "They will be all the more dreaded by our enemies, because every member will represent a man with two clenched fists." Through it all, however, he was careful to point out that "we preach attachment to the Crown and submission to the laws."

The membership subscriptions—called the Repeal Rent—were bringing in £2,000 a week. O'Connell opened a new headquarters, called Conciliation Hall, and put together a staff of fifty, many of them chosen for reasons other than talent. The monster meetings continued to draw astonishing numbers. Some 300,000 showed up in Kilkenny. An equal number were on hand in Tuam. The sheer numbers, and the discipline of the crowds, alarmed the government.

The largest monster meeting was held on the hill of Tara in County Meath, where the ancient high kings of Ireland were crowned. A million people, in a nation of eight million, attended. "Step by step we are approaching the great goal itself," O'Connell said. Another huge meeting was planned for October 5, 1843, at Clontarf, where Brian Boru defeated the Vikings in the eleventh century. It was to be O'Connell's greatest challenge yet to Peel's government. As the Repeal Association met in Dublin on Saturday, October 4, the day before the meeting, to discuss the arrangements, a document arrived from the Lord Lieutenant. With less than twenty-four hours' notice, the government informed O'Connell that his meeting was banned.

"This must be obeyed," O'Connell said. In no small feat of organization, word was dispatched that the meeting was canceled. Now it was Peel's turn to strike. O'Connell was arrested a week after the canceled meeting and charged with conspiracy.

The arrest outraged William Smith O'Brien, who had opposed O'Connell's election in 1828. The two men had, over their years together in the House of Commons, put aside their past disagreements. But while they found some common cause, O'Brien remained adamantly opposed to repeal. In fact, he had few qualms about imperial or colonial rule. He was an enthusiastic supporter of the British East India Company's plans to exploit the Indian subcontinent, and he believed French culture in Canada ought to be subordinated to English customs. He valued Ireland's legislative connection with England, which he regarded as a civilizing force. Thomas Davis, the intellectual force behind Young Ireland, complained that "he is not like us." Another peer joked that he was too much Smith and not enough O'Brien.

If he seemed too polite, too much the Englishman, he nevertheless opposed O'Connell's arrest and the government crackdown on monster meetings. Smith O'Brien visited O'Connell in Dublin on October 18, 1843, two weeks after the scheduled meeting at Clontarf, and he joined the Repeal Association a few days later. O'Connell was delighted, and announced that his colleague's decision was "of the utmost importance to the liberties of Ireland." But O'Brien's mother had a different view. In a letter to her son, she condemned the repeal movement as a "great evil," insisting that "even a child must know that nothing but misery [and] wretchedness" would follow repeal. "If you pursue the course announced in the paper," she wrote, "you will bring down my grey head with sorrow to the grave."

Smith O'Brien proceeded anyway, and eventually became a valuable liaison between O'Connell and Young Ireland. He was older than most of Young Ireland's members but younger than O'Connell—in a rare lighthearted moment, he declared that he stood for "middle-aged Ireland." The skeptical Davis welcomed him to the Repeal movement even though Smith O'Brien was still not quite pure on questions of nationality and identity. In a letter to *The Nation*, O'Brien pointed to the "similarity of institutions, connections of kindred, and community of glory" between Ireland and Britain. Davis was more interested in what set Ireland and Britain apart.

Young Ireland attempted to keep the Repeal Association from

stagnating while O'Connell prepared for his trial on conspiracy charges. It was no easy task. Within three months of the banned meeting at Clontarf, weekly contributions to the Repeal Association fell from £2,000 to £300. But the young men persevered, and implored the Irish to stand by O'Connell. And they continued their remarkable exploration of nationality in the pages of *The Nation* and during Saturday night salons held in various members' homes in Dublin. There, they debated history, critiqued poetry, and analyzed continental revolutionary movements. And they followed the progress of one of their favorite projects—the Repeal Association's establishment of reading rooms throughout Ireland, where books and periodicals, including *The Nation,* were circulated.

Young Ireland's task became even more difficult when Daniel O'Connell was found guilty of conspiracy in February 1844. Although sentencing was put off for three months, a prison term seemed certain. He was nearly seventy years old, and although healthy and strong, he feared the effect of jail time. His young allies feared the effects of his fear. Would he, in the time between verdict and sentencing, soften his views in hopes of avoiding prison? Davis certainly thought it was possible, particularly when O'Connell crossed the Irish Sea to England to deliver a series of utterly moderate speeches. *The Nation* ran an unsigned editorial warning of the dangers of compromise.

O'Connell's fears came true on May 30, 1844, when he was sentenced to a year in prison. Davis and Smith O'Brien took up the day-to-day running of the Repeal Association. Unity, Davis preached, was critical at such a moment: "Feud! Feud! Feud! That is our history," he wrote.

Then, in an astonishing development which the devout O'Connell described as a genuine miracle, Britain's House of Lords reversed the Liberator's sentence after three months. Bonfires, parades, and great demonstrations celebrated his return to liberty. But before long, it became clear that even ninety days had taken a toll. Observers noticed that he no longer had the energy he had once had. He left the running of the Repeal Association to others.

Young Ireland watched with growing anxiety as the movement drifted. Then, not long after O'Connell's release, the young nationalists received surprising news. In a letter to the Repeal Association, O'Connell said he would support a compromise rather than press for repeal, the cause to which he had rallied not only Young Ireland, but millions of Irish people. Some Protestant landlords supported a proposal to create a limited legislature for Ireland, one with far fewer powers than the Parliament of Henry Grattan's time. It was called the "federal solution," and O'Connell now seemed prepared to settle for it.

Davis and his colleagues at *The Nation* were stunned. The newspaper charged that the federalism plan would "teach the artistocracy still to turn their eyes to London as the scene of their ambition. It will continue to train them in English manners, feelings and prejudices." O'Connell soon reversed himself again, but the dynamic between the aging parliamentarian and his young allies had changed. Some Irish newspapers printed whispered accusations that the editors of *The Nation* were anti-Catholic. In a letter to Smith O'Brien, Davis asked O'Connell to disavow the "bigoted attacks" on the newspaper. O'Connell replied by referring to Davis's letter as a "Protestant philippic," telling him, with studied sarcasm, that, while writers for *The Nation* were entitled to scoff at what he called "the State Trial Miracle"—his release from prison—as well as "every other miracle from the days of the Apostles to the present . . . we Catholics on the other hand may be permitted to believe as many of these miracles as we may adopt either from credulity or convincing proofs."

At this extremely tense moment, Prime Minister Peel decided to introduce a series of concessions for Ireland. If he intended to exacerbate the sudden religious division between O'Connell and Young Ireland, he could not have been shrewder. Among other reforms, he proposed the creation of a network of colleges throughout Ireland to make higher education accessible to Protestant and Catholic alike. It was the sort of reform that Young Ireland would eagerly support, for its members regarded education as integral to the improvement of Ireland's national, cultural, and economic life.

At a meeting of the Repeal Association in early 1845, however, O'Connell denounced the proposed colleges as "Godless" because they would not require formal religious instruction, since Catholics and Protestants would be attending together. The battle lines, which had been forming for months, were drawn.

A climactic meeting was called for in Conciliation Hall. An ally of O'Connell's, Michael George Conway, made the astonishing assertion that Saint Patrick had been "no friend of . . . mixed education." O'Connell openly cheered him on.

Davis spoke next. He began by referring to Conway as "my old college friend—my Catholic, my very Catholic, friend."

O'Connell interupted: "It is no crime to be Catholic, I hope."

The interruption unnerved the young man: "No, surely no, for—"

O'Connell interupted again: "The sneer with which you used the word would lead to the inference."

"No, sir, no," Davis replied. "My best friends, my nearest friends, my truest friends are Catholics." He then delivered an impassioned speech, deploring "disunion." When he finished, O'Connell rose to reply, and he referred contemptuously to Young Ireland. "I shall stand by Old Ireland," he said. "And I have some light notion that Old Ireland will stand by me."

Once more Davis rose, and this time he spoke of his deep affection for O'Connell. And then he burst into tears.

O'Connell rushed to embrace and comfort him. But Davis's col-

Jane Francesca Elgee (Speranza)

leagues would not be so quick to forget what had transpired. And Davis would not be there to conciliate, for in September 1845, four months after his confrontation with O'Connell, Thomas Davis died after a summer of ill health. He was just thirty-one years old.

His friends were heartbroken. O'Connell wrote: "My mind is bewildered and my heart afflicted. What a blow—what a cruel blow to the cause of Irish nationality. . . . I can write no more—my tears blind me."

A vast funeral procession wound through the streets of Dublin. Watching the mourners pass by her home was a nineteen-year-old woman named Jane Francesca Elgee, whose family claimed a Member of Parliament, a writer, and a prominent Church of Ireland clergyman among its ancestors. Her father was a prosperous attorney, and she was reared in the comfort of affluent Dublin. As a child she learned Greek, Latin, Italian, French, and German, all the more impressive considering that the education of young girls was hardly a priority. She was most insistent, however, and at one point she told a governess: "If you won't educate me, I'll educate myself."

She was tall, dark-haired, and attractive, and still very much the voracious reader as she grew into adulthood. As she watched the funeral procession, she asked whose death had inspired such grief. She was told that the dead man was a poet named Thomas Davis. Without knowing him, she was a student of his, for she was a regular reader of *The Nation*. Her family was deeply conservative, but the young woman's reading was setting her on quite a different course.

After Davis's death, Jane Francesca Elgee adopted the pen name by which she would become famous, Speranza, and began contributing poems to *The Nation*. They were militant and blunt-edged, celebrating nationality and resistance:

> *Abject tears, and prayers submissive—*
> *Have they eyes, and cannot see?*
> *Never country gained her freedom*
> *When she sued on bended knee.*

The Nation added another new voice after Davis's death: thirty-year-old John Mitchel, an asthmatic son of a Unitarian minister and a native of County Derry in Protestant Ulster. Mitchel was nearly six feet tall and slender, with blue-gray eyes and a fine head of thick brown hair that he twirled when deep in thought, which was often.

He had no experience in journalism when he joined *The Nation*, but he leaped at the chance to escape the drudgery of law. Like Wolfe

John Mitchel

Tone, Smith O'Brien, and Davis, Mitchel had a law degree from Trinity College but loathed the profession's tedious work. His father, dubbed "Papist Mitchel" in Derry because of his support for Catholic emancipation, had hoped his son would join the ministry as well, but instead of following in Reverend Mitchel's footsteps, John inherited his father's politics. His sympathy for Ireland's oppressed Catholics led him to join O'Connell's Repeal Association in 1843, but he soon grew impatient with what he dismissed as "loud agitation."

At *The Nation,* Mitchel took over the assignment of writing the newspaper's political articles. The first one bore the headline "The People's Food." It called attention to reports that the season's potato crop had failed, an ominous development. "On this subject it will be well to think maturely and speak cautiously," Mitchel wrote, "but certainly, either for us or against us, the approaching season of suffering will be turned to political ends."

The first reports of potato failure had reached Dublin days before Thomas Davis's death. A Dublin newspaper noted that one farmer examined his field of healthy potatoes on a Monday, and by Tuesday morning, the entire crop was ruined.

Far from the debates in Conciliation Hall, far from the salons of Young Ireland, the Irish poor were staring at catastrophe. A young boy growing up near Skibbereen in County Cork recalled the horrible sight of blackened potato fields near his family's home: "The air was laden with a sickly odor of decay, as if the hand of Death had stricken the potato field." The young boy's name was Jeremiah O'Donovan Rossa, and he would soon witness the slow death by starvation of his father.

Before long, reports about the potato's failure were replaced by firsthand descriptions of suffering and starvation. The Duke of Wellington, the former Prime Minister, received a letter from a justice of the peace in Skibbereen describing the sight of "six famished and ghastly skeletons, to all appearance dead . . . huddled in a corner on some filthy straw, their sole covering what seemed to be ragged horsecloth and their wretched legs hanging about, naked above the knees. I approached in horror and found by a low moaning that they were alive, they were in a fever—four children, a woman and what had once been a man."

And yet food was plentiful in Ireland. Oats, barley, grain, livestock—all were in abundance, except for the potato. In accordance with Britain's policy of free trade, the government insisted that Ireland's harvests should continue to be shipped out of the country, most of it to Britain, which depended on Ireland to serve as its granary. Landlords began evicting starving tenants. As conditions worsened, the government appointed a religious, free trade ideologue named Charles Trevelyan to take charge of relief operations. Trevelyan saw in Ireland problems even graver than starvation: "The great evil with which we have to contend is not the physical evil of the famine, but the moral evil of the selfish, perverse and turbulent character of the people." England had been in Ireland for centuries, but the opinion of its administrators hadn't changed. The problem with Ireland was the Irish.

• • •

Politics went on as usual even as the Irish began to starve. O'Connell opened talks with his former Whig allies, now called Liberals, hoping to oust the Conservative government through the combined power of English Liberals and the nearly forty Irish repealers in Parliament. But one of those repealers, William Smith O'Brien, was dubious about entering into any such alliance. In fact, Smith O'Brien increasingly was dubious about anything related to Parliament, at least in matters Irish. In early 1846, as the prospective O'Connell-Liberal alliance was under discussion, Smith O'Brien declared that the Repeal movement's policy ought to be of "complete neutrality" in British politics. "I trust that the time is not far distant when men of all parties in this country will see that it is vain to place any trust save in ourselves—ourselves alone is the motto I would wish the Irish people to assume," he said.

Smith O'Brien's disgust was complete by spring of 1846. The House of Commons was fully aware of the famine in Ireland. O'Connell and O'Brien both had pointed out that food was leaving the country even though people were starving, and yet the government was proposing not relief, but yet another suspension of civil liberties, called a coercion act. Smith O'Brien decided he would no longer serve on committees if the work concerned the affairs of England or Scotland. But he continued to plead the case of Ireland's starving poor, saying that it was "the duty of the government" to provide work for the hungry able-bodied. His arguments went nowhere, and when, in April 1846, he was summoned to attend a meeting of the House's Scottish railway committee, he refused. The House found him in contempt, and Smith O'Brien was placed under arrest and given a one-month sentence in a cell in a basement adjoining Parliament.

He spent the sentence in a small room with a bed, a table, some chairs, and a few other bits of furniture. He had access to a toilet that, like the cell itself, was not well ventilated. With great understatement, he referred to his surroundings as "not cheerful." Young Ireland and *The Nation* rallied around him, with the newspaper describing him as "intensely Irish" as opposed to the endless number of "luke-warm" Irishmen.

O'Connell's allies, however, were not as enthusiastic. The Repeal Association passed a tame, watered-down proclamation of support, which infuriated Smith O'Brien and led him to complain bitterly about "the O'Connell creatures" who had "withheld approval of my conduct." He was released in late May, and immediately joined the effort to stop the coercion bill.

Working with his old allies in the Liberal Party, O'Connell was a key part of a coalition that rejected the coercion, leading to Peel's resignation. With O'Connell's collaboration, Lord John Russell became Prime Minister. A Liberal ministry meant that O'Connell once again could play a leading role in politics. But before any meaningful alliance could be worked out, there was the matter of the firebrands of Young Ireland, who opposed working with either of the two British political parties.

Debate over a Liberal alliance dominated discussions in Conciliation Hall through the spring and early summer of 1846. As the voices of dissent in Conciliation Hall grew louder, O'Connell proposed a resolution that pledged the Repeal Association to seek "amelioration of political institutions by peaceable and legal means alone, disclaiming all attempts to improve and augment constitutional liberty by means of force, violence and bloodshed."

The association met on July 13 to discuss the resolution. In a sense, the issue was merely hypothetical, for nobody was contemplating a violent rebellion. But the tensions that had been building for months could no longer be contained. O'Connell told his audience that he would no longer accept "the service of any man who does not agree with me both in theory and practice." The gauntlet had been thrown down.

A two-day debate opened on July 27. O'Connell was absent, but he sent a letter reiterating his determination to put the association on record against violent agitation. Smith O'Brien finally declared himself, abandoning his role as a mediator and aligning with Young Ireland against O'Connell. The two days of heated, angry debate culminated in a speech by a very young Young Irelander, twenty-three-year-old Thomas Francis Meagher, the son of a prosperous businessman in County Waterford. A spellbinding speaker with a gift for ornate phrases, he denounced O'Connell's peace resolutions:

"I do not condemn the use of arms as immoral," he said, "nor do I conceive it profane to say that the King of Heaven ... bestows His benediction upon those who unsheath the sword in the hour of a nation's peril. ... Abhor the sword; stigmatize the sword? No, my lord, for at its blow, a giant nation started from the waters of the Atlantic, and by its redeeming magic ... the crippled colony sprang into the attitude of a proud Republic—prosperous, limitless and invincible."

O'Connell's son John, also a Member of Parliament, tried to prevent Meagher from continuing. O'Brien protested that if Meagher were not allowed to finish, he would leave the meeting. O'Connell persisted, and Smith O'Brien marched out the doors of Conciliation Hall, taking with him Meagher, John Mitchel, and the rest of Young Ireland. They never returned, and in January 1847, they formed a new organization called the Irish Confederation.

Eighteen forty-seven would be spoken of as Black '47, the year in which the Irish died by the tens of thousands, in the fields as well as in the appalling workhouses in which the starving homeless took refuge. The parade of human skeletons to Ireland's ports continued, and scandalously unfit ships attempted to transport the remnants of a nation to America. Dozens of those ships sank along the way. In the midst of the dying Trevelyan announced that Ireland would be left to "the operation of natural forces." Parliament passed legislation demanding that the Irish gentry pay for further famine relief. Britain's treasury was to be closed to the dying Irish.

Finally, the fallacy behind the Act of Union was exposed—if England and Ireland were one country, after all, why were the Irish forced to fend for themselves in the midst of a calamity? In denying Ireland further assistance, the English government, consciously or otherwise, conspired in the depopulation of one of the United Kingdom's constituent provinces, and assisted in the obliteration of what was left of Gaelic Irish culture. There was no question that the English establishment understood what was happening, for the *Times* stated the situation clearly. Referring to the rural heart of Connaught, it said with obvious relief that "an Irishman will soon be as rare a sight in Connemara as a Red Indian on the shores of Manhattan." England had tried military conquest, plantation, and legislative union, and still Ireland resisted. But the combination of natural disaster and man-made deprivation offered a solution to England's Irish problem.

Starvation, or the operation of natural forces, not only would rid Ireland of its excess population one way or the other, but would destroy the potato-based culture that so offended British sensibilities. One newspaper remarked that finally the Irish would become meateaters, never mind that the starving poor would gladly have eaten meat if they could afford it. By demanding that Irish landlords pay for famine relief, the British foresaw the financial destruction of Ireland's landed gentry. The Ascendancy class, although Protestant and Anglophilic, was regarded in Britain as almost as lazy and indolent as the Irish poor. If they, too, could be forced out or reformed, Britain might finally achieve its goal of an Anglicized Ireland.

Jane Francesca Elgee's angry poetry in *The Nation* roused consciences among the relatively well fed in Dublin, especially when it became known that Speranza was a woman. While the men of Young Ireland were arguing about nationality, Speranza was reminding readers of the suffering and dying in the countryside:

> *Weary men, what reap ye?—Golden corn for the stranger.*
> *What sow ye?—Human corpses that wait for the avenger.*
> *Fainting forms, hunger-strircken, what see you in the offing?*
> *Stately ships to bear our food away, amid the stranger's scoffing.*

Daniel O'Connell deteriorated rapidly after Young Ireland split with the Repeal Association. He was seventy-one years old, and his energy and talent, even his once great voice, were spent. At his doctor's suggestion, he planned a trip to Rome for rest and relaxation, but first, he traveled to the House of Commons to make yet another appeal to his colleagues.

The House was still when he rose to speak. He could barely raise his voice above a whisper: "Ireland," he said, "is in your hands. If you do not save her, she cannot save herself." Watching from the opposition benches, future Prime Minister Benjamin Disraeli found the spectacle boring. He saw only "a feeble old man muttering from a table."

It was Daniel O'Connell's last speech in the House of Commons. He died on the road to Rome.

Without O'Connell, the Repeal Association began a slow slide into irrelevance. The Irish Confederation was now ascendant. Its leaders envisioned a network of confederation clubs throughout the island, organized through local leaders in the manner of the Repeal Association. The clubs took their names from the heroes of the past, Patrick Sarsfield, Jonathan Swift, Henry Grattan, Wolfe Tone, and Robert Emmet.

Though the organization's leaders were keenly aware of the suffering throughout the country, and Speranza's angry and defiant poetry reminded readers of *The Nation* that Ireland was dying all around them, they seemed unaware that the starving Irish masses could hardly concern themselves with questions of identity and nationality. While the nationalists argued that a self-governing Ireland surely would not be sending its food for export while its people were starving, the tenant farmers and their families had no strength for outrage.

John Mitchel saw firsthand the horrors of the rural west when he traveled to County Galway to campaign for a confederation candidate in a parliamentary by-election. "I could see, in front of the cottages, little children leaning against a fence . . . their limbs fleshless, their bodies half-naked, their faces bloated yet wrinkled, and of a pale, greenish hue—children who would never, it was too plain, grow up to be men and women," he wrote.

As Black '47 took its horrible toll and the Confederates struggled to respond, James Fintan Lalor, handicapped son of an Irish Member of Parliament, wrote a letter of introduction to *The Nation*'s editor, Charles Gavan Duffy. Lalor had been born around 1809—records were unclear—and suffered from poor eyesight and a spinal defect that stunted his growth and left him with a hunchback. Nevertheless, he attended college and became a voracious reader of English and Irish writers. Wordsworth was a favorite, as was Swift, but it was Thomas Davis who captured his imagination. Lalor was a devoted reader of *The Nation*. In his letter to Duffy, he wrote: "I owe you some gratitude. You have given me a country."

Lalor had been thinking about more than just nationality and identity. He had been considering the very practical matter of Irish poverty. In the letter to Duffy, he asserted that the land, not repeal, was the key to radical change in Irish society. "The owners of our soil must be Irish," Lalor said. If a movement could rally behind that simple slogan, there would be a real revolution in Ireland, he said. "Unmuzzle the wolf dog. There is one . . . in every cabin throughout the land."

Duffy was astonished, not only by Lalor's audacity but by his prose, which was powerful and passionate. "A new tribune!" Duffy said. "A new policy!" Duffy circulated Lalor's letter among his friends, and he invited Lalor to explain his policy in the pages of *The Nation*. In one long address and a series of letters, Lalor asserted that the system which led to the death and starvation of so many Irish people "can never again be resumed or restored." He proposed the organization of tenant associations; he discussed the possibility of rent strikes; and he insisted that the tenants who worked the land had rights, especially for improvements they made to the land.

Lalor anticipated an agrarian-based social revolution, which was not what Smith O'Brien, a landlord himself, and Gavan Duffy necessarily had in mind. Smith O'Brien worried that Lalor's radical ideas would frighten the middle and upper classes, whose support was necessary if the movement was to be broad-based and nonsectarian.

John Mitchel, who had seen the suffering in the west, was of a different view. He embraced Lalor's ideas, and when, in early 1848, he realized that Gavan Duffy and Smith O'Brien disagreed, he resigned his position with *The Nation* and founded his own newspaper, *The*

United Irishman. Its stated goal was to "prepare the country for rebellion." Smith O'Brien pleaded with Mitchel to soften his stance, arguing that the country wasn't ready for war. But Mitchel had lost patience with such arguments, and resigned from the confederation's leadership.

In the first issue of *The United Irishman,* Mitchel addressed an open letter to the Lord Lieutenant in which he declared that the only difference between the new generation of nationalists and "the illustrious conspirators" of 1798 was that the older generation "had not learned the charm of good, honest, outspoken resistance to oppression." In the House of Lords, Lord Stanley advised his fellow peers that they ought not to ignore the words of Mitchel and his allies: "These men are honest, they are not the kind of men who make their patriotism the means of barter for place or pension. They are not to be bought off by the government of the day. . . . No, they honestly repudiate this course; they are rebels at heart."

On February 24, 1848, another generation of Irish nationalists found itself enthralled by events in France. An almost bloodless revolution had broken out in Paris; the King, Louis Philippe, had been removed from his throne, and a republic had been declared. Enthusiasm was so high that Mitchel returned unabashedly into the confederation, and was welcomed with an ovation. Smith O'Brien was appointed to head a delegation to present the confederation's declaration of support to representatives of the new French republic. To a crowd of cheering Dubliners, Smith O'Brien said he would "cheerfully" give his life if it would "secure the redemption of this land." Ireland, he promised, would have its own Parliament within a year.

The confederation called for the establishment of a National Guard, in essence, a revival of the Volunteers of Grattan's time, and Smith O'Brien spoke of 300,000 recruits. In the midst of the sudden activity, Mitchel and Smith O'Brien were indicted for sedition. Smith O'Brien posted bail and carried out his mission to Paris, returning with a three-colored flag similar to the French banner, except this one was of green, white, and orange, representing Ireland's two traditions and the hope for peace between them. A nervous London deployed more soldiers to Ireland, increasing troop strength to ten thousand.

Though he was warned to avoid the House of Commons, where he still was a member, Smith O'Brien went to London after his French journey. He suffered the jeers of his colleagues as he defiantly declared that he would continue to try to "overthrow the dominion of this house in Ireland." It was his last speech as a Member of Parliament.

The government lost its sedition case against Smith O'Brien, and he was released to cheering crowds in Dublin. But the authorities were determined to make sure Mitchel did not enjoy such a moment. He was arrested again, this time charged with the newly created crime of treason felony, more serious than sedition. Mitchel was found guilty and sentenced to a forced exile for fourteen years. After the verdict and sentence, he addressed the jury: "I have acted all through this business . . . under a strong sense of duty. I do not repent anything I have done." Mitchel was hustled out of the courtroom and, within hours, he was put on a boat for a journey that would take him to a prison colony in Bermuda.

In the issue of *The Nation* dated July 22, 1848, Jane Francesca Elgee contributed an essay entitled "The Hour of Destiny." Though it didn't carry her pen name, it contained her characteristic deployment of exclamation marks: "Ireland! Ireland! It is no petty insurrection . . . that summons you to the field. . . . It is a death struggle between the oppressor and the slave. . . . Strike! Strike! Another instant, and his foot will be upon your neck—his dagger in your heart."

She wrote another inflammatory piece the following week, entitled "Jacta Alea Est."

"Oh! For a hundred thousand muskets glittering brightly in the light of heaven. . . . In the name then of your trampled, insulted degraded country . . . I call on you to make this aspiration of your souls a deed." The government suppressed that week's edition of *The Nation* and indicted editor Duffy for treason felony. As he was placed under arrest, a friend slipped close and asked, quietly: "Do you wish to be rescued?"

"Certainly not," Duffy replied. "You must wait for the harvest."

But there was to be no harvest. And there was to be no waiting.

On July 22, as William Smith O'Brien set out for County Wexford to inspect local confederation clubs, the government suspended the habeas corpus act and issued a warrant for Smith O'Brien's arrest. He still was not committed to armed rebellion, but the government's decision, along with pressure from more militant confederation leaders, left him with few options. Rather than flee the country, he decided that rebellion was the only honorable option.

With a few hundred armed men, he tramped the roads of County Tipperary, where he found scattered local support. After several days of marching, some of the would-be revolutionaries condemned their commander for his refusal to allow his troops to requisition food from local residents. (Smith O'Brien banned such tactics as unfair during a time of starvation.) Many demanded that Smith O'Brien call a halt to the rebellion in hopes of better success in the fall. The once reluctant commander was determined, however, to follow the course he had chosen.

The rebel band set up a barricade outside the town of Ballingarry, and, on July 29, a unit of about forty-five armed police officers spotted the obstacle, which they believed was held by as many as a few hundred insurgents. The police took refuge in the home of a widow named McCormack, who kept a cabbage patch adjacent to her home. Five of her seven children were in the house when the police comandeered it and prepared for a rebel attack.

Smith O'Brien arrived at the scene, and so did the Widow McCormack. She demanded that the rebels negotiate rather than burn down the house, as at least one of Smith O'Brien's men threatened to do. The rebel commander walked to a window and made friendly conversation with the police: "I am Smith O'Brien, as good a soldier as any of you," he said.

The standoff suddenly disintegrated from amiable to deadly. Stones flew toward the house and a shot rang out. The police opened fire. Two people outside the house were killed, one a young man who simply followed the crowd to see what the excitement was all about. A man standing next to Smith O'Brien was shot in the chest.

Police reinforcements eventually arrived, and the insurgent party slipped away, Smith O'Brien included. What became known as the Battle of Widow McCormack's Cabbage Patch was over. Smith O'Brien was arrested on August 5, convicted of treason, and condemned to death, although the sentence was commuted to transportation to the prison colony of Van Diemen's Land, now called Tasmania.

There was another attempt at revolution a year later, this one led by the crippled James Fintan Lalor among others, but it was a fiasco, and Lalor died three months later of a bronchial attack.

In Ireland the starvation continued. It would not end until 1851, after which a million people were dead and another two million had emigrated, many of them to America. It was the worst human catastrophe of nineteenth-century Europe, and, in nationalist lore if not in reality itself, the Famine became the defining moment of Anglo-Irish relations. Scholars would debate the extent of British culpability for the next century and a half, but in Ireland and in Irish America, there was little doubt about what had happened. Deliberate choices had been made in London, and because of those choices, the Irish had been nearly wiped out, driven from their land, starved to death in a land of plenty. Millions in Ireland had been presented with a modern version of Cromwell's choice of hell or Connaught: their choice had been death or America.

Ireland in 1851 was a country of abandoned villages and mass graves of orphans; of parents who had seen their children suffer terribly and then die a most horrible death. Traditional rural society simply ceased to exist, and a cruel sort of Anglo-Saxon individualism filled the void. With their communal society, the Irish were famously hospitable. But as famine fever and other communicable diseases descended upon the starving people, beggars and other victims were sent away, told to fend for themselves.

Smith O'Brien's brief rebellion didn't even rise to the level of fiasco. But later generations would consider it a point of honor that Ireland, starving Ireland, at least summoned some show of strength in the face of appalling death and cultural destruction. And the intellectual ferment that had caused this cautious Member of Parliament to lead a band of rebels through a famished land would inspire the generation that saw its parents and siblings and friends die of starvation, that saw no choice but to leave the land of their fathers and mothers. Generations of nationalists would interpret the Famine as the ultimate expression of England's cruelty in Ireland.

By the end of the nineteenth century, the population of Ireland had been nearly halved, and 150 years later Ireland would remain the only European country with fewer people at the end of the twentieth century than it had had in the middle of the nineteenth.

The Famine was so horrendous that it was not spoken of for decades. But it was not, and could not be, forgotten.

A disillusioned Speranza, whose poetry reminded her colleagues of the horrors in the countryside, drifted away from the nationalist movement and married a physician named William Wilde in the early 1850s. As Lady Wilde, she became a fixture in British society, and her son, Oscar, found fame as a writer. Before she died, Lady Wilde met a young poet named William Butler Yeats, who would one day tell of hearing Speranza describe Thomas Davis's funeral. From Davis to Lady Wilde to Yeats—three poets, three Protestants, and one continuous line of literary nationalism.

Like his protégé Speranza, Charles Gavan Duffy found only despair in post-Famine Ireland. The government had tried him nine times on treason felony charges after the failed rebellion of 1848, but Duffy was found innocent each time. He won election to the British Parliament and tried to organize a tenants organization after the Famine, but became embittered as some of his colleagues gave up the movement in exchange for government patronage positions. He decided to set sail for Australia in 1856, saying that Ireland was no more than "a corpse on the dissecting table."

CHAPTER FIVE

THE IRISH REPUBLICAN BROTHERHOOD

AFTER A SEVEN-YEAR exile in France, an itinerant teacher named James Stephens returned to Ireland in 1856, the very year that Charles Gavan Duffy pronounced the national spirit dead. Stephens himself had been assumed dead in 1848, after he was wounded slightly during William Smith O'Brien's skirmish in Ballingarry. Stephens went on the run after Smith O'Brien's men scattered, looking to evade the police while arranging a discreet escape.

His friends figured that his task would be made a good deal easier if the police thought he had died of his wounds. So they delivered the sad news to the editor of the *Kilkenny Moderator,* who composed a respectful farewell to the twenty-four-year-old rebel: "Mr. Stephens was a very amiable, and apart from his politics, most inoffensive young man, possessed of a great deal of talent, and we believe he was a most excellent son and brother." A headstone was carved, and a coffin placed in a plot in the local cemetery.

Stephens made his way to France, where he visited museums, audited lectures at the Sorbonne, studied philosophy, and experimented with radical politics. He lived on the Left Bank, taught English—he was fluent in French—and manned the barricades in Paris with another Irish exile and veteran of 1848, John O'Mahony, to oppose Louis Napoleon's coup d'etat in 1851. O'Mahony was a well-educated Gaelic scholar trying to make a living teaching Irish in Paris. The two men soaked up the fervor of European leftist politics, socialized with radicals and intellectuals, and inevitably thought of applying what they saw and learned to Ireland. It would not be enough, Stephens would later say, to simply change flags in Ireland. Echoing the teachings of James Fintan Lalor, he declared that "unless the Irish

James Stephens

land were given to the Irish people, Irish national independence was
not worth the trouble and sacrifice of obtaining it."

The two friends were young—Stephens was born in 1824, O'Mahony in 1816—and impassioned, and thought little of living in desperate poverty while they educated themselves in the art of
revolution. The room they shared had two backless stools, walls that
were covered with diagrams written in charcoal, and some straw for
bedding. A crucial partnership was born in that humble room in
Paris, one that would reinvigorate Irish nationalism and link the nationalist cause to the dreams of Irish America, home to two million
people who had fled Ireland during and immediately after the
Famine. Once they recovered from the shock of emigration and the
less-than-hearty welcome they received in the New World, the Irish
in America ensured that Irish freedom would become an interna-

tional matter and that Britain could not act in Ireland without considering the ramifications for American politics and public opinion.

Stephens and O'Mahony also sought to separate Irish nationalism, which had become so entwined with the Catholic liberator Daniel O'Connell, from the Roman Catholic faith of the Irish masses. Following the Famine the Church was a source of solace for the broken Irish, who responded with increased deference to clerical authority. Though Catholics themselves, Stephens and O'Mahony bluntly challenged the Church's leadership, leading to their condemnation not only by local clerics but by Pope Pius IX. They persisted nevertheless, insisting that the Church had no authority over political matters. Their argument became a central tenet of Irish republican doctrine.

James Stephens had been out of touch with his family during his long French exile. After landing in Dublin, he set out to visit his father, James, and his sister, Anne, who lived in the family's hometown of Kilkenny. He hadn't seen them since he had left his house armed with a dagger for a nighttime rendezvous that would take him to Ballingarry. He hadn't wished them farewell, for they were both sleeping.

Arriving in Kilkenny, he looked up an old priest who was a friend of the family. There was a pleasant reunion, followed by the most awful news: Stephens's father and sister were both dead. He was stunned. Nothing in Ireland was as before. Famine and death had changed everything. "Before the Young Ireland revolt a happy home was ours," he wrote. "My aged father felt the rude shock severely, and, as I was then informed, never recovered from the shock. My only sister followed him to the grave in the prime of girlhood; and thus was a household ruined and broken up."

Stephens had returned to Ireland expecting to find an aroused nation looking to finish the work that he and other veterans of 1848 had begun. Instead, to his bitter disappointment, he found his hometown and its surrounding areas completely moribund. "The ardour of Young Ireland had evaporated as if it had never existed," he lamented.

He decided to set out on a walking tour of the island to find out firsthand whether or not Ireland was beaten. If it was, he would return to Europe. If it wasn't, he would lead a new campaign to revive the Irish spirit of resistance. James Stephens was certain of his own abilities. Resuscitating a nation was, he believed, well within his power.

His journey took him the better part of 1856. He reckoned that he walked three thousand miles with little more than a walking stick and a knapsack, talking with farmers and tradesmen, shopkeepers and professionals, in city, town, and country. He made for a lonely, indeed a ghostly, figure as he tramped the depopulated, devastated countryside, for he met acquaintances who had read his obituary years before but had not been in on the deception. Some of these people really did believe him to be a ghost—"I had to give up the idea of ridding them of their ignorance and superstition," he complained.

He often heard exactly what he did not want to hear: that Ireland, with its Famine graves and its exiled children, finally was broken. A soldier told him that "in a few years more Ireland will be as content and as happy as Scotland." Even some of the men he knew in 1848 advised him that he was wasting his time. "Did Christ ever die for such a people," he wrote, bitterly. He found, perhaps not surprisingly, that the middle classes were content with the status quo, but he saw hope in farmers and laborers who, he said, "spoke to me with enthusiasm." And he discovered that the secret agrarian organizations of Ireland had not disappeared. They were called Ribbonmen now—they wore identifying ribbons when they went out at night to maim an offending landlord's cattle—and they were the descendants of the Defenders recruited into the United Irishmen by Henry Joy McCracken and Thomas Russell in the 1790s. Their presence, he believed, was a sign that not all Irish people were content.

Near Limerick, he learned that his onetime commander, William Smith O'Brien, had been released from his enforced exile in Van Diemen's Land and was permitted to return to his family's seat, Cahirmoyle, in County Clare. Stephens called on him, hoping for words of advice and encouragement from the man who had considered it a point of honor to rise in rebellion in 1848. O'Brien welcomed him but offered only discouragement. Cautious as he was even in his Young Ireland days, he said he feared that popular uprisings would lead to communism. "You see, Mr. Stephens, the respectable people of the towns . . . are quite indifferent to, if not hostile to, Irish nationality," Smith O'Brien said. Stephens tried to prod him, questioning him about the events of 1848, but Smith O'Brien's wife and children, hovering nearby, cut off the exchange. Stephens concluded that they found Smith O'Brien's past embarrassing.

He soon returned to Dublin and found a letter from his old friend John O'Mahony awaiting him. O'Mahony had left France and sailed to New York, where he joined a substantial Irish network in the teeming city. He and several other veterans of 1848 formed a group called the Emmet Monument Association, which secretly hoped to foment

John O'Mahony

revolution in Ireland from America. Its name subtly suggested its goal—after all, hadn't Robert Emmet commanded that no man write his epitaph until his country were free? O'Mahony and other Irish exiles in New York were prepared to begin the engraving process.

O'Mahony, a tall, well-built man with a head of brown hair combed back and emphasizing his forehead, had been reared in comfort in County Cork. He attended Trinity College, studied Latin and Greek, and despite his privileged upbringing became a student of the

Irish language, the language of the decimated poor, and of Gaelic culture, filled with stories of heroic and tragic warriors.

But his almost mystical view of Gaelic culture and language didn't blind him to the reality of Irish history: a substantial minority did not hail from Gaelic tribes and did not subscribe to the majority population's religion. That shouldn't matter, he wrote: "Every individual born on Irish soil constitutes . . . a unit of that nation without reference to race or religious belief."

He had lived off an inheritance until 1848, when he signed over his family's property to a brother-in-law. He was often impoverished for the rest of his life, as one colleague noted: "He had friends who were willing to sacrifice everything for him, yet he was often in need of a dollar, and when his poverty was discovered he declined to receive assistance in any shape or form."

He soon discovered that the leading Irish exiles in New York were more content to give speeches about Irish freedom than to take any action. In his letter to Stephens, he complained that he was "sick of Young Ireland and its theatrical leaders [in New York] . . . I am sick of Yankee-doodle twadle, Yankee-doodle selfishness and all Yankee-doodledum! The very names of parties are inverted here. Your slavery-man is a Democrat. A Republican . . . is an aristocrat!" He told Stephens he was ready to quit his involvement in the fledgling Irish-American exile movement—it was led, he said by "tinsel patriots."

Stephens counseled patience. He recalled that in his journeys throughout Ireland, he had excited interest among would-be nationalists when he talked of "their brothers beyond the seas, of the new and greater Ireland in the Western Republic." The Irish in America numbered in the millions, he knew, and they were beyond the control of Britain's laws, police, and military. One day, they could make all the difference.

"My three-thousand mile walk though Ireland convinced me of one thing—the possibility of organizing a proper movement for the independence of my native land," Stephens wrote. "I came to resolve that the attempt was not only worth trying, but should be tried in the very near future if we wanted at all to keep our flag flying." If a decade passed without "an endeavour of some kind," he wrote, "the Irish people would sink into . . . lethargy."

So on March 17, 1858, Saint Patrick's Day, Stephens assembled several supporters and proclaimed the founding of a group that would come to be called the Irish Republican Brotherhood. The IRB became, in its essence, a secret society writ large, and in time its leaders claimed to be the legal government of the nonexistent Irish republic. The IRB was the institutional Irish revolution, the force within the larger force of Irish nationalism. Over the next sixty years, it would infiltrate moderate nationalist organizations, set up front groups, recruit new generations to the cause of revolution, and otherwise seek to control the nationalist agenda. The IRB came to embody the idea of physical-force republicanism, disdainful of politics and reform. Members took an oath pledging their allegiance to the secret organization—this was not to be a public group like Young Ireland—and to the establishment of an "independent Democratic Republic" in Ireland. Later, the oath was changed to read:

"I . . . in the presence of Almighty God, do solemnly swear allegiance to the Irish Republic, now virtually established; and that I will do my very utmost, at every risk, while life lasts, to defend its independence and integrity; and, finally, that I will yield implicit obedience in all things, not contrary to the laws of God, to the commands of my superior officers. So help me God."

Of course, the Irish Republic was far from "virtually established," but exaggeration would become a hallmark of James Stephens's leadership.

In America, John O'Mahony formed a companion organization, similarly oathbound. The student of Gaelic mythology, he named his organization the Fenian Brotherhood in honor of a band of mythological Gaelic warriors, the Fianna. The label caught on, so much so that for the next 150 years, anybody espousing a nationalist or republican point of view in Ireland was usually called a Fenian.

O'Mahony reluctantly agreed that he and his organization would be subordinate to Stephens, and that their prime responsibility, for the moment anyway, was financial—the Americans would supply the money needed to spread the IRB near and far. It was a historic moment, one that would change the dynamic in Ireland. Irish America asserted its right to play a role in deciding Ireland's future.

Stephens constructed his new organization in a series of cells, or "circles," so that members would know only those in their own circles. Each circle had a commander, or center, referred to simply as A, several captains, known as Bs, sergeants, or Cs, and privates, or Ds. Stephens gave himself the title of Chief Organizer of the Irish Republic.

But he was not the only political organizer in Ireland.

Jeremiah O'Donovan Rossa had seen the hand of death in the blackened potato fields of Ireland, and had witnessed the slow death by

Jeremiah O'Donovan Rossa

starvation of his father in 1847. He was born in September 1831, in Ross Carbery, County Cork, and was raised on a moderately prosperous farm, with twenty cows and an assortment of barnyard animals. He described himself as "the pet of the house," whose mother so loved him that she breast-fed him until he was more than three years old. He grew up on folktales of fairies lurking in the bogs (and believed in them into old age) and of great injustices perpetrated against the Irish through the centuries. He would recall that his "fireside history" included stories of English soldiers putting infants on the tips of their bayonets and ramming them against stone walls in 1642.

He grew up speaking both Irish and English, and was enrolled in one of the new national schools that Britain began building in Ireland before the Famine. The failure of the potato crops, however, destroyed what had been a fairly pleasant rural existence. After his father died, Jeremiah himself became gravely ill, drifting in and out of consciousness. He heard a woman's voice near his bed saying, "Oh, he is dying now." He survived, only to see his family broken up when they were evicted from their farm. He was sent to Skibbereen, site of appalling suffering, to live with his father's relatives. He would later write of those terrible years that he had experienced "something that was worse than the hunger . . . and that was the degradation into which want and hunger will reduce human nature."

In the late 1850s, Rossa and several young men from Skibbereen banded together to form a nationalist organization called the Phoenix National and Literary Society, although its forty or fifty members did not intend to discuss the great works of Irish literature. Rather, they spent their nights drilling in the countryside, preparing for the day when they might take the field in earnest. Stephens got wind of Rossa's little society and made the long journey to Skibbereen—Rossa noticed that the soles of the Chief Organizer's feet were red and blistered from walking—to co-opt the Phoenix Society into the IRB. Stephens told Rossa's men that Irish-Americans would provide the means and even the manpower, an invading force of perhaps as many as ten thousand, for a revolution.

It was a nice story, designed to boost interest and morale in the organization Stephens was building, but it was a lie. In fact, Stephens was so dissatisfied with O'Mahony and the American effort that he set sail for New York shortly after visiting Skibbereen. He wished to see for himself why the Americans weren't doing their part. "One hundred and thirteen pounds from the whole American organisation in a whole year! . . . I cannot conscientiously defend the conduct of our brothers yonder," Stephens wrote. If O'Mahony could not persuade Irish America to give to the cause, Stephens would do it himself. He fantasized about returning from America with $1 million, thirty thousand rifles, and ten thousand Irish-American soldiers.

While he was aboard ship headed to America, the government swooped down on the Phoenix Society, arresting Rossa and nearly two dozen of his friends. The government, however, decided that it had no reason to take Rossa very seriously. He and his friends wisely agreed to plead guilty, and they were allowed to go free.

If Stephens believed that Irish America would open its wallets for him based on his magnetism, talent, and leadership, he soon learned exactly what O'Mahony was facing. "It is hard to get the mass of the Irish in New York to believe that any one can be serious who speaks of freeing Ireland," O'Mahony complained. The survivors and children of the Famine, crowded into the poorest parts of America's cities, may well have been burning for revenge, but their priorities were those of the poor everywhere—simple survival. It is hardly a wonder that John O'Mahony found it difficult to raise money from such impoverished people, not to mention that any money given to the Fenians would hardly have seemed like a sound investment.

Stephens spent an exhausting few days touring Boston, meeting and cajoling crowds of Irish-Americans. He raised five dollars. When he returned to New York, he sought out the support of another Irish exile, Thomas Francis Meagher, who had given the high-flown "sword speech" on that night in 1847 when Young Ireland broke with Daniel O'Connell. But the onetime firebrand said it would be "unworthy of me" to "urge or authorize a revolutionary movement."

The experience humbled Stephens. Once angrily impatient with O'Mahony, Stephens returned to Ireland with a greater appreciation for his colleague's plight. O'Mahony, he wrote, was "far and away the first patriot of the Irish race."

The transatlantic conspiracy was presented with an opportunity when an old 1848 man named Terence Bellew McManus died in San Francisco in January 1861. McManus had been in Ballingarry, was arrested, convicted, and sent to Australia. He escaped and fled to the American West Coast, where he lived in poverty until his death. San Francisco's Fenians suggested that McManus's body be returned for burial in Ireland. All agreed that McManus might perform one last service for Ireland by demonstrating the bond between Ireland and America. And so his body was transported by trains across the American continent, with stops at various centers of Irish population.

Before McManus's body was placed aboard ship in New York, it was brought with great ceremony to old Saint Patrick's Cathedral. Archbishop John Hughes, an Irish immigrant and a passionate advocate for his countrymen in America, gave a stirring eulogy that sounded like a blessing upon a rebel's life. "Some of the most learned and holy men of the Church have laid it down . . . that there are cases in which it is lawful to resist and overthrow a tyrannical government," he said from the pulpit. "The young man . . . to whose memory and remains you pay your respects . . . was willing to sacrifice—and I may say did sacrifice—his prospects in life, and even his life itself, for the freedom of the country he loved so well, and which he knew had been oppressed for centuries."

The corpse of Terence Bellew McManus did not meet with such warm sentiments once it arrived on Irish soil. Archbishop Paul Cullen, one of Ireland's leading clergymen and a man destined to become a Fenian nemesis, barred McManus's remains from Dublin's Catholic Pro-Cathedral. It was a powerful signal of disapproval. Stephens, however, found a sympathetic priest to perform graveside rites.

McManus's funeral and burial on November 10, 1861, a dreary, wet, and cold day, was a public display of the organization Stephens had been quietly building for three years. Trains brought thousands to Dublin for the ceremonies, and the streets were lined with onlookers. The procession made its way along Thomas Street, where Robert Emmet was hanged in 1803 and where Lord Edward Fitzgerald had been captured in 1798. Stephens would later claim that fifty thousand people marched in the procession, and that hundreds of thousands turned out to watch. At the graveside, a priest named Patrick Lavelle took note of the significance of the day's proceedings: "I am proud to see that the people of Ireland and of Dublin are not dead—that they have hope."

Stephens had achieved what nobody, save himself, thought possible when he was tramping the roads and lanes of Ireland in 1856. He had single-handedly revived a movement that even its passionate advocates regarded as dead. And nobody appreciated the accomplishment more than Stephens himself. A fellow Fenian watched Stephens as he soaked up the triumphant atmosphere at a reception following the McManus funeral: "He smiled and smoked, and walked about among his devoted lieutenants, receiving their congratulations . . . his small eyes twinkling all the while with a delight which only lovers of fame and human worship can understand. He moved that night in a sphere of glory."

With the able assistance of an aide named Thomas Clarke Luby, Stephens began a new recruiting drive throughout the country. Eventually, some eighty thousand men took the oath as members of the IRB. The typical recruit hailed from Ireland's poor and working classes, the very people O'Connell recruited into the Repeal Association in the 1840s. Stephens and O'Mahony, students of the European revolutions of 1848, saw the Irish struggle in class as well as patriotic terms. They took to heart the strategy of Wolfe Tone, who gave up on winning over liberal-minded gentry and proclaimed that he would rely on the men of no property.

As the organization grew, Stephens developed a strategy that would take the politics of Irish resistance to Britain, home to 600,000 Irish immigrants and their children, most of them concentrated in the country's leading cities. There, they suffered not only appalling poverty, but overt discrimination. A British periodical sneered that Britain's Irish immigrants were "unclaimed by civilization." Soon there were IRB circles in every major British city.

Even more boldly, Stephens ordered the subversion of Britain's garrison in Ireland, some 26,000 strong. More than half those soldiers were Irish-born, adding to the complexity of the struggle—the hated British soldiers were, at least half the time, Irishmen. Ingeniously, Stephens saw those troops not as traitors but as potential converts to the cause. Recruiters from the IRB gathered in pubs and other meeting places near army barracks to identify possible recruits. As many as eight thousand soldiers took the oath of allegience to the nonexistent Irish Republic; when the rebellion came, these men, Stephens hoped, would turn their weapons not on the rebels, but on other soldiers wearing the Queen's colors.

In the fall of 1863, the Irish Republican Brotherhood took the highly unusual step of creating its own newspaper, *The Irish People*. It was not the sort of tactic one would associate with conspiracy. Stephens, however, believed the paper was essential not so much as a vehicle for propaganda and education but as a source of revenue. Remittances from America continued to disappoint. The financial success of the paper, he said, was a "necessity—a matter of life and death to the organisation."

Stephens appointed as the paper's editor a cranky, onetime medical student named John O'Leary, a tall, thirty-three-year-old, blue-eyed man of letters who had earned Stephens's trust despite the fact that he refused to join the Irish Republican Brotherhood. O'Leary explained that he "could not in the least see that an Irish Republic was virtually established"—as the oath of membership claimed. Even if it were, however, O'Leary would hardly have supported it, for he was an aristocrat and a monarchist at heart. He was a nationalist, as were Stephens and the IRB, but he was no republican.

John O'Leary was reared in Tipperary in relative comfort (his father owned a good portion of the town), and was close to an elderly aunt who entertained him with stories of Irish warriors, both mythological and real. The shadow of 1798 was still a part of daily life in Ireland in the mid-1800s, and the old woman often shed tears as she talked about the bravery of the United Irish rebels.

Young John attended a private school where religion was given lit-

John O'Leary

tle attention. Although open to Catholics like young John, the school was run by a Protestant clergyman. The Catholic clergy did not approve of such schooling, but O'Leary's father didn't care. O'Leary grew up to become an agnostic, which allowed him to observe sectarian issues with a detached, intellectual attitude.

He still was in his teens when he began reading *The Nation,* and quickly became a disciple of Thomas Davis, who preached nationality above religion. After reading Davis's essays and poetry, he wrote, "everything was changed." Davis would be "the foundation and the origin" of "all that is Irish in me." At age eighteen, he was part of an ambush party that tried to rescue William Smith O'Brien as he was being transported to his trial in late 1848. The plan was betrayed, and O'Leary was arrested. Released soon afterward, he immediately returned to conspiracy, and fell in with James Fintan Lalor. Although the aristocratic O'Leary found Lalor's socialistic views on land "peculiar," he respected his intelligence and passion. He worked closely with Lalor in an ultimately vain attempt to foment a rising in 1849. Among the proposals under discussion was a plan to kidnap Queen Victoria during a visit to Dublin that year.

O'Leary knew Stephens and O'Mahony, admired them and shared their belief that revolution, and only revolution, would free Ireland. He had no patience for any nationalist who sought to play constitutional politics. As an accomplished writer and a fierce ideologue, O'Leary would help write Fenian dogma in the pages of *The Irish People.*

Working at his side was another curious specimen of Irish nationalism, Charles J. Kickham, also an intellectual with a passionate belief in revolution. Kickham was born in 1828 and shared Tipperary roots with O'Leary. He, too, had an atypical Irish Catholic upbringing, for his father was a merchant and businessman who made enough money to buy a twenty-acre farm on which young Charles was raised. His early education was rigorous, and like O'Leary, he seemed inclined to a career in medicine when, at age thirteen, his life changed quite literally in a flash. Gunpowder from his father's hunting rifle exploded in his face, leaving him half-blind, half-deaf, and disfigured.

Despite his wounded eyes, he read everything he could get his hands on. And when his father became a local agent for *The Nation,* young Charles read it, too. Like O'Leary, he was converted. He devoured the ballads and poems that were signed, simply, "The Celt," which was Davis's pen name. When it was announced that the Celt had died, Kickham recalled, his family grieved. "My mother . . . actually shed tears for a man whose name she had probably never heard while he lived," he wrote.

Like Davis, Kickham had a romantic streak in him. He had a profound belief in the simple decency of Ireland's rural people, the descendants of old Gaelic Ireland. He wrote fiction and poetry celebrating not only people, but place as well, specifically, the area of Slievenamon Mountain, just south of his hometown of Mullinahone in Tipperary. His signature work was a novel called *Knocknagow,* which offered a sympathetic portrayal of the rural Irish struggling to hold on to their way of life in the face of pressure from landlords and materialism itself. The book became one of the best-selling Irish novels of the nineteenth century.

Kickham joined the IRB in 1861. Just before taking up his new position with *The Irish People,* he traveled to America, and he found the republic much to his liking, in a romantic sort of way. (He said New Yorkers were "a polite people.") He described America as "an object more worthy of reverence ... than all the crumbling relics of nations that have withered put together. ... Magnificent Democracy! I kiss the hem of your garment."

At *The Irish People,* Kickham was called on to carry out one of the IRB's most important battles—not with the British, but with the Catholic Church. Under Archbishop Cullen's aggressive leadership, the Church was as eager as the government to wipe out secret revolutionary societies. Parish priests were instructed to withhold the sacraments from suspected members of secret societies, and they preached against such organizations from the pulpit. In a country still recovering from the Famine, a plague many took to be a signal of God's displeasure, the Church and the local priests had more power than ever over the ordinary people Kickham celebrated in his fiction. *The Irish People* was determined to fight the influence of the Church in Irish politics: "We never, of course, in the least denied the absolute right of a priest ... to hold any political opinion he liked," O'Leary wrote, "but we did wholly refuse to consider that a political opinion gained any weight or force from being held by a priest."

O'Mahony was fighting the same battle in America, where the Church provided Irish immigrants with a familiar institution in a hostile and alien new world. O'Mahony said that priests who denounced his Fenian Brotherhood were "either bad Irishmen, who do not wish to see Ireland a nation, or very stupid and ignorant zealots."

O'Leary, as a nonbeliever, was uncomfortable in the role of criticizing priests, for it was a delicate assignment. But it suited Kickham, for not only was he Catholic, but he was educated enough in Church practice to take on priests and bishops on matters of theology. It was Kickham who developed the IRB's position of "No Priests in Politics," and who noted that "to talk of submission to clergymen in politics would rather astonish the Catholics of any country in the world but Ireland"—a pointed criticism not of the Church in general, but of the Irish Church. Archbishop Cullen charged that *The Irish People* seemed "to have no other object but to vilify the Catholic Church." He called on Ireland's Catholics to "banish" the newspaper "from every house" and to "destroy" copies of it when they fell into pious hands. Kickham responded with a magisterial defense, challenging Cullen to produce "one ungarbled passage" to support his accusations, and reasserted IRB teaching that "Dr. Cullen or any other ecclesiastic is not to be followed as a guide in political matters."

Scarred and wounded, half-blind and half-deaf, Charles J. Kickham uncovered, in his "No Priests" campaign, an essential tenet of Irish resistance to British rule. Though often described as a Catholic movement, Irish nationalism in fact did not depend on the support of the Church.

With the subversion of the British Army well underway and the IRB established in England's cities, James Stephens prepared again to cross the Atlantic to deal with the one element of his revolution that was not living up to expectations. Irish America's financial contributions still seemed disappointing. In a hint of power struggles that would plague the movement in future decades, John O'Mahony was resisting Stephens's notion that as the Chief Organizer of the Irish Republic, he and only he was in charge of the sprawling, transatlantic conspiracy. As head of the movement in America, O'Mahony demanded equal status with Stephens. This would never do. Stephens decided that O'Mahony was "our stumbling block."

"I am sick—almost to death—of the man and his ways," he said. So he set out for America in early 1864 to set John O'Mahony straight.

He left behind in Ireland a mass of untested would-be soldiers. He stepped ashore in a land where more Irishmen were in arms than in any previous conflict. More than 150,000 Irish immigrants fought for the Union during the American Civil War, and another forty thousand immigrants served the Confederacy. Tens of thousands of first-generation Irish-Americans were in uniform, too, including, on the Confederate side, three sons of John Mitchel, the fiery and uncompromising agitator of Young Ireland days. After escaping from prison, Mitchel had become a journalist in New York, but his pro-slavery sentiments drove him south, to Tennessee, when war broke out. His bizarre support for the South cost him dearly. He lost one son in fighting at Fort Sumter. Another was killed at Gettysburg during Pickett's Charge. A third was wounded, but survived.

The Union army was among the greatest Irish armies that ever saw battle. Most of the Irish who put on Union blue did so in hopes of proving to the American elites that they were good and loyal Americans, even if they were Catholic. Others, however, had a more pragmatic view of the great struggle. American Fenians saw the Civil War as a chance to get battlefield experience before sailing back to Ireland and fighting the British. As many as ten thousand members of the Fenian Brotherhood joined one of the armies, although most sided with the North, for geographical if not ideological reasons. John O'Mahony himself had become a colonel in the 99th New York regiment, and some of the heavily Irish regiments from New York, Michigan, Ohio, and Massachusetts essentially were entirely Fenian outfits.

Federal politicians encouraged the desperately needed Irish to form their own regiments, to march with Fenian flags flying—the Irish Brigade flew a flag featuring a harp, shamrocks, and a sunburst—and to believe that after the war there would be a reckoning with Great Britain, which had granted the Confederates belligerent status. O'Mahony publicly stated that Secretary of State William Seward supported the Fenian Brotherhood's work. And, in the midst of the Civil War's carnage, Irish officers in the Union army were granted leave to attend a Fenian convention in Chicago in November 1863. It declared that the organization would "continue its labors without ceasing until Ireland shall be restored to her rightful place among free nations." The war itself received barely a mention—O'Mahony, in his address to the assembled delegates, complained that the war had "retarded the development of the Fenian Brotherhood" because "so many of our comrades" had joined the Union army. Some of those comrades who couldn't attend the convention sent messages of support and solidarity, including Thomas Francis Meagher, the very man who told James Stephens he could not condone a new attempt at revolution in Ireland.

Stephens arrived in America in March 1864. O'Mahony immediately took him aside and asked him to keep their differences to themselves. "I impressed upon him the ruinous effect of allowing any appearance of misunderstanding between us to be manifested in the organization," O'Mahony wrote. Still, he believed Stephens was ready to remove him and take personal control of the American movement himself. "He wants a money-feeder for the I.R.B. here, not a directing mind," he said.

In another sign of Washington's willingness to indulge the Irish nationalists in blue uniforms, Stephens was allowed to tour Union army camps to recruit soldiers into the IRB. He traveled under the alias J. Dailey, and obtained passes from various political and military figures to get behind the lines. He promised the troops that 1865 would be the year of action in Ireland. O'Mahony, who was trying to pacify militants in America who were ready to strike as early as 1863, wasn't consulted about this bold plan.

Stephens returned to Ireland in August, having raised $50,000 for the IRB. He also claimed that as a result of his recruiting, 100,000 Irish-Americans were ready for battle in Ireland. "Don't say anymore that I exaggerate," he told O'Mahony. If the tone seemed defensive, it was with reason. Back in Ireland, he told colleagues that he could produce three thousand Irish-American officers from Chicago alone. When he was challenged, he said, meekly, that by Chicago he was referring to all of America west of the Mississippi.

The American organization was prepared to take him at his word when he promised action in 1865. With the end of the Civil War in sight, and with it the demobilization of thousands of Irish-American soldiers, the Fenians convened again, this time in Cincinnati. O'Mahony declared that "this brotherhood is virtually at war with the oligarchy of Great Britain." It seemed like yet another Fenian overstatement, except that O'Mahony's view was shared by none other than Queen Victoria herself. She wrote in her diary on February 12, 1865, that she had been talking that day "of America and the danger, which seems approaching, of our having a war with her as soon as she makes peace; of the impossibility of our being able to hold Canada."

The Fenian proceedings in America were conducted openly; the threats that grew out of them were not hidden from either the broader public or the government. Nothing was done to suppress Fenian activities, leading O'Mahony and others to conclude that Washington supported the Fenians—a conclusion the British were beginning to share. The British consul in New York, Edward Archibald, was assigned the task of penetrating the Fenian Brotherhood. He found it a rather easy assignment.

The promised year of action, 1865, saw a quarter-million dollars move from Irish America to the IRB. The Fenian Brotherhood moved its headquarters to the Moffet Mansion, an elegant building near Manhattan's Union Square, and it took on the trappings of a capital in exile. At the insistence of some of the movement's grander members, the mansion was furnished lavishly, leaving O'Mahony to complain: "I fear the Moffet Mansion will be the tomb of the Fenian movement. It is want in Ireland, and waste in New York." But O'Mahony was desperately trying to keep the American movement together in the face of critics who demanded action immediately. He did nothing to stop the excesses.

The IRB was at its peak strength in 1865. Stephens reckoned that membership in Ireland and Britain had reached 85,000. Companies of men were drilling by moonlight in the Irish countryside. The movement had spread from Ireland to Britain; a significant portion of the British army garrison in Ireland had been subverted; there was money to buy and smuggle arms; and battle-tested Americans were free to display in Ireland what they learned at Antietam and Gettysburg. Irishmen who had opposed each other on American battlefields were beginning to show up in Irish ports, brothers now in the fight for Irish freedom.

The government in Ireland, relying on information from spies and informers on both sides of the Atlantic, made its move on September 14, 1865. Constables raided the offices of *The Irish People,* scooping up incriminating documents and arresting all present. The newspaper was suppressed.

John O'Leary, the paper's editor, was at the theater with a woman friend when the raid took place. Four detectives were waiting for him in his lodging house. O'Leary asked the detectives if their business could wait a few minutes. They agreed, and O'Leary set himself up in a comfortable armchair, a pipe in one hand and a whiskey and water in another. Thus fortified, he offered no further resistance. O'Donovan Rossa, the paper's business manager, was taken into custody a few weeks later.

Stephens went into hiding with Kickham and other IRB men, but not before dispatching a letter to O'Mahony telling him what to do if the Chief Organizer himself were rounded up: "Once you hear of my arrest . . . gather all the fighting men about you, and then sail for Ireland." The arrest he expected took place on November 9, 1865, when police raided the house he and Kickham were sharing. Both were taken away. By then, however, beleaguered John O'Mahony could hardly round up fighting men for an invasion of New Jersey, never mind Ireland.

The Chief Organizer of the Irish Republic never understood how delicate a task John O'Mahony had, although he seemed to appreciate that whatever the task was, O'Mahony was not the man for it. O'Mahony was a poor judge of people, and allowed a thoroughly unpopular character named Jim McDermott to rise to an important position in the Fenian Brotherhood. O'Mahony's colleagues were not surprised to learn later that McDermott was a British spy. The information McDermott passed on to the British consulate in New York was useful, but his ability to create dissension was even more helpful. Through gossip and outright lies, he helped create and then worsen factions and rivalries. O'Mahony, a scholar at heart, lacked the ruthlessness required of a revolutionary political leader. He allowed his critics to foment dissent, often with McDermott's help, rather than crush or mollify them. And when the dissidents decided that O'Mahony was not aggressive enough, they formed their own faction, splitting the movement in America at the very moment when Ireland seemed ripe for revolution.

The dissidents were known informally as the Senate wing of the Fenian movement, which had been modeled after the American federal government. O'Mahony, as president, represented an executive branch of the movement; his opponents were in the legislative, or Senate, branch. The leading dissidents were a wealthy immigrant businessman named William Roberts and a thirty-three-year-old brigadier general in the Union army named Thomas Sweeny, also an immigrant.

Sweeny, who had lost his left arm during the Mexican War, was convinced that Stephens would never send the IRB into battle. Like George McClellan, the twice-sacked commander of the Army of the Potomac, Stephens appeared to be so proud of the organization he had built that he couldn't bear to see it bloodied in combat. But Sweeny was skeptical of even the organization itself: "The most reliable accounts from Ireland have convinced me that our friends there are totally unprepared with the martial means necessary to contend, with any show of success, against the British troops," he wrote. He offered an audacious alternative plan: "The Canadian frontier," he wrote, "is assailable at all points." If the American Irish could not march against Britain in Ireland, they would do so closer to home, in the British-ruled country north of the border.

As a result of the split in America, the Irish Republic had two, competing capitals in exile: the dissidents flew their Irish flags on Broadway in lower Manhattan as they prepared to march north, and O'Mahony's flew from the Moffet Mansion on Union Square, as he waited to sail east. In his office in the British consulate in New York, Edward Archibald must have heaved a sigh of relief. Half of his work had been done for him: the American Fenians were now divided. It could hardly be long before they were conquered.

In Ireland, meanwhile, James Stephens had been placed in one of Dublin's most formidable prisons, Richmond, after announcing that he would make no defense against the charges arraigned against him. "In making a plea of any kind . . . I should be recognizing British law in Ireland. . . . I defy and despise any punishment it can inflict on me," he said.

None would be inflicted. The Irish Republican Brotherhood had penetrated the very gates of Richmond prison, and among those charged with guarding the Chief Organizer of the Irish Republic were secret members of the republican movement. It was a sign of just how well organized and dangerous the conspiracy had become. On November 24, 1865, an IRB party gathered outside Richmond's walls, while IRB men inside put an escape plan into action. Within minutes, James Stephens was a free man, and the IRB had a huge moral victory. A stunned British official lamented: "All our work is undone!"

But Stephens immediately made it clear that there would be no follow-up. Just as Sweeny feared, Stephens announced that 1865 would not be, after all, the year of action.

And so the action took place in America.

John O'Mahony pleaded with the Irish in America to stand by him. He summoned a rally in New York which the city's new Archbishop, John McCloskey—John Hughes's successor—condemned. Nevertheless, 100,000 people gathered in a park along the East River on March 4, 1866. O'Mahony told them that "what we want now is the means to procure arms . . . to fight the battles of Irish freedom." The British consul, Archibald, was mortified. He wrote back to London that he believed the Irish-Americans were planning "to set fire to London in several hundred places at the same time. . . . I am told that the phrase 'strike at the heart of the enemy' . . . means the burning of London."

There was no such plan. But Thomas Sweeny was proceeding with elaborate preparations for a ten-thousand-man invasion of Canada across a front extending from the American Midwest to New England. And the plan was hardly a secret—the New York Herald noted that "there is something of military system and calculation, and some probability of success, to this Roberts-Sweeny plan of operations." President Andrew Johnson and his Cabinet discussed the looming invasion—they decided to do nothing. Adding to tensions between Washington and London, the British had once again suspended habeas corpus in Ireland and were rounding up hundreds of suspected rebels, including Irish-Americans. Britain insisted that Irish-born American citizens still were subjects of the British Crown, sending Secretary of State William Seward into a rage. Disrupted and split, the Fenians at least were achieving one of their cherished goals—to sow dissension between London and Washington.

John O'Mahony believed he could no longer resist the pressure to act, somewhere, somehow. Members of his decimated Fenian Brotherhood began converging on the town of Eastport in Maine. Their target was the island of Campobello, part of the Canadian province of New Brunswick. A steamship loaded with weapons arrived in early April. American and British diplomats scrambled to the town to observe and file reports. The small army went into action on April 15, invading Indian Island, a small chunk of Canada. Irish America had struck its first blow against Britain.

And it was to be O'Mahony's last. Washington sent troops and warships to Eastport, and O'Mahony's Fenians immediately withdrew.

Now it was Sweeny's turn.

Sweeny's plan envisioned a winter assault on Canada, with troops moving across the border into Canada over frozen lakes and rivers. When O'Mahony beat his rivals to the punch, Sweeny's civilian commanders—William Roberts and his allies—ordered Sweeny to prepare for an immediate springtime attack. The assault force would be armed with weapons and ammunition purchased from federal arsenals, and would attack from several points along a one-thousand-mile front. And it would be known as the Irish Republican Army.

Thoroughly professional despite his growing apprehension, Sweeny tried to see to every detail, even issuing an order calling for each soldier to be supplied with towels, soap, combs, coarse needles and thread, socks, and, "if possible, a change of under clothing." He called on the "lady friends" of his soldiers to "parade . . . with flags and music" once the men were across the border.

The invasion was set for May 31, 1866. When the day came, Sweeny's carefully planned, three-wing invasion force collapsed through accident, apathy, and confusion—but not through U.S. government interference. Nevertheless, eight hundred men under the command of John O'Neill, a Civil War veteran like most of his men, crossed into Canada from Buffalo. They won their first engagement with Canadian militia, but after several days of fighting, the Johnson administration stepped in. Generals Ulysses S. Grant and George Meade—who had commanded some of the men now fighting in Canada—were ordered to Buffalo to put an end to the affair. With reinforcement impossible, O'Neill withdrew and was arrested by federal authorities. Sweeny, too, was arrested when he arrived on the scene. He bitterly blamed Washington for the invasion's failure. The carefully organized American wing of the Irish republican movement was now in tatters, reviled by a previously sympathetic press, treated as a dangerous joke by other Americans. And John O'Mahony, who had had the foresight to see in the great mass of Irish immigrants a nation in exile, faded into obscurity. Other, younger men soon would take over the movement he had founded with such hope before the Civil War. He lived out his years in poverty in a single room in a tenement in New York, forgotten and too proud to ask for help. Finally, a onetime colleague found him half-starved and unable to afford coal for a fire. He died shortly thereafter, in 1877, and became yet another corpse around which the nationalist movement rallied. In death, he was accorded a respect he was denied in the last decade of his life.

The rescue of James Stephens had been a moral victory for the IRB, but only a moral victory. As the American Fenians self-destructed on the Canadian frontier, the IRB was bleeding from a hundred wounds. In his hiding place adjacent to Leinster House, the home once occupied by Lord Edward Fitzgerald's family, Stephens could do nothing as, one by one, his closest and most reliable aides were brought in front of juries. The proceedings against those arrested during and after the raid on *The Irish People* were made memorable when Jeremiah O'Donovan Rossa agreed to prolong his trial for as long as possible in order to give the ailing Charles Kickham time to prepare a defense. Rossa chose to represent himself in front of a Catholic judge named William Keogh, who had been subjected to scathing attacks in *The Irish People*. Years before, Keogh had joined with Charles Gavan Duffy in agitating for tenant rights, but he sold out the movement in exchange for a government position. It was his treachery that helped persuade Duffy to leave Ireland for Australia.

Rossa's defense consisted of personal, sometimes brutal, attacks on Keogh, including long, verbal recitations from *The Irish People*'s bitter condemnations. This went on for days, which was precisely the idea. But when Rossa was through, Keogh exacted his revenge. The thirty-four-year-old Rossa was sentenced to life in prison for treason felony. Rossa gazed defiantly at the jury as he left the courtroom. He was not particularly well known before his arrest, but his contempt for Keogh and the entire courtroom proceeding transformed him into a nationalist hero and a symbol of Fenian defiance.

Kickham, O'Leary, Thomas Clarke Luby, and others followed O'Donovan Rossa to prison, despite an eloquent defense offered by the Anglo-Irish Protestant barrister Isaac Butt, who had successfully defended William Smith O'Brien and Charles Gavan Duffy in the days of Young Ireland. Deprived of the men who had helped him build the IRB, Stephens found himself relying on younger, less-experienced men, and even they were soon in custody as the police arrested up to three thousand Fenians in the early months of 1866.

When British military authorities realized the extent to which Fenianism had penetrated the army in Ireland, entire units were transferred, and soldiers who had taken the Fenian oath were drummed out and sent off to rot in the prison colony of Western Australia.

In the waning months of 1866, James Stephens announced to his colleagues that the rebellion once again would have to be postponed. His key advisers now were a cadre of Irish-American Civil War veterans from both North and South, most prominently a former Union colonel named Thomas Kelly and a former Confederate cavalry officer named John McCafferty. And they had had enough of Stephens's hesitation. Kelly and his colleagues stripped Stephens of his power over military planning, leaving him nominally in charge of the broader movement. Stephens protested that he fully intended to launch a rebellion in 1866, "but for the breakdown in my health." He had strained credibility many times in the past; now, nobody believed him. While Stephens would operate on the edges of Irish nationalism in decades to come, the Irish-American coup effectively ended his central position as the head of Irish resistance. He left for France, bitter and cruelly disgraced, in January 1867. Colonel Kelly, whose unaffectionate nickname for Stephens was "Little Baldy," unfairly accused him of making off with American money and living in luxury in France. In fact, he was desperately poor, moving from lodging house to lodging house with the landlord just behind him. He died in 1901, nearly unremembered and entirely discredited by his contemporaries, who had forgotten that James Stephens had found a broken country and a dead movement in 1856, and within a decade had built a formidable conspiracy that spanned an ocean.

The massive arrests and ensuing courtroom revelations shook British public opinion. Authorities checked for Fenians under every bed. The mayor of the English city of Chester notified London on February 11, 1867, that "about 500 Fenians arrived in Chester by various trains [and] it is reported from Liverpool police that 700 more will be here before tonight. . . . Further military assistance [is] urgently needed . . . to protect the city." The mayor's fears were well founded, for the Fenians were planning a raid on a military barracks and ammunition depot in the city. The mayor, however, wasn't breaking news to government officials in London. Thanks to their informers, they knew about the planned raid in advance, and had taken measures to foil it. In Ireland, a memo from the Dublin police asserted that "Irish American officers are in every county at the present moment waiting for orders."

Colonel Kelly could only wish his men were so well organized. Increasingly desperate, he decided to launch a rebellion on March 5, 1867. The commander in chief of the rebel forces would not be Kelly, who was hiding in London to evade the police, but a French officer and soldier of fortune named Gustave Clusert, who had fought not only in Europe, but in America as a brigadier general in the Army of the Potomac. On the eve of battle, however, Clusert abruptly resigned and returned to France, convinced that only failure would come of Kelly's plans.

He was right. There was indeed some sporadic fighting on March 5, an unusually cold and snowy late-winter day. But the Fenian rising was, for the most part, over within twenty-four hours. The speed with which it was put down came as a surprise to some thirty-eight Irish-American officers who set sail in a ship called *Erin's Hope* and arrived off the coast of Ireland, with guns and ammunition, in mid-April. It was too late by far. The brilliant and dangerous Fenian conspiracy, the greatest threat to British rule in Ireland since the United Irishmen, was broken.

In a sense, however, the Fenian movement's legacy of defiance, its claim to a place in Ireland's collective memory, was only just beginning. On September 11, 1867, Colonel Kelly and a comrade were arrested in Manchester, England. As they were being transported under a light guard a week later, a party of thirty Fenians ambushed the prison van and demanded that the police officers turn over their keys. The policeman inside the van, a Sergeant Brett, refused to do so. One of the Fenians fired a shot, perhaps to break the lock on the van door, perhaps to frighten Brett. Instead, the bullet fatally wounded the sergeant, and another prisoner inside the van took the key from the dying man and handed it to the Fenians. Kelly was set free.

The officer's murder, and the audacity of the ambush, shocked England. The police swept up dozens of Irish men living in Manchester. Eventually, five were put on trial for the crime. One was completely innocent; the other four were part of the ambush but none had fired the fatal shot. Nevertheless, they were convicted and sentenced to be hanged. Two of the suspects were naturalized American citizens, and one of them, Edward Condon, gave the Manchester rescue words that would be added to Irish nationalist lore. "I have nothing to regret, to retract or take back," he said in the dock. "I can only say: 'God save Ireland!'" Three of his co-defendants, William Allen, Philip Larkin, and the other American citizen, Michael O'Brien, took up the call: "God save Ireland!" they shouted.

Allen, Larkin, and O'Brien were hanged in Manchester on November 24, 1867. They became known as the "Manchester martyrs," and the anniversary of their executions would be commemorated in Ireland and in America for decades. Their courage inspired a ballad, entitled "God Save Ireland," that became an anthem of nationality and defiance.

> Whether on the scaffold high
> Or the battlefield we die,
> True to home and faith
> And freedom to the last.

A legacy of another sort grew out of another rescue attempt. In attempting to free an Irish-American officer, Richard O'Sullivan Burke, from Clerkenwell prison in London, Fenian conspirators not only blew open a hole in the prison wall using dynamite, but leveled nearby homes, killing twelve civilians and injuring thirty, some of them horribly maimed. The killing of innocents intensified English hatred of the Irish in general and the Fenians in particular. And, as it turned out, O'Sullivan Burke was nowhere near the hole the Fenians blew open in the prison wall.

Prison became the final battleground in the Fenian phase of the Irish revolution. The prisoners took their cues from Jeremiah O'Donovan Rossa, whose defiance of his jailers led to frequent punishments. (He was known for flinging the contents of his chamber pot at prison guards.) So often was he put on a bread-and-water diet that his colleagues scarcely recognized him, for he had become deathly thin. When starvation didn't subdue him his jailers tried humiliation. His hands were tied behind his back for nearly a month, forcing him to eat like an animal from his plate.

He managed to smuggle correspondence out of prison, describing conditions there and the punishments that were handed out routinely to all Irish prisoners. One of his letters was published in a national newspaper, *The Irishman*. A government commission was empaneled to investigate the charges, and Isaac Butt founded a campaign to win amnesty for the Fenian prisoners. After Manchester and Clerkenwell, the British public was not in a forgiving mood, but the amnesty campaign seized on a brilliant stroke of public relations. The name of Jeremiah O'Donovan Rossa, by now the most famous prisoner in Her Majesty's custody, was entered in a parliamentary by-election in Tipperary in 1869. To the astonishment of friends and foes, Rossa won.

The British Prime Minister at the time was William E. Gladstone, who regarded the events in Manchester and Clerkenwell as evidence that something new was required in Anglo-Irish relations. After Rossa's election to Parliament, Gladstone ordered a general amnesty for most remaining Fenian prisoners. Charles Kickham already was out of prison because of his poor health. His Fenian colleagues found themselves free again in early 1871.

Most of them sailed to America. There, far from the watchful eyes of the British government, they returned to the business of Irish rebellion.

CHAPTER SIX

THE LAND WAR

THROUGHOUT IRISH HISTORY, revolutionaries prospered when politics failed. But in the late nineteenth century, after the failures of the Fenian movement, politics nearly made revolution irrelevant. Emboldened Irish politicians questioned whether the revolutionaries had anything to offer besides the often-foiled dream of a republic free of Britain. Would it matter to the average tenant farmer if his landlord were Irish or English so long as he was nearly starving and subject to instant eviction? Such questions spoke to the everyday realities of Irish life in a way that assertions of political dogma did not. In the 1870s, fewer than two thousand people owned 70 percent of Ireland's land, and 3 million people, in a land that now held just over 5 million (down from 6.5 million in 1850), were landless tenants or laborers.

This more expansive and practical view of Ireland's problems came at a time, not coincidentally, when Irish women demanded a greater role in political life. They had little patience for romantic assertions that self-government would resolve in an instant all of Ireland's problems. Social conditions, and not just nationalist ideology handed down from their elders, inspired them to organize Ireland's first female-run political organization, the Ladies Land League, which proved to be more militant than its male-led counterpart.

The new political energy and creativity, and the emphasis on social justice as well as political independence, put the revolutionaries on the defensive, and persuaded some of them to break with rebel dogma which asserted that politics was no substitute for revolution. They understood the importance of a slow but significant expansion of democracy in Ireland, as well as the growing political and financial power of the Irish in America. To ignore these developments, to cling to the ideology of abstention at a time of increased participation in politics, was to invite irrelevancy and leave to others the task of defining the parameters of nationalism.

A series of important electoral reforms, beginning in the 1850s and continuing through the 1870s and 1880s, strengthened the power of the ballot box in Irish politics. The franchise in Ireland had been highly restricted since the British, in their pique over Daniel O'Connell's election to Parliament in 1828, raised the property qualification from 40 shillings to £10. But a reform in 1850 expanded the electorate from 45,000 to 164,000. A further reform in 1868 reduced the property qualification to £4, and allowed male lodgers—the village or town equivalent of tenant farmers—to vote if their premises were worth more than £10. The introduction of a secret ballot in 1872 made it easier for eligible tenant farmers to vote for their interests rather than those of their landlords. An equally significant reform in the mid-1880s gave the vote to all adult males over thirty who were heads of households. The electorate nearly tripled, from 226,000 to 738,000. While significant portions of Irish society were still excluded, most notably women, poor Irish farmers and laborers now had more political power than ever before.

Meanwhile, the Irish in America were becoming a potent force in urban government and in the fledgling trade union movement there. As Irish immigrants and their children began to take control of some of America's largest cities and their political machines, and as Irish workers pressed for reforms in the workplace, Fenian exiles in New York, Chicago, and Boston realized that they had an opportunity, and the power, to make Ireland an issue in mainstream American politics. A young Irish exile in New York named John Devoy, one of the IRB's best organizers, began searching for a way to take Ireland's cause out of what he called the "ratholes of conspiracy." Change, he believed, was coming, and the movement he devoted his life to would have to change too, or it would die.

Two politicians dominated the age: Charles Stewart Parnell, an Anglo-Protestant landlord from County Wicklow, and British Prime Minister William E. Gladstone, an earnest if occasionally tiresome Liberal who sought to reconcile Irish nationalist ambition with British imperialist control. Gladstone sought to correct past injustices in Ireland with political and social reforms that transformed the most basic relationship in the Irish countryside: landlord and tenant. The relationship between Parnell and Gladstone was tortured—Gladstone at one point threw Parnell into prison, and Parnell referred to the Prime Minister publicly as a "masquerading knight-errant"—but

Charles Stewart Parnell

ultimately the two men combined to make Ireland one of the most important issues in British politics at the height of empire.

Educated in Britain, given all the advantages that belonged to a child of Ireland's ruling class, Parnell became the spokesman for the country's landless farmers and the champion of Ireland's oppressed Catholics. Half-American on his mother's side, the grandson of an

American naval hero in the War of 1812, he was reared in a rambunctious household that was fiercely opposed to British rule and yet respectful of Britain's monarchy. He found in the country of his mother's birth an active Irish exile community eager to lend its support to a realistic, yet outraged, demand for change. His parliamentary seat gave him credibility with Irish America's middle classes; his contempt for British rule earned him the admiration of American Fenians.

Tall, with a bushy brown beard and thinning hair, he was aloof, charismatic, and inscrutable. He built a highly disciplined party organization, the first Irish political machine, and arranged alliances with revolutionaries who were willing to put aside dogma for the sake of achieving reform. But the unrepentant Fenians who refused to work with Parnell did not go away, even though they were overshadowed and seemingly irrelevant. They remained in the background, prepared to reassert themselves if Parnell stumbled.

Parnell, however, was nothing if not surefooted. His alliance with Gladstone in the mid-1880s demonstrated the absolute power he wielded in Ireland and the absolute faith he inspired in his supporters. When Daniel O'Connell had sought to realign himself with the Liberal Party leadership of the 1840s, Young Ireland walked out on him. Parnell's party and the Fenian supporters he attracted did nothing of the sort when their chieftain threw in his lot with Gladstone and his Liberals. That said something about Parnell's hold over his followers. It also said something about Gladstone, whose likes Irish nationalists had never seen before.

In the late 1860s, during his first term as Prime Minster, Gladstone had said that "my mission is to pacify Ireland." He demonstrated his seriousness by disestablishing the state-run Church of Ireland in 1869. No longer would the faith of Ireland's minority enjoy a legally protected and subsidized position in Irish life.

A further Gladstone reform, the Land Act of 1870, marked the first real attempt to resolve the eternal problems of land. The legislation did not protect tenants from eviction, but it required that tenants evicted for reasons other than the nonpayment of rent be compensated for any improvements they had made to the landlord's property. Like the act of disestablishment, the Land Act of 1870 sent a clear signal that the status quo in Ireland could change.

Gladstone broke with traditional British responses to discontent in Ireland even as Parnell was persuading some Fenians to reexamine their dogmatic opposition to constitutional politics. The failures of the past were explicit in the strong police presence and the frequency with which civil liberties were suspended in Ireland by Gladstone's rival, Benjamin Disraeli, an enthusiastic imperialist who was Prime Minister in 1868 and from 1874 to 1880. Disraeli cared little about Ireland and was happy to contain its discontents with armed enforcers. Gladstone, by contrast, was determined to try something new: an implicit acknowledgment of past injustice through corrective legislation.

Pacification seemed to bring immediate results. Ireland showed few signs of discontent in the early 1870s. The sprawling secret society known as the Irish Republican Brotherhood seemingly had left no legacy. The most effective young Fenian organizers were former prisoners who were living three thousand miles away in America. Ireland's farmers, although impoverished as before, at least had less reason to fear eviction, even before the Land Act of 1870. Evictions averaged fewer than one thousand annually in the years after the Fenian rebellion, down from nearly two thousand in 1864. Agricultural output steadily grew through the 1870s, from £38.4 million in 1870 to £43.7 million in 1877. Prices for the farmers' produce steadily rose, and rents were stable, even low in some parts of the country. One disappointed landowner remarked bitterly that "an Irish landlord is never so rich as when he is rid of his property."

Meanwhile, Irish children were attending schools in numbers as never before as a result of Britain's ambitious program of school construction. The national school system doubled in size in the fifty years following the Famine—nearly half the country was illiterate in 1851; by the beginning of the twentieth century, the percentage stood at about 12 percent.

So content was Ireland during Gladstone's first few years in office that the leader of the Irish delegation to Parliament, Isaac Butt, had trouble winning popular enthusiasm for a limited form of Irish self-government called Home Rule. Butt was a conservative, Anglo-Protestant barrister who believed in the union between Britain and Ireland until the Famine. He defended several Fenian suspects in the 1860s and then took advantage of the new secret ballot to form a political party pledged to winning an Irish legislature with limited powers over domestic issues. The Home Rule Party won fifty-nine of Ireland's 103 seats in the House of Commons in 1874, but many of the Home Rule Party members were Home Rulers in name only. They regularly voted against Home Rule bills brought before the Commons.

In April 1875, however, the dynamic began to change when the twenty-eight-year-old Parnell was elected as a Home Rule Member of Parliament for County Meath. In his first speech in the House of Commons in 1875, he noted that a colleague had referred to Ireland as a "geographical fragment" of England. "Ireland," Parnell replied, "is not a geographical fragment but a nation." He spoke out aggressively on Irish issues, condemning the ill treatment of several remaining Fenian prisoners and opposing suspensions of civil liberties, called coercion acts. He was equally forceful on more universal issues, criticizing the practice of flogging and arguing in favor of women's suffrage. When Parliament ignored Irish issues, Parnell joined his colleague Joseph Biggar in obstructing the House's business through the British equivalent of a filibuster, often forcing members to sit through tiresome parliamentary maneuvers until dawn. It was most ungentlemanly, and it offended the government, the opposition, and, especially, Parnell's putative party leader, Butt. The press and his colleagues publicly questioned his intelligence, and one journalist said in frustration that "something really must be done about Mr. Parnell."

His great strength was that he cared nothing for the good opinion of England's statesmen and politicans. Indeed, he seemed to welcome their scorn, and he returned it in full measure. From their exile in America, Fenians started paying close attention to this young Protestant landlord with an English accent and an icy demeanor.

Parnell was on holiday in France with his colleague Biggar in 1877 when he met a journalist named James J. O'Kelly, a onetime Fenian who had emigrated to America and had found work as a journalist in New York. They had a long talk, and O'Kelly was impressed. He praised Parnell in a letter to his lifelong friend and fellow journalist John Devoy, with whom, as a boy, he had made pikes and acted out battles from 1798. "I think he ought to be supported," O'Kelly wrote of Parnell. "He has the idea I held at the starting of the Home Rule organization—that is the creation of a political link between the conservative and radical nationalists. I suppose the lunatics will be content with nothing less than the moon—and they will never get it."

O'Kelly and Devoy were members of a secret American group called Clan na Gael (Family of the Irish), which had replaced John O'Mahony's Fenian Brotherhood as Irish America's most powerful revolutionary organization. Devoy, in fact, was one of seven members of a newly formed Revolutionary Directory made up of members of the Clan and the IRB, formally linking the two revolutionary organizations. He also was one of several trustees of a curious business called a Skirmishing Fund. It was a creation of fellow exile Jeremiah O'Donovan Rossa, who was making incendiary speeches in

John Devoy

America about his intentions to export war to Britain. He solicited contributions to the fund in the pages of *The Irish World,* a militant Irish-American weekly newspaper published in New York but circulated throughout the country and in Ireland. The newspaper printed a weekly list of contributors to the fund along with Rossa's ramblings about bringing fire to England's cities. Rossa's inflammatory remarks aside, the column indicated how well some Irish-Americans remembered the suffering they or their ancestors had endured in Ireland.

Devoy and O'Kelly considered Rossa an embarrassment. At the same time, they were growing weary of the nationalist movement's inaction in Ireland. They understood that they were on the verge of being left behind as new leaders like Parnell emerged. Although neither Devoy nor O'Kelly was prepared to renounce revolution, the two old friends were looking for a way out of an ideological bind. As revolutionaries pledged to the establishment of an Irish Republic, they were supposed to believe that only armed struggle could win

Ireland's freedom. But with a powerful young parliamentarian challenging the British in the House of Commons and an increasingly
powerful voting bloc of Irish in America, Devoy and O'Kelly understood that events were outpacing ideology. If they remained wedded
to Fenian orthodoxy, their purity would soon leave them paralyzed.

Devoy, a blue-eyed, dark-haired, iron-willed native of County
Kildare, already had demonstrated his abilities as a man of action. As
a young organizer for the IRB in the early 1860s, he was put in charge
of the subversion of the British army. After his arrest, imprisonment,
and amnesty, he joined O'Donovan Rossa and more than a dozen fellow Fenians in sailing to New York in 1871, where he immediately
resumed his agitations far from the clutches of the British government. He joined the Clan na Gael and very quickly made himself one
of the organization's key figures. His friend O'Kelly already was in
New York, working as a reporter for the *New York Herald*. Devoy
also became a reporter with the paper and, thanks to his command of
French and self-taught knowledge of international relations, went on
to become the *Herald*'s foreign editor.

Through his leadership of the Clan, Devoy rescued the credibility
of Irish-American nationalism after the disastrous splits and the fias-
coes on the Canadian border. In a superb bit of professional conspiracy, Devoy organized the rescue of six Fenians who were wasting
away in the prison colony of Western Australia in 1876. Several of the
prisoners had taken the IRB oath from Devoy when he was recruiting
Irish-born British soldiers into the movement, so he felt honor-
bound to free them from what one of the prisoners called a "living
tomb." The dramatic episode inspired world headlines, and led to
British charges that the American government had looked away while
Irish-American rebels interfered with Britain's criminal justice system. The rescue ship, named the *Catalpa*, sailed into New York Harbor in August 1876, and Tammany Hall sponsored a parade for the
liberated prisoners, which did nothing to soothe Britain's displeasure.

With the *Catalpa* rescue, Devoy demonstrated that the Irish-
American nationalist movement had reemerged from scandal and fiasco. So it was with some confidence that Devoy led a delegation of
Irish-Americans to the Russian consul in New York in the fall of
1876, hoping to arrange an alliance between Russia and the Irish nationalist movement as a Russian war with England over Bosnia-
Herzegovena seemed likely. The Russian diplomat politely turned
them away. He said he saw no sign that the Irish were discontent.
Where, he wondered, was the agitation for independence?

It was underground and inactive, in the hands of Charles J. Kickham, the half-deaf, half-blind old Fenian who was chairman of the Irish Republican Brotherhood and who seemed comfortable with inactivity. Aloof from politics, the movement was invisible to all but the closest observers of Anglo-Irish relations. Devoy burned with embarrassment, for he could hardly deny the plain truth. Isaac Butt, his onetime lawyer, was the public face of Irish nationalism, and his was too gentle and polite a face.

The Christmas holidays of 1877 saw a small victory for the Irish Home Rule Party. Its members won the release of one of the few remaining Fenians in British prisons. After serving seven years in appalling conditions, a thirty-two-year-old IRB man named Michael Davitt finally was given parole. Party members assembled in London to welcome the young man's return to freedom. He struck one of the politicians as looking "more like a starved poet than a revolutionary."

Few Fenians had suffered as Davitt had, but deprivation was nothing new to the native of the village of Straide, County Mayo. His family had been evicted from their farm during the Famine in 1850. With no home, no work, and no food, Davitt's parents, Martin and Catherine, and their four children showed up at the local workhouse, where there was a roof, food, and all manner of disease. Upon arriving, the Davitts were told that Michael, then four years old, would be housed separately. Catherine Davitt, a strong, independent woman who could neither read nor write, would have none of it, and the family set off for the English textile town of Haslingden. They were evicted there, too, and Michael nearly died when they were forced outdoors into a snowstorm. His life was spared when a neighbor, another Irish exile working and living in England, took in the family and allowed them to stay under his roof until Michael recovered.

The Davitts were part of the huge Irish Catholic underclass in the industrial cities of Victorian England. In their segregated ghettos, they reconstructed Irish village life, with music and dance and storytelling. And they did not forget the horrors they had witnessed during the Famine. Catherine Davitt told her son of the appalling sights around their old home in County Mayo, of three hundred corpses thrown into a mass grave outside the very workhouse the family came so close to entering.

Michael went to work in a factory at age nine, working twelve hours a day, six days a week. Two years into his "career" in the textile business, Michael was told to fill in for another boy on a piece of processing equipment. He protested that he was too small for the assign-

Michael Davitt

ment, but his supervisor insisted. Half an hour later, Michael's right arm became entangled in the equipment. It was badly mangled, and two weeks later it was amputated.

The loss of his arm meant that Davitt's dreary life in Britain's factories had come to an early end. Instead, he went to school. He was a hardworking student, and he made ample use of a local library, where he began reading books about Irish history.

Davitt took the oath of membership in the Irish Republican Brotherhood in 1865 in the Irish ghetto of Haslingden. Even after the botched rising of 1867, Davitt helped smuggle weapons and ammunition to the IRB in Ireland. He came to the attention of the authorities, and was arrested in 1870. His time in prison, which included a stretch in the notorious Dartmoor, was horrendous. "They have done their worst, and continued to deny me even the privileges accorded to the common herd . . . but I am sustained by the conciousness of my imputed 'crime' being an honourable one," he wrote from prison. He was forced to break stones despite his disability. He suffered from bronchitis. He lost nearly thirty pounds—from 151 to 122—in sixteen months. But he had promised that he would emerge from prison more dangerous than when he entered it. And so he did. "When I was in prison I spent my time thinking of what plans could be proposed which would unite all Irishmen upon some common ground," he wrote. "I made up my mind that the only issue upon which Home Rulers, nationalists, obstructionists, and each and every shade of opinion existing in Ireland could be united was the land question."

Such was the man Charles Stewart Parnell greeted in London during the holidays in 1877. Davitt had heard something of Parnell while in prison and was eager to meet this curious specimen of Anglo-Irish gentry. Parnell's "power and directness of personality" was immediately apparent, he later wrote. "There was the proud resolute bearing of a man of conscious strength, with a mission . . . but without a hint of Celtic character." Davitt sized him up as "an Englishman of the strongest type, molded for an Irish purpose." Parnell, for his part, was equally impressed with Davitt's strength. In discussing Davitt's prison stretch, Parnell showed a bit of himself to this stranger from Mayo: "I would not face it," he said of prison. "It would drive me mad. Solitude and silence are too horrible to think of. I would kill a warder and get hanged rather than have to endure years of such agony and of possible insanity." He asked Davitt what he planned to do next.

"I shall rejoin the revolutionary movement, of course," Davitt replied.

Parnell, a Member of Parliament who was pledged to uphold the law, said nothing.

Davitt did exactly what he told Parnell he would do, and he was immediately appointed a member of the IRB's governing body, its

Supreme Council. In July 1878, he set sail for America, where his mother lived, and where a core of young revolutionaries were trying desperately to find a way out of conspiracy's ratholes.

He showed up in the *Herald* newsroom in New York on a Sunday night in July 1878. He was looking for James J. O'Kelly, whom he had met in London earlier in the year, but instead he found John Devoy. He knew Devoy by reputation, and in fact they had a grim experience in common. At one point during his imprisonment, Davitt had spotted Devoy's name carved into the molding of his cell door. Devoy had served time in the same cell a few years before.

After Devoy finished his grueling overnight shift at the *Herald* at 4:00 A.M., the two new friends boarded a train to Philadelphia to attend a meeting of Clan na Gael.

Over the next few months, Davitt and Devoy filled in the details of the new agenda for Irish-American nationalism. With politics offering opportunities for mass agitation, they needed an issue around which they could rally not only Irish-American opinion, but mainstream America as well. Once again the issue was land. It spoke to the injustices that the Irish in America still remembered, either from firsthand experience or through the tales of parents and grandparents. Davitt and Devoy won great public support as they argued for the abolition of landlordism. In an impromptu speech in Brooklyn, Devoy declared that "the land question is the question of questions in Ireland, and the one upon which the national party must speak out in the plainest language. . . . The land of Ireland belongs to the people of Ireland and to them alone, and we must not be afraid to say so. . . . I believe in Irish independence, but I don't think it would be worthwhile to free Ireland if that foreign landlord system were left standing." Newspaper accounts noted that Devoy's speech was greeted with a "storm of applause."

In late October 1878, Devoy sent a telegram to Parnell offering the young Member of Parliament the support of Irish-American nationalists if he agreed to five conditions, including a "general declaration in favour of self-government" and "vigorous agitation on the land question on the basis of peasant proprietary," which meant ownership of Ireland's farms by Irish tenant farmers. This was heresy of the first order. Fenians did not accept "general" declarations in favor of self-government; they wanted a republic. And land agitation was regarded by Fenians as a mere distraction.

Devoy published the contents of the telegram in the *New York Herald* and it became a sensation in the Irish newspapers. He called his initiative a "new departure," and a departure it was indeed. Devoy later amplified what it meant for nationalists in Ireland and in America: it would, he wrote, make possible "the entrance into the everyday political life of a large class of men . . . who have hitherto held aloof from it." As a result of this apostasy, the chairman of Clan na Gael, Dr. William Carroll, eventually resigned, and Jeremiah O'Donovan Rossa set up his own propaganda organ to encourage what was called, euphemistically, an "active policy." Charles Kickham, the IRB chairman, wrote that "a Nationalist must of necessity cease to be a nationalist when he enters the House of Commons. . . . [The] English parliament is no place for an Irish patriot."

Davitt and Devoy profoundly disagreed with Kickham, and they prevailed in getting Clan na Gael behind the new policy. But, in a series of impassioned meetings in Paris in early 1879, they failed to win the IRB's approval. During one particularly bitter meeting, Kickham, now totally deaf and blind, rolled his left hand into an angry fist—the arguments were being translated for him by a colleague who spelled out words on the fingers of Kickham's left hand. No longer interested in the debate, Kickham verbally attacked Davitt, who burst into tears and fled the room.

Kickham and his chief ally, the ex-Fenian literary critic John O'Leary, won the battle, and so they would be bystanders in the coming war over land, a war that would result in the beginning of a social revolution in Ireland. Kickham continued to preside over an inactive, moribund IRB until his death in 1882. O'Leary returned to Paris to become what he was at heart, a professional critic. But his contribution to the Irish narrative of resistance was not yet complete. He would return to Ireland in the 1890s to become an oddly romantic figure, a literary revolutionary who never took up arms, an agent of republican revolution who didn't necessarily believe in republican government.

The pragmatists who were to define the new arrangements, Devoy, Parnell, and Davitt, met three times in Dublin in the spring of 1879. Devoy would later assert that he and Parnell agreed to form a working alliance, but Davitt said there was no such formal agreement. If not explicitly spelled out, however, certainly some kind of working relationship resulted.

Isaac Butt died in the midst of these meetings. He had come to public attention as a conservative Unionist in the 1820s. The Famine, however, persuaded him that the union between Britain and Ireland was hopeless, that Britain was not interested in seeing justice done in

Ireland. In his declining years, he tried in vain to keep control of a movement impatient with respectful argument. He was, in a sense, the mirror image of his counterpart in the revolutionary movement, Charles Kickham, a man who had outlived his time, but whose contribution to Irish nationalism was undeniable.

Butt's death moved Parnell closer to the role of the Home Rule Party's chief, although he did not formally win the chairmanship until mid-1880. Meanwhile, Davitt was monitoring conditions in his native County Mayo, where wet weather was threatening the coming harvest. The previous year's harvest had been poor, too. After nearly a decade of prosperity, Irish farmers and their families suddenly were faced with the terrifying prospect of hunger. Increased competition from America forced a drop in the price of wheat and other farm produce. Potato production fell by 75 percent. All the familiar signs of distress began to fall into place. Evictions increased, from 183 in the first quarter of 1878 to 261 in the same period in 1879. Predictably, agrarian crimes increased, too. There would be 863 in 1879, compared with 301 in 1878.

Davitt impressed Parnell with his accounts of growing desperation in the west, and he pleaded for a direct link between parliamentary politics and agrarian agitation. Davitt was organizing the tenants in Mayo, and he beseeched Parnell to lend his name to a demonstration planned for the Mayo village of Irishtown. Parnell agreed to speak at a subsequent demonstration in the town of Westport on June 8. "You must show the landlords that you intend to keep a firm grip of your homesteads and lands," he said. And, conjuring images of the Famine, he added: "You must not allow yourselves to be dispossessed as you were dispossessed in 1847." He made the case for immediate reductions in rents, without mentioning that he already had reduced rents on the lands he owned by some 20 percent.

Davitt organized similar demonstrations through the summer of 1879, as starvation grew imminent. Protest led to organization and the founding of the Land League of Mayo, and, in a sign that distress had reached every corner of the country, the league was reconstituted as the National Land League in October 1879. Michael Davitt was the league's founder. Charles Stewart Parnell was its president.

And so began a dramatic new phrase in Ireland's fight for freedom—the Land War. While hard-line rebels remained aloof, Davitt and Parnell set out on a course that would lead to a sweeping social revolution in Ireland and the eventual dismantling of landlordism there. The Land League became a public mass movement like none since the days of O'Connell. It sought to lower rents, reduce evictions, and agitate for peasant ownership, and while it was short-lived, its long-term achievement was remarkable. By the early twentieth century, its demands had been achieved. The landlord system was virtually abolished, and the vast majority of farm holdings in Ireland would be in the hands of those who occupied and worked them. Through tactics ranging from constitutional politics to social ostracism of land agents and farmers who replaced evicted tenants, the Land League formed a shadow social and political organization in rural Ireland in the early 1880s.

Meanwhile, in the United States, John Devoy helped organize the critical American political and financial support that made the agitation and organization possible. For the first time, the cause of Irish freedom became a mainstream American political issue, attracting the masses as well as the emerging Irish-American elites. It was in pursuit of political and financial support from America that Charles Parnell set sail for the land of his mother's birth in late December 1879.

In a measure of just how quickly events were taking charge of politics in Ireland, even while Parnell was aboard ship during the eleven-day journey, the situation in Ireland became even more desperate. Mass starvation seemed imminent. Parnell decided to split his fund-raising efforts; he would appeal for money to buy food and supplies for the hungry Irish as well as for the political work of the Land League. He visited more than sixty cities in just over two months, and was received with great enthusiasm almost everywhere, including in such distinctly non-Irish cities as Des Moines, Cincinnati, and Columbus. He addressed the House of Representatives, and was invited to the floor of the Stock Exchange in New York. He raised tens of thousands of dollars for the starving Irish farmers and for the Land League's political activities, proving the newfound power of Irish America.

His trip was cut short in March 1880 when Parliament was dissolved and a new election scheduled. Before returning to Ireland, Parnell brought together a disparate group of Irish-American reformers, revolutionaries, politicians, and labor organizers to form an American-based adjunct of the Irish Land League. The American Land League became the first mass political organization in the United States that openly agitated, and raised money, for reform in Ireland. It was a natural extension of Devoy's efforts, for it took Irish-American political agitation into the mainstream, and brought Ireland's grievances to a wider audience. Eventually the league would have 1,500 branches and more than 200,000 members, would raise more than

$500,000 to fund land agitation in Ireland, and would recruit priests, politicians, businessmen, lawyers, and others who would have either ignored or condemned the activities of Clan na Gael.

The British parliamentary election of 1880 demonstrated just how seriously Devoy's friend James J. O'Kelly took the idea of full Fenian participation in public life. While visiting Ireland on an aborted gun-smuggling mission, O'Kelly was persuaded to run for Parliament with Parnell's party. He won, and he became Parnell's closest male friend and confidant. All the while he kept up a regular correspondence with Devoy, who was the leading organizer of Irish America. There was a certain poetry to this highly intriguing relationship, for Devoy and Parnell were in similarly delicate situations. Both were committed to political agitation but were well aware of the need to keep the militants satisfied. Both relied on harsh rhetoric to keep a lid on discontent, and both often found themselves in close contact with men who were ready, and even eager, to pursue something more than mere speechmaking and argument. And both confided in the same man, James J. O'Kelly.

With Parnell back in Ireland, administration of the relief funds he raised passed into the hands of his two sisters, Fanny and Anna, who had opened a famine relief office in New York during their brother's tour.

Fanny Parnell had been living with the Parnell family's eccentric matriarch, Delia, in Bordentown, New Jersey, since the early 1870s. Fanny was not particularly healthy, but she followed politics with great enthusiasm. In addition to writing rebel poetry as an adolescent, she attended the trials of accused Fenians at a time when her brother, Charles, exhibited little interest in public affairs. Contemporaries noted her sharp wit and an independence of mind that she certainly shared with her sister, Anna. An acquaintance described her in 1879 as "a beautiful lady in all the enjoyment of youth"—she was thirty at the time—"with large, sparkling eyes, above the medium height, of willowy form, joyous in spirits, lively in expression."

Although she was attracted to Fenianism, it was the broader nationalism of the late 1870s and early 1880s, connecting politics to social reform, that stirred her passion and inspired her writing. In private, she was true to the principles she espoused in public: she politely but firmly refused an Irish-American delegation's offer to bring in the harvest from the fields near her home in New Jersey, explaining that "there are a number of poor people around me that I employ ever year. I have always employed them, and your doing the work would deprive them of their means of living."

Fanny Parnell and her mother, Delia

Along with Anna and their mother, she founded the Famine Relief Committee in New York, which managed the money Charles collected during his American tour. At the same time, she became famous for her poetry, earning comparisons to the muse of Young Ireland,

Speranza. Her most famous poem was entitled "Hold the Harvest," published in 1880 as the Land War was underway in Ireland.

> *But God is on the peasants' side,*
> *The God that loves the poor;*
> *His angels stand with flaming swords*
> *On every mount and moor.*
> *They guard the poor man's flocks and herds,*
> *They guard his ripening grain;*
> *The robber sinks beneath their curse*
> *Beside his ill-got gain.*

Michael Davitt described "Hold the Harvest" as "the 'Marseillaise' of the Irish peasant." The poem earned Fanny Parnell fame equal to her brother's, and established her reputation as a voice of the landless Irish peasant.

She was no less a populist in her prose. In a pamphlet entitled *The Hovels of Ireland* she sounded like one of the masses waving pitchforks outside the Bastille in 1789. "All through history it is the mob (so-called) that really ended [up] winning," she wrote. "In the warfare of plebeian against patrician it is the plebeian that scores the final victory. The blind instinct of the multitude, often wrong but much oftener right, is one of the most powerful of God's instruments of civilisation." But she was not prepared to rouse the tenants to violence. She argued that the Land League should "employ nothing but moral force."

Fanny and Anna often worked twelve-hour days on behalf of the Famine Relief Committee. Anna Parnell was something of a poet, too, although her verse never attracted public fanfare. She was three years younger than Fanny, and just as independent and strong-willed. (At one point during the land agitation in Ireland, she climbed on the back of another agitator so that she could cross a river to witness a police-supervised eviction.) She studied art as a schoolgirl, and, like Fanny, she took up politics at a young age.

She did not suffer fools gladly—a contemporary noted that "the mental inferiority to which women were condemned by ecclesiastical authority . . . galled Miss Anna." Her impatience extended to her brother, whose habit of ignoring paperwork drove her, and Fanny, to distraction, for it meant that invitations went unanswered and contributions unacknowledged. Anna made sure to acknowledge contributions of any size sent directly to the relief committee, and, in keeping with her egalitarian nature, she saw to it that even the smallest contribution was acknowledged. This was no small commitment, for most of the £60,000, some quarter-million dollars, that the committee raised came from the poor, slum-dwelling Irish of urban America.

In October 1880, with evictions and agrarian crimes commonplace in Ireland, Fanny Parnell called on Irish-American women to form their own organization to support the land agitation in Ireland. The New York Ladies Land League held its first meeting shortly thereafter. Encouraged by the response, Fanny soon suggested that the women of Ireland form an organization of their own. Shrewdly, she noted that women should be prepared to continue the agitation if its male leaders were arrested. And when Anna Parnell, who returned to Dublin after her stay in America, founded the Ladies Land League of Ireland despite her brother's skepticism, she sternly resisted suggestions that the Ladies Land League focus on charity work rather than the manly pursuit of political agitation. The Ladies Land League was to become a fomidable, militant, and effective organization in its own right.

Famine had been averted in 1879 and early 1880 thanks to the intervention of American dollars. But charity couldn't stop landlords from ridding their property of impoverished tenants. Evictions in 1880 more than doubled, to 1,893 families, compared to 1879, and agrarian crimes were nearly out of control, rising from 297 in 1879 to 2,590 in 1880.

By the closing months of 1880, Ireland was approaching outright rebellion, and the Land League, with 200,000 members in Ireland and another 200,000 in North America, functioned as a shadow government in the countryside. It used American contributions to set up special courts to dictate rents, it organized agitation against recalcitrant landlords, and, although pledged to nonviolence, it deliberately looked away as the rural population prepared for even stronger action. Michael Davitt, who returned to Ireland after guiding the American Land League's growth, wrote approvingly to Devoy that "it would take me a week to give you anything like an account of the immense growth and power of the [Land League]. It now virtually rules the country. . . . The courage of the people is magnificent. All classes are purchasing arms openly." The English Chief Secretary for Ireland, W. E. Forster, seemed resigned to war in Ireland. "We might pour in thousands of soldiers and occupy the disturbed districts as though they were an enemy's country, but these outrages are as difficult to deal with as guerilla warfare," said the Chief Secretary, who was the Lord Lieutenant's second in command. "I fear no troops will prevent them."

The league's most famous tactic was the boycott, which got its name from Captain Charles Boycott, a land agent who organized evictions in County Mayo. In solidarity with the evicted tenants, Irish farm laborers refused to harvest Captain Boycott's crops. A corps of Protestants volunteered to do the work, further adding to the tension, and, in a sign of how close the country was to outright rebellion, seven thousand British soldiers were called out to guard the volunteers. Many landlords who could not command the sort of protection accorded Captain Boycott decided they had no choice but to give in to the league's agitation, granting rent decreases of up to 50 percent. Those who refused sometimes paid a terrible price. A landlord in County Galway, Lord Mountmorres, was murdered in September 1880.

Parnell, now the official leader of the Irish Parliamentary Party, an independent political party made up of Irish nationalists, encouraged the newfound militancy of the Irish farmers even as he emphasized nonviolent agitation. At a huge meeting outside Limerick in early November, he reminded them of the need to "bring the strong force of public opinion to bear on any man who does take a farm from which another had been evicted." Through a combination of tactics borrowed from the secret societies and the modern strategies of political organization and propaganda, the Land League challenged British administration in Ireland as nobody had since the Repeal Association.

With the country in an uproar, the man who became known as Ireland's uncrowned king took a step that would plunge his life and career into unimaginable turmoil. In October 1880, Charles Stewart Parnell, a bachelor, took as his mistress Katherine O'Shea, the wife of one of his colleagues. She would become more than a lover. Politically astute and independent, she was Parnell's closest adviser in the tumultuous years to come. Parnell's colleagues apparently knew little or nothing of this, although it seems likely that Parnell might have confided in his new friend O'Kelly. It would seem natural enough, for O'Kelly was involved in a sensational divorce case in New York in the 1870s, having fathered a child out of wedlock with his French mistress.

Confrontation of one sort or another was becoming unavoidable in late 1880. Gladstone found himself presiding over a social revolution, and reverted to the tactics of his more belligerent predecessors by introducing a bill suspending habeas corpus and the regular rule of law in Ireland. This predictable response to discontent played into the hands of militants, who insisted all along that no good, and certainly no change, would come of politics and constitutional agitation. Their credibility at stake, Parnell, Davitt, and Devoy stepped up their tactics and their rhetoric. Parnell and his colleagues in the House of Commons brilliantly disrupted the debate over the latest coercion bill, at one point forcing the honorable members to sit through a forty-one-hour debate—the longest single session in House of Commons history—as the bill neared a vote. Devoy, addressing an American Land League meeting in New York on January 16, 1881, predicted that the land agitation inevitably would provoke a violent response from the British. "Will we, then, stand idly by and see our people and country devastated, and content ourselves with enthusiastic resolutions and sympathies," he asked. "No, for every Irishman murdered we will take in reprisal the life of a British Minister. . . . For a wholesale massacre of the Irish people we will make England a smouldering ruin of ashes and blood." That same day, Davitt addressed a shivering crowd in County Cork: "If your patience becomes exhausted by government brutality," he said, "the world will hold England, and not you, responsible if the wolfdog of Irish vengeance bounds over the Atlantic."

Devoy's words led to a bitter debate on the House of Commons floor. Davitt's prompted something more drastic: he was arrested on February 3, charged with violating the terms of his parole. One by one, Irish Members of Parliament denounced the government's actions. Parnell refused to allow Gladstone to speak, and was suspended and forcibly removed from the House floor. Each of his thirty-five colleagues in the Irish party was similarly dismissed from the proceedings.

A generation before, during the Young Ireland years, nationalists had talked about Irish Members of Parliament withdrawing from the House of Commons and unilaterally setting up a Home Rule assembly in Dublin. The moment for such action was at hand. Parnell, however, chose not to take such a drastic step, and the moment passed. But the Land League's money was transferred from London to Paris to preserve it from government seizure.

Gladstone then delivered a master stroke. He introduced a sweeping land reform bill, one that placed Parnell, Davitt, Devoy, and the entire land movement in an untenable position. The Prime Minister offered not just a conciliatory gesture, but genuine and long-sought reforms creating government land courts to set fair rents and offering tenants security so long as they paid their rents, among other provisions. It addressed the immediate grievances of the tenant farmers, although a loophole allowed the evictions of some tenants who were deeply in arrears on rent payments.

But it wasn't, of course, national self-government or independence. The militants who had agreed to back land reform as a tactic in a long-term strategy designed to win independence now faced an excruciating dilemma: support the bill, and perhaps see an end to agitation, or oppose the bill and spoil the chance for genuine relief. Before his arrest and imprisonment, Davitt foresaw Gladstone's move and the effect it would have on the movement he had built. "The government land bill will not be enough but it will satisfy a great number inside the [Land League]," he wrote to Devoy. "I anticipate a serious split in the league." Under immense pressure from both sides, Parnell allowed his members to vote their conscience. Parnell and six colleagues abstained on the bill's final vote in August 1881. The rest voted in favor.

Uncertain of his next move and aware that the revolutionaries in America were slipping out of Devoy's tight control, Parnell chose to attack Gladstone in insulting terms. The prime minister took the bait, reminding Parnell that the "resources of civilization in Ireland were not yet exhausted." No doubt delighted to have drawn Gladstone into the rhetorical battle, Parnell replied: "It is a good sign that this masquerading knight-errant, this pretending champion of the rights of every other nation except those of the Irish nation, should be obliged to throw off the mask . . . and stand revealed as the man who, by his own utterances, is prepared to carry fire and sword into your homesteads, unless you humbly abase yourselves before him and before the landlords of the country." Gladstone had heard enough. He ordered the arrest of Parnell, O'Kelly, and several others on charges of sedition. They were dispatched to Kilmainham jail while the country tested the new Land Act, and while Katherine O'Shea, Parnell's mistress, tried to cope with a difficult pregnancy. She was carrying her lover's child.

From prison, Parnell and his colleagues called on the Irish tenant farmers to stop paying rent. Of course, there was nothing Parnell could do to help enforce his manifesto. And there was nothing the Land League could do, either. It was officially suppressed on October 20, 1881.

With the country still in turmoil, the Ladies Land League stepped into the breach. Months before, the male leaders of the Land League had erupted in laughter when Davitt suggested that the Ladies Land League could carry on the agitation in the event of mass arrests. Parnell himself opposed the idea, saying the movement would "invite public ridicule" if women were seen as its leaders.

Several of the men asked: "Would you have the girls sent to prison, too?"

"In such a cause, why not?" Davitt replied.

Gladstone's land bill may have created a dilemma for Charles Parnell, but for Fanny and Anna Parnell, the issue was straightforward. The bill was not nearly good enough. It did not propose peasant proprietary, that is, ownership of the land by the people who worked the land. So they opposed the bill, and would not accept the argument that the farmers themselves might be content with something less than the Land League's stated goals. "Should this be true," Anna wrote, "then the Irish farmers are not worth fighting for." She threatened to "call on America to leave them to their fate."

The Dublin headquarters of the Ladies Land League became a whirlwind of activity. Anna saw to it that the league had a shadow executive ready to take over if the official leaders were arrested. And when a pro-Parnell newspaper called *United Ireland* was suppressed, Anna and her colleagues in the Ladies Land League arranged for it to be printed in Britain and in France, and then smuggled into Ireland.

The Ladies Land League had several critical duties, not the least of which was to make certain that the movement continued to grow in the face of coercion and the new land bill. It also was responsible for raising and spending considerable sums of money to help pay for the defense of agitators arrested under the coercion bill and to support the families of those arrested. But Anna Parnell's foremost obligation was in the countryside, attending to the thousands of families who continued to be evicted from their holdings. More than sixteen thousand people were evicted in 1881, and another 26,000 the following year. The evictions exposed just how large the arrears loophole in Gladstone's bill was.

The Ladies Land League fanned out into the countryside to witness the evictions, to protest against them, and to build rudimentary huts to provide families with at least some shelter. The work was more a symbol of solidarity than a substitute for a pulled-down cabin; nevertheless, it spoke to Anna Parnell's passionate belief in the cause of the impoverished tenants. The women built more than two hundred huts, and would have built a few hundred more if the authorities hadn't stepped in. Anna Parnell nearly attacked the Lord Lieutenant on a Dublin street after the hut-building project had been halted in Limerick.

Along with her sister, Fanny, Anna encouraged tenants to adhere to the no-rent manifesto that Charles and his colleagues proclaimed from their cells in Kilmainham jail. She was bitterly disillusioned when the farmers chose the assurances of Gladstone's bill over the fighting words of the Ladies Land League. "The first principle of the Land League was that the cultivator was entitled to the first fruit of his labours, while the landlord was entitled to nothing until the farmer's wants were satisfied," she wrote. "Its ultimate aim was the conversion of the tenants into owners of their holdings." She advised farmers to withhold their rents until all other expenses and outlays were accounted for, and she was disappointed when that advice was not taken, and angrier still when the Irish seemed appreciative of Gladstone's efforts at reform.

More than her sister, certainly more than her brother, and perhaps more than any of her brother's colleagues, Anna Parnell detested not only landlordism, but the landlords themselves. She bitterly condemned the landlords' treatment of their own wives and mothers, charging that inheritance laws favored men and forced women survivors to live in reduced circumstances. For their treatment of women alone, she wrote, Irish landlords deserved "extermination."

Given Anna's passion on the subject, it was not surprising that the Ladies Land League was more militant than the Land League itself in organizing boycotts and even in trying to intimidate tenants from taking advantage of the land courts provided for in Gladstone's land act. Michael Davitt later recalled that boycotting was "more systematic and relentless" under the Ladies Land League. "The result was more anarchy, more illegality, more outrages, until it began to dawn on some of the official minds that the imprisonment of the male leaders had only rendered confusion worse . . . and made the country infinitely more ungovernable under the sway of their lady successors."

The work of Anna Parnell and the other women in the movement earned the scorn of Catholic Archbishop John McHale, who complained that the women agitators were "forgetting the modesty of their sex and the high dignity of their womanhood." Several of the organization's agitators were arrested, as Davitt predicted they might be. And when the Ladies Land League itself was suppressed in December 1881, Anna Parnell organized such effective demonstrations that the government chose not to enforce its ban.

In late March 1882, the voice of Britain's establishment, the *Times* of London, conceded that the agitators in Ireland had won. "The Irishman has played his cards well and is making a golden harvest," the paper said. "He has beaten a legion of landlords. . . . He has baffled the greatest of legislatures and outflanked the largest of British armies in getting what he thinks his due. . . . Reason compels us to admit that the Irish have dared and done as they never did before." It was a startling admission of defeat, though the newspaper couldn't bring itself to admit that it was the Irish*woman* who had helped beat the landlords, baffle the legislature, and outflank the army. Irish women had made Ireland ungovernable through an ingenious campaign of moral force, intimidation, and mass protest. The British were paralyzed, for they could hardly call out troops to face protests led by women, however formidable. Nor could they force tenants to be sociable to other tenants who rented land from which others were evicted. The Ladies Land League had made its point.

On April 23, 1882, Captain William O'Shea wrote to a young colleague of Gladstone's, Joseph Chamberlain, after visiting his party leader, Parnell, in Kilmainham jail. He reported to Chamberlain that Parnell "is prepared, in case of . . . an arrangement on the question of arrears, to use his best energies to stop outrages, the circulation or support of No-Rent manifestos, and intimidation generally." Even as Anna Parnell carried on her campaign of confrontation in the countryside, O'Shea was conducting back-channel negotiations on Parnell's behalf with the British government. It was clear that Parnell was eager to cut a deal. Negotiations, however, were put aside for a few days when tragedy struck the O'Shea household. On April 25, Captain O'Shea wrote sadly: "My child is to be buried at Christchurch this afternoon." The daughter born to William and Katherine O'Shea, Sophie, died when she was just two months old.

But she was Parnell's daughter, not O'Shea's. Parnell wrote to Mrs. O'Shea on the day of the funeral: "I have indeed every hope and confidence that our separation will not now last very long."

He was released from Kilmainham on May 2. The conditions O'Shea outlined in his negotiations with Chamberlain became party policy under terms of what became known as the Kilmainham Treaty. The agrarian agitation was to be stopped. There would be no more boycotting, no more enouragement of rent strikes. In return, Davitt also was released from prison, and the government took up the issue of tenants deep in debt to their landlords. Parnell's party would now focus its attention exclusively on the attainment of Home Rule.

The Ladies Land League had served its purpose, but in the post-Kilmainham world, its militancy was instantly out of fashion. Parnell and Davitt were reunited outside Portland Prison, and on their way to London, they discussed the future of the Ladies Land League. The usually unemotional Parnell could hardly contain his anger. Davitt, who had been a supporter of the Ladies Land League from the beginning, defended the women, saying that they had kept the ball rolling while Parnell was in jail. "I am out now," Parnell replied, "and I don't want them to keep the ball rolling any more. The league must be suppressed, or I will leave public life."

His mood quickly changed, and turned lighthearted, as he speculated about winning Home Rule for Ireland and putting together a domestic government. Davitt, he joked, would be named director of prisons, having much experience in the field. Parnell also spoke warmly of the newly appointed Chief Secretary for Ireland, Lord Frederick Cavendish, who was preparing to replace W. E. Forster as the Queen's second-highest administrator in Ireland. Cavendish was married to Gladstone's niece, and although not very experienced, he had Parnell's respect for his sincerity and his modesty.

That same evening, Cavendish and an Irish civil servant named Thomas Henry Burke, who served Dublin Castle as an Under Secretary, were strolling through Dublin's Phoenix Park when a gang of men armed with surgical knives ambushed them and hacked them to death. The assassins were members of an obscure republican group called the Irish National Invincibles.

The public in Ireland as well as Britain was horrified. Parnell offered to resign his chairmanship of the Irish party, but Gladstone graciously said the gesture was unnecessary. With his equally stunned colleagues, Parnell issued a statement expressing "the universal feeling of horror which the assassination has excited," and assuring the world that the Irish people were "intense in their detestation of this atrocity." His sister Anna was not nearly as appalled. She wrote a letter to the *Times* of London that read very much like a justification of the killings. She said that Cavendish's predecessor, Forster, had "butchered men and women" and that the Lord Lieutenant, Lord Spencer, was responsible for "butchering children." It followed, she wrote, that "if there are any who are surprised that the assassin's arm is not idle . . . they must forget that there is such a thing as human nature among Irishmen."

The Phoenix Park murders emphasized Parnell's need to move away from confrontation. Although nonviolent in principle, the tactics of the land movement often inspired unsanctioned violence, or at least the threat of it. Anna Parnell clearly understood what might happen next. She defiantly announced that she would continue to organize the tenants, regardless of what politicians like her brother might say.

In the midst of this national and family drama, Fanny Parnell met with Michael Davitt, who sailed to America after his release, and a colleague at her home in New Jersey. Davitt, too, was disappointed in Charles Parnell's new course, believing that he had sold out the land movement, even though Parnell had demanded Davitt's freedom as part of the Kilmainham Treaty. Though he didn't break with Parnell, Davitt took up a cause Parnell certainly would not approve of. He argued that the ultimate solution to Ireland's problems was land nationalization, that is, government seizure of privately held land.

Davitt joined Fanny Parnell for a walk on July 20, a hot, midsummer afternoon. She had dinner shortly after returning, and after dinner, she died, at age thirty-two.

The exact cause of her death was never established. Parnell's colleague Timothy Healy said she died of an overdose of sleep medication, with the implication that she committed suicide. Her mother said simply that Fanny died of exhaustion. What is certain is that her death came as a shock, even though she was never particularly healthy. Her brother was grief-stricken, and Anna broke down completely, unable to work for weeks afterward.

With Anna distraught, Charles Parnell made his move against the Ladies Land League. Charging that it had spent too much money, he ordered it disbanded. Agrarian crimes promptly dropped from 3,433 in 1882 to 870 a year later. From the government's perspective, Parnell was a man of his word. But Anna Parnell would have nothing to do with her brother for the rest of his life, and, deeply bitter, she left Ireland to live in England. A quarter-century later, she wrote a long history of the Land League. She entitled the manuscript "Tale of a Great Sham."

Now completely committed to a constitutional campaign for Home Rule, Parnell set out on a course that would make him the arbiter of British politics. He made and broke governments, and, in a spectacular triumph, he won over Gladstone and the Liberal Party to the cause of Home Rule. His party, which grew from thirty members to eighty-six after a general election in 1885, became a highly disciplined machine, endowed with American money through an auxiliary organization called the Irish National League, which replaced the Land League. For several remarkable years, he held the balance of power in the House of Commons between the Liberals and the Conservatives, and he used that power to full advantage. After the general elections of 1885, the eighty-six votes Parnell commanded were exactly the difference between the 335 Liberals in the House of Commons and the 249 Conservatives. He threw his support to the Liberals and Gladstone.

He became enormously popular in Ireland and even in Britain, but

Conservatives and other British establishment figures regarded him as a traitor to both his class and the United Kingdom of Great Britain and Ireland. And they were convinced that he had ties to the sort of men who killed Lord Cavendish and Burke in Phoenix Park. Forster, the former Chief Secretary of Ireland, in fact accused Parnell of complicity in agrarian crime during a speech in the House of Commons in January 1883.

He was, by the middle of the 1880s, a walking target for Conservatives and the rest of the British establishment. By then, Katherine O'Shea, still married to Captain O'Shea, had given birth to two more of Parnell's children.

Parnell's bitter enemies, looking for any evidence of scandal, would have been interested in the letters his friend James J. O'Kelly was writing to John Devoy in New York after the Kilmainham Treaty. "When writing to me about Irish affairs, you should use a secret ink," O'Kelly advised, adding that he also would use invisible ink when he could. The elaborate precautions were understandable, given the nature of the correspondence. "With regard to the arms you are buying," O'Kelly wrote to Devoy in October 1882, "I consider the Colt revolver antiquated. Though a good shooting weapon . . . no man could reload the Colt during a fight—while the Smith and Wesson . . . could be easily and rapidly reloaded by even men new to the business." O'Kelly told Devoy that he could get "good imitations of the Smith and Wesson" in Turkey, and could have them "delivered in London or Liverpool."

While he carried on this intriguing correspondence with O'Kelly, Devoy was funneling tens of thousands of dollars raised from Irish-Americans to an inventor in New Jersey named John Holland. A native of Ireland who taught school in the city of Paterson, Holland was developing what would become a prototype for the first working American submarine. Shaped like a cigar, it soon attracted gawkers along the shores of New York Harbor as it cruised along the surface and then suddenly disappeared under the water. Devoy envisioned a day when the submarine would be put to use against British shipping. With that in mind, he spent $60,000 in the mid-1880s on the submarine, which the New York newspapers dubbed the "Fenian ram." Although Holland's invention never was turned against the British, his contribution to naval science was acknowledged when the American government christened its first submarine the USS *Holland*.

The Irish-American militants whom Devoy kept in line during the land war were considerably less inclined to support Parnell's new course. Clan na Gael had passed out of Devoy's control and was in the hands of more militant colleagues, who began to take their cues from the mercurial Jeremiah O'Donovan Rossa. After years of promising to bring death and fire to Great Britain, Rossa had finally made good on his threats. He drew blood—the blood of a seven-year-old boy—when an explosives team under his control blew up a military barracks near the English city of Salford. The young boy was the only person killed. Rossa nearly struck again in March 1881, when a bomb was discovered at the residence of London's Lord Mayor.

Clan na Gael began training teams of men in the use of dynamite. Among the trainees was an Irish immigrant named Thomas J. Clarke, who would be sent on a bombing mission to England in 1883 but would be arrested before he could carry out his assignment.

An internal Clan na Gael circular made the group's intentions clear: "We cannot see our way to an armed insurrection in Ireland. . . . But in the meantime we shall carry on an incessant and perpetual warfare with the power of England." Two bombs went off in London's subway system on October 30, 1883, injuring seventy-two people. A bomb went off in London's Victoria Station on February 26, 1884. There were three more explosions on May 30, including one in Scotland Yard. The British were furious with the American government and made their complaints known through diplomatic channels, to no avail. Prime Minister Gladstone told Queen Victoria that "no other civilized country in the world would tolerate the open advocacy of assassination and murder." What became known as the "dynamite war" against Britain reached a climax in January 1886, when Irish-American bombs went off at the Tower of London and in the Houses of Parliament.

Devoy opposed the terror campaign, but he was powerless to stop it. The campaign continued sporadically until 1887, when members of the Clan turned on each other in a series of invective-filled disagreements. The Irish-American movement was split and discredited yet again, and would remain in the shadows for nearly twenty years.

John Devoy, however, had many years of agitation left, and once he reestablished control over the Irish movement in America, he would never again cede power to anybody. Even if that person claimed to be the head of an Irish Republic.

In December 1885, there was an explosion of a different sort in London. Prime Minister Gladstone announced that he would support a

Home Rule bill for Ireland. It was an enormous personal triumph for Parnell and his method of nonviolent confrontation.

Throughout most of Ireland, cheers greeted Gladstone's conversion. But there was only a foreboding gloom in the island's northeastern corner. The 500,000 Protestants in the northern province of Ulster, accounting for about half the island's non-Catholic population, bitterly opposed the prospect of home rule. In the years since the Act of Union, Protestant Ulster had seen the economic benefits of direct British rule, and it had begun to carve out its own identity, separate and distinct from the rest of Ireland, indeed, separate and distinct from its Catholic neighbors. The dissidents were neither Irish nor British, but something unique: they were Ulstermen—Protestant, industrial, and, in their eyes anyway, modern. That some 600,000 people in the nine counties of Ulster were Catholic didn't seem to matter to the Ulstermen.

The center of discontent was Belfast, a thriving capital of industry, and the home of a huge shipbuilding company called Harland & Wolff. Unlike Dublin or any other Irish city, Belfast was integrated into the greater British economy. Catholics, who made up about 30 percent of the city's 230,000 people in the 1880s, were relegated to jobs with the lowest wages and most arduous conditions. The Protestant-only Orange Order, established in the 1790s to carry out sectarian warfare against the Catholic Defenders in the countryside, functioned as a shadow government that enforced the rules of Ulster's religious caste system. Its sprawling network of lodges controlled private sector hiring and public sector services. The extent of the discrimination was clear at Harland & Wolff shipyards in Belfast, where there were only 225 Catholics in a work force of three thousand in 1887.

The Protestants of the Orange Order understood that this blatant discrimination would not continue if a Dublin-based legislature were established. So, speaking the language they believed Britain would understand, they argued that Home Rule would be Rome rule, that in a self-governing Ireland, they would be subjected to the canon law of the Roman Catholic Church. Seeing a chance to win support for his Conservative Party, Lord Randolph Churchill told colleagues that "the Orange card would be the one to play." With that in mind, he sailed to Ulster and delivered a rousing call to arms in Belfast, predicting civil war if Home Rule passed. And, in a later visit, he delivered a line by which he is remembered in the north of Ireland: "Ulster will fight, and Ulster will be right," he said, consciously linking the entire province with Protestantism and loyalism, even though a slim majority of Ulster's Members of Parliament were, in fact, pledged to

Home Rule. (Seventeen of Ulster's MPs in 1886 were Parnellites; sixteen were Conservatives.) The leader of the Conservative opposition,
Lord Salisbury, asserted that Ireland's Catholics were no more capable of self-government than the barbarians in some of Her Majesty's
far-flung holdings. "You would not confide free representative institutions to the Hottentots, for example," he said. Democracy, he went
on, "works admirably when it is confined to people who are of the
Teutonic race."

Parnell was not deaf to the militant language shouted from the
Protestant steeples of Ulster. He advised his supporters in the
province to give "every possible regard and consideration [to]
the susceptibilities of our Orange fellow countrymen. . . . Our policy
is one of generous toleration and consideration for all sections of the
Irish nation."

Gladstone introduced his Home Rule bill on April 8, 1886. It called for
a legislature in Dublin that would control certain domestic issues such
as education and taxation, but would not have any power over foreign
affairs, trade, or the armed forces. Speaking directly to the sentiment in
Protestant Ulster, Gladstone said: "I cannot allow it to be said that a
Protestant minority in Ulster . . . is to rule the question at large for Ireland." He reminded his colleagues of the injustices for which they
could make amends. "Find, if you can, a single voice, a single book . . .
in which the conduct of England towards Ireland is anywhere treated
except with profound and bitter condemnation," he said.

Those were couragous words. But when the measure came to a
vote, ninety-three members of Gladstone's Liberal Party abandoned
their leader. The bill failed, 341 to 311. Gladstone resigned, a general
election was called, and a Conservative government came into power.
It seemed to be a bitter defeat. Oddly enough, though, the Irish regarded it as something of a moral victory, and Parnell's standing was
undamaged.

Less than a year later, in March 1887, the *Times* of London began a
series of articles entitled "Parnellism and Crime." The newspaper reported that it had letters signed by Parnell that indicated his approval
of the Phoenix Park murders. A special parliamentary commission
was assembled to investigate, with the new Conservative government's Attorney General assuming the role of prosecutor. The specific accusation, that of complicity in the Phoenix Park killings, fell
apart when it was proved that the *Times* letters were a forgery. But
the Attorney General pressed on, determined to link Parnell to agrar-

ian crimes during the Land War and to the militants of the Irish-American movement. Parnell endured questions about his American tour of 1880 and his links to John Devoy. O'Kelly and Davitt were called to testify, too, with Davitt giving a long and brilliant speech justifying his actions during the land agitation. The commission exonerated Parnell, humiliating the *Times* and the Attorney General, and he returned to a standing ovation in the House of Commons.

But there still was the matter of Mrs. O'Shea.

Captain William O'Shea's petition for divorce came before a London court on November 15, 1890. Charles Parnell was named as a co-respondent, but neither he nor Mrs. O'Shea appeared in court to contest the charge. The *Times,* sensing a chance for revenge, gleefully published scandalous details of the adulterous relationship. In the ensuing uproar of condemnation from the press and clergy, Gladstone made it clear that he could no longer do business with the Irish Parliamentary Party if Parnell remained its chairman. And by now, Parnell had linked his fate to England's Liberals. Without Gladstone, and with a hostile Conservative government in power, the Irish party had nothing.

Party members met in Committee Room 15 of the House of Commons on December 1, 1890, to decide Parnell's fate. The bitter debates lasted a week. A pro-Parnell member named John Redmond made the case that if his colleagues dumped Parnell at Gladstone's behest, then Gladstone would be master of the Irish party.

Timothy Healy, one of the bright young men recruited under Parnell's leadership, sneered: "Who is to be the mistress of the Party?"

Parnell lost. The party split into a Parnellite wing, with twenty-six members, and an anti-Parnellite faction, with forty-four members. Parnell bravely carried on, taking his case to the country in a series of by-elections in 1891, trying to turn them into referenda on his leadership. It was to no avail. The country he once all but ruled as its uncrowned king now rejected him. At one election appearance, somebody in the crowd threw lye in his face.

Parnell and the former Mrs. O'Shea married during the summer of 1891, in the midst of terrible exertions. He tried to rally Irish America through Devoy, who gave him encouragement and support, but had precious little else to offer.

Unlike Devoy, Michael Davitt publicly condemned Parnell for misleading his friends and colleagues. A friend of Davitt's named Dr. Dixon suggested that the earnest reformer shouldn't act so surprised. After all, Dr. Dixon said, Davitt had mentioned something about the affair years before. "I am not prepared to put my imperfect recollection against your more accurate memory," Davitt wrote in a huff. Nevertheless, he subconsciously suggested that perhaps Dr. Dixon's memory was correct. "Until Captain O'Shea took public action [against] Mr. Parnell, the latter's relations with Mrs. O'Shea did not materially concern the movement of which Mr. Parnell was the leader. . . . When you talk about 'stomaching the affair for years,' you are speaking arrant nonsense. I stomached nothing. I heard only what rumour was saying and not what facts and evidence could prove."

In other words, he, and no doubt many others who so cruelly abandoned Parnell, indeed *had* "stomached" the affair for years.

After a summer of intense activity and bitter disappointment, Charles Stewart Parnell and his wife went to London to rest in the fall of 1891. He became delirious on the night of October 5, asking Katherine to "hold me tight . . . so I can fight those others." He died the next day, probably of heart disease, at age forty-five.

His body was brought back to Dublin. Abandoned and rejected in his final crisis, he was given a splendid funeral.

CHAPTER SEVEN

TO SWEETEN IRELAND'S WRONG

ABOARD THE BOAT that brought Charles Parnell's body back to Ireland was a tall, striking-looking young woman dressed entirely in black. Her fellow passengers assumed the display was an extravagant tribute to the dead Irish leader, but in fact Maud Gonne was in mourning for her infant son, Georges, who had died in France in late August 1891. Awaiting her arrival into Kingstown was the man who had proposed marriage to her some months before, a pale poet with an oval face, pince-nez eyeglasses, and flowing hair, William Butler Yeats.

It was pure chance that Gonne shared Parnell's final journey to Ireland, for she was not among those who believed he was the next great Irish chieftain. Although she didn't know Parnell's sister Anna, she certainly shared her radical politics, her militant attitude toward landlords, and her contempt for Irishmen who went to London in hopes of effecting change in Ireland. Like Anna Parnell, Maud Gonne received her education not in the cloistered, clubby atmosphere of constitutional politics, but in the unforgiving fields in the west of Ireland. She became a legend among the farmers of County Donegal in the late 1880s as she personally witnessed a new round of evictions and sought to rally the tenants with sentiments officially declared inappropriate during the Home Rule campaign. "Irish homes and lives are being destroyed by Englishmen," she said. "Irishmen must hit back."

At this stage in his life, Yeats would have cheered those sentiments, so long as they came from Maud Gonne's mouth. Deeply and famously in love with this astonishing woman, Yeats would have cheered anything Maud Gonne said. "If she said the world was flat, I would be proud to be of her party," he wrote.

William Butler Yeats

Yeats also was not a Parnellite. Like the object of his obsession, the young Yeats sat at the knee of the old Fenian John O'Leary, back in the literary drawing rooms of Dublin from his long exile in France. There, O'Leary reprised the arguments he had made against Parnell and constitutional politics in the early 1880s. The pure revolutionary, as O'Leary still considered himself, could have nothing to do with corrupt politics in London. Once a dangerous felon filled with ideas

Maud Gonne

of physical force and revolution, O'Leary had lived long enough, and had been ineffectual enough, to become a grand old man delivering such wisdoms as: "There are some things a man must not do to save a nation." First among these proscribed activities, he said, was crying in public.

With his great white beard and professorial demeanor, and with a record as a revolutionary unblemished by any action, he was a safe tutor to romantic nationalists, and regularly held court in the salon of a remarkable literary association called the Contemporary Club. It was there that the painter John Butler Yeats heard O'Leary talk about letters and politics. Soon, the painter's son began stopping by the club, if for nothing else then as a remedy for his painful shyness. He, too, was taken with O'Leary's charm, intelligence, and integrity, and he was not alone. Writers and artists regularly made a pilgrimage to the home O'Leary shared with his poet sister, Ellen, and there they were told that they ought to infuse their art with a sense of nationality. Ireland, O'Leary said, would never achieve political nationhood without a strong cultural identity. Nothing he did as a revolutionary could have had a more profound impact. It was thanks to O'Leary's dreamy-eyed politics that William Butler Yeats joined the Irish Republican Brotherhood, and while he was but a short-lived member, the admonitions of O'Leary to bring politics to art were evident in Yeats's work. He wrote that he "would accounted be" in the company "who sang to sweeten Ireland's wrong."

It was through O'Leary's sister, Ellen, that Yeats heard of an extraordinary young woman who had abandoned the life of a British army officer's daughter and taken up the cause of Irish nationalism. A meeting was arranged, via a letter from Ellen O'Leary to the twenty-three-year-old poet's father. The younger Yeats was so infatuated with Maud Gonne's beauty that he forgave the young woman's militant talk in praise of war. And he discovered how much they had in common: "She, like myself, had received the political tradition of [Thomas] Davis, with the added touch of hardness and heroism from the hand of O'Leary." Gonne and Yeats later founded a literary group together and called it Young Ireland, in tribute to their shared influence, Thomas Davis—a man who had died decades before either one was born.

By the time Yeats greeted the grieving Gonne on the day Parnell's body returned to Ireland, she was emotionally and physically spent. "She was plainly very ill," Yeats wrote later. She couldn't sleep without using chloroform.

They were together frequently in the ensuing months, which pleased Yeats greatly. He believed she found his "spiritual philosophy" a great comfort, and he convinced himself that her emotional dependence on him would lead to love. It was, he admitted, a cruel calculation on his part. But it was what he wanted.

His ministrations, then and in later years, did not win his heart's desire. She eventually returned to her lover in France, Lucien Millevoye, the father of her dead son. Yeats settled for her companionship. And as friends, they became, in a mystical sense, the First Couple of a spectacular revival of Irish literature and culture that was quietly underway even before Parnell's death, but which reached its creative climax in the years afterward. Maud Gonne would become Yeats's obsession and his inspiration, the model for his *Cathleen ni Houlihan,* a play set during the rebellion of 1798 that stirred national-ist passions thought to be buried in Parnell's grave. Maud Gonne's performance in the leading role so roused the audience and public opinion that Yeats was left to consider what he had accomplished. "I went home asking myself if such plays should be produced unless one was prepared for people to go out to shoot and be shot. . . . Miss Gonne's impersonation had stirred the audience as I have never seen another audience stirred," he wrote.

Yeats and Gonne were part of an extraordinary collection of intel-lectuals, artists, and writers who operated in neither the ratholes of conspiracy nor the committee rooms in Parliament, but in salons, stu-dios, theaters, and country houses. And there they kept alive the idea of an Irish nation, separate and distinct from England. Many years later, Yeats would ask if his play had sent out "certain men the En-glish shot."

In a sense, the answer to the question, as he surely knew, was a re-sounding yes. The revival of Irish folklore, language, sports, theater, and poetry in the late nineteenth and early twentieth centuries created an alternative expression of Irish identity at a time when politics was discredited and revolution discarded. The country was not only de-moralized, it was depopulated. The mass emigrations that began dur-ing the Famine continued to bleed Ireland of its young, so that its population in the 1890 census was 4.7 million, or just over half what it was before the Famine, and it continued to fall.

Some of those who remained benefited from the social changes brought about during the Land War. A succession of land reforms followed Gladstone's sweeping land bill of 1881, so that the relation-ship between landlord and tenant began to resemble a partnership of sorts. It obviously was not a partnership of equals, but the tenants at least had security, stable rents, and a measure of prosperity. The ten-ants could afford housing unimaginable during the depths of the Famine; in 1841, only 17 percent of Ireland's tenant farmers lived in houses with five rooms or more. By 1901, 56 percent lived in such housing, and their numbers were growing. In 1903, a massive land purchase act offered financial incentives to landlords to sell to ten-ants, and also offered tenants reasonable terms to take ownership of the land they worked. It was, in fact, the realization of peasant own-ership, one of the goals of land reformers in the 1880s.

As tenants' fortunes improved, the nature of Irish poverty was changing. No longer did economic injustice take the form of a mud-walled cabin. Instead, it was the urban ghetto, where the slumlord replaced the landlord, and the boss replaced the estate agent as the tormentors of the population.

In the last years of the nineteenth century and the early years of the twentieth, Dublin was home to some of Europe's most appalling slums. Not far from the splendor of the Georgian buildings along the River Liffey and the walls of Trinity College was a city of poorly paid, cruelly treated workers. The city's infant mortality rate was 27.6 per 1,000, the highest in Europe. While the farmers in the countryside saw great improvements in their housing, 21,000 Dublin families, representing as many as 100,000 people in a city of about 300,000, lived in single-room apartments. "Even homelessness is preferable to some of these wretched abodes," said one government investigator.

Dublin's population density of 38.5 people per acre was double that of every major British city. Disease was rampant, as was malnutrition. Officials from charity organizations were shocked when they met "with pregnant mothers not having anything to eat for as long a period as four days." Efforts at reform were thwarted because the city's local government was in the hands of the industrial barons and urban landlords, most of them Irish, who ruled the city as surely as the absentee landlords once ruled the countryside. One landlord told a would-be reformer, "If you wish to do the people good, teach them to be content with what the Almighty sends them."

The labor organizer began to replace the agrarian agitator as the voice of economic discontent in Ireland.

It was a measure of the country's disgust with politics that when Gladstone succeeded in getting a Home Rule bill passed in the House of Commons in 1893, few bothered to make note of the achievement. Part of the apathy was based on political reality. Even Gladstone knew that the conservative House of Lords would veto his Home Rule bill, which the Lords did, rendering it null and void. Even though Britain's Liberal Party was committed to Home Rule and Gladstone was intent on finding a compromise settlement that would satisfy Irish nationalists, the undemocratic House of Lords, a bastion of conservative imperialists, was determined to keep the status quo in Ireland.

But Ireland's apathy was based on more than an understanding view of British politics. Parnell's fall and death were crushing blows, and there was nobody large enough to take his place. The Irish realized that the greatest leader of their generation was dead and buried at age forty-five, and they would not see his like again. Politics, in his absence, seemed pointless. The party he so memorably led continued to be bitterly divided into pro-Parnell and anti-Parnell wings, even though Parnell himself was gone. The party was utterly ineffective, and would remain so until it finally reunited in 1900.

The cultural movement offered an alternative to dreary politics. Its claims to be purer and more spiritual registered with an apathetic public, but given Irish history, any movement that sought to find identity and authenticity in the folktales, language, and customs of the Irish peasantry could not help but be perceived as political.

The rediscovery of a culture that had been scorned as backward and barbaric since the days of Henry II and Pope Adrian came at a particularly poignant moment. For the celebration of Gaelic Catholic Ireland's rural-based culture and ancient language came even as the Protestant Irish in Ulster were defining themselves as citizens of Victorian Britain and children of the Industrial Revolution, a people very different from the descendants of Gaelic Ireland. And in yet another startling twist of history, the rediscovery of Gaelic Ireland was the work of Anglo-Irish Protestant elites, like Yeats, who were smitten with the romance of a rural, traditional culture they saw as untainted by modern industrialism—in other words, untainted by the economic and social forces that were defining the shape and the identity of the Ulstermen.

"Wherever men have tried to imagine a perfect life, they have imagined a place where men plow and sow and reap, not a place where there are great wheels turning and great chimneys vomiting smoke," wrote Yeats, who was born in rural County Sligo in 1865. "Ireland will always be a country where men plow and sow and reap. . . . We wish to preserve an ancient ideal of life."

Barely a half century had passed since those who lived that ancient ideal had starved to death by the hundreds of thousands. A decade had not yet passed since the plowers and sowers and reapers in the province of Yeats's birth, Connaught, rebelled against the arbitrary evictions and high rents that were part of that imagined perfect life. But now Yeats, along with a dazzling circle of friends and artists, found in the rural and long-suffering west not poverty but the richness of a forgotten culture.

This was not the rural Ireland Maud Gonne knew.

The daughter of a British army officer, Edith Maud Gonne was born in England in 1866, the first child of Thomas and Edith Gonne. The family moved to Ireland in 1868, when Colonel Gonne was transferred there in the aftermath of the Fenian rising, and Maud's sister Kathleen was born soon afterward. The happy little family was not together very long. Edith Gonne died when Maud was just four years old. One of Maud's earliest childhood memories was the sight of her mother in a coffin, dressed in white and blue and wearing pearls and turquoises. Her father held Maud in his arms and whispered: "You must never be afraid of anything, even of death."

A single parent, Tommy Gonne tried to balance the emotional and educational needs of his two daughters with his professional obligations as a military attaché and adviser to the diplomatic service. Maud and Kathleen were well traveled by the time they were in their teens, as would be expected of the children of a soldier with imperial duties, and were educated by a series of relatives, tutors, and governesses as they moved from Ireland to England to France, Italy, and Switzerland. With a father in the Queen's service, and a continental education and a European outlook, Maud Gonne's upbringing was far removed from the childhoods of most Irish republicans.

The family returned to Dublin from Rome in 1885 when Tommy won an appointment as Assistant Adjunct General for the British army in Dublin. As the daughter of a prominent officer of the British garrison, Maud was formally presented at Court in Dublin, where, during the course of the debutante ball, she caught the famously wandering eye of the Prince of Wales, the future King Edward VII. The Prince took her by the arm and escorted her to the royal dais. She was in her mid-teens, but with her breathtaking looks, her gold-brown hair, and astonishing height—she was five feet, ten inches, when she was fourteen—she was often mistaken for her father's wife. That she called her father "Tommy" no doubt added to the confusion. As he fulfilled the social obligations of a high-ranking British officer in Ireland, Tommy Gonne turned to his precocious daughter to serve as a hostess and companion. She delighted in being close to the father she adored, but socializing with the Anglo-Irish gentry was not her favorite activity. "I had to sit through seven-course dinners and, in the drawing room with the ladies, receive absurd compliments for wearing poplin dresses," she recalled.

That world came to an end in November 1886 when Tommy Gonne died after a brief illness at age fifty. Maud was not quite twenty. While she and her father had flouted social convention with the delightful intimacy of their relationship, she showed no signs of political rebelliousness, save for one unpleasant incident when she cut short a visit to a local landlord who regaled a dinner party with talk of his cruelty toward an evicted family.

Maud went off to find her place in the world, her financial security

ensured thanks to her father's will. To the horror of her aunts and un-
cles, after abandoning the idea of taking up nursing, she decided to
become an actress. But the stage was put on hold when she developed
a lung illness—she went to France to recuperate, and there met her
future lover, Lucien Millevoye, a young French nationalist and the
grandson of a poet. Millevoye was determined to help France regain
Alsace-Lorraine, which the Germans had seized after the Franco-
Prussian War of 1870. An Anglophobe like so many Frenchmen, he
impressed Gonne with his belief that Ireland, too, should reclaim its
national territory, and he told her that she could become Ireland's
Joan of Arc. Though they never married, Millevoye and Gonne lived
together in France and had another child, a daughter named Iseult, in
1894.

She met John O'Leary during one of her periodic visits back to
Ireland, and like Yeats she fell under his spell. "I want to work for
Ireland," she told him. "I want you to show me how." O'Leary was
more than happy to do so, prescribing a regimen of history books and
great works of Irish literature. She rented an apartment near the National Library of Ireland and Trinity College, the heart of intellectual
Dublin, and invited artists, writers, and scholars to join her for late
night discussions about poetry, language, literature, and, above all,
nationality. "A big black kettle and a tea and coffee pot in the cup-
board in the wall supplied us with refreshments and our talk was the
wine on which we used to get satisfactorily drunk," she wrote. Yeats,
of course, was among those in attendance, as were a shy, serious-
minded compositor at the *Irish Independent* newspaper named
Arthur Griffith and an earnest student of the Irish language named
Douglas Hyde. They represented an array of opinions and backgrounds, but were brought together in the cause of Irish identity.

Hyde was the son of a Protestant clergyman from County
Roscommon. He learned Gaelic culture from his Irish-speaking
neighbors in the west. He was a determined proselytizer for Gaelic,
and he marked Maud Gonne as a potential convert, in part, it would
appear, because of her looks. "My head was spinning with her
beauty," he wrote. But Gonne characteristically dismissed Hyde's notions as impractical. She was, she said, "trying to spread revolutionary
thoughts and acts." For Maud Gonne, learning the Irish language did
not qualify on either score. Resisting evictions was a much more
practical course of action.

In the late 1880s, just before Parnell's death, several of his radical
parliamentary colleagues combined with rural agitators and sympathetic priests to form what was called a Plan of Campaign against land-

lords. Gonne was an enthusiastic supporter of the campaign, and was a conspicuous figure at evictions, a beautiful woman of Olympian height, a well-dressed stranger from the city who moved among the fields with a Great Dane at her side. Although evictions were much rarer than they had been in the early 1880s, their brutality made a deep impression on this strong-willed woman raised far from potato patches and thatched-roof cabins. She described one of the many evictions she witnessed: "It was a small two-roomed cottage inhabited by a bed-ridden old woman, her daughter and two children; the man was in Scotland seeking work. . . . [The old woman] was carried out on a mattress clutching in claw-like hands a little statue of the Blessed Virgin . . . her eyes blinked sightlessly in the light—she had not been outside the house for years. She and her mattress were deposited on the roadside, and her daughter and the children cried beside her."

Maud Gonne's work for Ireland spanned the worlds of politics and culture. With Yeats and other notables, she helped found the Irish Literary Society in 1892, bringing the fledgling revival of Irish culture to the countryside through the founding of reading rooms and libraries. In her heart, however, Gonne was an activist and agitator, not a literary nationalist. In fact, she thought Yeats's selection of books for the society reading rooms too elitist. She served as a passionate reminder that there were practical, down-to-earth issues at hand, and they could not simply be dismissed as beyond the concern of an Irish language enthusiast or a collector of Irish folktales, or even a love-struck writer of dazzling poetry.

The fine line between the celebration of Irish culture and the implications for nationalist politics was evident in a speech given on November 25, 1892, in Leinster House. In front of an audience of literary and artistic luminaries, Douglas Hyde, the president of the National Literary Society delivered an address entitled: "The Necessity for De-Anglicising Ireland." It was an emphatic plea for a revival of an Irish Ireland, a re-creation of the world he had known as a teenager growing up in County Roscommon in the west. He argued for a distinct Irish identity, common to nationalist and Unionist alike, and an end to what he called West Britonism, that is, Irish imitation of English customs and culture.

"I wish to show you that in Anglicising ourselves wholesale we have thrown away with a light heart the best claim we have upon the world's recognition of us as a separate nationality," he said. Ireland, he claimed, was losing its connection with "Brian Boru . . . with the

Douglas Hyde

O'Neills and O'Donnells . . . and even to some extent with the men of '98. It has lost all that they had—language, traditions, music, genius and ideas." If Ireland wished to claim a separate nationality, he asserted, it must re-create its separate cultural identity, in dress, in art, in everyday custom, and nothing would establish it more clearly than a return to the Irish language.

Hyde fervently believed in the separation of culture and politics. But his invocation of Ireland's lost connection to the O'Neills and

O'Donnells, and the men of 1798, was explicitly political. The leaders of 1798—Wolfe Tone, Henry Joy McCracken, Lord Edward Fitzgerald—were not Irish speakers, nor did they wander the countryside in search of authentically Irish experiences. They were entirely political and nationalist. They didn't read tales from the Gaelic countryside; they read Thomas Paine. They sought not a restoration of Gaelic Ireland, but a country free of British imperial rule.

When the speech was over, William Butler Yeats overheard another member of the audience say that Hyde had just delivered "the most important utterance of its kind since '48." In that year, a small column of Irishmen under the leadership of William Smith O'Brien had fought with police during a botched attempt at rebellion. Where Hyde saw identity, others saw politics. The connection was inescapable. As for Yeats himself, he differed with Hyde's assertion that an Irish literature required the use of the Irish language, for he believed Ireland could and would produce a cosmopolitan but distinctly Irish literature in the English language. He was content, however, with Hyde's general call for a de-Anglicized Ireland.

With his great walruslike mustache and tweedy demeanor, the man who had passionately argued for an Ireland purged of English influence, if not rule, was the very picture of an Anglo-Irish squire. And so he was. The thirty-two-year-old son of an Anglican vicar delighted in hunting and shooting, two of the gentry's favorite pasttimes, held a law degree from Trinity College, and spent his nighttime hours in the Victorian clubs of Dublin.

As a child in the rural west, however, Hyde grew up in a culture far different from that of the polished wood, leather chairs, and polite society of his adulthood. Gaelic Ireland, mysterious, exotic, and authentic, surrounded him and led him away from the life of his aristocratic Anglo-Irish parents. His father, who despised Parnell, wanted his son to follow him into the ministry. But young Douglas had found a second father in Seamas Hart, an Irish-speaking gamekeeper who lived near the Hyde home. Hart helped introduce the eager adolescent not only to the language, but to the agrarian, Gaelic culture of his neighbors, kept alive in the villages and at the rural fairs, passed along verbally from generation to generation.

At age thirteen Douglas Hyde discovered his life's purpose. While in his teens, he traveled throughout the west, gathering tales from the countryside and studying the Irish language. He was fluent in Irish by the time he entered Trinity, and he began writing poetry in Irish under the pseudonym An Craoibhín Aoibhinn, Irish for "delightful little branch."

His speech at Leinster House created a sensation in the Irish press, and led to the founding, a year later, of the Gaelic League, an Irish language organization which in time would prove to be an inculcator of more than mere pride in Irish culture. From the ranks of the avowedly nonpolitical Gaelic League would come the political revolutionaries of the next generation. Old-style political nationalism was not what Hyde wanted from the Gaelic League, but a contemporary description of the league's effect on the country suggests the power of the forces he had identified. The Gaelic League's celebration of Irish folk culture, wrote an affluent Anglo-Irish woman named Lady Isabella Augusta Gregory, "was the small beginning of a weighty change. . . . The imagination of Ireland had found a new homing place."

The unasked question was: whose Ireland? For the Gaelic League did not capture the imagination of the Ireland at work in the shipyards and factories of Belfast. Although Hyde argued for an Irish identity that included Unionist and nationalist, Protestant and Catholic, the movement he helped inspire would prove to be only slightly less divisive than the political movements. Gaelic Irish Catholics and Anglo-Protestant elites took up the Irish language and Irish theater. But, for the most part, the Presbyterian working classes in Ulster did not, and they regarded such pursuits as suspicious and subversive.

Lady Gregory was yet another member of the Anglo-Irish aristocracy to find authenticity in Ireland's most remote province. Like Yeats and Hyde, she was a native of Connaught, born in County Galway in 1852. At the time of Hyde's de-Anglicization speech, she was a forty-year-old mother and widow living on the estate of her late husband, Sir William Gregory. Sir William had been a colonial governor of Ceylon and was a full-fledged member of Ireland's Anglo-Protestant landed aristocracy, with a home in London as well as the estate in Galway, called Coole Park. The Gregorys were on intimate terms with the most powerful politicians in Britain. But Lady Gregory herself was not from such rarefied circles. Hers was a middle-class family, and her mother and sister were both fierce Protestants who trolled the countryside in search of Catholics to convert.

She, however, exhibited no inclination to convert the natives. Rather, she sought to learn from them. She was artistically inclined, with an artist's free spirit. Her love affairs were the talk of Ireland's cultural elite.

Lady Augusta Gregory

If her personality didn't seem suited to the stuffy world of the Anglo-Irish gentry, however, at least her politics were more conventional. She was suspicious of the Land League, which she regarded as run by "ruffians," although she made a point of noting that her husband was a "land reformer" because he supported measures to grant tenants a certain degree of stability. And, like her husband, she vehemently opposed Home Rule.

But even as a child, she was intrigued by the culture of the native Irish. Her interest in the romantic poetry and literature of Young Ireland added to her curiosity. "Once in childhood I had been eager to learn Irish," she wrote. After her marriage to Sir William, she asked one of the gardeners at Coole for help in learning the language, but to no avail. The gardener thought she was mocking him.

She found renewed determination to pursue her interest in language and folklore following Hyde's speech and the publication of two small books that caught her attention. After several years of work, Hyde published a volume called *Love Songs of Connacht,* a collection of folktales from the west of Ireland that won rave reviews from Yeats. And Yeats himself published *The Celtic Twilight,* a series of essays, poems, and tales based on the folklore of the poet's native County Sligo. The two books of folklore made Lady Gregory "jealous" for the people and tales of Galway, and she set out to demonstrate that her neighbors had stories of their own to tell.

She went to the local workhouse, the last refuge for the poor, and interviewed its residents about folktales, legends, oral histories, and culture, what she would call "that poetry of the soil." They would provide her with material for a wonderful career as a playwright, poet, folklorist, and theater producer. A witness to social injustice like Maud Gonne and Anna Parnell, this anti–Home Rule widow of an imperial governor would become, in time, a fervent nationalist.

In the summer of 1897, Lady Gregory's home, Coole Park, became the headquarters for the revival of Irish arts and culture. Yeats and Hyde both were guests of Lady Gregory's that year, and both became friends and creative partners with the woman of the house. Coole, with its large library, bucolic surroundings, and access to the original keepers of Galway folklore, became both a refuge and an inspiration for the poet and the linguist. And Lady Gregory, in the process of becoming an artist in her own right, became muse, collaborator, and patron of the Irish revival.

Of the three, Yeats played the most active role in politics, and while his Anglophobia and Irish patriotism were genuine, it surely was no coincidence that he was found on the march when Maud Gonne was leading the column. During the late 1890s there were several battles to be fought. Yeats and Gonne helped organize an anti-English protest in Dublin on June 22, 1897, the day that the British Empire celebrated Queen Victoria's sixtieth anniversary as monarch.

Not surprisingly, the peaceful protest deteriorated when demonstrators carried a coffin with the words "The British Empire" written on it through the streets of Dublin. Accompanied as the coffin was by written displays of the number of starvation deaths and evictions that had taken place during the Queen's long reign—how many Irishmen had been hanged, and so forth—the authorities sought to show their displeasure as memorably as possible. In the resulting riot, two hundred people were hurt and an elderly woman killed. Yeats and Gonne were together on the streets that night. He remembered that she walked "with a joyous face."

Both Yeats and Gonne then turned their attention to the centennial commemoration of the 1798 rebellion. At a meeting of a centenary committee, Yeats cited examples from the Irish rebel pantheon, Robert Emmet, Wolfe Tone, Thomas Davis, and John Mitchel, and condemned the English as "evil." Ireland's freedom, he predicted, would come eventually, "though not, perhaps, in our day." Gonne, in the meantime, gave even more militant speeches in the west of Ireland, where she and Yeats occasionally listened for the music of the fairies said to inhabit the rural landscape. The centennial year saw the largest gatherings of nationalists in years, and it had barely passed when the Boer War presented the couple with yet another reason to agitate together. Irish nationalists sympathized with the Boers, or Dutch settlers, of South Africa, who were fighting a guerrilla war against the might of the British Empire, and some joined an Irish brigade to fight alongside the Boers.

Gonne addressed a meeting of twenty thousand pro-Boer demonstrators in Dublin in 1899, while Yeats organized rallies aimed at discouraging enlistment in the British army. Gonne was by now among the most popular women in Ireland. When she showed up at rallies in a horse-drawn coach, people in the audience unhitched the horses and pulled the carriage themselves. Her ferocity knew few bounds—she proposed to a Boer representative in France that bombs be secretly placed on board troop ships taking British soldiers to South Africa. The Boer was appalled. Gonne said, simply: "Whether you kill your enemies on land or at sea, it does not seem to me to make any difference."

The pro-Boer work was done so well that Irish enlistment in the flagging British army was nonexistent. So desperate were the British for Irish bodies to fling at the Boers that the aging Queen herself was dispatched to Dublin as a recruiter. Yeats countered with a ferocious public letter: "Whoever stands by the roadway cheering for Queen Victoria cheers for the Empire, dishonours Ireland, and condones a crime." When the authorities sought to win the hearts of Dublin children by giving away treats in Phoenix Park in conjunction with the Queen's visit, Gonne organized a counter-giveaway, attracting thirty thousand children to the five thousand who attended the official commemoration. The royal visit was a failure, but Gonne's success inspired Yeats to wonder: "How many of these children will carry bomb or rifle when a little under or a little over thirty?"

Such activities and sentiments were not part of the regimen at Coole Park. Although their politics differed, Lady Gregory, Yeats, and Hyde agreed that it was imperative to show the value and importance of the culture surrounding their palatial retreat. Lady Gregory delighted in taking Yeats on jaunts through the countryside, searching for folklore, or in taking aside "whoever came to the door, fisherwoman or beggar or farmer," and interviewing them about their legends and customs. Hyde organized entertainments in Irish for poor children in the area, and he and Lady Gregory discussed plans to revive the ancient sagas of vanished Gaelic Ireland. The movement they led was finding expression in new literary journals, including one called *Shan Van Vocht* ("The Poor Old Woman") in Belfast, edited by two women poets, Alice Milligan and Anna Johnston, and in a revival of ancient Irish games, such as hurling, organized by the new Gaelic Athletic Association.

The outpouring of culture that followed was yet another unexpected twist in the epic narrative of Anglo-Irish history. Gaelic Irish culture, repressed and virtually exterminated under British colonial rule, found its way into the canon of literature and onto the stages of London and New York under the sponsorship of the sons and daughters of the Anglo-Protestant Ascendancy. Determined to produce authentic Irish theater, and filled with material gathered from workhouses and rural festivals, Yeats and Lady Gregory founded the Irish Literary Theatre, later to become internationally prominent as the Abbey Theatre. Lady Gregory embarked on a playwriting career that would produce more than thirty plays based on folktales, legends, and Irish history. Her play *The White Cockade* told the story of the Battle of the Boyne, casting Patrick Sarsfield as a hero trying bravely to revive the national spirit after defeat. With her translation and retelling of the story of Cuchulain, she revived the ancient myth of the great, defiant hero of Ulster who died fighting rather than surrender. She won Yeats's admittedly subjective praise for "the best [book] that has come out in Ireland in my time ... for the stories which it tells are a chief part of Ireland's gift to the imagination of the world."

A collaboration of the three friends led to the adaptation of a folk-tale to stage comedy sponsored by the Literary Theatre. In the creative hothouse of Coole Park, Yeats and Hyde sketched out their interpretations of the tale, called *Casadh an tSúgáin,* or *The Twisting of the Rope,* a story about a poet from the west of Ireland and his pursuit of a village woman. Hyde took the notes, spent two days writing the play in Irish, and dictated the results to Lady Gregory. It debuted in Dublin on October 21, 1901, on the same bill with an English-language adaptation, co-written by Yeats, of the story of the mytho-

Arthur Griffith

logical Gaelic lovers Diarmuid and Grainne. *Casadh an tSúgáin* demonstrated yet again how fine was the line between culture and politics. While *Diarmuid and Grainne* won polite applause and reviews, *Casadh an tSúgáin,* with Hyde himself playing the role of the poet, had the audience on its feet. Thought to be all but extinct, the Irish language was reborn on the Dublin stage. One reviewer said the performance was "a memorable one for Dublin and for Ireland."

But it wasn't enough for those who were beginning to appreciate art for more than just art's sake. "Let Mr. Yeats give us a play in verse or prose that will rouse this sleeping land," wrote the very same critic who wrote so glowingly of *Casadh an tSúgáin.* "This land is ours, but we have ceased to realise that fact. We want drama that will make us realise it."

Cathleen ni Houlihan made its debut on April 2, 1902. Although it seemed as though Yeats had supplied what his critic had asked of him, in fact the play was a collaboration with Lady Gregory, with Yeats apparently the junior partner. Maud Gonne became the personification of suffering Ireland, giving meaning to the lives of an eighteenth-century farming family concerned about their limited means. Gonne was a sensation. "In her, the youth of the country saw all that was magnificent in Ireland," wrote one observer. At the play's climax, the hushed audience heard her recite the playwright's salute to the heroes of the past:

> They shall be remembered for ever
> They shall be alive for ever,
> They shall be speaking for ever
> The people shall hear them for ever.

The overwhelmed audience sang the stirring ballad by the Young Ireland poet Thomas Davis, the inspiration of Yeats and Gonne:

> Let Ireland, long a province,
> Be a Nation Once Again!

As the curtain rang down on *Cathleen ni Houlihan,* a visibly moved Arthur Griffith joined in the singing from his place in the audience. Griffith was among the young middle-class intellectuals who set out for Maud Gonne's apartment in Dublin in the early 1890s to absorb the thoughts and wit of Yeats, Hyde, and of course Maud Gonne herself. In the decade that followed, Griffith had come into his own as an important thinker, and he looked the part, with thick glasses, a serious public demeanor, and a down-at-the-heels appearance. A friend watched his reaction as the audience cheered Gonne's performance: "I can still see his face as he stood up . . . to join in the singing of what was then our national anthem. . . . It was the face of a self-contained man who was moved to his depths."

The literary and cultural revival profoundly affected Arthur Griffith, a man whose name would be connected with politics, not with art. He surely was not the first to make the connection between culture and politics, but it was he who built a political organization to take advantage of the sentiments the artists had so clearly identified. He founded a political party called Sinn Féin, Irish for "Ourselves," which captured in a phrase his vision for an Ireland that not only governed itself, but looked after itself by itself, with neither help nor hindrance from the outside world. Sinn Féin would become the party of republican revolution in Ireland, and would survive to become the political arm of the Irish Republican Army late into the twentieth century, but its founder was no republican. Arthur Griffith fervently believed in a self-governing Ireland, an Ireland that was an island unto itself, but he had no difficulty accepting the crown of Britain as a symbolic authority in Ireland.

Arthur Griffith was born in Dublin on March 31, 1871, the son and grandson of printers. Griffith himself took up the printing trade, although he would win attention as a writer and publisher of his own propaganda. Griffith's paternal grandfather must have been an extraordinary and complex man. Born into a sturdy Protestant farming family in Ulster, he converted to Catholicism as a teenager. He was cast out of his family and disinherited.

As a teenager and young adult Griffith followed the fortunes of Charles Stewart Parnell, who loomed so large in Ireland during the 1880s and even larger in the imagination of an impressionable, intelligent young man. Parnell's reserve and his sometimes icy distance impressed the serious-minded Griffith.

His formal education ended at age fifteen, when he took up printing, but he was a voracious reader of books and newspapers. Griffith associated with other well-read young men in the printing trade and together they formed debating societies and literary associations. While very much a child of the Gaelic revival, Griffith was practical enough to realize that there was more to Ireland and Irish culture than the music of the fairies in the west.

"Ireland is truly no longer the Gaelic Nation of the fifth or the twelfth or even the eighteenth century," he wrote. "The Gael is gone . . . and the Irishman is here." And he asserted, as others had asserted before him, that the Irishman had a right to an identity distinct from his powerful neighbor's. "Since the Almighty forbade us for all time to merge our frontiers and invested us with a nationality that we cannot escape," he wrote, "it is of no earthly consequence whether we are a small nationality. . . . It is of no earthly consequence because we have got to accept it."

He lived a life of hard work and poverty, eventually marrying and raising a family even as he published a series of poorly financed nationalist newspapers, organized the Sinn Féin movement, and furthered his self-education in the reading room of the National Library of Ireland in central Dublin.

In 1904, Griffith published in pamphlet form a series of newspaper articles he had written on the history of Hungary. It was by no means an academic treatment of the subject; rather, it was a political argument. The hero of *The Resurrection of Hungary* was Francis Deak, a patriot who led Hungary to self-government within the Austro-Hungarian Empire through nonviolent resistance to Austrian imperialism. "The Irish Deak," he wrote, "must be like his Hungarian prototype—a man who can honestly say that he desires no more, while he refuses to accept less, than the acknowledgement of the Constitutional rights of his country." He quoted approvingly a wryly phrased formula from Jonathan Swift: "The people of England having obliged themselves to have the same monarch as ourselves, we will oblige ourselves to have the same monarch with them."

Griffith proposed a good deal more than just a renewal of the parliament that Henry Grattan won in 1782. He believed all top administrators should be Irish. And he demanded that the Irish Parliamentary Party in the House of Commons withdraw from London to set up the Irish Parliament he proposed. The party, now reunited and revived under the leadership of John Redmond, one of Parnell's former colleagues, greeted Griffith's demands with steely indifference. Redmond was intent on winning what had eluded Parnell: a Home Rule Parliament with far fewer powers than Griffith proposed. No unilateral gesture would achieve Home Rule, Redmond knew.

Griffith's pronouncement became known in shorthand as "the Hungarian policy." It was a brisk seller in its pamphlet form, with thirty thousand copies sold in three months, and it aroused the interests of a scattering of young Irish people, reared on the Irish cultural revival, who were looking for a new political vehicle, untainted by the faction fights and failures of the past. Some were republicans who abhorred the notion of a shared monarch with Britain, but who saw in

Griffith a defiance they admired (he would soon join the revived Irish Republican Brotherhood, even though he was willing to settle for something less than an Irish Republic) and a sense of Irish identity they shared.

Griffith's economic ideas, too, promised a break with the dreary status quo. Although not nearly radical enough to please a burgeoning trade union movement in Dublin, Griffith's proposals of greater use and exploitation of Ireland's natural resources, mandatory arbitration in labor-management disputes, and the protection and encouragement of native Irish industries won a following.

He became, in a sense, leader of the opposition to the established Irish Parliamentary Party. But he soon was without some of his initial allies, most notably Cathleen ni Houlihan herself. In an ill-considered moment in 1903, Maud Gonne agreed to marry John MacBride, a seemingly dashing veteran of the pro-Boer Irish Brigade. In fact, he was a boor himself, often drunk and menacing. The couple divorced and she and their young son, Sean, left for France in 1906, not to return for more than ten years. Yeats effectively dropped out of politics for the time being, concentrating with Lady Gregory on the development of the Abbey Theatre. Hyde attended to the Gaelic League which grew to 100,000 members in nine hundred branches.

Griffith, then, became the political hair of the Irish revival. The aging John Dillon, a onetime Parnell deputy and still a Member of Parliament, dismissed Sinn Féin's threat to the Parliamentary Party. Sinn Féin, Dillon wrote, "has no one with any brains to lead it."

Dillon's contempt was understandable, for Arthur Griffith and Sinn Féin were mere annoyances, not genuine political players. After some initial electoral success, Sinn Féin's popularity crested, and it remained very much in the margins. And beyond even the margins was the tiny remnant of the Irish Republican Brotherhood, which attracted a few hundred true believers to small commemorations of dead heroes.

The spokesman for mainstream Irish politics was the colorless but earnest John Redmond, chairman of the reunited Parliamentary Party of eighty-two members. With the help of Irish-American dollars and a fund-raising organization called the United Irish League, Redmond was as much in command of the party as Parnell had been. Redmond's goal was the same as Parnell's—Home Rule, through an alliance with the British Liberal Party. And under Redmond, it seemed attainable.

A constitutional confrontation in 1910–11, coinciding with the death of King Edward VII, stripped the House of Lords of its power to kill Commons legislation. Bills were still subject to the Lords' veto, but any bill that passed the Commons three times would become law regardless of the upper house's vetoes. A Liberal government, with Redmond's support, prepared a Home Rule bill to be introduced in 1912. As long as the Liberals remained in power, its passage in the Commons was assured, and the House of Lords could only delay its implementation. But there was one obstacle that Redmond and the Liberals underestimated: the Ulster Protestants, who called themselves Orangemen, in honor of William of Orange.

The Orangemen didn't recognize themselves in the drama of Yeats and Lady Gregory. They were not interested in folktales from Connaught. They didn't speak Irish. They were Unionists, pledged to the Act of Union linking Ireland and Britain in one United Kingdom. Their lives were entwined with Britain, not with the rest of Ireland. Families sent sons into the British army. They looked to London, not Dublin, as their ancestral seat of government. Their children learned British history in school. Their prosperity was the product of British investment. Their Protestant religion was the faith of Britain (although the Presbyterianism of many Ulster Protestants once was considered as heretical by the Church of England as Roman Catholicism). They believed they were not only a nationality apart from the Irish, but a race apart.

And so, as Orangemen, as Ulstermen, they were prepared in the name of loyalty to Britain to resist British law. A new leader emerged to speak for the militant Unionists: a forceful barrister and Member of Parliament named Edward Carson. He had been born in Dublin, not in Ulster, but he understood the Ulstermen. "We must be prepared ... the morning Home Rule passes," he said, "to become responsible for the government of the Protestant Province of Ulster." At the time he spoke, the province contained about 885,000 Protestants and 690,000 Catholics. In the language of identity politics, however, Ulster was not so much a geographic location as it was a separate race and a state of mind.

Prime Minister Herbert Asquith introduced the third Home Rule bill, which was very much like the previous two, on April 11, 1912. John Redmond was in his glory, and Ireland was ablaze in celebration. Few took Carson's fiery speeches very seriously. At last, it seemed, the solution was at hand. Arthur Griffith was among the few critics, appalled by a provision barring an Irish Home Rule legislature from collecting taxes—a fundamental duty of any legitimate legislature. But he and Sinn Féin essentially stood aside, acknowledging the bill's popularity. A nationalist newspaper declared that Home Rule meant that Ireland would be both "trusted" and "liberated." Speaking at a huge outdoor rally outside the General Post Office in Dublin, an obscure cultural nationalist named Padraig Pearse declared that "the bill which we support today will be for the good of Ireland and we shall be stronger with it than without it." He added a warning, however: "Let the foreigner understand that if we are cheated now there will be red war in Ireland."

Pearse delivered his speech in Irish. Few of his listeners understood it.

A month after Asquith introduced the new Home Rule bill, the leader of Britain's Conservative Party, Andrew Bonar Law, gave an astonishing speech in the House of Commons. In siding with Irish Protestant militants of Ulster, he warned that "there are stronger influences than parliamentary majorities"—a clear incitement to violence. He later elaborated on the point. "We regard the government as a revolutionary committee which has seized upon despotic power by fraud," he said of the mild-mannered Asquith and his Cabinet appointees. "In our opposition to them we shall not be guided by the considerations or bound by the restraints which would influence us in an ordinary constitutional struggle. . . . I can imagine no length of resistance to which Ulster can go in which I would not be prepared to support them."

With this sort of encouragement, Carson prepared to demonstrate just how far he was willing to go in defying democracy. On September 28, 1912, after ten days of anti–Home Rule demonstrations in the north, Carson summoned the Protestant population of Ulster to Belfast to sign a pledge vowing resistance to Home Rule. He was the first to sign. Some 218,000 men followed, and a similar number of women signed a separate petition—fully half of the Protestant population of the nine counties of Ulster. The strategy was clear: they would resist Home Rule to the death. The threat horrified Winston Churchill, whose father had urged the Ulstermen to resist the first Home Rule bill in 1886: "Think of the consequences to Ireland if Home Rule were defeated now by violence or threats of violence," he said. "[If] we are now to be told . . . that a minority in a single province is by audacity to bar the way for all time to the whole progress of the Irish nation . . . then . . . constitutional and parliamentary actions and patient law-abiding agitation for the redress of grievances would in every part of the British Empire, and indeed throughout the civilized world, be discredited and mocked."

Though he opposed Home Rule for all Ireland as a matter of principle, Carson soon realized that his position was untenable. So he introduced a bill in Parliament to exclude Ulster's nine counties from the Home Rule legislation. Of those nine counties, five had a majority Catholic (and presumably pro–Home Rule) population. Arthur Griffith, who had not done or said much since the bill was introduced, charged that any Irish leader who agreed to the surrender of "a square inch of the soil of Ireland" would be treated as a traitor to Ireland and would be dealt with accordingly. His threat was directed squarely at the determined but accommodating Redmond.

Protestant Ulster's political leaders began 1913 with a new organization, the Ulster Volunteer Force. Within a matter of months, it recruited 100,000 men, who drilled and trained in preparation for civil war. The Ulstermen were on the verge of treason, challenging a piece of democratic legislation with the force of a private army. Nationalist Ireland looked on with amazement, imagining how quickly the fury of the British Empire would descend on them if they tried such a tactic.

Amazement, however, gave way to a grudging admiration, and admiration turned to imitation. If the Ulstermen could organize, why couldn't nationalist Ireland? The Irish National Volunteers, a pro–Home Rule militia, were formed in late 1913, near the close of an eventful year in Irish history. And so two private armies were on the march in Ireland, and British politicians in London were faced with the prospect of civil unrest on its western flank as Europe's imperial powers drifted toward war.

Dublin, in the meantime, saw brutal confrontation in its streets, but the issue at hand had nothing to do with Home Rule. The city's oppressed workers, literally sick of their appalling conditions, walked off their jobs in the fall. They did so at a time when nearly half of all annual deaths in the city took place in workhouses, asylums, and prisons. Most workers put in seventy-hour workweeks for pay that kept them in dire poverty. At a time when officials reckoned that a typical family required 22 shillings a week for subsistence, many Dublin families were earning 10 shillings.

A fiery, Liverpool-born organizer named James Larkin founded the Irish Transport and General Workers Union and, in 1913, began pressing for better wages and working conditions. An alarmed coterie of Dublin employers sought to break the union. When that failed, they imposed a general lockout of the city's unionized workforce. Twenty-five thousand people were thrown out of work, causing immense suffering. Confrontations with the police were so common, and so one-sided, that the unions organized a militia of their own called the Irish Citizen Army. Although the workers returned to their jobs by the beginning of 1914 without winning management concessions, the lockout brought their terrible plight to the attention of the cultural nationalists as well as the hard-line republicans. Both camps realized, as Maud Gonne reminded them in the last days of land agitation, that politics and culture meant nothing if they did not offer relief from economic oppression.

And so militant language and confrontation began to replace genteel discussions of Irish cultural identity. Within the scrupulously nonpartisan Gaelic League, restless members called for a more direct engagement in the nation's political affairs. Douglas Hyde, who insisted on keeping the league out of political disputes, bitterly resented criticisms from Arthur Griffith, who demanded that the league become less academic and more confrontational. Hyde dispatched a pointed letter to Griffith: "If your policy is to prevail, then I think I foresee the discredit and defeat of the Gaelic League. . . . Its defeat and discredit does not mean much to you, no more than any other public question. It means everything to me. I watched it at its cradle but I'm not going to burden its hearse with tears if I can help it."

Padraig Pearse, who had been one of Hyde's lieutenants in the Gaelic League's early years, declared that the league's contribution to Irish nationalism had run its course. With Ulster prepared to wage war, Pearse argued that the time had come for more aggressive tactics. "The vital work to be done in the new Ireland will be done not so much by the Gaelic League itself as by men and movements that have sprung from the Gaelic League," Pearse said. "We must accustom ourselves to the thought of arms, to the use of arms. We may make mistakes in the beginning and shoot the wrong people, but bloodshed is a cleansing and a sanctifying thing, and the nation which regards it as the final horror has lost its manhood."

Such words made an impression on a tiny group of republicans that often gathered in a tobacco shop in central Dublin run by Thomas J. Clarke. Given amnesty in 1898 after imprisonment for his part in the failed bombing mission in England, he had gone to America and come back, and was now one of the organizers of the Irish Republican Brotherhood, an organization that, in the rush to Home Rule, seemed as archaic, and as doomed to failure, as the Fenians.

But with Home Rule under threat from armed Unionists in the north, and with nationalists parading around openly as members of the Irish National Volunteers, the IRB saw an opportunity. Slowly, it began to infiltrate the Irish National Volunteers, who would unknowingly become a perfectly legal front group for the conspiracy's revolutionary dreams. Of the thirty members of the Volunteers' steering committee, twelve were IRB members, and three more were sworn in later. The IRB, with no more than two thousand members, watched and waited for the chance to launch the next rebellion.

Early in the terrible year of 1914, Winston Churchill, the First Lord of the Admiralty, who was preparing for an inevitable conflict with Germany, charged that Edward Carson and the Ulstermen were engaged in a "treasonable conspiracy." The British government began to act accordingly, preparing its garrison in Ireland to move against Ulster. But in March, when the commander of the Curragh army barracks in County Kildare was consulted about plans to enforce Home Rule in Ulster by force of arms, he and nearly sixty other officers submitted their resignations. The government backed down, and the officers were reinstated.

A month later, members of the Ulster Volunteer Force marched to two beaches in Ulster and unloaded ships carrying 25,000 rifles and three million rounds of ammunition. The weapons had been purchased secretly in Germany, which was soon to be at war with Britain. It was an astonishing show of defiance, and it proceeded unimpeded. The Ulstermen now had a formidable arsenal to back up their threats of civil war.

An era that began as a search for identity was ending with Irishmen preparing for battle.

CHAPTER EIGHT

BLOODY PROTEST FOR A GLORIOUS THING

MEMBERS OF THE Irish Republican Brotherhood were fervent though few in 1913, as resurgent politics once again appeared to have displaced revolution. Despite the militant attitude in Ulster, the popularity of Home Rule and the likelihood of its passage in Parliament seemed to satisfy all but the most adamant nationalists, who knew they were a distinct and isolated minority. The IRB's small-circulation propaganda organ, *Irish Freedom,* bitterly took note of reality in the fall of 1913: "Ten years ago, the Parliamentary Party was losing its grip on the country. . . . Today the Parliamentary Party controls more thoroughly than ever the daily press and the public mind in Ireland." When the newly crowned King George V arrived in Ireland in 1911, great crowds cheered him while militant republicans tore down banners celebrating the King's visit.

The revolutionaries of Irish America were as distraught as their co-conspirators in Ireland. The fund-raising arm of the Parliamentary Party, the United Irish League, had won over mainstream Irish America and even two consecutive U.S. Presidents, Theodore Roosevelt and William Howard Taft, to the cause of Home Rule. One Irish-American militant in Clan na Gael knew exactly what Home Rule meant for people like himself: "We are reaching what seems to be the end," he wrote, though not the end the revolutionaries had envisioned.

John Redmond's hold over the Irish Parliamentary Party was indisputable, and the party's hold over nationalist Ireland was unquestioned. By 1913, Arthur Griffith's Sinn Féin seemed a spent force as an opposition political party. Winston Churchill looked across the Irish Sea with satisfaction. "Rebellion, murder and dynamite, these have vanished from Ireland," he said. Nearly forty years after William

E. Gladstone vowed to pacify Ireland, the Irish at last seemed pacific indeed.

As the bulk of nationalist Ireland marched behind Redmond, the IRB organized small ceremonies to honor the martyrs of the past, whose bones remained pure and uncompromised. Annual commemorations celebrated the memory of Robert Emmet and Wolfe Tone,

Padraig Pearse

two republican nationalists who died uncompromised and untainted. However lonely they were, the two thousand or so stalwarts of the IRB knew they were playing a familiar role: they were keeping alive an alternative to constitutional politics, preparing for the inevitable disillusion that seemed to follow so many political agitations.

Eager though the IRB was for members, at least some of its leaders had no use for thirty-four-year-old Padraig Pearse, at least not right away. They turned down his first attempt to join because they didn't trust this mystical poet-schoolmaster who spoke in favor of Home Rule and opposed the politicization of the Gaelic League, and who had praised local government reforms that a Conservative-led British government put in place in 1907. Though he was gaining renown as an orator capable of Fenian-like rhetoric, Pearse had a difficult time shaking his image as a right-wing nationalist willing to settle for what the IRB regarded as an unacceptable compromise.

Pearse knew better. After drawing hoots from a militant audience when he condemned Redmond's critics, Pearse told a friend: "Let them talk! I am the most dangerous revolutionary of the whole lot of them."

Pearse was one of four children born in six years to James Pearse and Margaret Brady. James Pearse was an Englishman and convert to Catholicism from Unitarianism who moved to Ireland from England in search of work. A stone carver, he found plenty of jobs building Catholic churches, and so the family was comfortable, though not affluent.

Pearse's elderly aunt was a frequent visitor to the household, and she regaled the children with tales of Ireland's martyrs, heroes, and glorious failures. Wolfe Tone and Robert Emmet were particular favorites of hers, and so they would become of her great-nephew. James Pearse also was intensely political, and was a strong supporter of Parnell's Home Rule campaign. His admiration for Parnell was passed on to Padraig, who would later annoy militant republicans with his unstinting praise for the fallen leader.

As a boy, Padraig's best loved playmate was his brother, Willie, younger than Padraig by two years. They attended a Christian Brothers school in Dublin, where they received a conventional education, one designed to provide children with skills—measured by exhaustive examinations—they would need in the workforce. Young Padriag was a good student, but in later life, he looked back at the prosaic education he received with contempt. In an essay he entitled "The Murder Machine," he denounced the Irish educational system as "devoid of understanding, of sympathy, of imagination. . . . Into it is fed all the raw material in Ireland . . . what it cannot refashion after the regulation pattern it ejects."

School at least offered Pearse a chance to learn Irish, and the old language struck a chord with this quiet young man who wore glasses and a serious demeanor and seemed so different from the boys who preferred sports to study. He was among the early members of the Gaelic League, and through the league he pursued his interest in Irish literature, poetry, and folklore. He tried his hand at teaching Irish, but his earnest proselytizing was a bit too much for some of his students. One of them, a young man named James Joyce, decided to drop out after hearing Pearse speak disparagingly of English.

Pearse earned a law degree from the Royal University in Dublin, but in the grand tradition of Irish rebels with law degrees, he found the work tiresome and turned to more heroic, if less financially rewarding, pursuits. After a visit to the Aran Islands off County Galway, where the native language and culture remained relatively unchanged, he devoted himself to the Irish cultural revival. He edited an Irish language literary journal, wrote long journalistic descriptions of life in the Irish-speaking west, and opened a school for boys called Saint Enda's that was his reply to the "murder machine." Saint Enda's became an inculcator of Irish language, culture, and history.

His intense interest in Gaelic Ireland did not lead him to insist that the Gaels were the only authentic Irishmen. In fact, he said that an Irish nation must include the traditions of all who wished to be part of that nation. "I challenge again the Irish psychology of the man who sets up the Gael and the [Anglo-Irishman] as opposing forces with conflicting outlooks," he wrote. "He who would segregate Irish history and Irish men into two sections—Irish speaking and English speaking—is not helping toward achieving Ireland a Nation."

Writing in English as well as Irish, he became a prolific and noteworthy poet and playwright, and very much the product of the Gaelic revival. His work resonated with themes of nationality, from folklore to politics: his three-act play, *The Defence of the Ford,* offered a worshipful interpretation of the folk hero Cuchulain and his battles against the enemies of ancient Ulster. Indeed, as much as Pearse revered the memory of Wolfe Tone and Robert Emmet, it was Cuchulain who inspired and informed so much of his art. The great hero's words were emblazoned on a fresco at Saint Enda's: "I care not though I were to live but one day and one night if only my fame and my deeds live after me."

It was his speechmaking, not his art, that brought Pearse to the attention of one of the IRB's key organizers, Thomas J. Clarke.

Through Clarke's influence, Pearse finally was invited to join the IRB in 1914. He soon became an extremely valuable recruit, for not long after taking the IRB oath, he was named the director of organization of the Irish National Volunteers. From that position, Pearse organized the Volunteers in the secret interests of the IRB, which meant organizing not for the protection of Home Rule, but for revolution.

By late spring 1914, the Irish National Volunteers were more than a match for the 100,000 men who had enlisted in Edward Carson's Ulster Volunteer Force. The Volunteers' membership eventually would reach nearly 200,000. From its headquarters on Great Brunswick Street in Dublin, its self-styled officers created a small military bureaucracy, issuing orders for the formation of companies and instructing recruits to study the British army's standard infantry manual for basic instructions in combat. The manual, headquarters noted, could be purchased for a shilling.

On the eve of World War I, then, the two large private armies in Ireland were watching each other with suspicion. Ironically enough, the nationalist private army was sworn to uphold an act of the British Parliament—Home Rule—while the Unionist army was preparing to fight Home Rule. Even as Britain prepared for conflict with Germany, its leaders had an eye on the powder keg that Ireland had become. Civil war, it seemed, was but one false move away.

Tom Clarke, the dynamiter turned IRB operative, was delighted to see armed columns marching through the streets of Dublin. As a hard-line republican, he had no use for John Redmond and Home Rule, but any display of militancy was preferable to apathy. "It is worth living in Ireland [in] these times," Clarke wrote to a friend in America. "There is an awakening—the slow, silent plodding and the open preaching is at last showing results . . . and we are breathing air that compels one to fling up his head and stand more erect."

Clarke turned fifty-six years old in 1914, but after spending fifteen years in prison, he looked at least a decade older. Gaunt and gray, with round spectacles and a bushy mustache, Clarke might have been mistaken for a retired clerk, and certainly not for a hardened ex-felon intent on bringing revolution to Ireland. Instead of breaking him, prison only reaffirmed Clarke's militant politics. He saw men with whom he was arrested slowly go insane after years of hard labor, special punishments, isolation, sleep deprivation, and silence. "Harassing morning, noon and night, and on through the night . . . harassing with bread and water punishments . . . with 'no sleep' torture and other tortures," Clarke wrote of his prison years. "This system was

Thomas Clarke

THOMAS CLARKE (1858-1916) born in the Isle of Wight, was a son of a Leitrim Protestant father who was a sergeant in the British army. His mother was a Catholic from Co. Tipperary. Sentenced to life imprisonment in 1883, for his part in the London campaign, he spent over 15 years under the most brutal prison conditions. More than half of his fifteen comrades were driven insane. First to sign the Proclamation of 1916 he was also the first to die in the executions which followed. He was executed at dawn on May 3rd, 1916 in Kilmainham Jail.

Printed in the Republic of Ireland by DAOL, Cork

Thomas Clarke

applied to the Irish prisoners, and to them only, and was specially devised to destroy us mentally and physically."

Tom Clarke's father was a Protestant and a British army sergeant who served part of his career as a member of the Crown's forces in Ireland. His mother was Catholic. The father of the future rebel was an exemplary soldier, so much so that when he retired in 1868, his discharge noted that "his conduct has been very good, and he was, when promoted, in possession of two Good Conduct Badges."

It was with horror, then, that this upstanding retired member of Her Majesty's armed forces realized that his son not only refused to follow his father's footsteps, but had become a member of the Irish Republican Brotherhood in 1878. He also was dabbling as an actor; it is not known which avenue Sergeant Clarke regarded as a surer path to infamy.

Clarke emigrated to New York in 1880, became a naturalized American citizen, joined Clan na Gael, and eagerly responded when a militant clan faction asked for volunteers to plant dynamite bombs in Britain. He was arrested long before he could strike the planned blow against Britain. Not long after his release in 1898, he married Kathleen Daly, the young niece of a comrade of his, and the couple emigrated to America. He rejoined Clan na Gael but, in 1907, he crossed the Atlantic one last time. His revolutionary work, he decided, had to be done in Ireland.

By 1914, he was the father of three boys, and his wife was a full partner in his revolutionary activities. Kathleen Clarke was one of the founding members of a women's organization called Cumann na mBan ("Council of Women"), which was to the Irish National Volunteers what the Ladies Land League was to the Land League. In the spirit of Anna Parnell, the women of Cumann na mBan were not about to serve as a mere auxiliary to the men's organization. Not only did they learn first aid, but they were instructed in the cleaning, loading, and firing of rifles.

Kathleen Clarke strove mightily to balance the duties of a revolutionary's wife, a revolutionary in her own right, and a mother. She once left the boys home alone when the oldest, John, was about twelve so she could preside at a lecture at Cumman na nBan headquarters. It was the first time the boys would be alone, and their mother struggled with guilt and fear. Before leaving, she took them aside: "Now boys," she said, "my duty to Ireland tonight is to go and make this lecture a success, and your duty to Ireland is to stay in bed until I return. You are not to light paper, matches or anything else. . . . Will you promise to do your duty to Ireland?" They did.

In June 1914, Padraig Pearse proclaimed that the Volunteers were "a dream coming true." For John Redmond and his colleagues in the Irish Parliamentary Party, however, the Volunteers were a potential nightmare. Everywhere Redmond looked he saw only instability.

Britain was moving closer to war with Germany; the Ulstermen continued to drill and train; and the Home Rule bill was lumbering its
way through the parliamentary process. One of Redmond's colleagues pointed to the dangers the Volunteer movement posed for the
Parliamentary Party: "It could not be controlled, and if the [Volun-
teers] met some day and demanded an Irish Republic, where would
our Home Rule leaders be?" It was a legitimate concern, because
Redmond was about to offer a major concession to Unionist Ulster.
The Irish Parliamentary Party would support a compromise allowing
six of Ulster's nine counties to opt out of a Home Rule government
for six years after the bill's passage. The six counties, Antrim, Down,
Derry, Tyrone, Fermanagh, and portions of Armagh, formed the
heart of Protestant, Unionist Ulster; the nationalist, Catholic counties
of Donegal, Cavan, and Monaghan would be included in the Home
Rule Parliament. A form of partition, anathema to republicans, was
under discussion.

Confident that he had the power of public opinion behind him,
Redmond demanded that he be allowed to nominate half the members of the Volunteers' provisional executive committee. Combined
with committee members who already supported him, Redmond
would effectively take control of the burgeoning movement. The IRB
contingent within the Volunteers, of course, bitterly opposed Redmond's proposal, but a majority of the committee reluctantly agreed
to accept his nominees.

Though Pearse voted against the Redmond takeover, in the bitter
aftermath he showed a calculating and practical side for which few
later observers gave him credit. "I voted against surrender . . . but I
do not regard the cause as lost—far from it," he wrote. "We will remain in the movement, and shall be watchful to checkmate any attempt on Redmond's part to keep us from arming. This is the real
danger. The future of the movement depends upon our remaining at
our posts to see to it that the Volunteers are a real army, not a stage
army. The movement at present is sweeping through the country like
a whirlwind, and the one cry is: 'Give us arms.' " Pearse appealed to
Irish America, which he had visited in early 1914 on a fund-raising
tour to benefit Saint Enda's, for help in getting weapons. "It will be
an irony of ironies if this movement comes and goes and leaves us—
the physical force men!—the only unarmed group in the country."

Arms were soon on their way, not from America, but from the nation that was preparing to go to war with Britain—Germany, which
had supplied arms to Carson's Ulster Volunteer Force earlier in 1914.
On Sunday, July 26, a yacht called the *Asgard*, under the command of

Erskine Childers, an Anglo-Irish Protestant writer who had served in the British army and worked as a clerk in the House of Commons, sailed into the port of Howth, County Dublin. The *Asgard* carried about nine hundred rifles and 25,000 rounds of ammunition bought from German agents in Hamburg. A contingent of eight hundred Volunteers was on hand to unload the weapons and dispatch them to secret storage places.

As an imitation of the Ulster gunrunning, it was pale, indeed. Even when another shipment landed off County Wicklow was accounted for, the Irish National Volunteers had brought in only about 1,500 weapons, a far cry from the 25,000 rifles and three million rounds which the Ulster Volunteers had imported in April. There was another difference, far more telling. The Ulster gunrunning went unchallenged. But after the Howth landing, a contingent of British troops, the King's Own Scottish Borderers, unsuccessfully tried to stop a small party of Volunteers bearing rifles. When the troops marched back to Dublin, crowds along a street called Bachelors Walk greeted them with taunts and jeers. A shot rang out, then a volley. Three civilians were killed and more than two dozen injured. The country was stunned. For militant nationalists, the killings on Bachelors Walk were a reminder that there were two sets of rules in Ireland. Pearse believed that events had played into the IRB's hands: "The army is an object of odium and derision," he wrote with obvious glee. "The whole movement, the whole country, has been re-baptized by bloodshed."

Days later, the nations of Europe summoned their young men to battle. There would be rebaptism aplenty during the next four years as the world's great imperial powers attempted collective suicide on Flanders fields.

Fenian doctrine had it that England's difficulty was Ireland's opportunity, and with the first cannon shot of World War I, opportunity had arrived at last. With Britain at war, the IRB's ruling executive, the Supreme Council, decided that it would stage a rebellion before the war was over. Planning eventually was turned over to a Military Council of three, later expanded to seven. The council's chief strategist was a poet named Joseph Mary Plunkett, who dabbled in military history. That was his sole qualification for the job.

The extent to which the IRB was utterly unrepresentative of the mass of Irish opinion, at least at the moment, was made clear in a speech in the House of Commons on August 4, the day Britain declared war. The Foreign Secretary, Sir Edward Grey, noted that "the

one bright spot in the very dreadful situation is Ireland." It was a remarkable assertion, given Ireland's long history of resistance, but it
was true all the same. The Irish were fully behind John Redmond and
his loyal Parliamentary Party. "The position in Ireland—and this is a
thing I should like to be clearly understood abroad—is not a consideration among the things we have to take into account now," Grey said.

So it seemed, and it was no small relief. The Irish, nationalist and
Unionist alike, eagerly heeded the call of the recruiter—there was no
conscription, at least not yet. Meanwhile, the long-awaited Home
Rule bill finally became law on September 14, 1914, without an
amendment allowing exclusion for parts of Ulster. Conservative
members of the House of Commons staged a walkout in protest, but
they knew their actions were mere theater. The historic passage of
Home Rule was followed by a companion bill suspending implementation of Home Rule for a year or for the duration of the war,
whichever was longer. The explosive question of Ulster was to be put
off until the British could restore tiny Belgium, occupied by the German military, to its rightful place among free nations.

Six days later, a triumphant John Redmond publicly pledged that
the Irish National Volunteers, 188,000 strong, would be available to
serve with British regulars on the European battlefields instead of
serving merely as a home defense force. The militant faction of the
Volunteers wanted nothing to do with Britain's war, and so the Volunteers split into two unequal groups. Some thirteen thousand dissenters, led by Pearse and his fellow IRB infiltrators, formed their
own militia, renaming themselves the Irish Volunteers. The rest, more
than 170,000, stayed true to Redmond's pledge, and so threw themselves into the trenches of France in hopes that a grateful Britain and
Ulster would notice their loyalty to the Crown. Eventually, more
than 200,000 Irishmen voluntarily enlisted in the British army during
World War I.

An Irish peer of the realm, Sir Roger Casement, was in America
when war was declared. Like Hugh O'Neill during Elizabethan times
and Wolfe Tone and Lord Edward Fitzgerald in the late eighteenth
century, Roger Casement was prepared to do business with England's
enemy of the moment. He envisioned a formal alliance between the
Irish revolutionary movement and the Kaiser's government, negotiated through the services of Irish revolutionaries operating in neutral
America. Casement drew up a petition to the Kaiser himself, asking
for Berlin's help in fomenting a rebellion on Britain's western flank.
"Thousands of Irishmen are prepared to do their part to aid the Ger-

man cause, for they recognize it as their own," Casement wrote, discreetly avoiding a mention of the tens of thousands of Irishmen who were volunteering for the British army.

Casement's German strategy was not his alone. John Devoy, the aging Fenian, already was in touch with German diplomats in New York. Devoy and two younger allies, an Irish-American judge named Daniel Cohalan and a wealthy businessman from County Tyrone named Joseph McGarrity, were an integral part of the fledgling plans to bring rebellion to Ireland. They would provide money, arms, and diplomatic contacts with Germany, contingent on America's continued neutrality.

Casement, a handsome aristocrat with a well-trimmed brown beard and an upturned mustache, was yet another curious recruit to militant Irish nationalism. He was a fifty-year-old member of the Anglo-Irish gentry who had gained fame and a knighthood as a member of Britain's foreign service. While in the Belgian Congo at the beginning of the century, he witnessed and exposed the colonial government's appalling treatment of the natives. He found evidence of forced labor and resettlements, of torture, mutilation, and murder, and he compiled the evidence in reports back to London. He later traveled to South America to investigate charges that Indians in the region bordering Peru and Colombia were serving as slaves for rubber companies. At one point, he examined the effects of whippings on one thousand Indian men, women, and children: "I never saw anything more pathetic than these people," he wrote. "They move one to profound pity."

It wasn't until he was forty years old that Casement began to take an interest in the island of his birth. His family had lived in landed comfort in County Antrim, the heart of Ulster Protestantism, although the family was Anglican, while the bulwark of Protestant Ulster was Presbyterian. After returning to Ireland in 1904 following his stint in the Congo, Casement met several fledgling nationalists. An enthusiastic and passionate man by nature, Casement took up the cause of Irish culture after meeting Douglas Hyde. He set out for his first trip to the west of Ireland in the middle of 1904, and was soon immersed in learning the Irish language. The west also brought out his humanitarian instincts. He started a fund-raising campaign for a group of poor Irish-speaking children in County Galway whose school had closed.

The journey from cultural nationalism to militant republicanism was common enough, although it received an assist when Casement observed the tactics of his fellow Ulstermen preparing to resist Home

Rule with force. His conversion to militant nationalism was complete. Germany, he decided, represented "European civilization at its best" while Britain was "European civilization at its worst." After retiring from Britain's foreign service, Casement was one of the founding members of the Volunteers and was among the organizers of the Howth gunrunning, although he was not a member of the Irish Republican Brotherhood, a fact that weighed against him when he met with Devoy in the summer of 1914. Still, even the grumpy Devoy was taken with Casement's evident sincerity and enthusiasm. Devoy's co-conspirator, McGarrity, was a great deal more impressed. He told Devoy that Casement was the greatest Irishman since Wolfe Tone.

After attending a rally in Philadelphia to protest the Bachelors Walk killings, Casement explained his plans to Devoy and McGarrity. He would, Casement said, set sail as soon as possible for Germany to serve as the Irish revolutionary movement's liaison with the German government and to raise a brigade made of Irish-born British soldiers whom the Germans would be holding as prisoners of war. He had dreams of persuading Germany to provide an invasion force of fifty thousand to support an Irish-led rebellion. In order to carry out these ambitious plans, he explained, he needed contacts, money, and false identification papers. Devoy and McGarrity approved. Through Devoy, Casement met with German diplomats in New York, who agreed to the plan.

As Casement was making final preparations to leave for Germany, he told his American supporters that he intended to bring along a Norwegian sailor he had met in New York, Adler Christensen. Devoy, who had been played the fool at least once by spies and informers in Clan na Gael, was appalled. Devoy may have suspected that there was more to the Casement-Christensen relationship, for when Christensen returned to New York sometime later, Devoy had him watched carefully. With noticeable disgust, Devoy reported to McGarrity that Christensen was often in "the neighborhood of the Tenderloin" and was meeting with suspicious characters in a disreputable New York hotel. Devoy was a prudish old bachelor who had left behind a fiancée in Ireland, but he also was a professional conspirator. He believed Casement and Christensen were homosexuals. But if Casement's sexual orientation offended him, it was in part because of the security risks it posed.

Under the cover of American neutrality, Devoy, McGarrity, and other Irish-Americans acted as German agents in America in return for Germany's promise to support rebellion in Ireland. The IRB, distrustful of the mails, sent messengers via ship to Devoy in New York.

Devoy, in turn, forwarded the messages—which included specific requests for guns, ammunition, and manpower, as well as broad outlines of the IRB's strategy—to German diplomats in New York. The messages were then sent in code by telegraph to Berlin via the German embassy in Washington.

In addition to their work as agents of intrigue, Devoy and McGarrity helped raise tens of thousands of dollars for the IRB, transmitting the money in increments of $5,000 and $10,000 through the couriers that regularly reported to Devoy in his newspaper office in downtown Manhattan or in his hotel room in midtown.

Soon, however, Devoy had to send something else across the Atlantic. On June 29, 1915, Jeremiah O'Donovan Rossa died a confused and lonely man at the age of eighty-four on Staten Island. In his declining years, he was a far cry from the fiery and furious organizer of the bombing campaign against London in the 1880s. He lived in a mist, unable to recognize his daughter, shouting out commands in Irish to unseen comrades. In a coherent moment less than two years before his death, he sent a letter to Devoy, pleading for his company. "I am home and in bed every day," Rossa wrote. " 'Tis a lonesome kind of life."

When Rossa died, Devoy sent a telegram to Tom Clarke in Dublin: "Rossa dead. What shall we do?"

Clarke replied: "Send his body home at once."

Jeremiah O'Donovan Rossa became in death what he was surely not in life: an effective advocate of Irish republicanism. Clarke set out to add Rossa's name to the list of posthumous recruiting agents for the Irish revolution. While the body was en route from New York, Clarke set up committees and subcommittees to look after the smallest details (seventeen special trains would be required to bring in mourners from the countryside), making sure that IRB members controlled the arrangements. One of Clarke's committees was in charge of putting together a program of literary tributes to Rossa, and a committee member solicited a contribution from James Connolly, a labor leader and head of the union movement's private militia, the Irish Citizen Army. "When are you fellows going to stop blathering about dead Fenians," Connolly replied. "Why don't you get a few live ones for a change?"

Clarke's choice to give the traditional graveside oration was obvious. It would be Padraig Pearse. Before setting out for his cottage in County Galway to prepare the speech, Pearse asked Clarke how far he should go in summoning a new generation to follow in the spirit of the deceased. "Make it as hot as hell," Clarke said. "Throw discretion to the winds."

On August 1, 1915, a gray, rainy day, thousands gathered in Dublin's streets as the body of the dead Fenian made its way to sprawling Glasnevin Cemetery, the final resting place of Daniel O'Connell, Charles Stewart Parnell, and James Stephens, among others. The Irish National Volunteers, wearing splendid uniforms and bearing rifles, shared escort duty with Connolly's Irish Citizen Army and a contingent of young boys enrolled in a quasi-military Boy Scout organization called Fianna na hEireann. Its president was one of Connolly's most devoted acolytes, Countess Constance Markievicz, the wife of a Polish count and yet another member of the Anglo-Protestant gentry who embraced militant Irish nationalism.

Once the mourners reached Rossa's graveside, Pearse stepped forward to deliver his much anticipated eulogy. He was dressed in the uniform of the Irish National Volunteers, a man in young middle age with a solid build but with little in the way of military bearing. But his words were as charged with emotion as any call to arms delivered on history's battlefields.

"Life springs from death, and from the graves of patriot men and women spring living nations," he said. "The defenders of this realm have worked well in secret and in the open. They think that they have pacified Ireland. They think that they have pacified half of us and intimidated the other half. They think that they have foreseen everything, think that they have provided against everything, but the fools, the fools, the fools! They have left us our Fenian dead, and while Ireland holds these graves, Ireland unfree will never be at peace."

Pearse's words were those of a man far removed from mainstream Ireland. Some six thousand Irishmen a week were volunteering for service in the British army, to be, in fact, defenders of the realm. But he had no illusions he would sway public opinion. All he needed were a few true believers, and they could reclaim nationality from the moderate Home Rulers.

One of Britain's top administrators in Ireland, Sir Mathew Nathan, watched events with some apprehension, but, as it turned out, imprecise information. He reported back to London that "I have the uncomfortable feeling that the Nationalists are losing ground to the Sinn Feiners and that this demonstration [the Rossa funeral] is hastening the movement." In fact, the militants had moved far beyond Sinn Féin's doctrine of dual monarchy and passive resistance. It was a distinction that continued to escape the authorities. Still, there was little Dublin Castle could do but watch. With bodies piling up on the Continent, the British army could hardly spare the effort and manpower to take more aggressive action against the militants, no matter what they might call themselves. Besides, they represented such a minority that to suppress them would be to create martyrs—exactly what John Redmond didn't need as he drained Ireland of extremists.

James Connolly was growing impatient with the words that so frightened Dublin Castle. Connolly was slowly amassing a small cache of arms in the basement of the Irish Transport and General Workers Union headquarters, Liberty Hall. An independent thinker as well as an ideologue, he was both a nationalist and a socialist, and he was tired of waiting for the chance to fuse the two. Outside Liberty Hall, a huge banner asserted that "We Serve Neither King nor Kaiser, but Ireland."

Connolly had no idea what the IRB's Military Council was planning. He saw only what the public saw: a private army of significant numbers, marching, drilling, and training, but to no apparent end. Writing in the union movement's newspaper, the *Worker's Republic,* Connolly demanded an end to mere talk of revolution. "The time for Ireland's battle is NOW, the place for Ireland's battle is HERE," he wrote in January 1916. Pearse, Clarke, and their colleagues knew that Connolly had the means to preempt the IRB's plans. He was the commandant of the labor movement's private militia, the Irish Citizen Army. Although the ICA had been formed to protect workers from police attacks during strikes, Connolly seemed to be suggesting that its 350 or so members might launch a nationalist rebellion on its own. The time had come for a long talk with this passionate socialist who had the courage of his convictions.

Short and stout, with a reputation as a devoted humanitarian and a prickly colleague, Connolly was forty-seven years old as the fateful year of 1916 began. He was married with six children—a seventh, Mona, the firstborn, died in 1904 at age thirteen when her clothes caught fire while she was preparing a meal. The tragedy came on the very day Mrs. Connolly and their children were to sail to America to join James, who went to New York the year before. The family postponed their journey by a week so they could mourn and bury the oldest child. Connolly spent the days waiting at the piers in New York, wondering why his family was late in arriving. His questions were answered when the sad little party arrived on Ellis Island without Mona.

Friends said the gregarious Connolly who left for America never returned, that the man who came home to Ireland in 1910 was more quarrelsome and difficult. They attributed it to his bitter and impoverished life as a socialist organizer in America, but surely the horrible death of his daughter three thousand miles away, far from his protec-

James Connolly

tion, had had something to do with the change. "The blow darkened my life, and changed all our hopes and prospects," he wrote.

Connolly was born in 1868 not in Ireland, but in Edinburgh, Scotland, to a pair of Irish immigrants living in poverty in the city's Irish slums. Though he spent his work-shortened childhood in Scotland, and later returned to spend part of his adult life there, he didn't consider himself Scottish or even British. He described himself as "an Irishman who has always taken a keen interest . . . in Ireland." Like the young Michael Davitt, Connolly was reared in what amounted to an Irish village transported into industrial, Victorian Britain, and his accent was neither Scottish nor Irish, but a blend that was unique to the Little Ireland of Edinburgh. His father worked for the city as a street cleaner. The family was so poor that James developed rickets, probably as a result of malnutrition. But his parents impressed on their children the value of education, and their efforts were not in vain. James was so earnest a scholar that he read at home by the dim light of embers, and wrote with charred sticks.

But, at a certain point, education was a luxury for families like the Connollys, and James was dispatched to the workforce at age twelve, taking a job with a bakery that required him to be at work before sunrise. Two years into this draining routine, young James followed the footsteps of many a poor boy with few options: he joined the British army, after lying about his age to the officers of the Royal Scots Regiment. He got his first glimpse of the land of his parents' birth when he was deployed to Ireland in the 1880s.

Connolly deserted the army four months before his seven-year enlistment was up, shortly after falling in love with a twenty-one-year-old Protestant Irish woman named Lillie Reynolds, a domestic servant. She followed him back to Scotland, where he fled after his desertion (his company's records were so jumbled that his superiors assumed his enlistment was up), and they were married in 1890. The newlyweds lived in the same frightful conditions in which Connolly was reared. The Irish slums of Edinburgh were statistically only slightly better than the slums of Dublin. Cholera was a killer, infant mortality was high, and the crowded living conditions bred the usual social pathologies associated with the urban poor.

Through his older brother, John, Connolly came in contact with socialist agitators in Edinburgh, and eventually he succeeded John as secretary of the Scottish Socialist Federation. The pattern of his life was set. He spent the rest of his days as a wandering agitator, pamphleteer, and union organizer, a voracious reader of socialist theory, and a self-taught intellectual. Such work didn't pay well, and his growing family lived a life of extreme hardship and poverty. But through his journalism, he became a prominent voice in European socialism, and one of very few who had no university training, who was, in fact, an unskilled laborer.

Connolly returned to Ireland in 1896 to take a job as a union organizer, and he quickly became an important figure as both a socialist and a nationalist, organizing unions and promoting socialism while joining Maud Gonne and William Butler Yeats in protesting Queen

Victoria's sixtieth anniversary celebrations. He would later say that his comrades in Britain and on the Continent never really understood him. "They all forget that I am an Irishman," he told his wife.

His fellow socialists elsewhere were awaiting a worldwide revolution of the proletariat. Connolly, however, struggled to provide the missing link between the nationalist revolutionaries of the IRB and Ireland's social agitators and union organizers. His vision was embodied in the political organization he founded in 1898, the Irish Socialist Republican Party. "The man who is bubbling over with love and enthusiasm for 'Ireland' and yet can pass unmoved through our streets and witness all the wrong and the suffering, the shame and degradation, wrought upon the people of Ireland . . . without burning to end it is, in my opinion, a fraud," he wrote.

Connolly had a profound effect on Padraig Pearse, a middle-class intellectual who suffered none of the deprivations that Connolly knew firsthand. Nearly alone among his IRB colleagues, Pearse sounded themes of social justice as well as political separatism, and while he wrote approvingly of the mystical properties of bloodshed, in his less passionate moments he sounded a great deal like Connolly on the subject of the war in Europe. "You can see the rich men are making [a profit] on the war while the very poor are on the verge of starvation," he wrote. "And yet they want the poor to work at home and fight abroad so that so-called noblemen may sit at ease . . . and congratulate each other on the glory and greatness of the British Empire."

Unlike Pearse, however, Connolly had little patience for the romantic visions of the cultural nationalists. Like his friend Maud Gonne, he believed the bulk of the Irish poor faced more immediate problems. "You cannot teach a starving man Gaelic," he said. But you could teach him to rebel, and that seemed to be Connolly's plan. The IRB's top leaders decided the time had come to take this formidable man into their confidence.

In mid-January 1916, emissaries from the IRB's Military Council passed word to Connolly that Padraig Pearse wanted to meet with him. "There's no man in Ireland I'd rather meet," he said. Connolly immediately was taken to see not only Pearse, but other members of the Military Council as well. Over the course of several extraordinary days, Pearse revealed that the IRB was planning a rebellion on Easter Sunday, April 23; that his fellow poet, Joseph Plunkett, had devised a plan for an assault on Dublin with five thousand troops to coincide with a rising in the countryside with an equal number of rebels; and that assistance from Germany was being arranged through their allies in New York. After three days of intense discussion, James Connolly was sworn into the Irish Republican Brotherhood and made a member of its Military Council. Labor and nationalism were officially joined together.

A courier was dispatched to New York with a message to Devoy. He received it in early February and was stunned when it was decoded. "We have decided to begin action on Easter Sunday," it read. "We must have your arms and munitions in Limerick between Good Friday and Easter Saturday. We expect German help immediately after beginning action." Devoy knew his co-conspirators in Ireland were planning a rebellion, but he thought it was at least a year away. Now he was being told that he had less than three months to make the necessary arrangements. Over the next few weeks, Devoy and his allies raised and dispatched $100,000 to the IRB to buy weapons. Devoy became a frequent visitor to the German consulate in New York, a place the old, gray-bearded conspirator regarded as scandalously loose with sensitive documents, which were often lying openly on desks. Devoy asked for 100,000 rifles, artillery, and a cadre of German officers to lead the earnest but inexperienced rebels. The Germans told him that they would ship twenty thousand rifles, ten machine guns, and ammunition to Ireland in time for the rebellion. He took what he could get. He wrote to his ally Joseph McGarrity in thinly veiled language: "I have received an answer to my application for the position. . . . It is favorable, but the salary is not as big as I expected, but it is a living wage."

Meanwhile, the man who was supposed to be acting as the movement's ambassador to Germany, Sir Roger Casement, was in a sanatorium, his mental and physical health broken. His plan to recruit a brigade made up of Irish prisoners of war in Germany was an embarrassing failure. Devoy told Berlin to keep Casement in the dark, and to make sure he remained in Germany when the rebellion broke out. Casement was distraught and paranoid, and when the Germans refused to acknowledge his request to send a messenger to America, he bitterly condemned "the customary form of official courtesy in this country." He had no idea that by ignoring him, the Germans simply were following Devoy's request.

The military plan for Dublin, the fulcrum of the rebellion, called for the seizing of several strongpoints, with a headquarters established in the General Post Office building on the city's broad boulevard, Sackville Street. The GPO was a prominent neoclassical structure with elegant columns reaching to the curb. To the south rose a statue of Daniel O'Connell, while a statue of Charles Stewart Parnell guarded the street's northern approach. The rebel leaders, then, would carry out their revolution in the shadow of the nine-teenth century's great constitutional agitators.

Although there was some tactical logic in Plunkett's choice of tar-gets, the overall strategy of intentional sacrifice seemed clear: by bar-ricading themselves in static positions, the rebels would not win Irish freedom, but would, by dint of their martyrdom, demonstrate unvan-quished Irish resistance to false promises, duplicity, and popular opinion. Even James Connolly, the hardheaded Marxist, was won over to religious imagery. "In all due humility and awe, we recognize that of us, as of mankind before Calvary, it may truly be said, 'with-out the shedding of blood there is no Redemption.' " Pearse indicated exactly what he had in mind in a poem he called "The Mother," in which he spoke of "two strong sons" who die "in bloody protest for a glorious thing."

A German ship disguised as a Norwegian trawler slipped into the North Sea on April 8, headed for the Irish coast with the promised shipment of rifles. Named the *Aud,* the ship took a circuitous route to its destination, cleverly evading British navy patrols. Another Ger-man vessel set sail for Ireland three days later. This one, a submarine, carried no arms, but on board were three Irishmen, Sir Roger Case-ment and two friends. Distraught and disillusioned, convinced that the devious Germans were offering only token help to the rebels in Dublin, Casement demanded that Germany return him to Ireland. The Germans were glad to be rid of him. He intended to stop the re-bellion in its tracks.

In New York, an IRB courier showed up at Devoy's doorstep on April 14, nine days before Easter, bearing another message from the Military Council. Again, Devoy was stunned. The council suddenly decided that early delivery of the German arms might compromise the rebellion. Devoy was instructed to tell the Germans that the arms ship should rendezvous no earlier than Easter Sunday night. Previous instructions put the delivery between Good Friday and Saturday. A panic-stricken Devoy delivered the message to the Germans in New York, but it was in vain. The *Aud* had no radio. Four days later, armed agents from the U.S. Secret Service raided the German con-sulate in New York. Among the documents scattered on desks were copies of Devoy's communications with Berlin. The information would have been greatly appreciated in London, but British intelli-gence already was well informed of the rebels' intentions. They had cracked the German code, and were intercepting Devoy's communi-cations with Berlin.

In his capacity as director of military organization for the Volunteers, Pearse scheduled a series of manuevers for Easter Sunday. It was the ideal cover under which to launch the rebellion. But now the time had come for the IRB to show itself. Aides to Eion MacNeill, a college professor who was the putative chairman of the Volunteers, convinced him that Pearse and his fellow militants had something in mind for Easter besides a military parade.

MacNeill confronted Pearse on Holy Thursday evening at Saint Enda's school, and the headmaster admitted the truth: the IRB had in-

Countess Markievicz

filtrated the Volunteers and was ready to launch a rebellion. Furious, MacNeill said he would do all he could to cancel the unauthorized and, in his mind, untimely rebellion. Pearse calmly told him it was out of his hands, that any action he took would lead to confusion and thus to certain, and bloody, failure. After another meeting on Good Friday, MacNeill conceded that a confrontation was unavoidable. As long as the German arms were on their way, he decided he would do nothing to stop the rebellion.

Meanwhile, the *Aud* was off the coast of County Kerry, signaling to the shore. Nobody was there. The *Aud*'s captain, of course, didn't know about the change in schedule, and the Military Council hadn't considered the possibility of an early arrival.

As the *Aud* waited patiently at sea, Countess Constance Markievicz was trying to resolve a dilemma in her Dublin home. She needed material for a flag, but the shops would be closed the next morning, Good Friday. The four young people who were sharing her increasingly shabby house were puzzled. The Countess had been a nervous wreck all week, and this new and quite unexplained need for a flag only added to the tension in the household.

She was a lieutenant in the Irish Citizen Army, the highest-ranking woman in the fledgling rebel unit, and she knew the rebellion was imminent. She and a friend had already tested several detonators that had been smuggled into Ireland from England. They demolished a wall on her property in the Wicklow Mountains south of Dublin.

Confronted with the fact that she could not buy any material, the forty-eight-year-old Countess disappeared for a moment, and then returned to her young friends with a green bedspread. She placed it on the floor of her drawing room and cut it into a more manageable shape, while her little dog, Poppet, created a nuisance, tearing at the material until a bit of it ripped away. The Countess asked one of her friends to find some gold paint, but there was only a small bit left, and it was dry. Undeterred, the Countess found some mustard and mixed it with the paint, and, as her friends held the former bedspread taut, she carefully painted the words IRISH REPUBLIC on the material. She was pleased with the final product.

Before her marriage, she was known as Constance Gore-Booth, daughter of a prominent Anglo-Protestant landlord in County Sligo. She was born in London in a town house near Buckingham Palace, but the family seat was an estate called Lissadell in Sligo. Her paternal grandfather was a member of the British Parliament.

At the age of nineteen, she was presented at court to Queen Victoria in the standard coming-of-age ritual of the ruling class, and she spent most of her early adulthood in the manner expected of a rich, beautiful young woman. She married Count Casimir Markievicz of Poland in 1900, and they settled into a life revolving around art and literature. Her only contact with politics came when she and her husband were summoned to Dublin Castle, seat of the British administration, for a social event.

Inevitably her contacts in Dublin's cultural community put her in touch with Yeats, who had been an occasional visitor at Lissadell, as well as Maud Gonne and Arthur Griffith. She told Griffith in 1904, when she was thirty-six years old, that she had only recently realized that there were people in Ireland who opposed the authority of the British monarch. Griffith introduced her to a world she knew nothing about; within five years, she helped found the Fianna na hEireann, a nationalist Boy Scout organization. She also joined an early manifestation of Cumann na mBan called Bean na hEireann ("Women of Ireland"), and delivered a lecture to the group asserting that "a free Ireland with no sex disabilities in her constitution should be the motto of all Nationalist women."

She became a familiar sight at nationalist demonstrations and at suffragist rallies, and then completed her remarkable political journey when she met the labor leader James Larkin and then, especially, James Connolly, who converted her to socialism. She fed workers and their families during the lockout of 1913, and a friend watched her "with sleeves rolled up, presiding over a cauldron of stew, surrounded by a crowd of gaunt women and children carrying bowls and cans." Liberty Hall became her second, or third, home, while her actual residences became auxiliary headquarters for union organizers, socialists, and members of the Irish Citizen Army.

As she prepared women for the battle she knew was coming, she told them that they should "get away from wrong ideals and false standards of womanhood. . . . We have got to get rid of the last vestige of the harem before woman is free as our dream of the future would have her." Her commitment was not without personal sacrifice. Her daughter, Maeve, was being reared by her own mother, and she was growing apart from her husband.

As the battle drew near, she took it upon herself to make a flag of green. When it was finished, Countess Constance Markievicz returned to her nervous sense of anticipation. She didn't have much longer to wait.

Good Friday brought double disaster. The British navy spotted the *Aud* and ordered it to proceed to the port of Queenstown, County Cork. The German captain scuttled the *Aud* while sailing into port, and the arms and ammunition intended for the rebellion sank to the bottom. Meanwhile, Roger Casement and his two friends landed on a beach called the Banna Strand in County Kerry after their German submarine escort placed them in a rubber raft and sent them on their way. Police were on the alert in the area, and Casement was arrested within a few hours. He refused to give his name, claiming to be an ordinary English traveler. A district inspector from the police force, the Royal Irish Constabulary, was brought in to question him. "I think I know who you are," the inspector said, "and I pray to God it won't end the way of Wolfe Tone."

Everything, it seemed, had been betrayed. When MacNeill heard about the disasters on Easter Saturday morning, he rescinded his pledge to allow the rebellion to proceed. He got on his bicycle and pedaled to the offices of the *Sunday Independent* newspaper, where he placed a prominent announcement canceling the scheduled Easter Sunday maneuvers. The careful plans, the years of international intrigue, were in ruins. As Pearse and his brother, Willie, left Saint Enda's, their mother shouted: "Now, Pat, above all, do nothing rash."

"No, mother," Pearse replied.

The Military Council assembled in Liberty Hall on Easter morning. A dejected Pearse had no great fighting words to rally flagging spirits. He believed they had no choice but to flee to the west, the mystical west of folklore and fairy tales, where the spirit of Cuchulain resided in front of many a turf-burning hearth. There, he said, they could start anew. Connolly, an urban man to his marrow, disagreed. The fight, he said, would be in the streets of Dublin, where Ireland's oppression and exploitation had taken on its modern character in the festering slums and crowded lanes. Tom Clarke argued that the rebellion should go forward, same place, same day. After a long discussion, the council decided to postpone the rebellion for a day. There was no talk of scrapping it altogether, despite the certain knowledge that the government was on high alert. Even if they didn't act, they would be arrested anyway in the inevitable, and no doubt imminent, government crackdown. (Dublin Castle, as the rebels deduced, was preparing a list of suspects to be rounded up.) Their contacts with Germany made them, in Britain's eyes, traitors subject to a traitor's death. If they didn't act, their names would be attached not to a bloody protest, but to a fiasco. They would be bunglers, not martyrs.

The rebellion was fixed for noon on Easter Monday. Printers working elsewhere in Liberty Hall produced a copy of a proclamation Pearse had drafted. Because of a shortage of type, the document

The Easter Proclamation, 1916

POBLACHT NA H EIREANN.
THE PROVISIONAL GOVERNMENT
OF THE
IRISH REPUBLIC
TO THE PEOPLE OF IRELAND.

IRISHMEN AND IRISHWOMEN: In the name of God and of the dead generations from which she receives her old tradition of nationhood, Ireland, through us, summons her children to her flag and strikes for her freedom.

Having organised and trained her manhood through her secret revolutionary organisation, the Irish Republican Brotherhood, and through her open military organisations, the Irish Volunteers and the Irish Citizen Army, having patiently perfected her discipline, having resolutely waited for the right moment to reveal itself, she now seizes that moment, and, supported by her exiled children in America and by gallant allies in Europe, but relying in the first on her own strength, she strikes in full confidence of victory.

We declare the right of the people of Ireland to the ownership of Ireland, and to the unfettered control of Irish destinies, to be sovereign and indefeasible. The long usurpation of that right by a foreign people and government has not extinguished the right, nor can it ever be extinguished except by the destruction of the Irish people. In every generation the Irish people have asserted their right to national freedom and sovereignty; six times during the past three hundred years they have asserted it in arms. Standing on that fundamental right and again asserting it in arms in the face of the world, we hereby proclaim the Irish Republic as a Sovereign Independent State, and we pledge our lives and the lives of our comrades-in-arms to the cause of its freedom, of its welfare, and of its exaltation among the nations.

The Irish Republic is entitled to, and hereby claims, the allegiance of every Irishman and Irishwoman. The Republic guarantees religious and civil liberty, equal rights and equal opportunities to all its citizens, and declares its resolve to pursue the happiness and prosperity of the whole nation and of all its parts, cherishing all the children of the nation equally, and oblivious of the differences carefully fostered by an alien government, which have divided a minority from the majority in the past.

Until our arms have brought the opportune moment for the establishment of a permanent National Government, representative of the whole people of Ireland and elected by the suffrages of all her men and women, the Provisional Government, hereby constituted, will administer the civil and military affairs of the Republic in trust for the people.

We place the cause of the Irish Republic under the protection of the Most High God, Whose blessing we invoke upon our arms, and we pray that no one who serves that cause will dishonour it by cowardice, inhumanity, or rapine. In this supreme hour the Irish nation must, by its valour and discipline and by the readiness of its children to sacrifice themselves for the common good, prove itself worthy of the august destiny to which it is called.

Signed on Behalf of the Provisional Government,

THOMAS J. CLARKE,
SEAN Mac DIARMADA,   THOMAS MacDONAGH,
P. H. PEARSE,   EAMONN CEANNT,
JAMES CONNOLLY.   JOSEPH PLUNKETT.

was printed in different fonts, giving it its distinctive look. Addressed, significantly, to "Irishmen and Irishwomen," it proclaimed the existence of an Irish Republic:

"In the name of God and of the dead generations from which she receives her old tradition of nationhood, Ireland, through us, summons her children to her flag and strikes for her freedom. . . . We declare the right of the people of Ireland to the ownership of Ireland, and to the unfettered control of Irish destinies. . . . In every generation the Irish people have asserted their right to national freedom and sovereignty; six times during the past three hundred years they have asserted it in arms. . . . The Republic guarantees religious and civil liberty, equal rights and equal opportunities to all its citizens."

The document paid tribute to Ireland's "exiled children in America" and to "gallant allies in Europe"—meaning, of course, Germany. And it declared that the Republic was "oblivious" to "the differences carefully fostered by an alien Government."

Tom Clarke, at fifty-eight the oldest member of the council and a symbol of the link between generations, was the first to sign. Six more signatures followed: Connolly, Pearse, Thomas MacDonagh, Joseph Plunkett, Eamonn Ceannt, and Sean MacDiarmada. Three of the signatories, Pearse, Plunkett, and MacDonagh, were poets.

There was no turning back now.

Countess Markievicz was shocked to read MacNeill's announcement in the *Sunday Independent.* She had spent part of Easter Saturday afternoon in Liberty Hall, copying and dispatching orders for a general mobilization of the Irish Citizen Army on Easter Sunday afternoon. A friend dropped by and saw her busy giving directions. The friend assumed that the Countess was in the midst of rehearsing a play, not an unreasonable conclusion given that Liberty Hall had put on a play of Connolly's the previous weekend.

"Is it for children?" the friend asked of the presumed play.

"No," the Countess replied. "It's for grownups."

After reading on Sunday morning that the Volunteers' maneuvers were canceled, the Countess knew that something had gone wrong. She immediately set out for Liberty Hall, carrying her homemade flag with her. It was, she later wrote, "the busiest day I ever lived through." In the late afternoon, she joined Connolly at the head of an Irish Citizen Army march through Dublin, after which Connolly delivered a speech that asserted Ireland's right to a place in any postwar negotiations.

The Countess retired for the night in a friend's house knowing that in the morning she would march with the Irish Citizen Army and take her place as second in command of a rebel contingent in Saint Stephen's Green in the center of fashionable Dublin. As her comrades prepared for bed, they heard a gunshot from the Countess's room. Her nerves strained, her body exhausted, she accidentally fired her pistol while unloading it. The bullet pierced a door. It was the rebellion's first casualty.

Easter Monday was a holiday in Ireland. Army officers happily headed off to the Faireyhouse Races, delighted that the weather was sunny and splendid. Dublin Castle was convinced that Casement's arrest and the failed arms shipment meant an end to any immediate trouble, although arrests surely would have to be made soon. For the moment, however, there seemed to be no need to interrupt anybody's day off.

The rebels assembled at Liberty Hall before noon. Padraig Pearse, who bore the titles of Commandant in Chief of the Army of the Republic and President of the Provisional Government, cycled to his date with destiny. He wore the green uniform of an Irish Volunteer, a South Africa–style slouch hat, and, in a display of the old-fashioned military dash that was being blown apart by the killing machines on the Western Front, a sword. Countess Markievicz, Connolly, Clarke, and the other members of the Military Council prepared to take up their assigned positions. Joseph Plunkett, the poet and amateur tactician, also brandished a sword. His throat was covered in bandages, the aftermath of surgery he had endured three weeks before. The operation was of no use. Tuberculosis was killing him. Nearby, another signatory of the proclamation, Sean MacDiarmada, leaned on a cane. He had survived polio years before, but it had left him partially crippled.

Plunkett's plans called for a force of five thousand rebels in Dublin. Just over one thousand showed up. But ahead they marched. Countess Markievicz wore a green blouse, knee britches, an ammunition belt, and a hat like Pearse's, although hers was decorated with feathers. She and the contigent's commander, Michael Mallin, marched into Saint Stephen's Green at the head of a party that included fifteen women. The rebellion was only a few hours old when the Countess spotted several British soldiers outside the rebel emplacement. She aimed her rifle and fired. Two men fell to the ground.

Other small parties made their way to their assigned targets. A tall, American-born professor of mathematics named Eamon de Valera was put in charge of capturing Boland's Mill, which commanded a key approach to central Dublin. Pearse, Connolly, Clarke, and the rest of the headquarters staff marched north up Sackville Street toward the General Post Office. As they marched, Connolly whispered to a comrade: "We are going out to be slaughtered."

When they neared their target, Connolly yelled out a command worthy of Pearse's sword: "Left turn! The GPO!/Charge!" The column of about 150 burst into the building, cut telegraph cables, smashed windows, and began turning the place into a fortress. When stunned customers were cleared from the building, Pearse stepped outside and read his proclamation. It was greeted with profound curiosity. An ebullient Connolly shook Pearse by the hand. "Thanks be to God, Pearse, that we've lived to see this day," he said. A rebel party raised two flags from the GPO's roof. One was a tricolor of green, white, and orange. The other was Countess Markievicz's homemade banner.

A few hundred miles away, on Valentia Island off the coast of County Kerry, a small rebel party invaded a telegraph office and dispatched a coded message to Devoy and his allies in New York: "Tom successfully operated today."

Amazingly, the rebellion took authorities by surprise. Martial law wasn't declared until Tuesday night, thirty-six hours after the rebels seized the GPO. But as the government and the military emerged from their sunny holiday, the forces at their command soon demonstrated the truth in Connolly's prophecy of slaughter.

With reinforcements pouring into Dublin, the army had 6,500 soldiers in the city by Tuesday night. The outnumbered rebels in their exposed positions made for easy targets. While the rebels dug trenches in Saint Stephen's Green, as if the fighting would resemble the stalemate in Flanders, the army took up positions in the Shelbourne Hotel overlooking the park and fired with deadly effect. The rebels retreated from the green on Tuesday night, taking shelter nearby in the Royal College of Surgeons. The retreat did nothing to dampen the Countess's enthusiasm: "We've done more than Wolfe Tone already," she told her troops. At one point, orders went out to set fire to neighboring buildings thought to house British snipers. When the order was rescinded, the Countess crawled from room to room to pass along the news. In midweek, one of the women under her command, Margaret Skinnider, was wounded when the British opened fire on the college's ground floor. The Countess held her hand as a nurse attended to her serious, but not life-threatening, wounds.

The rebels in the GPO were likewise under heavy fire by Tuesday night. Machine guns and snipers deployed on the roof of Trinity College to the south had a clear shot at the rebel headquarters. By Wednesday, the toll of rebel, military, and civilian casualties was mounting. The government issued a directive ordering that "persons discovering dead bodies should inform the police or the Chief Medical Officer . . . immediately." Tom Clarke, who had impressed his comrades on Monday at Liberty Hall with his quiet but obvious joy, told a friend: "The game is up. We have lost."

Perhaps not surprisingly, the only man with military experience on the Military Council, James Connolly, became the de facto rebel commander as the battle took shape. Pearse, for all his tributes to battle and bloodshed, actually couldn't stand the sight of blood or suffering. Placid, almost passive, he observed the gunfire and chaos around him without saying much. Connolly, on the other hand, ordered the erecting of barricades, sent out patrols, inspected rebel positions in and around the GPO, and continued to insist that the forces of British capitalism would never shell private property. He found out otherwise on Wednesday, when the gunboat *Helga* steamed up the River Liffey and opened fire on rebel positions, including Connolly's Liberty Hall. A young officer, already regarded as one of the best fighters in the GPO, watched Connolly's vibrant, aggressive leadership with increasing admiration. "I would have followed him through hell had such action been necessary," the young officer, Michael Collins, wrote. He had less admiration for Pearse, whom he regarded as a dreamy, ineffective romantic.

By Thursday, the center of Dublin was aflame. Several women at headquarters, nurses and members of Cumann na mBan, were ordered to evacuate, for the rebel position was becoming increasingly untenable. Although the rebels under de Valera's command had beaten back an attack, other positions were weakening. The rest of the country had not risen. Dubliners themselves became increasingly hostile as destruction and civilian casualties mounted. Pearse knew exactly what would happen: "When we are all wiped out," he told one of his men, "people will blame us for everything, condemn us." But, he added, "in a few years they will see the meaning of what we tried to do."

With fires threatening to engulf the GPO, Connolly led a patrol outside the building to set up a command post elsewhere. A bullet smashed into his ankle as he scurried back to the GPO. The wound was terrible, as was its effect on morale. Connolly was on his back, out of action, relying on morphine to dull the awful pain. "Oh, God," he moaned, "did a man ever suffer more for his country."

The rebels evacuated the burning GPO on Friday. Pearse ordered a surrender on Saturday, April 29. A young woman from Cumann na mBan was sent to the College of Surgeons to alert the rebels there of the surrender. With the commander, Mallin, asleep, Countess Markievicz was summoned to receive the messenger and her news that the rebellion was over. She was stunned. "We could hold out for days here," she said. "Let's die at our posts." She finally was persuaded to obey Pearse's order.

The rebellion had lasted six days, the longest stretch of fighting in Ireland since 1798. Sixty-four rebels, 130 soldiers or police officers, and more than three hundred civilians died in the fighting. Hundreds more were wounded. The heart of Dublin was a smoking ruin. Ordinary business ground to a standstill, and soon some 100,000 Dubliners, a third of the city's population, were on relief. More than three thousand people, including seventy-nine women, were arrested. Many had had nothing to do with the rebellion.

The reaction in Dublin was exactly as Pearse had anticipated. The rebels, now prisoners, were bombarded with insults and jeers as they were marched to jail. As Countess Markievicz marched at the head of her small command, she heard shouts of "Shoot the traitors" and "Mad dogs!" Thousands of Dubliners were related to Irishmen fighting in the British army in France, fighting because they believed their loyalty would ensure that Home Rule would take effect as soon as the war in Europe ended. The rebellion seemed a violent repudiation of their sacrifice and courage. The rebels had claimed to speak and act in the name of Irish men and women. But now those very people rejected their claim.

The rebellion's leaders were taken into custody, and courts-martial began almost immediately. There was little doubt about the outcome, although a member of the Irish Parliamentary Party, John Dillon, feared what might happen next. He told his party leader, John Redmond, that he should "urge strongly on the government the extreme unwisdom of any wholesale shooting of prisoners. . . . If there were shootings of prisoners on any large scale the effect on public opinion might be disastrous in the extreme. So far the feeling of the population in Dublin is against the Sinn Feiners. But a reaction might very easily be created." Dillon understood the role that corpses played in Irish history. But, like the British authorities, he didn't understand that the rebellion was not the work of Sinn Féin.

Despite Dillon's advice, Pearse, Connolly, Clarke, Countess Markievicz, and more than one hundred others were condemned to death in front of a firing squad. The court-martial's presiding judge had little stomach for the task that was assigned him. After hearing Pearse deliver a speech from the dock worthy of his heroes Wolfe Tone and Robert Emmet, the judge told a friend: "I have just done one of the hardest tasks I have ever had to do. I have had to condemn to death one of the finest characters I have ever come across. There must be something very wrong in the state of things that makes a man like that a rebel."

Pearse and Clarke, along with the poet Thomas MacDonagh, were executed on May 3. Kathleen Clarke was summoned to her husband's cell in Kilmainham jail the night before. "I am to be shot at dawn," Clarke told her. "I'm glad it's a soldier's death I'm getting. I feared hanging or imprisonment. I had enough of imprisonment." He told Kathleen that he and his comrades had "struck the first successful blow for freedom." "It will not come today or tomorrow, and between this moment and freedom, Ireland will undergo hell." Kathleen Clarke underwent a personal hell. Not only was her husband executed, but so was her brother, Edward Daly, a prominent member of the Volunteers.

In his last hours, Padraig Pearse wrote two final poems, one to his mother, the other to his beloved brother, Willie, who also was under a death sentence. Willie Pearse ("You only have been my familiar friend," his brother wrote) was shot on May 4. So was Joseph Plunkett, the poet turned military planner. Several hours before Plunkett faced the firing squad, he and his fiancée, Grace Gifford, were married in the prison chapel. A priest performed the ceremony by candlelight. The groom wore handcuffs, and twenty soldiers with fixed bayonets were on hand as witnesses. After the ceremony, the groom was taken back to his cell. Later, the newlyweds spent fifteen minutes together before Plunkett was taken out to be shot.

John MacBride, the former husband of Maud Gonne, who had joined the rebellion at the last moment, was shot on May 5. On May 8, four more men, including Countess Markievicz's commander, Michael Mallin, were executed. The Countess herself was spared, her sentence commuted to life imprisonment. The special treatment infuriated the socialist and feminist in her.

The British military commander in Ireland, Major General Sir John Maxwell, was determined to see that those who led the rebellion pay in full for their treachery. But his pursuit of rough justice was fulfilling the second part of Pearse's prophecy. As each day brought either news of more executions or rumors of more, the public began to turn against Britain's pursuit of vengeance. The spat-upon rebels were becoming martyrs. In the House of Commons, John Dillon again warned the government of the cost of vengeance. Of the rebels, he said, "I am proud of their courage and if you were not so dense and stupid, as some of you English people are, you could have had these men fighting for you." History, he said, was slipping out of Britain's hands. The Easter Rising "is the first rebellion that ever took place in Ireland where you had a majority on your side. It is the fruit of our life work . . . and now you are washing our whole life work in a sea of blood."

In America, politicians who supported John Redmond and Home Rule found themselves reconsidering their opposition to the rebels and the tradition they represented. A prominent New York congressman, William Bourke Cockran, told an anti-execution protest rally in Carnegie Hall that "for thirty years I have been one of those who had believed . . . that it was the part of prudence for Irishmen to forget . . . the wrongs of the centuries. . . . And now, behold the consequences of this attempt. The vilest murders ever committed in Irish history are fresh before our eyes. The noblest Irishmen that have ever lived are dead . . . shot like dogs for asserting the immortal truths of patriotism!" In Washington, President Wilson's foreign affairs adviser, Colonel William House, warned that the executions would "come back to haunt us." An American ally of Redmond's sent a cable to the embattled parliamentary leader, with a brutal but candid analysis: "Your life-work destroyed by English brutality. Opinion widespread that promise of Home Rule was mockery."

James Connolly's wife, Lillie, and their oldest child, Nora, were summoned to Kilmainham jail just before midnight on Wednesday, May 10. "Well, Lillie, I suppose you know what this means," Connolly said when they arrived at his cell.

"But your beautiful life, James," a distraught Mrs. Connolly replied. "Your beautiful life."

"Hasn't it been a full life, Lillie, and isn't this a good end?"

At dawn on May 11, James Connolly was taken to the jail yard by stretcher. He was placed in a chair in front of a firing squad. A priest asked him if he would say a prayer for his executioners. "I will say a prayer for all brave men who do their duty according to their lights," he replied. And then the firing party did its duty. His body, like those of his comrades, was covered in lime and buried in the jail yard. There would be no corpses to mourn, no great funeral processions to join.

Fifteen rebels had been executed. Next in line was the mathematics instructor, Eamon de Valera, whose American citizenship represented a diplomatic disaster in the making. Britain, poised to send its divisions into action in the Battle of the Somme, was clinging to the hope that sooner or later America would enter the war against Germany. David Lloyd George, about to become Prime Minister, was convinced that Irish-American opinion could sway Washington to Germany's side. And so the British government was loath to alienate American public opinion by shooting one of its native-born citizens.

Roger Casement

(Shooting the naturalized American Tom Clarke apparently posed no such dilemma.)

Suddenly, then, the firing squads stopped. De Valera was spared, as were the remaining rebels given death sentences—all except one, Roger Casement, who hadn't actually taken part in the rebellion, but who had consorted with Britain's enemies in Germany. Casement was different from the others. He was a peer of the realm.

While in prison Casement told a friend that he knew he would never see Ireland again, and that he hoped that the Irish language would survive him. "I wonder how it will all be in a hundred years hence," he wrote, "and whether any of the old speech, and thoughts that sprang from it, and prayers that grew from it, will still survive." He was hanged on August 3, 1916. By the time he climbed the gallows, Irish opinion had been transformed, and the men and women Britain condemned as traitors were being hailed as heroes. In his tribute to the rebels of 1916, Yeats wrote that in Ireland all was "changed, changed utterly" by the Easter sacrifice.

And so it was.

Today, in the lobby of the General Post Office in Dublin, a statue of the dying Cuchulain commemorates the Easter rebels.

CHAPTER NINE

LIBERTY

As a BLOODY protest, the Easter Rebellion accomplished its goals. But the next generation of revolutionaries, while finding inspiration in the example of the Easter martyrs, would not be content with suicidal sacrifices or with eloquent speeches from the dock. Suicidal sacrifices ended as glorious failures; eloquent speeches preceded a trip to the gallows.

Inevitably, as control of Ireland passed from civil authorities to the military in the rebellion's aftermath, thousands of Irish men and women were arrested and detained without formal charges. The rebellion had hardly been the work of a massive conspiracy, but the authorities acted as if it were. Trade union members were suspected of Sinn Féin sympathies, never mind that Sinn Féin and the union movement were mortal enemies, and, moreover, that Sinn Féin had had nothing to do with the rebellion. General John Maxwell declared that he intended to "arrest all dangerous Sinn Feiners, including those who have taken an active part in the movement although not in the present rebellion."

General Maxwell was the de facto military dictator of Ireland, with some forty thousand troops at his disposal. No hint of unrepentant nationalism was beyond his reach—he even attempted to persuade the Bishop of Limerick, Edward O'Dwyer, to discipline two priests he judged to be too nationalistic. The Bishop replied: "I regard your action with horror, and I believe that it has outraged the conscience of the country. . . . Your regime has been one of the worst and blackest chapters in the history of the misgovernment of this country." Like nearly all of his clerical colleagues, the Bishop opposed the Easter Rebellion and the physical force tradition of Irish nationalism. Crude oppression, however, reminded him why that tradition existed in the first place.

The mass arrests and stepped-up military presence demonstrated bluntly that Ireland was in the control of an oppressive and alien government that could rule the country only by force. Nearly two thousand prisoners were transported en masse to an internment camp in north Wales called Frongoch and held without trial. The prisoners organized themselves into military units, and drilled and paraded. Officers met secretly to rehash the strategic mistakes of the Easter Rising. Those who wished to succeed Pearse, Connolly, and Clarke understood that they couldn't win pitched battles with a mighty army. The next rebellion would be brutal and ruthless, a war of skirmish and ambush, hit and run. And, unlike the Easter Rising, it would require the tacit support of at least a portion of the population. For the first time in Irish nationalist history, physical force separatism and political agitation would be made to work together rather than against each other, or despite each other. The movement would contest elections as well as the presence of the British army in Ireland.

A glimmer of support already was evident as the Irish began to agitate for release of those held in Frongoch and elsewhere. Kathleen Clarke, grieving over the loss of her husband, Tom, and her brother, Ned Daly, and struggling to raise her three boys, founded an Irish Volunteer Dependents Fund to raise money for the families of dead and imprisoned rebels. In an act of extraordinary selflessness, she and her husband had made provisions for the fund well before the rebellion, so she had slightly more than £3,000 for start-up money. The legacy would have spared Mrs. Clarke considerable financial difficulty in the coming years, particularly when, as a matter of principle, she refused government assistance for her family after her husband's death. She chose instead to apply her savings for the relief of women like herself and children like hers.

During the late summer of 1916, Clarke planned to sell a series of commemorative flags to raise money for the fund. A member of the dreaded intelligence division of the Royal Irish Constabulary, the so-called G Division, showed up at her door with a written notice from General Maxwell. The flag sale, Maxwell wrote, was likely to "prejudice recruiting of His Majesty's forces." The appalling, aimless slaughter at the ongoing Battle of the Somme probably was a more effective anti-recruiting device than anything Mrs. Clarke could dream of. Nevertheless, Maxwell informed Mrs. Clarke that she would be "liable to arrest and prosecution" for "taking part in such public collections."

Though she lost the battle over the flags, Clarke continued to raise money and recruit members for the fund. As undaunted as she had ever been, Clarke fought off the Parliamentary Party's attempts to use the money for partisan political agitation. The fund attracted not only militants like herself, but the suddenly sympathetic middle class and professionals who made up the core of support for Home Rule.

The fund eventually grew large enough to require the services of a paid, full-time secretary. It was for that task that Kathleen Clarke hired a young man from West Cork who had fought with her husband at the General Post Office, Michael Collins.

Collins was a Frongoch man who used his time in prison to great effect. He was among the camp's most active organizers, noted for a swaggering, cocky presence that earned him the nickname "The Big Fellow." It was less a reflection of his stature, although at six feet he was above average in height, than it was an indication of his sense of self-importance. He was the camp's champion in the hundred-yard dash and a ferocious wrestler known for gnawing on an opponent's ear. He was also the "head center," or chief organizer, of the Irish Republican Brotherhood's contingent in the camp. Not only did Collins befriend many a future ally and comrade while in His Majesty's custody, but he helped reorganize what became the core of the IRB's new leadership. In the battle to come, Collins's dual roles within the IRB and the rebel government made him the most powerful man in Ireland before he turned thirty.

Some of Frongoch's prisoners were released in midsummer, and the remainder, about six hundred, were allowed to return to Ireland in time for Christmas. At the same time, Lloyd George invited Andrew Bonar Law, a Conservative who sided with militant Unionists against Home Rule, to join the government in a coalition war cabinet. And Edward Carson, the instigator of armed resistance to Home Rule, became Great Britain's Attorney General, the chief enforcer of British law. The message to nationalists seemed clear: those who threatened treason in the name of Unionism could be forgiven and even rewarded.

Michael Collins and Arthur Griffith were among the beneficiaries of Lloyd George's Christmas gesture. Griffith had been imprisoned for a rebellion he had had nothing to do with. His Sinn Féin organization was in shambles, but, ironically, its mistaken association with the rebellion now gave it an aura of heroism and sacrifice.

Collins returned to his birthplace in west Cork, and was startled to discover that only two people in his native town of Clonakilty offered to shake his hand. He soon decided his place was in Dublin,

Michael Collins

where people were a bit more demonstrative toward the former prisoners. One of those who greeted him eagerly was Kathleen Clarke. Impressed by his "forceful personality," "wonderful magnetism," and "organizing ability," she hired him.

"After talking to him for a while, I decided he was just the man I had been hoping for," she wrote. Collins eagerly agreed with Clarke's insistence that the Easter Rising was not the end of another glorious failure, but simply the first shot in a revolution that would continue. She not only gave Collins the job of secretary of the dependents fund, she turned over to him all the information her husband had given her about IRB members throughout the country. As secretary of the fund, Collins had an excuse to travel around the countryside, soliciting support for the dependents in one conversation and reorganizing the IRB in another.

Michael Collins was twenty-six years old when he went to work for Clarke. Suspicious of the romantic cant that was as much a part of Irish revolutionary tradition as betrayed plans and generational succession, Collins himself was about to become one of Ireland's great romantic heroes and the most effective revolutionary leader in the long centuries of Irish rebellion. With a square jaw and sturdy shoulders, he looked the part of a military man. He stood out in the GPO as a highly competent junior officer who nevertheless had a delightfully irreverent sense of humor, and was not reluctant to display it in front of some rather unlikely people. After a heavy skirmish toward the end of the week's fighting, Collins asked Padraig Pearse if he and a friend could be excused from the GPO because they had dates on Saturday night. Pearse's reaction is not recorded. But when Pearse issued a stirring directive in mid–Easter week comparing the rebellion favorably with his hero Robert Emmet's "two-hour insurrection," Collins shook his head. Emmet, after all, wound up giving one of those great speeches from the dock and died a failure. "I do not think the Rising week was an appropriate time for . . . poetic phrases," Collins wrote. "[It] had the air of a Greek tragedy about it."

In the new strategy of revolution, Michael Collins determined that poetic phrases would be no substitute for effective political organization followed by ruthless action.

The first test of the changed public mood in Ireland came in early 1917, when James J. O'Kelly, the Fenian rebel turned Member of Parliament for Roscommon, died. A by-election to fill the vacant seat gave Sinn Féin and the IRB a chance to capitalize on the public's changed mood. The Parliamentary Party nominated one of its local operatives. The revolutionary movement supported the independent candidacy of George Plunkett, father of Joseph Mary Plunkett, the poet executed for his role in the Easter Rising. Plunkett was a papal count, from an old and distinguished Catholic family. He was a noted patron of the arts, a member of the Irish bar and of the Royal Dublin

Society—that is, until the society banned him because of his son's involvement in the rebellion.

Collins and Griffith, representing the military and political factions of a movement that was reviving and evolving by the day, threw themselves into the Plunkett campaign. Neither was quite sure what their candidate stood for and, in fact, Collins and Griffith had several intense quarrels over what would constitute a final settlement of the revolution. Griffith clung to his notion of a separate Parliament under a joint crown; Collins was pledged to bring about a republic with no ties to the British monarchy. Plunkett himself was silent on such issues, for he was ill for most of the campaign. He, too, had been rounded up and sent to prison after the rising for the crime of being his son's father.

Collins demonstrated a talent for one of the dark political arts that, many years later, would be called spin. He posted banners reading, "Plunkett is winning," although he had no such evidence. Griffith organized a get-out-the-vote drive, a task made no easier when a rare snowstorm fell on polling day. Nevertheless, not only did Count Plunkett win, he collected more than double the votes of the Parliamentary Party machine's candidate.

Padraig Pearse was right after all. The people had come to understand what he and his friends had tried to accomplish. By the summer of 1917, Sinn Féin's membership reached a quarter million in a country with just over four million people. Rallies around the country featured a ballad called "A Soldier's Song":

> Soldiers are we
> Whose lives are pledged to Ireland
> Some have come
> From a land beyond the waves.

"A Soldier's Song" would become Ireland's national anthem.

There were more electoral victories to come. In May, one of the remaining rebel prisoners, an IRB man named Joe McGuinness, won a seat in the House of Commons from County Longford. Once again, despite their differences, Collins and Griffith worked together to achieve a mandate. McGuinness won by thirty-eight votes. Lloyd George sought to break the nationalist momentum by putting together a conference to discuss a compromise settlement, including the possibility of partition. The conference included no militant nationalists, and the compromise went nowhere.

On June 18, 1917, the last prisoners held since Easter 1916 were released and sent home to Ireland. Six months had passed since Michael
Collins had walked the streets of his hometown unwelcomed. Now,
cheering crowds gathered to welcome the prisoners, including the senior surviving commandant of the rebellion, Eamon de Valera, who

Eamon de Valera

had, in fact, come "from a land beyond the waves." He had no trouble finding people to shake his hand. And on July 11, 1917, he was elected to Parliament from County Clare in an overwhelming victory with Sinn Féin's support. The election was a stinging blow to the Parliamentary Party and to Redmond personally, for the seat de Valera won had been held by Redmond's brother. Willie Redmond was among the tens of thousands of pro–Home Rule Irishmen who flocked to Britain's colors as a sign of their loyalty and gratitude. A captain in the Royal Irish Regiment, he was killed in France.

De Valera delivered his victory speech wearing the uniform of the Irish Volunteers, and declared that his victory was a "monument" to the men of Easter week. In October, Arthur Griffith, the founder and guiding light of Sinn Féin, stepped aside as the organization's president to allow de Valera to succeed him. The governing committee of Sinn Féin was reconstituted to include Collins and other physical force men, marking a break in the movement's insistence on passive resistance. It became a well-organized political party, prepared to contest the Parliamentary Party for control of the Irish political agenda as the country drifted ever closer to renewed crisis.

With Sinn Féin under his direction, de Valera then was elected president of the resurgent Volunteers. The strategy of combining physical force nationalism with political agitation could be summed up in a single name: Eamon de Valera.

He was thirty-five years old, the father of four young children. Though he would one day assert that to know what Ireland wanted he need only search his own heart, he was born in New York to an Irish immigrant mother and a Spanish father. He was sent to Ireland to live with his mother's relatives after his father died, although his mother continued to live in America. It was a curious decision, one that would later inspire grumblings that his mother had abandoned him, and that his paternity was in question. What is certain is that after making the transatlantic journey to Ireland in 1885, he was raised in a one-room, thatched-roof cottage in County Limerick in the impoverished, rural town of Bruree. It was a lonely place in any case, all the more so for a boy who was an emotional orphan and who bore an odd surname. He learned the daily chores of a farm, which gave him firsthand experience in the life of the improverished Irish farmer. He later developed a romantic, Yeats-like mystical belief in the purity and innocence of rural Irish life. As a teenager, however, he found that the romance of chores was lost on him. He decided he would not spend his life milking cows and digging potatoes.

Education was his way out. He earned a bachelor's degree at

Blackrock College and set out on a career as a mathematics teacher just as the Gaelic revival was reaching its zenith. He began studying the Irish language, and fell in love with both the ancient tongue and his slightly older instructor, Sinead Flanagan, whom he married. His pursuit of language prompted an interest in politics, and from politics the journey took him to militant nationalism. He joined the Irish Volunteers in 1913, and participated in the Howth gunrunning in 1914. He impressed his colleagues with his sincerity, devotion, and bravery, and, after joining the IRB, he rose through the Volunteer ranks to assume the post of commandant during Easter week. Troops under his command outside the main battle zone fought an effective engagement with British troops attempting to advance toward central Dublin, giving him the aura of a man who had beaten the British in a fair fight.

After the surrender in 1916, he was not among those dispatched to Frongoch, but was moved to five prisons during his stay of just over a year. He agitated for better food, organized work stoppages to protest unfair punishments, and otherwise made his presence known to the authorities as well as his fellow prisoners. And so it was the tall, austere, and devoutly Catholic native New Yorker who assumed the combined role of political chieftain and military commander as the Irish prepared to make full use of their two traditions of resistance.

To help those preparations along, the British continued their remarkable series of blunders.

Thomas Ashe, who had commanded a successful skirmish against the Royal Irish Constabulary outside Dublin in 1916, was one of the IRB's key reorganizers as well as one of Michael Collins's close friends. As the RIC began to crack down on Sinn Féin rallies during the summer and fall of 1917, Ashe was arrested and sent to Mountjoy jail in Dublin, where he joined more than two dozen Sinn Féiners arrested in the police sweep. They demanded status as prisoners of war, and commenced a hunger strike to press their demands. Ashe was subjected to an assortment of abuse for his obstinacy, including the removal of his bed.

Several days into the hunger strike, prison authorities decided to force-feed the malcontents. It was not a pretty process. A tube was shoved down their throats or nostrils and food, a mixture of beaten eggs and milk, was poured in. A doctor performed the task.

Though always gruesome, the procedure went terribly wrong when Ashe's turn came. He didn't resist, but somehow the doctor botched the force-feeding. Ashe died several hours after the tube was removed.

The Volunteers organized yet another spectacular nationalist funeral, which further demonstrated the changed attitudes in Ireland. Nearly forty thousand people marched in the funeral procession, including nine thousand uniformed Volunteers and nearly twenty thousand representatives of various trade unions. Countess Constance Markievicz, the veteran of 1916 whose life was spared because of her gender, followed the casket wearing her Irish Citizen Army uniform. Collins was chosen to give the funeral oration. Clad in his uniform and stricken with grief, he stepped forward after a squad of Volunteers fired a volley over Ashe's casket. There would be no Pearse-like celebrations of martyrdom, no citations of past failures. He spoke briefly in Irish and English: "Nothing additional remains to be said. That volley which we have just heard is the only speech which it is proper to make above the grave of a dead Fenian." A British newspaper complained that the bungled force-feeding had "made 100,000 Sinn Feiners out of 100,000 constitutional nationalists."

It didn't seem that way at first. Sinn Féin faltered during the next series of by-elections for Parliament in 1918, losing three straight to a seemingly revived Parliamentary Party. One of those losses came in an election in County Waterford to fill the seat of the Parliamentary Party's leader, John Redmond. Patient and trusting, but ultimately too passive and blind to the fact that he was being undercut by the very government to which he vowed allegiance, Redmond died in March 1918. His son campaigned while wearing a British army uniform, and won handily. Momentum seemed to be swinging against Sinn Féin. But then Britain blundered again.

Ireland had been exempt from Britain's conscription law since its passage in January 1916. The exemption was one of the wartime government's few politically sensitive decisions on Irish policy. But as World War I entered its final year, Britain had nearly exhausted its supply of young men. A revived Germany launched a huge offensive and was threatening to overrun Allied positions in France. In mid-April 1918, the government announced that conscription would be extended to Ireland. At the same time, Lloyd George offered to implement Home Rule immediately. It was a cynically diluted form of Home Rule, far less than what had been passed into law in 1914. The proposed Irish Parliament would not even control the country's post office, never mind taxation, policing, and other basic government functions. In addition, 40 percent of the seats in the Parliament's lower house would be reserved for Unionists, although they made up no more than a quarter of Ireland's total population.

It was an insult to Irish nationalists, and was immediately recognized as such despite Lloyd George's soothing words. "When the young men of Ireland are brought into the fighting line, it is imperative that they should feel they are not fighting for establishing a principle abroad which is denied to them at home," he said. The principle in question, of course, was self-determination for small nations, the reason given to sanctify the waste of a generation of England's young men.

Even for a man with a reputation for duplicity, it was an astonishing statement. The young men of Ireland had been on the fighting line all along. Another fourteen thousand had volunteered for service in 1917. And while they were fighting Britain's battle on behalf of small nations, the British government not only parlayed with Unionists who vowed to fight Irish self-determination in the name of loyalty to Britain, but interned and executed those who took up arms in the name of self-determination.

No Irish nationalist could possibly regard Lloyd George's gambit as a satisfactory settlement of a centuries-old conflict. The Irish conscription bill passed the House of Commons on April 16. Outraged members of the Irish Parliamentary Party walked out of the House in protest. It was to be their final gesture of defiance, and it was too late.

When the Home Rule proposal failed to win any popular support, the British government announced that it had uncovered evidence that Sinn Féin leaders were negotiating with the Germans to launch yet another rebellion in Ireland. Arrested in the so-called German plot were Eamon de Valera, Arthur Griffith, Kathleen Clarke, Countess Markievicz, and seventy others, including Count Plunkett.

The British tried mightily to persuade American political leaders of the enormity of the charges against the Sinn Féiners, implicitly connecting Irish-American militants like Devoy and his friends to pro-German sympathies. The proof they offered was nothing more than a rehash of the IRB's connections with Germany before the Easter Rebellion. The pro-British administration of Woodrow Wilson declined to publicize the dubious information. Secretary of State Robert Lansing told the President that colluding in such an obvious smear would "involve us in all sorts of difficulties with the Irish in this country."

Irish voters had an immediate chance to express their disgust at the turn of events. On June 19, 1918, prisoner Arthur Griffith was elected to Parliament in the first critical by-election since Sinn Féin seemed to be running out of steam earlier in the year. Voters in County Cavan turned out in huge numbers in response to Sinn Féin's brilliant election slogan for their imprisoned candidate: "Put him in to get him out."

The Sinn Féin leaders were still in custody when the world war ended at 11:00 A.M. on November 11, 1918. The British had promised that Home Rule would follow the war's end. Instead, Lloyd George announced that its implementation would be postponed indefinitely, and the military would continue to govern Irish affairs from Dublin Castle. In the meantime, with the war emergency over, Britain's Parliament was dissolved and a general election scheduled for mid-December. With the bulk of Sinn Féin's leadership in prison, it fell to Collins and his allies to organize a massive political campaign that would transform the election into a referendum on Ireland's claim to independence. Forty-eight Sinn Féin candidates were chosen from the ranks of the prisoners, and the party's literature made clear that they stood not for Home Rule, but for independence. One piece of campaign literature listed the great heroes of the past whose names were not on the ballot, but whose place in folk memory was assured: Brian Boru, Father John Murphy, Lord Edward Fitzgerald, Wolfe Tone, Robert Emmet, Padraig Pearse, James Connolly, and the most recent martyr, Thomas Ashe. "Why did they die?" the poster asked. "They died to rescue the liberation of the oldest political prisoner in the world—Ireland!"

Working to Sinn Féin's advantage was the greatest expansion of the franchise since the 1880s. More than 800,000 women over thirty were eligible to vote for the first time, and the total eligible electorate, including all males age twenty-one or over, was just short of two million. Elimination of the last property qualifications had increased the electorate from about 700,000 people before the war.

The results were spectacular. Sinn Féin won seventy-three of Ireland's 105 seats. The Parliamentary Party, the dominant force in Irish politics since the days of Isaac Butt and Charles Stewart Parnell, won just six seats. Before the election, the party had held eighty seats.

Nearly three quarters of Ireland's elected representatives in Parliament were commited to full independence in an undivided Ireland. The world war had been fought for the rights of small nations and to make the world safe for democracy, or so the victorious Allies had asserted. The small nation of Ireland made its claim to self-determination through a peaceful and democratic election. Sinn Féin hoped the demonstration would persuade the victorious powers,

America in particular, to give Ireland a hearing during the redrawing of the world's borders.

Failing that, there could be only one other alternative. On January 17, 1919, the military authorities in Ireland telegraphed Sir Henry Wilson, the chief of the Imperial General Staff—the highest-ranking army officer in Britain—with a request for tanks and machine guns. Wilson, an Anglo-Irishman born in County Longford, was astonished. "We are sitting on top of a mine which may go up at any minute," he wrote in his diary.

The victorious Sinn Féin candidates who were not in prison or abroad, about twenty-seven total, gathered in Dublin's Mansion House on January 21, 1919, to proclaim the founding of an Irish Parliament, or as it was formally known, the Dáil Eireann. The Dáil issued a declaration of independence, saying that "we declare that the nation's sovereignty extends not only to all men and women of the nation, but to all its material possessions . . . we re-affirm that all rights to private property must be subordinated to the public right and welfare."

Among the Dáil's other pronouncements was a casual reference to hostilities between the Irish and English. "The existing state of war between Ireland and England can never be ended until Ireland is . . . evacuated by the armed forces of England," the Dáil declared. On the day the Dáil met, a party of Volunteers killed two members of the Royal Irish Constabulary in County Tipperary as they transported explosives to a quarry. The constables were the first casualties of what became Ireland's War of Independence. They not only were Irish themselves, but were Catholics. The Volunteers, however, were ruthlessly nonsectarian in their choice of targets. To wear the uniform of British administration, whether as a soldier or a police constable, meant that one would be considered an enemy of the rebel government and its army. Eighteen more constables were shot in 1919 during a series of uncoordinated attacks.

The police, many of whom were unarmed, were easy targets, so easy in fact that the attacks on them were bitterly condemned in the press and in the broader forum of public opinion. But as the Volunteers evolved into a force that became known as the Irish Republican Army, the nine thousand members of the Royal Irish Constabulary came to be regarded not as cops on a beat, but as the eyes and ears of the British administration, not very different from the 38,000 British soldiers in Ireland. And if they could be intimidated, if recruits could be scared off and older constables persuaded to retire while they still had their lives, Britain would have no choice but to consider wholesale military action with the bodies of nearly a million young men in the freshly dug graves of France.

And so rebellion broke out again in Ireland, not with a great demonstration, not with futile marching, not with pitched battles, but with brutal ambushes designed to demoralize representatives of the British government.

With Ireland drifting toward all-out war, a young medical student and onetime altar boy in Dublin reported to his sister that he had taken the Volunteers' oath of allegiance to the newly created Dáil. "That's good," she said. "Now you're a real army."

Seventeen-year-old Kevin Barry joined the Volunteers in the fall of 1917, after the brutal death of Thomas Ashe by botched force-feeding. He had shown a keen interest in nationalism years earlier, thanks in part to the unending rituals of unrepentant Irish nationalism. He was only six when his father, who owned a dairy farm and business, died. But the family was comfortable enough to send young Kevin to some of Dublin's most renowned schools, including the Jesuit-run Belvedere College, whose alumni included James Joyce.

When he was thirteen, he attended a concert commemorating the memory of the Manchester Martyrs, the three men hanged for murder in Manchester, England, in 1867 whose cry of "God Save Ireland" was part of the Fenian canon. The young Barry came away from the concert filled with martial spirit and ready to join Countess Markievicz's Fianna na hEireann Boy Scout movement, but his family talked him out of it.

In 1919, Kevin Barry was a first-year student of medicine at University College, Dublin. He was bright enough to win a merit-based scholarship given annually by the Dublin Corporation, the city's governing body, and, when not immersed in his studies, he was a scholastic rugby player known for his energetic tackles although he was of average size at about five feet, nine inches. Portraits taken at the time show a young man with slicked-back hair, slightly protruding ears, and a cocky half-grin. Young Kevin liked to dance, too, but the friends he made and who followed him to socials in Dublin had no idea that he was leading a double life. In addition to his studies, his rugby, and his dancing, he was drilling at night with the Dublin Brigade, Irish Volunteers.

As part of his schoolwork, he kept a journal of essays in which he expounded on a range of topics. One of his favorite books, he recorded, was *A Tale of Two Cities*. "The chapters relating the outbreak of the Revolution are especially fine," he wrote. "They show how the patience of a long-suffering people is tested to the utmost;

Kevin Barry

how they worked and plotted secretly to regain their freedom and how when the chance came they seized it. The outburst of long bottled-up fury, of pent-up hate, and long-standing grievances, is splendidly described." In an essay entitled "Uses of History," he wrote: "The British have tried for 700 years to abolish Irish tradition and write false histories, but owing to the effects of the poets . . . they have failed."

He would later be described as a born soldier, but to his friends at college, Kevin Barry seemed to be no more, and no less, than a young man from a respectable home who scrapped like hell in rugby matches and spent his weekend nights at dances. Just like any other young man with a bright future.

While in Lincoln jail, Eamon de Valera, a devout Roman Catholic, not only attended Mass but assisted the chaplain. He was, in essence, an adult altar boy. Rewards for such piety were supposed to come only in the hereafter. De Valera, however, didn't have to wait that long.

The chaplain regularly left his key to the prison's inner doors and gate exposed in the chapel's small sacristy, a routine de Valera couldn't help but notice. He found an excuse to retreat to the sacristy before Mass, quickly made an impression of the key using warm wax from the chapel's candles, and then drew a replica of the key to its exact dimensions. The seemingly harmless drawing found its way to Michael Collins, who immediately began preparations for what promised to be the latest in a long tradition of Irish nationalist jail-breaks. A copy of the key was sent to de Valera in a cake. It didn't work. Neither did the next two. The fourth, however, fit perfectly. Collins and his comrade Harry Boland showed up outside Lincoln jail in the dark of night on February 3, 1919, with a key of their own. De Valera made his way through the prison's inner doors with his key, and within minutes, he was outside and being hustled into a waiting car. He remained a fugitive as news of the audacious adventure captured headlines.

Collins arranged hiding places for de Valera in England until he could be brought back to Dublin with great fanfare. But while de Valera was underground, Britain released all those arrested in the German plot crackdown, making his return to Ireland a good deal less dramatic. He took his place in the Dáil in April, and was elected Prime Minister. Collins was named Finance Minister, Arthur Griffith, Minister for Home Affairs, and Countess Markievicz, Labor Minister.

Though he was the political leader of a rebel government about to fight for its very existence, de Valera decided that his place was in his native country—America. There, he believed, he might win for the rebel Irish government the recognition it was not going to receive among the Allied powers remaking the world in the postwar meetings at the Palace of Versailles. Even with a new generation of formidable rebels, the Irish could not take on the British Empire by themselves. Irish America, with its money, its political clout, and its underground network of revolutionaries, would be Ireland's ally in its decisive hour.

Collins, preparing to unleash a brutal war on Crown forces, was asked to make the necessary arrangements to smuggle de Valera to his native city of New York. De Valera refashioned his Irish title of Pri-omh Aire, or Prime Minister, into that of President of the Irish Republic, boarded a ship as a stowaway, and landed in Manhattan on June 11, 1919. After allowing him time to rest and visit his remarried mother in Rochester, New York, the Irish-American network arranged a press conference worthy of de Valera's title. A motorcade whisked him to the Waldorf-Astoria hotel, where he addressed dozens of reporters and held forth very much like a man on a vital diplomatic mission. It was an emotional moment for the American Irish. A man bearing the title of President of the Irish Republic had come to America to enlist their support—and he was a native-born American himself. During a reception that lasted long after midnight, the aging leader of the Irish-American revolutionary movement, John Devoy, sized up this man half his age. De Valera, he decided, "is the best leader Ireland has had for a century."

De Valera spent the next eighteen months in America. And while Ireland went to war, so did he. His enemies, however, were the established leaders of Irish America. Though he raised $5 million for the Dáil and its war effort (some $3 million of it remained in America for the duration of the war) and commanded great public attention, he and Devoy and their respective allies engaged in a quarrel the likes of which had been seldom seen in the annals of Irish factional fighting. When it was over, Devoy had been ousted temporarily from the Irish revolutionary movement after more than five decades of agitation, and de Valera, incredibly, stepped on so many toes with his clumsy political lobbying that neither of the two U.S. presidential nominating conventions of 1920 issued a statement about Ireland's claim to self-government. The Republican Party had been prepared to pass a Devoy-authored statement of sympathy for Irish self-determination, but de Valera exploded when he realized that the plank contained no specific mention of the Irish Republic. The plank was withdrawn, and the Democrats, under no pressure from their partisan foes, chose to ignore the issue despite, or because of, de Valera's presence at their convention.

Just after de Valera left for New York, Michael Collins added two new titles to that of Minister of Finance for the rebel Irish government. In June 1919, he was named Director of Intelligence, a job he had been performing long before he received official recognition from his colleagues. And in July, he was named President of the Supreme Council of the Irish Republican Brotherhood. According to the brotherhood's constitution, the Supreme Council was, in fact, the government of the Irish Republic, and its President was the legal head of that government. Members of the IRB pledged their loyalty to that secret government. With the formation of the Dáil, IRB loyalties were conflicted. But as war slowly crept through the countryside, there was little point in dwelling on such matters of ideology.

Throughout 1919, as the Volunteers carried out their intermittent attacks on the Royal Irish Constabulary, the Dáil sought to establish itself as a genuine government in at least some parts of the country, meeting openly in Dublin's Mansion House, organizing a loan to finance its growing administrative and military costs, appointing local government officials, and establishing its own courts. Among the rebel judges was Kathleen Clarke, who served as chairman of the Republican courts for north Dublin despite her lack of legal experience. Sessions were held wherever space could be found, and special care was given that the space was beyond the reach of British raiding parties. In establishing its own institutions, the Dáil furthered its claim to be a legitimate government, one deserving of support not only from the local population, but from the Irish-Americans who were flocking to see de Valera and opening their wallets for the cause.

Meanwhile, the Volunteers, with an effective fighting force of no more than about five thousand, continued to carry out small-scale attacks on constables through 1919, while Collins's counterintelligence agents targeted detectives. The fighting was raised a notch in September when the Cork Brigade attacked a party of British soldiers, killing one and wounding four. A jury refused to rule that the soldier's death was a murder, prompting some two hundred British soldiers to wreck portions of the town of Fermoy, County Cork. British authorities then took the drastic step of suppressing the Dáil, Sinn Féin, Cumann na mBan, and any propaganda organs tied to the groups. Military rule was stepped up, and soldiers and police regularly raided homes and arrested suspected Sinn Féiners. Twenty thousand homes were raided in 1919 and the first three months of 1920, and some four hundred people arrested and transported to prison in Britain. Soldiers with fixed bayonets patrolled the streets of Dublin.

In de Valera's absence, Michael Collins became both the military and political leader of the Irish rebellion. As Minister of Finance, he was charged with the critical job of financing an unrecognized government as well as an army dismissed as a band of cutthroat terrorists.

As Director of Intelligence, Collins turned Britain's centuries-old game of spying on its ear as he built an astounding system of intelligence of his own, penetrating the police, the military, and even Dublin Castle itself. He broadened his portfolio to build a counterespionage unit that came to be known as the Squad. Trained as assassins, the Squad targeted individual police constables, detectives, and military intelligence officers. Such targets could not be killed in traditional, set-piece battles. They would be killed one by one, in their own homes, in front of spouses, as they left church. They were killed not to gain a territorial advantage; they were killed because of what they knew.

Through the power of the Squad, his leadership of the IRB, and his role as director of organization of the Volunteers, Collins was recognized as the de facto commander in chief of the army, even though others held the appropriate titles. The Defense Minister was the brave and fanatical Cathal Brugha, who suffered from grave wounds he received during the Easter Rebellion. Brugha, however, was a part-time minister, and he deferred to the Volunteers' chief of staff, Richard Mulcahy, a thirty-three-year-old engineer, Gaelic Leaguer, and veteran of the Easter Rebellion who unselfishly allowed Collins to break down traditional chains of command in his pursuit of a hit-and-run war. Mulcahy was a friend and ally of Collins, a fellow graduate of Frongoch, and he understood Collins's importance as a Cabinet officer, a rebel, an organizer, and a man of action. He also knew that Collins was the president of Ireland's ultimate secret society, the IRB. Mulcahy and Collins worked side by side, the staff officer and the freelance, one a cautious organization man who was a master of logistics, the other a high-spirited, instinctive, and natural-born leader who was far more willing than Mulcahy to sanction uncoordinated raids and ambushes of constables. Together, they made a formidable team.

Born in 1886, Mulcahy was one of eight children in a devout Catholic family from Waterford—four of his five sisters became nuns. He was a married man and a father when he became the day-to-day organizer of the Volunteers. Reserved, disciplined, and dignified, Mulcahy was yet another rebel who made the journey from the cultural nationalism of Yeats, Douglas Hyde, and Lady Gregory to the revolutionary republicanism of Padraig Pearse, Tom Clarke, and Countess Markievicz.

Politics and nationalism were absent from the Mulcahy household when he was a child, but as a young adult working in a civil service job with the post office, Mulcahy began reading one of Arthur Grif-

Richard Mulcahy

fith's newspapers, *The United Irishman.* The effect was transforming: Griffith, Mulcahy later wrote, explained "the traditions and resources of Ireland, portrayed its mission and gave us . . . our dream." Mulcahy was a cautious man, as his first career choice—the post office— indicated, and his fledgling nationalism reflected his sober-minded moderation. So Griffith, who argued for Irish self-government under a joint crown with Britain, was a natural mentor. But as Mulcahy pursued his dream, he joined a particularly militant branch of Hyde's Gaelic League in Dublin. There, he met Thomas Ashe, Michael Collins, and his future superior, Cathal Brugha. He joined the Irish Republican Brotherhood soon afterward, around 1908.

He was Ashe's second in command during Easter week as they fought a brief but successful skirmish with the Royal Irish Constabulary in Ashbourne, in County Meath. After Pearse's surrender, Mulcahy was arrested and sent to Frongoch, where he renewed his friendship with Collins. Upon his release, he rejoined the Volunteers and the Gaelic League, and was appointed the Volunteers' chief of staff in 1918. A young recruit named Ernie O'Malley, a onetime medical student who witnessed the Easter rebellion and became a rebel as a result, described Mulcahy as "neat and trim, quiet. He had a shrewd cold look. . . . He spoke slowly, stressing words nasally. His face was of the thin type, clean-shaven with bushy eyebrows." His grasp of detail, patience, and organizational skills marked him as a logical choice for chief of staff. But while Collins received credit as the guiding spirit of the guerrilla war, Mulcahy also played a critical role in developing the IRA strategy of hit-and-run. With 38,000 British troops in Ireland in 1919 (and more on the way) to complement ten thousand members of the Royal Irish Constabulary, Mulcahy's assignment was daunting, and the odds against him overwhelming.

In late December 1919, British Prime Minister Lloyd George delivered his country's first political, as opposed to military, response to the changed sentiment in Ireland. He offered another Home Rule bill.

This one was quite different from the Home Rule that had been passed into law in 1914 but never implemented, even after 200,000 Irishmen joined the British army. The new bill set up not one, but two Home Rule Parliaments in Ireland. One, in Dublin, would control a few local government functions in twenty-six counties, from Donegal in northern Ulster to Galway in the west and Cork in the south. The other Parliament would be based in Belfast, and would control six of Ulster's nine counties that made up the heart of Protestant, Unionist northeast Ireland. It was, then, a bill to partition Ireland, and was called the Better Government of Ireland bill of 1920. The *Irish Times,* the voice of the Anglo-Irish Protestant Ascendancy in Dublin, made its view clear: "We yearn for peace, but in Mr. Lloyd George's proposal we see not peace but a sword."

In 1920, sporadic attacks on the police gave way to a more systematic and coordinated campaign against Crown targets. In reply, the

British unleashed a paramilitary force that brought war to Ireland's civilian population, viewed as co-conspirators with the rebel army. The rebels, increasingly referred to as the IRA, wore no uniforms to distinguish combatant from civilian, and, in 1920, British policy also refused to recognize such distinctions. Troops and police enforced a curfew in Dublin, and the whole of Ireland was in a state of siege. Two hundred unarmed civilians were killed by Crown forces before the year was out. The Irish called 1920 the Year of the Terror.

Early in the year, Mulcahy ordered the Cork Volunteers to escalate the war by attacking RIC barracks. Soon the tactic was put into place wherever possible. The RIC operated two thousand barracks, some of them thinly defended, and they functioned as both a symbol of Ireland's massive police presence and a genuine threat to rebel operations. A series of attacks led the police to abandon some of their facilities in the countryside, and as they did, Mulcahy ordered the simultaneous burning of 150 deserted barracks in early April. Tactically, the action was of little value. Symbolically, however, it was a spectactular demonstration of defiance. Members of the RIC resigned by the hundreds, and there were few fresh bodies with which to replace them. Sir Henry Wilson, chief of the Imperial General Staff, saw a bad ending if more aggressive steps weren't taken. "I really believe that we shall be kicked out" of Ireland, he confided to his diary.

The attacks on police earned the rebels the stinging condemnation of the Catholic Church. Priests and bishops, like many later commentators, took note that the rebels' victims tended to be Irish and Catholic. British observers in particular found the IRA's attacks on Irish Catholics worthy of contemptuous irony. But while men like Richard Mulcahy were devout Catholics, they were fighting what they regarded as a war of liberation, not of religion. To the political and military leadership of the rebel movement, it was a question of choosing sides, not denominations.

British policy had it that the Irish were engaged not in warfare but in criminal activity, and so the government continued to regard the conflict as a matter mainly for the police, not for the troops it had on hand in Ireland. Rather than deploy them wholesale and declare martial law, the British decided to recruit new members for the RIC from former soldiers in Britain. Their mix-and-match uniforms gave them their name—the Black and Tans, after a pack of race hounds of similiar hues. Combined with other new recruits for the RIC's auxiliary division, known as the Auxiliaries, the deployment of this new force led to horrors reminiscent of General Lake's march through Ulster and County Wexford in 1797–98.

The Black and Tans concluded that the guerrillas could operate only through the tacit, or even outright, support of at least a sizable portion of the citizenry. If the citizens could be intimidated, it was thought, they would pretty soon give up their rebel sympathies.

When the Volunteers killed a constable, the Black and Tans responded with outright murder, beatings, torture, or destruction of important rural facilities like creameries. Families often left their homes at night and slept in fields to escape the nighttime maurading of His Majesty's forces. To do otherwise was to risk torture or summary execution.

Kathleen Clarke and her family came in for special attention throughout the terrible year. Her house was a favorite target of the rampaging security forces, who invited themselves in during the early morning hours. Clarke was, admittedly, not a neutral observer but an out-and-out supporter of the rebel government. But her elderly mother could hardly have posed a threat to the administration of British law and justice, and yet she was beaten with a rifle butt during a raid. She never recovered from the injury, and died five years later in terrible pain.

But the raiding parties never got their hands on the man in charge—Michael Collins, who chose to hide out in the open, where nobody was looking. Collins brazenly carried out his business, often meeting his agents in Vaughn's Hotel in central Dublin, while rumors circulated of a £10,000 price on his head. Cocky by nature anyway, Collins's refusal to go into hiding also was a tribute to the work of his spies, who seemed to know what the police were up to before the police themselves knew. Mulcahy, too, managed to evade arrest, although he was not as dashing as Collins, who daily cycled through the streets of Dublin to his job as director of political assassination.

The IRA's general headquarters was, like the IRA itself, often just a half-step ahead of the police. And as the war intensified and the IRA's strategy centralized, Mulcahy's role at GHQ became critical. A guerrilla war might seem to an outsider to be formless and chaotic, but the paper flow at GHQ indicated otherwise. Local commanders requested not only arms, ammunition, and provisions, but direction on such matters as reprisals, the execution of spies, the treatment of deserters, and an IRA-enforced boycott of merchants who did business with Crown forces. Mulcahy issued a series of general orders offering guidelines to his local commanders on their conduct of the war. While Collins was the swashbuckler, the intuitive, combative guerrilla genius, Mulcahy was a steady hand who understood that success depended not only on audacity, but on public support.

And so, when a rogue IRA member or an agent provocateur threatened a doctor in Galway who was treating a member of the hated RIC Auxiliaries, Mulcahy ordered the local brigade commandant to see to it that the doctor was "given any protection that may be necessary." When a brigade commandant in Limerick asked for advice about dealing with ordinary citizens who spoke with British soldiers or police, Mulcahy said that such people should be advised "in a formal and dignified communication . . . that their association with the enemy at the present time places them in the position wittingly or unwittingly of being potential spies."

In keeping at least a portion of the public sympathetic to the rebels in an awful and intensely personal war, Mulcahy received no end of assistance from his enemy, particularly as the terrible year of 1920 drew to a close.

On August 12, 1920, an IRA commandant named Terence Mac-Swiney was arrested outside Cork City Hall. MacSwiney was the city's Lord Mayor, succeeding another republican activist, Tomas MacCurtain, who was assassinated in his bedroom in February 1920. Men in blackened faces shot him, fled, and were never apprehended. But a coroner's jury, made up of local citizens, issued a verdict of murder against Prime Minister Lloyd George and other officials, including a local supervisor of the RIC named Swanzy. The IRA assassinated Swanzy in the Ulster town of Lisburn, County Antrim, and, in turn, Catholic homes in Lisburn were set on fire, and in Belfast, sixteen Catholic men and women were killed in an anti-Catholic pogrom.

In his inaugural speech as MacCurtain's successor, MacSwiney had made it clear that he was not intimidated. "This contest on our side is not one of rivalry or vengeance, but of endurance," he said. "It is not those who can inflict the most, but those that can suffer the most, who will conquer."

When MacSwiney was brought before a court for possessing documents "likely to cause disaffection to His Majesty," he announced that he would immediately begin a hunger strike. "I have decided that I shall be free, alive or dead, within a month," he said. He misjudged his power to endure, and Britain's power to inflict, punishment. After two months, he was neither dead nor free, but was a powerful symbol of the rebellion. As he deteriorated, longshoremen in America prepared to call a work stoppage to demand his release. A quarter million South American Catholics petitioned the Pope to intervene on his behalf. In New York, the rebel government's envoy to the Irish-American movement, a physician named Patrick McCartan, noted that "from the banker in his club to the tramp in the ditch, few ate without at least a passing thought of the Lord Mayor of Cork."

Lloyd George refused to back down, saying that if he did so, "a complete breakdown of the whole machinery of law and government would follow." But that vaunted machine already was broken.

After fifty-seven days without food, MacSwiney issued a statement, in the form of prayer, to his fellow rebels. "I offer my pain for Ireland," he wrote. "I offer my suffering here for our martyred people, beseeching Thee, oh God, to grant them the nerve and strength and grace to withstand the present terror in Ireland."

On the morning of September 20, 1920, as MacSwiney was into his second month without food, Kevin Barry went to Mass, received Holy Communion, and then joined a small party of his IRA comrades on Bolton Street in Dublin. Barry and the others had orders to ambush a British army truck as it picked up a consignment of bread from a nearby bakery. Conveniently enough, the ambush was scheduled for 11:00 A.M., giving Barry time to conduct his business and return to class in time for an examination at 2:00 P.M.

The IRA men wanted weapons, and the soldiers had them. Armed with a .38 Mauser, Barry and his fellow members of Company C were to surround the truck, disarm the soldiers, take the weapons, and flee. Although the truck was about thirty minutes late, everything else seemed to fall in place at first. Barry covered the back of the truck, and when the five soldiers in the back realized they were surrounded, they complied with the order to lay down their weapons.

Then a shot rang out, possibly a warning shot from an uncovered soldier in the front. Barry and the rest of the ambush party opened fire. Barry's gun jammed twice; by the second time, he was alone. His comrades had fled. He dove under the truck, hoping nobody would notice him in the confusion, but it was to no avail, and he was placed under arrest. One of the soldiers he had shot was dead.

Barry was taken to a military facility, where an officer asked him about the identity and whereabouts of his comrades. He declined to give them, even though a sergeant held a bayonet to his stomach. "The sergeant was then asked to turn my face to the wall and point the bayonet at my back," Barry later testified. "I was so turned. The sergeant then said he would run the bayonet into me if I did not tell." He didn't. The sergeant put away the bayonet, ordered Barry to lie face down on the floor, and then, with his knees planted on Barry's back, the sergeant twisted the suspect's arm for about five minutes. An officer continued to ask Barry to identify his comrades. He continued to refuse.

He was removed to Mountjoy jail, and his case was brought before a court-martial. On October 20, the court found eighteen-year-old Kevin Barry guilty of murder and ordered him to be hanged. The execution was scheduled for November 1.

Terence MacSwiney died on October 25, on the seventy-fourth day of his hunger strike. His was yet another huge Irish funeral, with an archbishop and two bishops presiding over the requiem Mass. His sacrifice had won admiration throughout the world at a time when Prime Minister Lloyd George and Colonial Secretary Winston Churchill were insisting that the rebels in Ireland were nothing more than, in Churchill's words, a "murder gang." A placard was raised in front of Cork's City Hall, where two consecutive Lord Mayors had fallen victim to the war: "Terence MacSwiney, murdered by the Foreign Enemy, in the Fourth Year of the Republic."

The public outcry that MacSwiney's suffering inspired was transferred to the condemned Kevin Barry, awaiting his fate in Mountjoy jail. Foreign newspapers covered the countdown to November 1 as world opinion cried out for mercy. In New York on October 30, Eamon de Valera recorded a statement paying tribute to MacSwiney and calling further attention to Barry's case. He then recited lines that once thrilled a Dublin theater audience:

> *They shall be remembered forever*
> *They shall be alive forever,*
> *They shall be speaking forever*
> *The people shall hear them forever.*

They were the words of Yeats, spoken by Maud Gonne, in *Cathleen ni Houilihan*.

Kevin Barry went to his death on a Monday morning, November 1, 1920, after hearing two Masses in his cell. A priest who walked with him to the scaffold, Father John Waters, wrote to Barry's mother: "You are the mother, my dear Mrs. Barry, of one of the bravest and best boys I have ever known. His death was one of the most holy, and your dear boy is waiting for you now, beyond the reach of sorrow or trial."

The execution further outraged public opinion, in Ireland and throughout the world. Young Barry's courage, his refusal to inform on his comrades, earned him a revered place in the nationalist pantheon. Poems and ballads were written to his memory, the most famous of which contained the lines:

> *In Mountjoy Jail one Monday morning*
> *High upon the gallows tree*
> *Kevin Barry gave his young life*
> *For the cause of liberty.*

A little more than a week after Kevin Barry's death, Prime Minister Lloyd George announced that Britain had "murder by the throat" in Ireland. It was a premature assessment, for on Sunday morning, November 21, Michael Collins sent his team of killers into action. Within a matter of hours, a horrified Dublin Castle realized that its counter-intelligence operation no longer existed. Murder, in fact, had Britain by the throat. Twelve British intelligence officers were executed, some of them shot in front of their wives while in bed.

It was brutal, ruthless, and classic Michael Collins. He was rewriting the rules of warfare, anticipating the day when information was as important as territory and armament. He was also rewriting history, avenging long-dead Fenians done in by Britain's spies and informers. In the British press, the mysterious Michael Collins was condemned as a murderous gangster and a vicious terrorist—the sort of man one does not invite to the negotiating table. Churchill contended that Britain would never "surrender to a miserable gang of cowardly assassins," likening them to "the human leopards of West Africa."

When the extent of the horror became apparent that Sunday afternoon, a troop of Auxiliaries and Black and Tans made their way to Croke Park, a sports stadium in Dublin and the site of an Irish football match that afternoon. The troops opened fire on the crowd, spraying bullets at random. Fourteen people, including one player, were killed. Hundreds more were wounded. The troops suffered no casualties. There were more horrors to come. After an IRA ambush killed seventeen Auxiliaries on November 28, British troops burned the center of Cork city, the home of Tomas MacCurtain and Terence MacSwiney.

Unbeknownst to the combatants, by the end of 1920, Lloyd George was sending peace feelers to Arthur Griffith, standing in for de Valera as the head of the Dáil government. In the meantime, the Better Government of Ireland Act formally became law, officially establishing a six-county state called Northern Ireland and governed by a Parliament in Belfast. The Dáil and the IRA refused to recognize the partition and continued to fight for a united Ireland under a single, independent legislature.

De Valera finally returned to Ireland in late 1920 as back-channel peace talks were underway in earnest. His American mission was a financial success, but he failed in his stated objective of winning American political support for the Dáil. He went to his native land certain that he could persuade the Wilson administration to support not just the ambiguous idea of Irish self-determination, but an Irish Republic. Irish-American agitators like Devoy understood that Wilson would not antagonize Lloyd George and the British, and pleaded instead for vaguely worded declarations of support for the Irish. De Valera refused to compromise, so he returned to Ireland with no declarations from America. And his obstinacy split the Irish-American movement, the wild card in Anglo-Irish relations, while an Irish army fought desperately for long-sought liberty.

Although Sinn Féin didn't recognize the Better Government of Ireland Act, it chose to contest elections for the new Home Rule Parliament in Belfast and the proposed Home Rule Parliament in Dublin in May 1921. Sinn Féin used the election to its own end, winning 124 of 128 districts in the twenty-six counties outside the northeast. The Sinn Féin victors met and constituted themselves not as a Home Rule Parliament, but as the Second Dáil, claiming legal governing authority over all of Ireland, including the northeast. The anti-nationalist Unionist Party dominated the election in Northern Ireland.

As murmurs of peace made their way to Dublin, de Valera argued for a dramatic show of traditional military force. He had never been entirely comfortable with the guerrilla tactics of Collins, Mulcahy, and their commanders in the field. So on May 25, an IRA contingent of one hundred men attacked the Custom House, an eighteenth-century landmark along the River Liffey and, as the repository of administrative records, a symbol of British rule. The rebels set the building afire and won a dramatic publicity victory, but at considerable cost. Six IRA men were killed, which, in a small army, was bad enough, but eighty were captured, and many of the prisoners were among the rebel army's top men. The venture into traditional warfare was a disaster, and Collins knew it. The next day, British troops raided an office Collins used, and just missed capturing Collins himself.

The Custom House assault did not stop the discreet peace talks. King George V, in Belfast to open the Home Rule Parliament for Northern Ireland on June 22, held out an olive branch to the rebels as he presided over a ceremony that officially partitioned the island. De Valera was arrested the same day, but in a sign of how events were moving, an embarrassed British government ordered his release the next day. Lloyd George then made official what was happening behind the scenes: to the astonishment of the Cabinet colleagues he had kept in the dark for six months, Lloyd George sent a letter to de Valera inviting him to a conference in London.

It was a moment of breathtaking significance in the long history of Anglo-Irish conflict. And from the talks with de Valera came another milestone: a formal truce between Crown forces and the IRA. It was signed with appropriate ceremony in Dublin's Mansion House, where the Dáil had declared Ireland's independence in 1919. The Irish rebels hadn't necessarily won, but they hadn't been beaten, either. They were still in the field when the British Empire sued for peace. After centuries of conflict, after the sacrifice of dedicated and patriotic men and women easily ridiculed because they were always on the losing side, the Irish had forced the British to the bargaining table.

About 1,500 people had died in the war, nearly three hundred of them civilians. The rebel army suffered about 750 dead and had killed about six hundred Crown forces, most of them police officers. Thousands more were wounded, and parts of Cork and Dublin were in ruins. The casualties and damage were nothing compared with the slaughter of World War I, but this had been a personal war. There were no great killing machines. The combatants looked into the eyes of the people they shot.

The truce was not a peace treaty, but the Irish people, or at least the Irish people outside the six counties in the northeast, acted as though the war was indeed over, and that they had won. But what exactly constituted victory? Could it be anything less than the ideal of a united Irish Republic, the dream of Wolfe Tone, Robert Emmet, James Stephens, Padraig Pearse, and James Connolly? Could a guerrilla army that counted its bullets before setting an ambush make demands of an empire without a thought to compromise? Would compromise taint victory and betray the blood of martyrs past? Did Kevin Barry and Terence MacSwiney die for anything less? The ghosts of Ireland's past, distant and recent, haunted the warm summer nights of 1921. The ghosts were pure and uncompromised, forever pledged to the dreams for which they died.

But none of those ghosts had ever been invited to parlay with the

Prime Minister of Great Britain. None had lived to see a day when Fenians in jacket and tie and bearing diplomatic credentials from a rebel Irish government were treated as equals by the men who ran the British Empire.

Eamon de Valera decided to monitor the historic negotiations from Dublin, and dispatched Arthur Griffith, Michael Collins, and three other men, including the grandson of the Young Irelander Charles Gavan Duffy, to London to negotiate a peace treaty with the men who ruled a quarter of the world's population: Lloyd George, Churchill, and their colleagues, men who were running risks of their own. Hard-line Conservative and Unionist critics were horrified that government ministers were willing to sit down with terrorists.

Negotiations began on October 11, 1921. Michael Collins was thirty years old, the youngest principal in the talks and surely one of the most unlikely envoys the British Empire had ever invited to Downing Street. He and Griffith quickly became the outstanding figures in the Irish party, summoned to meetings without the others, taken into the confidence of their famous counterparts.

From the beginning, it was clear that Lloyd George was not about to grant a republic to the men he faced across the bargaining table. That would have been unconditional surrender, and the Irish were in no position to expect it. Nor were the British about to undo the partition of the island. The six-county state of Northern Ireland already was functioning with a Home Rule Parliament, a Prime Minister, and a Cabinet. Lloyd George, who brought the arch-Unionist Edward Carson into his wartime Cabinet, had made his position clear long before negotiations began.

Following weeks of intense talks, Griffith, Collins, Lloyd George, Churchill, and their fellow negotiators signed a treaty on December 6, 1921, after Lloyd George threatened to bring renewed war to Ireland. Collins, for one, didn't think the Prime Minister was making an empty threat. With the IRA out in the open, with its de facto commander exposed, and with the public grown accustomed to life without terror, Collins could hardly have relished a return to bloodshed.

The Anglo-Irish Treaty called for the creation not of a thirty-two-county Irish Republic, but a twenty-six-county entity to be known as the Irish Free State. It would share the island with Northern Ireland, which would continue to be a province of the United Kingdom. The Irish did win a seemingly significant concession. Britain agreed to set up a boundary commission that would redraw portions of the border between the two Irish states to allow nationalist areas, such as parts of southern County Armagh, to be included in the Free State.

The Irish Free State would have the same relationship to the British Crown as Canada, a self-governing nation with what was called dominion status within the British Empire. Canada enjoyed more independence than mere Home Rule offered, although its legislature technically, but often only technically, was subordinate to the British Parliament. Members of the Irish Free State's Dáil would swear to be faithful to the King and his successors.

From the Irish perspective, the Anglo-Irish Treaty was a flawed document and a bitter compromise. And the promise of the boundary commission would never be fulfilled. Still, Collins and Griffith won for Ireland more than Britain was willing to grant Parnell in 1886 or Redmond in 1914. After eight hundred years of conflict, the British army would march out of most of Ireland, accomplishing what all the great heroes of the past could only dream of in their jail cells or their exile.

Collins and Griffith knew the treaty would not please the hardliners, but Collins at least had gotten approval from the IRB on the wording of the oath of allegiance to both the new Irish state and the British Crown. As president of the IRB's Supreme Council and by now a living legend, Collins commanded the support of many of the fighting men who might have been expected to oppose compromise. One of his intelligence officers told Collins that his men were behind him. "What is good enough for you is good enough for them," Collins was told.

But it was not good enough for the rebel government's political leader. Griffith and Collins thought Eamon de Valera would support the compromise. They were wrong. When the treaty was brought to the Dáil for debate in late December, the divisions of ideology and personality that had always existed were put on public display. De Valera condemned the treaty as a sell-out of the Republic, although his alternative treaty, which he called Document No. 2, read very much like the one Collins and Griffith signed.

At a critical juncture during the debate, Collins delivered an impassioned speech that betrayed his own ambivalence but nevertheless stated the case for peace after so long a struggle: "In my opinion, [the treaty] gives us freedom, not the ultimate freedom that all nations desire ... but the freedom to achieve it." Later, Collins took aside Kathleen Clarke, one of six women elected to the Dáil. She was on de Valera's side, bitter and angry with Collins for what she regarded as a betrayal of her husband and the Republic. Collins knew he could not persuade her to accept the treaty. "All I ask is that, if it's passed, you give us a chance to work [on] it."

It did pass, on January 7, by a vote of sixty-four to fifty-seven. But opponents would not give it a chance to work. De Valera immediately resigned as head of the government. The hardest of the hard-liners with him were the women members, among them Kathleen Clarke, Countess Markievicz, Margaret Pearse, mother of Padraig and Willie Pearse, and Mary MacSwiney, sister of Terence MacSwiney. De Valera led the anti-treaty contingent from the assembly on January 10, after the Dáil voted to accept his resignation.

A democratically elected body of Irish men and women had spoken, but de Valera, who claimed to know in his heart the wishes of his adopted countrymen, refused to accept the vote as binding. The treaty's supporters elected Arthur Griffith as president of the Dáil and Michael Collins as Chairman of the Provisional Government. Richard Mulcahy was named the new government's Minister of Defense. Collins sent messages of conciliation across the Atlantic to John Devoy, apologizing for de Valera's treatment of him and making it clear that the old man's support was important. In the crisis to come, the vast majority of Irish America stayed with Collins.

On January 18, 1922, two days after the new Provisional Government took office, the British administration surrendered Dublin Castle, seat of imperial power for centuries. The Union Jack was lowered, and the Irish tricolor of green, white, and orange was raised in its place. After the bitter split over the treaty, it was almost an anticlimactic moment. And yet it was the day that the men and women of decades and centuries past had longed to see. Michael Collins, the political and military leader of the new government, took a taxi to the ceremony and accepted possession of the castle in the name of the free Irish people. The Lord Lieutenant, Lord Fitzalan, greeted Collins: "I'm glad to see you, Mr. Collins," he said.

"Like hell you are," Collins replied.

Collins was laughing. It was one of the few lighthearted moments in what should have been a celebration of a glorious and historic landmark in the fight for Irish freedom.

In mid-March, de Valera made a series of inflammatory speeches encouraging the anti-treaty soldiers of the IRA to wage war against Griffith and Collins. He talked about wading through "the blood of some of the members of the Government in order to get Irish freedom." An anti-treaty armed force took de Valera at his word on April 14, 1922, by seizing another eighteenth-century Dublin landmark, the Four Courts, which had served as the center of Britain's legal system. It was a high-profile show of defiance, made with de Valera's encouragement. Meanwhile, an appalling anti-Catholic pogrom was underway in the north, claiming the lives of nearly two hundred. The Belfast government had recruited Sir Henry Wilson, who had retired as Britain's highest military officer, to take charge of the province's law enforcement, and Michael Collins saw his hand in the sectarian slaughter. Men in uniform were among the murder gangs roaming the province.

With the Free State and Northern Ireland on the brink of civil war, Collins and de Valera met face-to-face and agreed to hold a general election for a new Dáil. The election would be, they knew, a referendum on the treaty. The vote took place on June 16. Ninety-four of the 128 victorious candidates were pro-treaty. There could no longer be any argument about which side spoke for the mass of Irish people.

Sir Henry Wilson, successor to Edward Carson as the most virulent opponent of Irish nationalism, was assassinated in London on June 22 in retaliation for his complicity in the murder spree underway in the north. The assassins were two IRA men who had served in the British army during World War I. One, in fact, had left a leg on the battlefield in Britain's service. The British government was appalled, and assumed that the anti-treaty IRA was responsible. Actually, responsibility lay with Michael Collins.

It was the beginning of renewed violence. The Free State army opened fire on its former comrades in the Four Courts on June 28, not quite a year after the Anglo-Irish truce had seemingly liberated the people from war and fear. Civil war then engulfed Ireland. Few wars are as bitter as civil wars; few civil wars were as bitter as the Irish Civil War. More than five hundred combatants died in the summer of 1922, surpassing in a few weeks the IRA's casualties in the fighting from 1919 to 1921. The conflict divided those whose work and art during the Gaelic revival had so influenced a generation of revolutionaries: Maud Gonne, who had returned to Ireland after a long exile in France, sided with the anti-treaty forces; William Butler Yeats and Douglas Hyde went on to serve in the Free State's Senate.

The tension showed in the demeanor of Arthur Griffith, the Free State's Prime Minister. He worked himself to exhaustion, and spent a few days in a hospital in early August 1922, trying to regain his strength. It was to no avail. He died of a brain hemorrhage on August 12. Michael Collins marched in the funeral procession with Richard Mulcahy.

Collins went south, to his native Cork, a week after Griffith's funeral. The anti-treaty IRA found out that he was in the vicinity and set up an ambush as his small motorcade made its way near the town of Bealnamblath. After a battle of about thirty minutes, a bullet struck Collins in the back of his head. The commander in chief was dead at age thirty-one.

The war sputtered on for another nine months. Its brutality was appalling, and the tactics of both sides did no justice to the cause to which they claimed allegiance. The anti-treaty IRA threatened to assassinate members of the Free State government. No such assassinations took place, but relatives of Free State officials were murdered. The Free State ordered the summary executions of captured IRA men, and at one point, prisoners were tied together and blown to pieces by a land mine. The government imprisoned about thirteen thousand treaty opponents, a total that Oliver Cromwell, General Lake, General Maxwell, and Sir Henry Wilson no doubt would have envied.

De Valera ordered the anti-treaty IRA to end its resistance in the spring of 1923. He was arrested and taken prisoner by the Free State government, and released in 1924. The divisions of the Irish Civil War would last for generations, and the patriotic men and women who died during those bitter months were lost as the Irish people in the Free State set about governing themselves for the first time in centuries. There was, however, at least this redeeming feature: in 1932, Eamon de Valera, the political leader of the defeated anti-treaty forces, was elected Prime Minister of the state he had made war against in 1922. In a tribute to Ireland's democratic spirit, the victorious government in the civil war peacefully handed over power to a man it had imprisoned as the leader of an insurgency.

The Free State and Northern Ireland went their separate ways, viewing each other with suspicion and contempt from across a border that ran through the fields of farmers. Though some politicians in the Free State paid lip service to the injustice of partition, few took their speeches seriously. It took an Irishman from America to acknowledge reality. The old Fenian John Devoy was a guest of the Free State in 1924, invited to public ceremonies at the request of a member of the new Free State Senate, William Butler Yeats. During a dinner in his honor in Dublin, Devoy acknowledged that war would not make Irishmen out of Orangemen. "The only solution of the boundary question is the abolition of the boundary by the consent of the people of the Six Counties," he said. "I want it to be done peacefully." Force, he later said, would accomplish nothing.

Those words were his last great service to Ireland. He died four years later, and was buried in Dublin's Glasnevin Cemetery, the final resting place for generations of Irish patriots.

. . .

On December 21, 1948, the Irish Prime Minister, John Costello, head of a government that included Richard Mulcahy, announced that henceforth the twenty-six counties of the old Irish Free State would be known as the Republic of Ireland and would no longer be a member of the British Commonwealth. As Michael Collins contended, the treaty of 1921 had granted the freedom to win freedom.

But in the province known as Northern Ireland, where a group called the United Irishmen once agitated for an end to religious distinctions in Ireland, freedom was parceled out carefully, and only to those judged to be sufficiently loyal. There would be no freedom for Northern Ireland's Catholics.

CHAPTER TEN

THE ORANGE STATE

PERHAPS THE MOST celebrated episode in the Orangemen's history took place in 1689, when stouthearted defenders of Protestant Ulster closed the gates of the walled city of Derry in the face of James II. The King and his army laid siege to the city for nearly five months. The Protestants inside suffered terribly, but they never surrendered.

From the moment of its creation in 1922, Northern Ireland institutionalized the siege of Derry, codifying its mentality into law and slamming the gates of government in the faces of the province's Catholics. More than fifty thousand heavily armed police officers and trained reservists, nearly all of them Protestant, were prepared to enforce the government's wishes.

Northern Ireland was home to 1.2 million people at its founding. Two thirds were Protestant and, presumably, Loyalists or Unionists—both terms signified loyalty to the Union of Great Britain and Northern Ireland, but the terms later took on a class association. Working-class Protestants called themselves Loyalists while their better-educated political leaders were Unionists. Whatever name they went by, however, the Protestants of Northern Ireland constituted a formidable majority. But majority stature was not nearly enough for the state's founders, who wished to ensure a Protestant monopoly on political power through the ruling elite's Unionist Party. Catholics were effectively disenfranchised through manipulation of the province's political institutions, rendering the Catholics' main political voice, the Nationalist Party, utterly powerless.

A succession of Prime Ministers and top government officials had in common more than their membership in the Unionist Party. They also were members of the Orange Order, which meant that they took an oath to protect the Protestant church from conspiring Catholics. The province's first Prime Minister, James Craig, was proud of his role as a grandmaster in the Orange Order. "I have always said that I am an Orangeman first and a politician and a member of this parliament afterwards," he said in 1932.

Craig and his colleagues acted accordingly. The Orange lodges provided Northern Ireland with recruits for its new paramilitary police force, the Royal Ulster Constabulary, and its part-time reserves, called the B Specials. Another Prime Minister of Northern Ireland, Sir Basil Brooke, made it clear why the province seemed to be on a war footing. "The fight is only beginning and it will have to go on until Italy and the Church of Rome are submerged in the waters of the Mediterranean," Sir Basil said.

Translating sectarian rhetoric into law was easy enough for a one-party government. The Unionists drew the boundaries of local political districts to make sure that the Catholic vote was rendered meaningless. The most egregious example of sectarian gerrymandering took place in Derry, where nearly 90 percent of the city's Catholics were jammed into a single ward and the rest scattered harmlessly into two Protestant wards. The result was a rigged system in which a Protestant monolith ruled a city that was more than half Catholic. All public buildings, including the city's two hospitals, were built in the Protestant section of the city.

Behind the manipulation was a strategy aimed at more than just the political exclusion of Roman Catholics. The system required enemies and scapegoats, because, in fact, many working-class Protestants were only slightly better off than Catholics. The fruits of loyalty were few, but at least there were some. Protestants had first claim on government-built housing, they knew they would get jobs ahead of Catholics, and they were inculcated with the spirit of embattled Loyalism, which submerged all other differences in the name of the eternal siege.

There was good reason to keep the secretarian pot boiling, for beyond the control of Northern Ireland's political leaders were economic forces that threatened the province's principal industries of linen and shipbuilding. More than half of Northern Ireland's labor force worked in the linen industry in 1924, making the province especially vulnerable to the emerging market of synthetic fibers. Shipbuilding, too, responded to larger economic forces, for slowdowns in international trade inevitably meant slowdowns in orders for new ships.

A decline in both industries was underway during Northern

Ireland's infancy, but decline became near-collapse during the world-wide depression of the 1930s. There were twenty thousand shipbuilding jobs in Belfast in 1924. By 1933, there were just two thousand. The effect was catastrophic, and ironically enough, the suffering was disproportionately Protestant. Catholics did not have shipbuilding jobs to lose in the first place.

The province was on its way to becoming a rusting relic of the Industrial Revolution. The statistics in employment and public health demonstrated that working-class Protestants were getting hit nearly as hard as Catholics. Unemployment throughout the province before World War II was about 25 percent. Tuberculosis ran rampant, accounting for half the deaths of the province's young adults. Belfast's infant mortality rate went from the best among cities in Great Britain and Ireland early in the twentieth century to the worst by 1938. So appalling were conditions in both communities that in 1932 some Catholic and Protestant workers banded together to protest the government's refusal to deal with joblessness. At one point, Catholic workers attempted to rescue Protestant strikers whom the police were hauling off for violating a government ban on labor demonstrations.

The British government, which retained ultimate power over Northern Ireland, chose to ignore the sectarian system the Unionists had put in place. And the Free State in Dublin not only was powerless, but was consumed with problems of its own. The freedom to win more freedom did not include the ability to provide jobs and a future for the young people of the Irish Free State, and so independence did nothing to reverse Irish emigration. The Free State population in 1926 was just shy of three million; by the fiftieth anniversary commemoration of the Easter Rebellion in 1966, the population in the twenty-six counties had shrunk another 100,000. The talented and ambitious were lost to America, to Australia, and, ironically enough, to Great Britain.

Although the ascension of Eamon de Valera as the country's Prime Minister in 1932 was a credit to the Free State's democracy, the Unionists of Northern Ireland saw it in quite a different light. De Valera was a symbol of hard-line republicanism, and the IRA still was a small presence in both the Free State and the North. (Its chief of staff during a portion of the 1930s was Sean MacBride, the son of Maud Gonne and John MacBride.) In the North, de Valera and members of his new political party, Fianna Fáil ("Soldiers of Destiny"), were regarded as secret IRA sympathizers, never mind that de Valera ruthlessly cracked down on the IRA during the 1940s when guerrillas tried to launch a campaign in Northern Ireland using the Free State (briefly renamed Eire) as a base. De Valera ordered IRA members interned, as the British had after 1916, and several died on hunger strike, protesting their treatment at the hands of an Irish government. Other IRA members were executed after attacking police in the twenty-six counties. Finally, a member of Eamon de Valera's government, Minister for Justice Gerald Boland, announced in the mid-1940s that the IRA was dead.

De Valera's volatile mixture of nationalism and devout Catholicism seemed to confirm the Orangemen's worse suspicions. In 1937, de Valera sponsored a new constitution for the Irish state that included a clause recognizing "the special position of the Holy Catholic Apostolic and Roman Church as the guardian of the Faith professed by the great majority" of the state's citizens. The clause eventually was abolished, but it was a fair indication of de Valera's vision. He had resisted calls to establish the Catholic Church in Ireland as the Church of England was established in Great Britain, but he believed in the Church's "special position" in Irish society. His Ireland was Catholic, it was rural, it was patriarchal, it was conservative, and, inevitably, it was impoverished, isolated, and an exporter of people. De Valera was the dominant figure in the twenty-six counties until his death in 1975 at the age of ninety-three. The state he created in his own image was free of British political hegemony, but it did little to inspire Northern Irish Protestants to wish for reunification. Within two decades of his death, however, the Ireland he served as Prime Minister for nearly twenty years and as President for fourteen more would change, utterly.

London and Dublin may have been bystanders as Northern Ireland created a single-party, Protestant-only state, but they were hardly uninformed. Northern Ireland's founders made no attempt to disguise what they were doing. Prime Minister Craig articulated Northern Ireland's founding principle in 1934, when he told his colleagues, "All I boast is that we are a Protestant parliament and a Protestant state," despite the fact that a third of the population was not Protestant.

One of the first pieces of legislation to make its way through the Northern Ireland Parliament was called, euphemistically, the Civil Authorities Act. It was known more commonly as the Special Powers Act. It gave the government the right to intern citizens without formally charging them with a crime, and gave police the right to search any home without a warrant. It was clear who had the most to fear from random arrests. The law also banned political organizations espousing republican principles, gave the province's Minister for Home Affairs the power to suppress newspapers, magazines, and books and to impose curfews, gave police the power to break up any gathering of three or more people, and even reintroduced flogging as a form of punishment. Political debate within the province would be tightly controlled and relentlessly patrolled. Critics could be silenced or imprisoned at the whim of the police and government.

Beginning in 1932, the Northern Ireland Parliament met in a massive and unyielding building in an area just outside Belfast called Stormont. There, with a permanent majority of four Unionists for every Catholic, lawmakers invented new ways of making life difficult for the province's minority population. A statue of Edward Carson, looking defiant, graced the Parliament building's grounds. Carson, the Dublin-born barrister who famously argued that the Protestant people of Ulster were so loyal to Britain that they would take arms against Home Rule, died in 1935. As the province's grand old man, he reminded his fellow Unionists that their cause was not only about religion, but about nationality and, as he saw it, race. "The Celts have done nothing in Ireland but create trouble and disorder," he said during his retirement. "Irishmen who have turned out successful have not in any case that I know of been of true Celtic origin."

To further ensure a Unionist monopoly on power, Northern Ireland's founders gave affluent property owners extra opportunities to vote in local government elections. The franchise itself was limited to the owners of property and the heads of households and their spouses in rental housing. Children of voting age who lived with their parents in rented homes were ineligible to vote, as were any other lodgers. A quarter of the population was thus deprived of votes in local elections. But well-off property owners could cast as many as six votes by proxy based on the value of their holdings.

Those local rules didn't apply to elections for members of the British Parliament, to which Northern Ireland sent twelve members. But that didn't matter. Thanks to gerrymandering, the Unionists had a lock on ten of the twelve Northern Irish seats in Parliament. And as Charles Parnell once linked his Nationalist Party to the British Liberal Party, the Unionists aligned with Britain's Conservatives, seeking to pry concessions when their votes made or broke governments.

Rigging the political system and suppressing criticism were powerful instruments of control, but there were also informal methods of marginalizing the province's Catholic minority. Sir Basil Brooke put forward the argument that employment discrimination against Catholics was to be encouraged and indeed commended. He noted with disapproval in 1933 that some Protestants were giving jobs to Catholics, and he made clear his opinion of the practice. "I have not one about my place," he said with pride. He returned to the theme a year later, urging "people who are loyalists not to employ Roman Catholics, 99 percent of whom are disloyal."

The province's employers were more than happy to oblige Sir Basil. As late as 1970, one of Northern Ireland's largest employers, the giant Harland & Wolff shipyard, employed four hundred Catholics in a workforce of ten thousand. Catholics who managed to find work despite the attitude of Northern Ireland's leading statesmen inevitably occupied the lowest rungs of the labor force. There were no Catholics among high-ranking civil servants, and few if any among the public bodies that controlled local government functions. Among the most important portfolios in local government, and one of the most corrupt and patronage-ridden portfolios, was housing.

Catholics suffered from overt bias in housing. In predominantly Catholic County Fermanagh, a government survey in 1944 found that more than 50 percent of homes in rural areas were in desperate need of replacement. But the local government bodies, in Protestant hands, stopped building new housing until after World War II, and then, 82 percent of the new units were allocated to Protestants. Again, there was nothing secret about what these policies were designed to achieve. A Unionist Member of Parliament named E. C. Ferguson complained in 1948 that "the Nationalist [Catholic] majority in the County Fermanagh, notwithstanding a reduction of 336 in the [last] year, stands at 3,604. This county, I think it can safely be said, is a Unionist county. The atmosphere is Unionist. The Boards and properties are nearly all controlled by Unionists. But there is still this millstone around our necks. I would ask [local authorities] to adopt whatever plans and take whatever steps, however drastic, to wipe out this Nationalist majority."

There were in Northern Ireland people fully prepared to take steps, however drastic, against Catholics. On the Shankill Road in Belfast, the heart of the city's working-class Loyalist community, Augustus Spence, known by his nickname, Gusty, was on the verge of young adulthood and considering the options available to a poorly educated Protestant. Born in 1934, one of seven children living in a two-bedroom home, Spence would later refer to his neighborhood as "the heartland of the Empire, where we ruled over nothing except poverty." He was considered a good student, but he left school early because his parents couldn't afford to pay for books and the uniform required of high school students. He went to work at age fourteen, earning 85 pence a week in the Belfast mills.

Gusty Spence

In another kind of society, he might have wondered about the sort of government that neglected basic social and economic conditions but demanded absolute loyalty all the same. But in the Protestant state of Northern Ireland, there was no questioning the leaders of the eternal siege, for they were busy men, constantly on the lookout for signs of disloyalty. "We were made conscious by politicians, our politicians, [that] if we criticized the government, the border was likely to fall, the Jesuits would move in and all hell would break loose," he later said. So he asked no questions, went to work, and then, in the late 1950s, joined the British army unit known as the Royal Ulster Rifles, which was deployed to Cyprus. When he returned to Belfast, he found work in the city's shipyards, places where the province's Protestant blue-collar workers were accorded their rewards for loyalty. There, and elsewhere along the Shankill Road, the talk was of the IRA. At the time it was moribund, but in the dockyards and in the Protestant neighborhoods, it was ever-present. "Everyone was told there was a resurrection of the IRA," he said, "and that they were about to pounce."

To counter the coming threat, Spence became one of the founders of a new paramilitary organization that took its name from the days of Edward Carson—the Ulster Volunteer Force. Its mission was sectarian murder in the defense of Protestant Ulster.

On the night of June 26, 1966, four young Catholic men were walking home from their jobs as bartenders near the Shankill Road when five members of the new UVF opened fire. One of the young Catholics, Peter Ward, was killed, and two others were wounded. Among those arrested for the random murder was Gusty Spence. Though he protested his innocence, he was found guilty and sentenced to life in prison. With his limited prospects ruined and the parameters of his life defined by his jail cell, he decided to educate himself in "the political circumstances which led me to be in jail," he later said. The first book he read was entitled *My Fight for Irish Freedom,* the memoir of a famed IRA guerrilla from the 1920s, Dan Breen.

The education denied Gusty Spence was, ironically enough, provided to a promising young Catholic in Derry named John Hume. Growing up in the 1940s, Hume was a witness to the injustices heaped upon Northern Ireland's Catholics. One of seven children, he was reared in the city's Catholic ghetto, called the Bogside. His mother, Annie Doherty, was illiterate. But his father, Sam Hume, not only knew how to write, but was proud of his wonderful penmanship. That skill helped him get a job in a government office during World War II entering names on ration books. Later, the senior Hume found work in the shipyards. But when the war ended, so did his job. In his late fifties, Sam Hume never again found work. He devoted his time to assisting others in filling out job applications and encouraging his eldest son to "stick to the books."

John Hume's childhood home in the Bogside was similar to Gusty Spence's in Belfast. It had two bedrooms, not nearly enough for a family growing by the year, and no bathroom, only a backyard toilet. There was little in the way of relief from the local authorities, for the government was firmly in the hands of Unionists even though Catholics made up 65 percent of the city's population during Hume's early years.

The injustice and discrimination didn't convert Sam Hume into a nationalist or a republican. When John was about ten years old, he and his father went to an election rally near their home. The Nationalist Party, whose representatives were powerless and confined to gerrymandered, all-Catholic districts, tried to stir up passions with talk about putting an end to partition. The rhetoric, not surprisingly, had an effect on the impressionable young John as he listened to speakers seemingly offering a solution to the poverty and political impotence of Northern Ireland's Catholics.

Sam put a hand on his son's shoulder. "Son, don't get involved in that stuff," he said.

"Why not, Da?"

"Because you can't eat a flag," Sam Hume replied.

Opportunity presented itself when Great Britain reformed its educational system, and Northern Ireland's, as World War II was coming to an end. In 1948, Hume took a government-administered examination for eleven-year-olds that was designed to put high achievers on a university track. Because it was a London initiative, there was little Northern Ireland's leaders could do to foil the program's lack of discrimination between Protestant and Catholic students. The program came too late, however, for Gusty Spence in proud, impoverished Protestant Belfast.

John Hume finished in the top 25 percent in his class, thus qualifying for a government scholarship to the school of his choice. He chose a Catholic school in Derry called Saint Columb's, a place his family could never have afforded on its own. In fact, he was the only one of the seven Hume children to receive a full, formal education.

The scholarships were the first step toward the creation of what would become a broad-based, educated Catholic middle class in Northern Ireland, a middle class that the young Daniel O'Connell would have recognized. Just as O'Connell chafed at the barriers placed in the way of his professional advancement in the 1820s, when Catholics were barred from Parliament and the highest honors in law, so, too, the well-educated children of the Catholic ghettos in Northern Ireland would not stand for publicly sanctioned discrimination. Two years later, another young Catholic boy destined for achievement and fame entered the school—Seamus Heaney. Long after they were graduated from Saint Columb's, Hume and Heaney would win Nobel Prizes within three years of each other, Hume for peace and Heaney for literature.

Hume gave serious thought to the priesthood, and enrolled in Ireland's most famous Catholic seminary, Maynooth in County Kildare, across the border in the Republic. He majored in French and

John Hume

in history, and one of his instructors was a gregarious, whiskey-drinking, pipe-smoking lecturer in modern history named Father Tom Fee. Father Fee, a small man with a receding hairline, came from the town of Crossmaglen in the southern part of County Armagh, just over the border from the Republic. Crossmaglen was and remained a bastion of unreconstructed Irish republicanism. Even while Father Fee was instructing his charges at Maynooth in modern history, a few IRA diehards commenced another guerrilla campaign in border areas such as Crossmaglen. It ended in failure in 1962, and an IRA statement to the press complained that the Irish people were "distracted" from "the supreme issue," meaning partition. In fact, they were distracted by dismal economic prospects and were leaving their country in search of work, for the 1950s was yet another dreary decade of stagnation and widespread emigration in the Republic.

Fee was born in 1923 amid the terror of the Irish Civil War and the anti-Catholic pogroms in Belfast, and he grew up to become an expert in Gaelic culture and the Irish language, a fiddle player, and a devoted fan of Gaelic sports. At Maynooth, he was known for his casual, friendly manner, a far cry from the stiff, pre–Vatican Council II priests who remained aloof from their students. John Hume was one of his prize students, and Hume rewarded Fee's interest by taking top honors in history.

Hume, however, would not follow in Father Fee's footsteps. He dropped out of the seminary in 1957, returned to Derry, and found work as a French teacher. His were the first paychecks in the Hume household since the end of World War II. He married in 1960, the same year he took the first steps toward a political career. He and several friends, determined to find a way to help neglected, impoverished Catholics help themselves, founded a credit union in Derry. From an initial deposit of £7, it grew to more than £20 million and more than fourteen thousand members. Within a few years, he became president of a network of credit unions throughout Ireland. And, in another affirmative action to counter government neglect, Hume and his growing network of allies founded a housing organization that proceeded to do what the Unionist-controlled government of Derry refused to do: build or help finance decent housing for its majority population of impoverished Catholics. After the organization's successful beginning in the mid-1960s, the Derry city government stepped in and refused Hume's plan to build seven hundred homes in 1968. The ban was in keeping with Northern Ireland's permanent state of siege. Nothing was to be done to ease the plight of the Catholics, for they were not true citizens of the Protestant state of Northern Ireland.

Two pictures of famous Americans adorned the walls of John Hume's office. One was of President John F. Kennedy, the great-grandson of immigrants from County Wexford whose achievements in America represented the dreams of Catholic Ireland. The other was that of Martin Luther King, Jr., whose crusade against discrimination in America had a profound effect on Hume. African-Americans had marched for the very same rights denied to Catholics in Northern Ireland. The Nationalist Party, the supposed voice of Catholics in

Northern Ireland, was useless as a vehicle for protest. "Nationalists in opposition have been in no way constructive," he wrote. "It is this lack of positive contribution and the apparent lack of interest in the general welfare of Northern Ireland that has led many Protestants to believe that the Northern Catholic is politically irresponsible and therefore unfit to rule." Something new, he decided, was required to bring about change.

As if he anticipated the rumblings of Northern Ireland's Catholics in the mid-1960s, a fiery Presbyterian minister and politician named Ian Paisley began making a name for himself with anti-Catholic diatribes so extreme that they seemed like parodies, except that irony was not among the gifts for which Paisley was noted. Paisley became a powerful voice of reaction, a Northern Irish George Wallace, as the old social order began to unravel. His favorite bogeyman was the IRA, which he saw, or said he saw, lurking under every Catholic bed in the province. But the IRA was practically nonexistent in the mid-1960s. Catholics looking for change were not about to turn to a discredited paramilitary organization. Instead, like John Hume, they looked across the Atlantic to see the revolution African-Americans were achieving by their moral force alone. In 1967, middle-class, moderate Catholics who benefited from Great Britain's educational reforms came together to found a new organization, the Northern Ireland Civil Rights Association. It was agnostic on the question of a united Ireland. Instead, it sought to win pragmatic reforms for Northern Ireland's Catholics: an end to discrimination, fair elections, and equal citizenship. While Paisley and his allies saw the IRA's hand in the civil rights movement, in fact, the organization's goals of winning reforms within the system were the antithesis of the IRA's. The IRA and its sympathizers didn't wish to reform the Northern Ireland state. They sought to destroy it.

The fledgling civil rights movement decided to begin its campaign of nonviolent protest with a short march on August 24, 1968. A petite twenty-one-year-old student at Queen's University in Belfast named Bernadette Devlin read of plans for the march in a campus newspaper. "Excellent idea," she thought.

Devlin was yet another example of the changes that education was bringing to Northern Ireland as liberal policies were put in place throughout the United Kingdom. She was the daughter of a poor, working-class Catholic family in County Tyrone. Neither of Devlin's parents was involved in politics, although her father certainly had rea-

Bernadette Devlin

son to question the methods of the Northern Irish state. When Bernadette was a schoolgirl, her father, John Devlin, a carpenter, went to Britain in search of work. It was a common enough journey, given the high unemployment in the province, but there was another, more insidious reason why John Devlin was unemployed. For reasons that were never explained to him, he discovered that his government insurance card, the equivalent of an American Social Security card, had been stamped with the phrase "political suspect." The card had been in his employer's file. His employer fired him, and nobody else would hire him. He died not long afterward, when Bernadette was nine years old.

If John Devlin was suspected of republican sympathies, Bernadette Devlin pleaded guilty to them by age twelve, when she entered a local talent contest and recited selections from the works of Padraig Pearse and portions of Robert Emmet's famous speech from the dock. She won first prize. By the time she entered Queen's University in Belfast in 1965, she had developed a critique of the society she was raised in that was a good deal more complicated than mere recitations from dead patriots. She had only scorn for the Catholic Church, which she regarded as "among the best traitors Ireland has ever had" because of its traditional social conservatism. And she had little patience for traditional nationalism. She decided that she wanted not simply a thirty-two-county Irish Republic, but a socialist republic, one in which Protestants and Catholics would work together to tear down the power structure that kept them apart.

That, of course, was a tall order. First there was the fledgling crusade for civil rights for Catholics. In August 1968, she joined the civil rights march from Coalisland to Dungannon, along with about 2,500 others, many of them students. The marchers were under strict orders that there were to be no republican banners. The march was uneventful, more like a pleasant stroll than a political demonstration, until marchers approached Dungannon, where four hundred members of the Royal Ulster Constabulary blocked the route and 1,500 counter-demonstrators taunted the marchers from behind a barricade. The march was rerouted to a Catholic area of Dungannon, and it ended with marchers singing the American civil rights anthem, "We Shall Overcome." To keep the momentum going, plans were made for a second march, to be held in Derry on October 5.

John Hume had mixed feelings about the coming march. His first priority was the growing credit union movement, which he wished to keep separate from partisan politics. But his sympathies were with the nonviolent civil rights protesters, and when the Northern Ireland government stepped in and banned the march, Hume's decision was made easy. He was in the streets as the marchers stepped forward toward Derry's city center. Elsewhere in the crowd of five thousand marchers was Bernadette Devlin, along with several Labour Party Members of Parliament from England. Banners read: "Class, Not Creed."

The marchers had walked only a few hundred yards when the RUC moved in. Wielding their nightsticks, or batons as they are called in Ireland and Britain, they hit anything that moved, including some local elected officials and an elderly woman who was standing near one of the English MPs when a constable struck her in the head. A water cannon hosed down the marchers, including Hume. As marchers scurried for cover, Devlin stood in the street, paralyzed with horror as she examined the faces of the police. They were, she thought, delighted, absolutely delighted.

A cameraman from the Republic's national television service filmed the police rampage, and when the brutal images were shown not only in the Republic but throughout the world, public opinion galvanized just as it had in America when a television audience saw police attacking civil rights demonstrators in Alabama. British Prime Minister Harold Wilson arranged for a private screening of the film. Among the images he saw was that of blood pouring from the head of Gerry Fitt, one of the two Catholic Members of Parliament from Northern Ireland.

Demonstrations became part of daily life in Northern Ireland in late 1968 as emboldened Catholics demanded an end to the province's blatant discrimination in housing, employment, and government. Within two weeks of the Derry march, Bernadette Devlin and a group of her fellow students at Queen's University formed a nonsectarian organization called the People's Democracy. It called for six basic reforms that were nothing less than a call for the dismantling of the Unionist Orange state: one person, one vote; an end to gerrymandering; allocation of housing according to need; a ban on job discrimination; a right to freedom of speech; and a repeal of the Special Powers Act.

Protests continued through the winter. The police fought back, and so did militant Protestants. Devlin was part of a march from Belfast to Derry in January 1969 that came under vicious attack from mobs throwing bricks and bottles. The RUC made no move against the assailants; some of the assailants, it turned out, were members of the police reserve, the B Specials.

Throughout the unrest, the demonstrators made it clear that they were not marching for an end to partition. They were marching for their rights, and marching to bring an end to the Unionist monopoly on power in Northern Ireland. But militant Protestants saw the students and agitators as agents of the virtually nonexistent IRA. Ian Paisley held a counterdemonstration, calling on "all Protestant religions" to make sure that "Republicans" and the IRA were stopped in their tracks.

But there was no stopping what had been started in Derry. The Northern Irish Prime Minster, Captain Terence O'Neill, told the protesters that their complaints had been heard, and they should now await the changes they demanded. The London-born, Eton-educated O'Neill was not the sort of overt anti-Catholic that his predecessors were. Trained as a functionary of the system, he was lost when the system was challenged. In desperation, he called for an election in the Northern Ireland Parliament in early 1969. The campaign became yet another landmark in an era of change. The Unionist monolith shattered as hard-line Protestants campaigned, and won, on the strength of their opposition to the Unionist Prime Minister.

The election was a milestone for the province's minority community as well. The traditional party of Catholics, the Nationalist Party, suffered a string of defeats to younger, more aggressive candidates. Among these was John Hume, who won a seat from Derry after conducting a campaign calling not only for civil rights, but for "radical social and economic politics" to benefit all people in the province. Tellingly, Hume's platform was based on Northern Irish politics. There was no smash-the-border rhetoric to stir up Nationalists. The people, he knew, couldn't eat flags.

Hume originally was asked to run in a pending by-election for a seat in the British Parliament, but he declined. So the Nationalists and civil rights agitators turned to a highly unlikely alternative, Bernadette Devlin. With the Unionist Party divided, the civil rights movement saw an opportunity to put forward one of its own, a student with no experience, no money, and no love of establishment politics. She was nominated fifteen days before election day. But in that short span, she had little problem capturing the attention, pro and con, of voters in her proposed constituency in mid-Ulster. On April 18, less than a week before her twenty-second birthday, she became the youngest woman ever elected to the House of Commons and the youngest MP in more than two centuries. In her victory speech, she said: "I was elected by the oppressed people of Ulster, and I shall work for them."

Prime Minister O'Neill granted the principle of one person, one vote throughout Northern Ireland a few days later, on April 22. He resigned on April 28. The hard-liners thought he was too weak, too willing to give Catholics what they demanded.

The change in government brought no change to the streets of Derry, where demonstrators and police dueled with each other throughout the summer of 1969. The climactic moment came on August 12, the day the gates of the city were shut as King James's forces approached in 1689. To commemorate the occasion, young Protestants traditionally marched through the city in fife and drum corps, reminding Catholics of the order of things in Protestant Ulster. The march in 1969 deteriorated into a rock- and missile-throwing contest as the marchers paraded through the Catholic ghetto of the Bogside. The police fired tear gas. What became known as the Battle of the Bogside had begun.

The fighting lasted for three days. Bernadette Devlin, MP, manned hastily built barricades and hurled stones and bits of pavement at the police, who responded with even more tear gas. John Hume walked the streets, urging negotiation rather than violent confrontation. He was laid flat when a gas canister hit him in the chest. The Battle of the Bogside led to street fighting in Catholic west Belfast. Police officers fired machine guns at the unarmed demonstrators. The toll of dead reached six, the toll of wounded in the hundreds. Hundreds more were burned out of their homes. The Prime Minister of the Irish Republic, Jack Lynch, delivered a momentous speech on television. He declared that it was "evident" that the government in Northern Ireland "is no longer in control of the situation," he said. "It is clear, also, that the Irish Government can no longer stand by and see innocent people injured, and perhaps worse." He announced that army units would be deployed close to the border.

It sounded like a threat to use the army of the Irish Republic to defend Northern Ireland's Catholics. It was worth noting that nothing had been heard from the Irish Republican Army. The graffiti on the walls of Belfast read: "IRA—I Ran Away."

On August 14, the British government stepped in. Soldiers from the Prince of Wales's Own Regiment relieved the RUC of its law enforcement duties in Derry. The British army had returned to Ireland.

They came to protect Catholics in the North from the police, and they were greeted with tea in Catholic neighborhoods. Many astonishing things already had happened by the time the British soldiers arrived, but the friendly reception might well have been the most astonishing. It certainly testified to Catholics' utter alienation from the Unionist government. Just before the troop deployment was announced, John Hume was in the Northern Irish Parliament building in Stormont when he heard Northern Ireland's Deputy Minister for Home Affairs, John Taylor, say that he had mobilized the exclusively Protestant B Specials, all eleven thousand of them. Hume was furious. "I do not wish to engage in any verbal battles with anyone," Hume said from the floor, "but after listening to Taylor's speech, which was a jackboot speech in the present crisis, I can only say this in reply: we are quite firm, we shall not be moved." With that, he left the building. Within a year, Hume formed a new political organization, the Social Democratic and Labour Party, pledged to nonviolent, constitutional agitation. And while Hume believed that a reunified Ireland was the ultimate solution to Northern Ireland's problems, he challenged the Republic to respect the traditions and culture of Protestant Ulster.

There was little question that in Northern Ireland and in the Republic there were men, and some women, too, who were members of the Irish Republican Army. Firsthand evidence, however, was scanty. Since the suspension of its border campaign in 1962, the IRA's most public activity occurred the evening of March 6, 1966, as the Irish Republic was preparing to celebrate the fiftieth anniversary of the Easter Rebellion. That night the IRA, such as it was, blew up a monument to Britain's Lord Horatio Nelson, a relic of the old order that stood outside the General Post Office in Dublin.

By the time Derry exploded, the IRA had few arms and fewer members. A political party aligned with the IRA boasted a famous name but precious little support—Sinn Féin, an utterly revamped organization with little connection to the Sinn Féin of Arthur Griffith's day. And in January 1970, the IRA split into two factions, the Official IRA and the Provisional IRA. The bulk of Sinn Féin aligned with the Provisionals, or Provos, as they were called.

Bloody riots continued as the two IRAs quarreled. Six people were killed in Belfast in July 1970. Ian Paisley was elected to the British Parliament; Bernadette Devlin was reelected, and then arrested for her part in the Derry riots. The IRA had yet to show a presence. But on February 6, 1971, the Provisional IRA claimed its first victim, shooting a British soldier to death. A paramilitary and terrorist campaign that would last more than a quarter century was underway. The Stormont government responded with internment, which granted police the right to imprison political suspects without formally charging them with a crime. The new policy was put into effect on August 9, 1971. British soldiers, so recently considered the Catholics' protectors from the Northern Irish government, were sent into Catholic neighborhoods just before dawn to arrest nearly 350 suspects. That was just the first day's haul. More than 1,500 were arrested before the year was out.

In using the army to round up citizens in so brutal a fashion, the British government made it clear that the soldiers were not in the north to defend Catholics from the Orange state. The soldiers, in fact, were an instrument of the Orange state. In Catholic areas, women no longer gave the soldiers tea. Instead, they began banging garbage can lids on the pavement as a warning signal when they spotted an army patrol in the neighborhood.

Internment led to greater tensions, more demonstrations, and increased IRA violence in the form of hundreds of bombings. A bomb planted in a pub in Belfast killed fifteen people, all civilians. Another bomb in a furniture store on the Shankill Road killed four people, two of them children. A doctor and two police officers were on hand when the dead children were brought to a mortuary. "We cried our eyes out," the doctor said.

The Civil Rights Association scheduled a huge anti-internment rally in Derry on January 30, 1972. As usual, the march was banned. As usual, the marchers chose to defy the ban. Perhaps as many as 15,000 people joined the march, Bernadette Devlin among them. Members of Britain's 1st Parachute Regiment recently had been deployed to the city, and had forcefully prevented Hume from leading a smaller march on January 22. Hume retreated from confrontation, fearful of the hate he saw in the soldiers' faces.

The January 30 demonstration included all of the rituals that had become familiar to marchers and security forces. Barricades were put up to reroute the marchers; marchers pelted the soldiers manning the barricades with rocks. The paratroopers were not on the front line, but were in reserve. As Hume had seen several days earlier, they were ready for a fight.

Unprovoked and without warning, they moved in and opened fire just after four o'clock. Bernadette Devlin was on a platform with a microphone in her hand. "Don't be afraid . . . ," she was starting to say. She dove under the platform and silently said a prayer she had memorized in childhood: "Protect me in the hour of death." The demonstrators, in the thousands, were sitting ducks in an open courtyard. Devlin shouted to some marchers lying nearby to crawl away toward cover. They didn't. They were dead.

The soldiers fired 107 rounds in twenty terrible minutes. Thirteen people were killed on the spot. Eighteen more were wounded. The soldiers claimed they opened fire when they heard shots. None of the dead and wounded were armed. Television film showed a priest waving a blood-soaked handkerchief as he scrambled to give last rites to the dying. John Hume heard the shots as he was sitting in his home. "That's it," he said to his wife, Pat. "The lid's really off now."

It was an appalling massacre, made worse, if that were possible, by the callous behavior of government officials the next day. The Home Secretary was a pompous nonentity named Reginald Maudling, a man who had pronounced Northern Ireland to be "a terrible country" after his first visit there. He offered no apologies and no regret, stating that the soldiers had opened fire on marchers who were attacking them with firebombs. He referred to the march as a riot.

Bernadette Devlin, who returned to Parliament when it reconvened, attempted to address the House under a rule that gave priority to Members of Parliament who were witnesses to an event under discussion. The Speaker refused to recognize her, and then censured her when she refused to sit down. She could take no more. She leapt from her seat and physically attacked Maudling, pulling his hair and pummeling him as she screamed: "Murdering hypocrite!" Maudling's eyeglasses were sent flying, and parliamentary reporters were sent scurrying through House of Commons records to find out whether an MP had ever physically attacked a colleague. (To the reporters' surprise, Devlin's behavior was not so uncommon. One report noted that Winston Churchill had once thrown a book at an opponent during a debate.) Afterward, she said her only regret was "that I didn't seize him by the throat while I had the chance." A government whip who was standing near Maudling noted that "for such a small lady she packs a pretty powerful punch."

The city's coroner found that most of the victims were shot in the back. "I say it without reservation—it was sheer, unadulterated murder," he said. An official British Army report the day after the killings described the victims as either gunmen, bombers, or nail bombers— several soldiers had been attacked with nail bombs in Derry in mid-January. Later investigations, however, would show that all the dead and wounded were unarmed. Evidence of the Army's concern over what had transpired was obvious in the report's conclusion. "It is suggested that the following points can usefully be emphasised in public . . . that the investigations confirm that all Army shooting was . . . in self defence [and] that the IRA fired first," the report stated.

At a tense meeting of the British cabinet at 10 Downing Street on February 4, Prime Minister Edward Heath brought up a remarkable suggestion. According to the minutes of the meeting, Heath asked Northern Ireland Prime Minister Brian Faulkner, who was in attendance, if there was any support for a proposal to cede two Catholic neighborhoods in Derry—the Bogside and Creggan—to the Irish Republic. Such a startling move would have meant redrawing the borders of Northern Ireland, which even the most moderate Unionist would have regarded as a stunning betrayal of Britain's commitment to the province's Protestants.

Not surprisingly, Faulkner told Heath that the proposal should not be taken seriously, noting that once begun, the redrawing of Northern Ireland's boundaries might never end. Besides, he noted cryptically, giving the Irish Republic parts of Derry would not resolve the core of the problem, which he described as the attitude of Belfast's Catholics.

Heath pressed the point, however, asking Faulkner why Unionists wouldn't consider giving the Republic Catholic areas in Derry or in the city of Newry, County Down. Faulkner maintained that not everybody in those areas was an Irish Republican. The Secretary of State for Foreign and Commonwealth Relations, Sir Alec Douglas-Home, put Faulkner further on the defensive by asking whether an exchange of population in such areas could be arranged. Faulkner said he didn't believe Catholics would willingly move from the North to the Republic because they would face a drop in living standards.

Later in the meeting, which barely touched on the Army's deadly assault on civilians, Heath wondered about the stability of the Irish Republic's government. He asked Faulkner if he thought it was possible that the IRA could take over Dublin. Faulkner said he could by no means rule out the possibility.

The Stormont government, the political manifestation of that entity known as the Ulster Orangemen, neither British nor Irish, Roman Catholic nor Church of England, fell in March 1972. Even a Conservative-led British government, usually the Ulsterman's best friend, could no longer allow the men of the Orange Order a free hand to deal with the province's minority population. Britain suspended Northern Ireland's Parliament and imposed direct rule on the province, meaning that Northern Ireland no longer had a Prime Minister and Cabinet to govern its domestic affairs. Direct rule from London didn't mean an end to British army presence in Northern Ireland, nor did it mean an end to internment. The army continued its wholesale arrests of young Catholic males, its predawn raids, and its use of persuasive if painful methods of interrogation. It set up small businesses as fronts to gather intelligence in Catholic areas and colluded with Gusty Spence's successors in the growing Loyalist paramilitaries as they widened a campaign against Catholics in general and those suspected of republican sympathies in particular.

With the North drifting toward all-out guerrilla war, there was a brief interval beginning with the fall of Stormont when the IRA and the British government both seemed eager to ease tensions and head off a prolonged battle of attrition. The IRA's leadership issued a statement in June 1972 hinting at the possibility of talks with representatives of the British government. The idea intrigued John Hume, who quietly offered himself as a go-between. After weeks of secret meetings, British government officials agreed to meet face-to-face with a young republican prisoner named Gerry Adams, who was among the Catholics rounded up and sent to internment camps. It was a highly sensitive move on Britain's part, for it would hardly do if the public realized that the government was talking to outlaws branded as terrorists.

Adams had been hauled off to prison in March 1972. A few days before his arrest, four of his friends blew themselves up when a bomb prematurely exploded. They were members of the IRA. The oldest of the four was twenty-year-old Tom McCann, and when he wasn't found in the rubble, his friends thought that somehow he had escaped. Their hopes were shattered when searchers finally found a piece of McCann's scalp in the wreckage.

In his talks with senior British officials, Adams put foward the IRA's demand that their prisoners be given special status, with the right to wear their own clothes, to refrain from forced labor, and to associate freely with other special category prisoners. In essence, the IRA was asking for political recognition. The British agreed to create what it called a special category prisoner in return for an IRA cease-fire. The cease-fire was granted, although it didn't last.

There were other, more public deliberations that showed some promise. Political leaders from Northern Ireland, the Republic of Ireland, and Great Britain began a series of talks leading to a dramatic announcement at Stormont in November 1973 that political leaders in the North had agreed to form a new government with power to be shared, for the first time, with Catholics. Called the Sunningdale Agreement, it brought together leaders of the old Unionist Party with members of John Hume's new Social Democratic and Labour Party. Hume was one of several Catholics nominated to an eleven-member executive that would govern the North in a new assembly. There was also to be a Council of Ireland, made up of representatives of the Republic as well as the North, to share in administrative tasks affecting the whole island.

It seemed, for a brief moment, that peace was at hand. But the Loyalist paramilitaries immediately announced their opposition. The IRA set off a series of explosions to show its disapproval. And when the politicians seemed determined to go forward anyway, Loyalist-dominated unions called a general strike, shutting down the province for more than two weeks.

The government caved in and scrapped the agreement. The war went on, terribly, with the toll of dead and wounded rising by the hundreds every year. The IRA stepped up its terror campaign with an offensive in Britain, killing more than two dozen civilians in no-warning attacks in pubs in Guildford and Birmingham. Those atrocities inspired further injustice when British police rounded up Irish males in the vicinity of the bombings. Ten men would be convicted for the pub bombings. They would become known as the Guildford Four and Birmingham Six, and they would serve sixteen years before Britain finally conceded that they were, in fact, innocent.

The collapse of Sunningdale put an end to political initiatives. John Hume's dream of nonviolent resistance to Unionist injustice was dead. Bernadette Devlin lost a reelection bid in 1974 when Hume's SDLP ran a candidate against her, splitting the Catholic-Nationalist vote and handing the seat to a Unionist. She never again held elective office, although she continued to agitate and display her contempt for the province's politics. Though far more radical than the people she spoke for, she was an articulate and brilliant advocate, so much so that in 1981, a Protestant paramilitary gang burst into her home, opened fire, and left her and her husband gravely wounded. Both eventually recovered.

Northern Ireland in the mid-1970s became a full-fledged battle-ground for one of the bitterest and least-understood conflicts in the world. Often portrayed in America as a tribal war between the province's Catholics and Protestants, with the British as the hapless and frustrated middlemen, it was in fact a war of terrorism pitting the Provisional wing of the IRA, armed with weapons from Irish America, the Middle East, and Eastern Europe, against the combined forces of the British army, the Royal Ulster Constabulary, and Loyalist paramilitary organizations. A crack British army unit known as the Special Air Services was dispatched to Northern Ireland, allegedly to implement a policy known as shoot-to-kill, that is, they were given license to shoot suspected IRA members on sight. The British government, for its part, denied that such a policy existed.

Appalling atrocities were commited on all sides. A group known as the Shankill Butchers, made up of members of the Ulster Volunteer Force, tortured, slaughtered, and dismembered at least nineteen Catholics in the mid- and late 1970s. So odious were the crimes that when the gang's leader, a man named Lanny Murphy, was released from prison after beating murder charges, the UVF leaked word of his whereabouts to the Provisional IRA, who took their revenge in the expected fashion. The IRA, meanwhile, expanded its targets to include part-time members of the Ulster Defense Regiment, a reserve unit of the British Army. They were killed while off-duty, unarmed, and defenseless. IRA bombings during the mid- and late 1970s in Protestant areas had the smell of sectarianism about them, although the IRA was as likely to kill a Catholic soldier as a Protestant.

The British army itself continued to act as an agent of the Unionist system, even if the Unionist government no longer existed. There were seventeen thousand soldiers in the North, to supplement members of the Royal Ulster Constabulary, and they existed, it seemed, to harass Irish Catholic males, all of whom were presumed guilty of the crime of nationalism. Army patrols regularly sealed off streets in Catholic neighborhoods to conduct raids and general harassment, and individual soldiers in full battle dress regularly kept passersby in their gun sights.

Still, the British wished to be seen as idealistic peacemakers trying to keep two barbaric tribes from killing each other. That self-created image took a beating in the late 1970s when a series of international bodies, including the European Court of Human Rights, criticized Britain's treatment of paramilitary prisoners and for other violations of human rights. The criticisms generally were accorded little attention in the British press.

For a short time in 1976, it seemed as though public opinion alone might bring an end to the conflict when thousands of Catholic and Protestant women banded together after one of the province's most horrible tragedies. Two IRA men in a car were trying to escape British army pursuers. Shots were fired; the IRA man at the wheel was killed. The car rammed into Anne Maguire and her four children, three of whom died. Anne Maguire spent weeks in a coma. When she came out of it, she was told what had happened to her family.

The women who took to the streets to protest the violence became known as the Peace People. The organization's two founders, Betty Williams and Mairead Corrigan, the latter an aunt of the Maguire children, won the Nobel Peace Prize in 1976 for their efforts. But the movement built no networks and no momentum. The Maguire children were not the last innocents, not even the last children, to die in Northern Ireland. Going into the last year of the grim 1970s, the province had settled into a terrible little war, not nearly as intense as 1972, when nearly five hundred people died, but horrible all the same for the hundreds of people who were in the wrong place at the wrong time.

On August, 27, 1979, Lord Louis Mountbatten was in a small fishing boat off the coast of County Sligo with his fourteen-year-old grandson, three friends, and a fifteen-year-old crew member. The seventy-nine-year-old Mountbatten was a member of Britain's extended royal family, one of Britain's great heroes of World War II, and the last British viceroy in India prior to its independence and partition in 1947.

The IRA had put a bomb on the vessel. It exploded as the boat was making its way out of the small harbor of Mullaghmore, killing Mountbatten, his grandson, and the teenage crew member. Another passenger died the next day. At about the same time, bombs went off

Cardinal Tomas O Fiaich

in County Down, killing eighteen British soldiers. It was one of the bloodiest days of Anglo-Irish conflict in the twentieth century, and chilling proof that the IRA could strike at any time, even against so seemingly secure a target as a member of the royal family. The new British Prime Minister, Margaret Thatcher, flew by helicopter to Northern Ireland and, wearing a flak jacket, led a chorus of denunciations that spanned the globe.

Tomas Cardinal O Fiaich was on his way to Rome when the bombs went off. As Archbishop of Armagh, O Fiaich was the highest-ranking Roman Catholic clergyman on the island of Ireland, the Primate of All Ireland, successor to Saint Patrick. He had come a long way indeed from the days when he was known as Father Tom Fee and was tutoring John Hume in modern history. Immersed in Irish culture and fluent in the language, Father Fee Gaelicized his name when he was named Archbishop. He decreed that the motto for his office would be "Fratres in Unum," Latin for Brothers in Unity.

The Cardinal's business in Rome took on added gravity in the wake of Mountbatten's murder. He was putting together last-minute details for Pope John Paul II's visit to Ireland, scheduled for late September. There was talk of having the Pope visit the Roman Catholic cathedral in Armagh town, the ancient seat of the Irish Catholic Church, but Ian Paisley demanded that the government ban the Pontiff from setting foot on Northern Irish soil. Paisley's opposition was not enough to change the Pope's schedule, but after the Mountbatten killing, O Fiaich and the Vatican decided against a trip to Armagh. Instead, the Pope went to Drogheda in the Irish Republic, where he made a direct plea to the IRA. "On my knees," he said, "I beg you to turn away from the paths of violence and return to the ways of peace."

The Pope's message and the public outrage over Mountbatten's death made little impression on one IRA man serving fourteen years for possession of a gun. Bobby Sands, a twenty-five-year-old father who had spent most of his adult life in prison, justified the IRA's killing of Mountbatten. "He knew about the problem [in Ireland] and did nothing about it," Sands said. He was a Catholic reared in predominantly Protestant neighborhoods in Belfast and elsewhere, and his family was subjected to cruel taunting and worse. When a legal Protestant paramilitary organization, the Ulster Defense Association, led a menacing march near the Sands home, young Bobby, not yet a teenager, spent the long night awake and with a knife in his hand. The family finally fled to a Catholic neighborhood after a Protestant mob threw a garbage can through their window. He dropped out of school at fifteen and, with no prospects save poverty and the dole, he joined the IRA while still in his teens.

Soon after Mountbatten's state funeral, the unlikely trio of Cardinal Tomas O Fiaich, Bobby Sands, and Margaret Thatcher came together in what amounted to a second front in the Northern conflict. This battle took place not in the streets of Derry or the rural lanes of south County Armagh, but in the prisons of Northern Ireland and, eventually, in 10 Downing Street itself.

The British government ended the special category status for paramilitary prisoners arrested after March 1, 1976. From then on, prisoners charged with terrorist crimes were to be treated like any other criminal. Bobby Sands was among the new prisoners denied the special category privileges. He and several other IRA men were arrested in 1977 when soldiers stopped their car and found a pistol inside. That was enough for him to be sentenced to fourteen years. He was remanded to a prison built specifically for the paramilitary prisoners. The British called it Her Majesty's Prison, the Maze. The Irish called it Long Kesh, the name of the town in which it was located. From the air, the facility resembled a huge H, and thus was given yet another name: the H Blocks.

Following the elimination of special category status, IRA prisoners in Long Kesh refused to wear prison-issue uniforms, and clothed themselves instead in blankets. They contended that they were not common criminals, that their crimes were political and should be recognized as such. Prison authorities responded by confining the protesting prisoners to their cells. The protest escalated when some prisoners refused to wash and took to smearing their cells with excrement from their chamber pots. By 1980, more than 1,300 prisoners were on the blanket in Long Kesh—a little less than half of them members of Loyalist paramilitary groups whose special category privileges also were taken away.

Sands was one of the leaders in the prison, entertaining his fellow prisoners with memorized passages from Leon Uris's novel *Trinity*, which was set in Ireland in the early twentieth century. He kept a diary and wrote poetry and short stories, although he had to do his writing by stealth because the protesting prisoners were denied writing privileges. He wrote on toilet paper with a pencil he kept hidden from authorities.

Cardinal O Fiaich was a regular visitor at Long Kesh, beginning in the late summer of 1978. He issued a statement bitterly condemning the "inhuman conditions" at the prison, and took note that Northern Ireland had three thousand men and women locked up throughout the province, with more than half in Long Kesh. "One would hardly allow an animal to remain in such conditions" as he saw in Long Kesh, he said. "The stench and filth in some of the cells, with the remains of rotten food and human excreta scattered around the wall, was almost unbearable." In two cells he visited, he said, "I was unable to speak for fear of vomiting."

His criticisms led to a round of fierce condemnations, not of the conditions in the prison, but of his statement. He was accused of giving aid and comfort to terrorists. The government fired back at the Cardinal, issuing a statement saying that the prisoners were to blame for the appalling conditions. The prisoners, at least, appreciated his efforts. The Cardinal received a letter at Christmastime in 1979 from a prisoner who thanked him for his efforts but said that "our cells are even more terrible than they were . . . if there is a hell in this world it is surely in the H-Blocks." The prisoner said he hoped to see the Cardinal in Long Kesh again sometime soon, and signed his name Riobard O Seachnasaigh—the Irish form of Bobby Sands.

O Fiaich returned to the prison in March 1980, and among the prisoners he visited was a Protestant paramilitary serving a life sentence for murder—Gusty Spence. The onetime commander of the Ulster Volunteer Force was being held in the same facility that was bursting with captured IRA men. When Spence spotted the Cardinal, he offered his hand and a traditional Irish greeting: "A hundred thousand welcomes!"

"You should say *Cead mile fáilte*," the Cardinal replied with a smile, referring to the Irish-language rendering of the welcome phrase. Spence noticed that the Cardinal had a bad cough, which he attributed, rightly, to smoking. He offered the Cardinal a pipe with tobacco drenched in poteen, or homemade alcohol. The two men spent some time talking about the Irish-language classes the Loyalists had organized in prison. O Fiaich met several other prisoners that day, and he took note that Spence was the only one, Catholic or Protestant, to address him as "Your Eminence."

Gusty Spence had vowed to educate himself in "the political circumstances which led to me being in jail," and he had. He turned away from traditional Unionism, and decided that he wished he had never heard of Ian Paisley. He did not renounce Loyalism, but he came to the conclusion that violence would resolve nothing, and that working-class Protestants had been manipulated into hating Catholics instead of insisting on decent jobs and housing. Politics and education, he decided, were preferable to the gun. On July 12, 1977, Spence commemorated the Battle of the Boyne with a startling address to his fellow Loyalist prisoners in Long Kesh. "We are living in the most socially and legalistically oppressive society in the Western hemisphere, the manifestations of which are strewn over that society like scabs," he said. "The fears of the Roman Catholics will not go away because a bunch of bigoted Unionist politicians say so, and make no mistake about this word 'Unionist,' because we are Unionists, too, even though we could never agree with those fascists who hold the reins of power. Do they not realize that the IRA was a natural manifestation of Catholic fears just as the UVF and UDA were born from Loyalist fear?" He called on "all the warring factions" to put aside their weapons. "Eventually Loyalist and Republican must sit down together for the good of our country."

He became a father figure to a generation of Protestant paramilitaries held in Long Kesh in the late 1970s and early 1980s. Though he swore off violence, he played the part of commander, installing a military-like discipline among his fellow prisoners while questioning their instinctive resort to the gun and bomb. Two of his prized converts were Billy Hutchinson, who was sent to Long Kesh for his role in the murder of two young Catholics, and David Ervine, who was caught with explosives.

As the Christmas holidays approached in 1980, Gusty Spence sent a card to his new friend, His Eminence Tomas Cardinal O Fiaich. He enclosed a line wishing that 1981 would be "a period of happiness and peace in our country."

A hunger strike had just ended in Long Kesh when Spence sent his card to the Cardinal. It had lasted for more than fifty days, and it ended with at least one prisoner near death when prison authorities seemed to concede some demands for a return to special category privileges. O Fiaich, as Ireland's leading Catholic prelate, and Sands, as the new commanding officer of republican prisoners in Long Kesh, had been in the middle of negotiations leading to the strike's conclusion.

The compromise collapsed almost immediately, and on the evening of February 28, 1981, Bobby Sands ate his weekly allotment of fruit. It was an orange, and it was to be his last bit of solid food. He had asked a prison chaplain about the morality of hunger strikes, whether they were considered suicide under Church law. The chaplain tried to talk him out of such a dramatic gesture.

"Greater love hath no man than this that he lays down his life for his friends," Sands replied.

On the morning of March 1, Bobby Sands refused to eat the meals left in his cell. A new hunger strike was underway, and Sands would not be alone. Plans called for new strikers to join periodically until the British granted the Irish prisoners the privileges they had enjoyed before 1976.

Sands's friends and colleagues knew not only that there would be no turning back, for Sands was a determined young man, but that the British government was unlikely to concede. Margaret Thatcher made her opinions quite clear. Murder, she said, was murder. Sands, of course, was not in prison for murder, but for being in a car in which a gun was found.

"I am standing on the threshold of another trembling world," Sands wrote on the first day of his fast. "May God have mercy on my soul." He turned twenty-seven years old on March 8, the eighth day of his strike. "I am awaiting the lark, for spring is all but upon us," he wrote that day. "Now lying on what indeed is my deathbed, I still listen even to the black crows."

As Sands's protest gained worldwide publicity, high-ranking American politicians, including House of Representatives Speaker Thomas O'Neill, Senator Daniel Patrick Moynihan, New York Governor Hugh Carey, and Senator Edward Kennedy, pleaded with Margaret Thatcher to soften her position. So did politicians from the Irish Republic. And so did Cardinal O Fiaich, who was invited as a matter of courtesy to the Prime Minister's residence at 10 Downing Street. Thatcher said to one and all that she would not concede to terrorists. At one point during a contentious meeting with Cardinal O Fiaich, Mrs. Thatcher wondered aloud why the British and Irish couldn't get along. "We fought the Germans and the French, and now we're on the best of terms with them," she said. "Why are we fighting the Irish?"

"But Prime Minster," the man from Crossmaglen replied, "you're not occupying the Rhine."

Asked if he wanted a drink, the Cardinal ordered an Irish whiskey, only to be told there was none in the house.

Hunger strikes had a long and tragic history in Ireland, and the sense of déjà vu became even more eerie when a Member of Parliament from parts of Counties Fermanagh and Tyrone, Frank Maguire, died on March 5, five days into Bobby Sands's strike. A by-election to fill the vacancy was scheduled for mid-April. A coalition of republican sympathizers nominated Bobby Sands to run for Maguire's seat as the candidate of an ad hoc political party called the H-Block Movement. Faced with a critical dilemma, John Hume's moderate Social Democratic and Labour Party chose not to split the nationalist vote with a candidate of its own. The ensuing campaign became a referendum on Britain's policy of criminalizing IRA prisoners. The British, faced with a public relations nightmare, tried to persuade voters that a vote for Sands was a vote for the murderers of Lord Mountbatten. To no avail. On April 10, 1981, Bobby Sands won the seat from his cell. He was now Robert Sands, MP.

It was a bitter blow for Margaret Thatcher and her Conservative government, who had argued that there was no public support among Catholics in Northern Ireland for the prisoners' demands. The votes of thirty thousand people refuted the Prime Minister. And now, in accordance with the hunger strikers' plans, three more prisoners had joined Sands in the protest.

Still, the government conceded nothing, even as world opinion rallied around the young man with long brown hair who defied the notion that he was but a common criminal. Pope John Paul II sent a personal envoy to plead for a compromise. A delegation from the Irish Republic, including Sile de Valera, granddaughter of Eamon de Valera, tried to meet with Thatcher, but she declined. She said that it was not her practice to meet with "MPs from a foreign country."

Bobby Sands died on May 5 after sixty-six days on hunger strike. More than 100,000 people attended his funeral and burial ceremony. News cameras from around the world recorded the massive display of grief. From a purely propaganda standpoint, the Thatcher government had stumbled into disaster.

Still the strike went on, and more men died, slowly, inexorably, during the summer of 1981. O Fiaich met again with the Prime Minister, but the meetings were bitter and acrimonious. The Cardinal heatedly told the Prime Minister that Northern Ireland had been a lie from its creation. Thatcher took this as evidence that he was an IRA sympathizer at heart. The British press agreed with the Prime Minister. The *Sunday Express* referred to him as the "Chaplain in Chief of the IRA."

Ten men died before the hunger strike was called off in late August. Their courage and determination turned them into highly sympathetic characters, even though some of them were in prison for murder. In the war for public opinion, the British had suffered a catastrophe. In America, Irish-Americans who had given little thought to Northern Ireland marched outside the British consulate in New York. Other Irish-Americans chose a more lethal way of showing their support: they arranged new arms shipments to an IRA whose ranks grew as each hunger striker was buried.

Almost lost in the drama of the dying men was a startling political development. With Sands dead, another by-election was scheduled to fill the vacancy in Tyrone-Fermanagh. A republican named Owen Carron, who had served as Sands's campaign manager in April, was nominated for the seat. Carron was neither a prisoner nor a hunger striker, not a man who could appeal for a sympathy vote. He won anyway, with an increased margin of victory.

Sinn Féin, the political party aligned with the IRA, had stood aloof from politics in both the Irish Republic and Northern Ireland. With great republican purity, the party denounced both governments as illegitimate. Carron's surprisingly easy victory, however, indicated that politics might be effective after all.

And that was exactly what Gusty Spence was preaching in the very prison that had held Bobby Sands and his nine dead comrades.

CHAPTER ELEVEN

THE COMMON CAUSE OF PEACE

THE YEARS FOLLOWING the hunger strike were filled with bitterness and despair in Northern Ireland and the Irish Republic.

The conflict in the North became a terrible stalemate, with neither side capable of military victory but both unwilling to concede. The number of annual deaths was low compared with the early 1970s, usually in double digits, but that only magnified the horror as each new victim represented yet another sacrifice to hopelessness. The urban battleground and symbol of division switched from Derry—where an end to gerrymandering and the imposition of one-person, one-vote resulted in a transfer of power to Catholics—to Belfast, the capital of Protestant Ulster. The duel between the IRA and the security forces took on an added dimension when Loyalist paramilitaries stepped up a campaign of sectarian assassination against Catholics. Some Catholics were targeted simply because of their religion; others, however, were chosen with greater care. In April 1984, three armed men fired twenty shots at the new president of Sinn Féin, Gerry Adams, outside a courthouse in Belfast. The bearded thirty-six-year-old native of Belfast's Catholic ghetto was hit four times. One of the bullets just missed his heart.

The attempt on Adams's life was a clear indication that Loyalist paramilitaries were prepared to eliminate those they blamed for disturbing the power structure that existed in Northern Ireland before 1968. But there was an added element of desperation to some of the seemingly random murders in the 1980s. The civil rights movement of the 1960s and the educational reforms of the 1950s were bearing fruit in the form of a fledgling Catholic middle class blossoming in parts of formerly Protestant Belfast. But when middle-class Catholics began moving up, Protestants moved out, displaced in the province they still regarded as theirs. A Presbyterian church and a lodge of the Orange Order in the Protestant working-class neighborhood of Belfast's Ormeau Road soon became symbols of changing times. Both would be abandoned before the end of the 1980s as the neighborhood changed from Protestant to Catholic.

Evidence of Catholic economic gains came even as the province's old industrial core continued to rot, swelling overall unemployment to 21 percent in the early 1980s. Hundreds of factories closed, and the number of manufacturing jobs in the province dropped from 177,000 in 1970 to ninety thousand by the end of 1983. The province's two anchor industies, linen and shipbuilding, suffered terrible losses. Employment in the linen trade fell to about six thousand in the early 1980s, from 45,000 in the late 1950s. And the shipyard of Harland & Wolff stayed in business only through government contracts. Employment, nevertheless, continued to fall, from more than seven thousand in the late 1970s to five thousand in the early 1980s. By the end of the 1980s, London was spending nearly £2 billion a year to subsidize the North's economy.

The economic suffering fell on Protestants who once counted on their domination of manufacturing as part of the reward for remaining loyal to the Crown and identifying themselves as British, not Irish. Protestant unemployment was about 12 percent, double what it was in the early 1970s. Catholic unemployment grew, too, from about 17 percent in the early 1970s to 35 percent in the early 1980s. But the sting was worse for Protestants, because their political leaders told them that Northern Ireland was run by and for Protestants, that they were, in fact, the ruling class. Catholics had learned long ago that flags made for paltry meals. And as the 1980s wore on, Protestant working-class neighborhoods like the Shankill and Sandy Row began to take on the same gray, dreary look of Belfast's Catholic ghettos of the Falls Road and Andersontown, where some families hadn't worked in generations. The frustration was palpable, and led at least some Loyalists to question the very idea of Protestant privilege upon which the Northern Ireland state was founded.

The Loyalist murder squads, however, were not so interested in asking questions. Instead, they set out to undo the effects of the new, albeit uneven, social mobility for Catholics through random murder in neighborhoods changing from orange to green. And in yet another sign that the police and army were not the impartial arbiters the government claimed them to be, Loyalist killers sometimes received information surreptitiously from the Crown's security forces in setting up members of Sinn Féin or suspected republican sympathizers for assassination. Among the murders believed committed in collusion with the security forces was that of a Catholic lawyer named Pat Finucane, who was killed in 1989 after a British Member of Parliament complained that something had to be done about lawyers who defended republican suspects. Finucane fit the description, and something was done. He was shot in front of his wife, a Protestant.

In the Republic, meanwhile, economic progress made in the mid-1960s under Prime Minister Sean Lemass—a member of Michael Collins's assassination team in 1921—collapsed in the early 1980s, sending tens of thousands of young people abroad in search of work. Unemployment in the Republic reached nearly 20 percent, and the dole became a way of life in places like Cork city. The border and the conflict in the north were constants in the Republic's political debate, but the people had far more immediate concerns. During the 1960s and 1970s, they had been led to believe that emigration was a tragedy of the past, but now their children, blessed with good educations and part of a vibrant youth culture, were boarding planes and boats because there was no future at home. The Republic was once again unable to provide jobs and opportunities for its young people. And when, in the mid-1980s, voters approved a continued ban on divorce in keeping with Catholic teaching, few could argue that the Republic was a hospitable place for already wary Northern Protestants. As for Northern Ireland's Catholics, it was noted with characteristic dark humor that the British dole was more generous than the Republic's.

In an attempt to change the status quo and to counter a startling upswing in support for Sinn Féin after the hunger strike, John Hume and other moderate nationalists connected to his Social Democratic and Labour Party convened what they called a New Ireland Forum in the early 1980s to discuss a range of possible political solutions to the violence. With the enthusiastic support of the Dublin government, they spent months in earnest conversation with leading figures from north and south about the island's future. The forum followed Hume's position that Unionism and the Ulster Protestant tradition were not going to simply disappear, that they had to be accepted as authentically Irish and dealt with accordingly. This inclusionary vision contrasted with Sinn Féin's simple message that the Unionists were welcome to join in a reunited, thirty-two-county Republic, which Unionists by definition opposed. And Hume's vision was a far cry indeed from the message of the Gaelic-Irish cultural movement of Yeats, Hyde, and Lady Gregory, Anglo-Protestants all.

But Hume also made it plain to the British that many Catholics in

Northern Ireland were not simply alienated from the government and society, but regarded the state itself as hostile to themselves and their ambitions. Speaking in the British House of Commons in early July 1984, Hume recalled seeing a group of youths gathered outside his home in Derry and in the act of preparing Molotov cocktails, or, in the local vernacular, petrol bombs. He didn't call the police, he explained, because that would have only made the situation worse. "That is a stark reality of life in areas of Northern Ireland that do not give their allegiance to the Union [of Britain and Northern Ireland]," he said.

Irish Prime Minister Garret Fitzgerald traveled to Britain in November 1984 to hold what was billed as a crucial summit meeting with Prime Minister Margaret Thatcher to discuss the New Ireland Forum's efforts, which outlined several possible options for the North, including an end to partition. Fitzgerald had persuaded Thatcher that some gesture was necessary to bolster moderate nationalists in the North. Otherwise, he warned, the SDLP could follow the path of John Redmond and the old Parliamentary Party, which the old Sinn Féin demolished in 1918. Thatcher seemed to agree. But with Fitzgerald at her side and the press assembled for the ritual post-summit news conference, Thatcher said: "I have made it quite clear . . . that a unified Ireland was one solution that is out. A second solution was confederation of the two states. That is out. A third solution was joint authority. That is out."

The press in Ireland and in America boiled down her sentiments in three caustic words: Out, out, out! A mortified Fitzgerald hung his head and returned to Dublin, where the leader of the opposition, Charles Haughey, accused him of leading Ireland "into the greatest humiliation in recent history." Haughey, who would experience humiliation firsthand in the late 1990s in a series of personal and professional scandals, was not exaggerating. Thatcher's contemptuous remarks were nothing short of a diplomatic embarrassment for nationalists searching for a peaceful way out of murderous civil unrest.

A furious John Hume bitterly condemned Thatcher and her allies: "We may yet be driven to the conclusion that no serious business can be done with this particular British government," he said.

Thatcher's contempt for her Irish colleague seemed to capture the spirit of Tory imperialists such as Benjamin Disraeli and Randolph Churchill. But only a month before her dismissal of Fitzgerald, she had barely escaped with her life when the Provisional IRA bombed the hotel where she was staying during a Conservative Party conference in the seaside resort of Brighton. The bomb killed six people, three of them wives of midlevel Conservative figures. In missing their target but killing innocents, the IRA at Brighton set a pattern for the mid- to late 1980s, when lethal mistakes became frequent. In claiming responsibility for the attack, the IRA chillingly directed a comment to the Prime Minister: "Today we were unlucky, but remember, we have only to be lucky once. You will have to be lucky always."

After a cooling-off period, the Irish approached London again, and this time they were not crudely rebuffed. In the intervening months, Thatcher had traveled to America to meet with her friend and ideological soul mate, Ronald Reagan, grandson of Michael Reagan of County Tipperary. Reagan had become convinced that Thatcher had made a critical mistake during her meeting with Fitzgerald. The two leaders discussed Ireland during a summit at Camp David just before Christmas 1985. Two months later, House Speaker Thomas O'Neill of Massachusetts told British diplomats and then Thatcher herself that she ought to say something conciliatory about Northern Ireland in a scheduled address to a joint session of Congress in February 1985. She did, telling Congress that she and her Cabinet recognized "the differing traditions and identities ... in Northern Ireland, the Nationalist and the Unionist. We seek a political way forward acceptable to them both and which respects them both."

The Unionists took a deep breath and detected an odor of betrayal in Thatcher's remarks. She was discussing their future, which was a matter of internal British politics, with outsiders. Worse yet, they were American politicians, a group Unionists regarded as advocates of a pro-IRA, Irish Catholic viewpoint. The British tabloid press, appealing to the lowest common denominator, had always been happy to fuel such fears. When an IRA bomb killed two people in October 1981, just after the last of the ten dead hunger strikers was buried, Britain's *Daily Express* featured a front-page editorial blaming O'Neill, Massachusetts Senator Edward Kennedy, New York Governor Hugh Carey, New York Senator Daniel Patrick Moynihan, and New York City Mayor Ed Koch, the son of Polish Jews, for the blast because they had criticized Britain's hard line during the strike. The *Express* headline read: "Five Guilty Men."

Worse yet from the Unionist view, Thatcher's Washington speech seemed to make no moral distinction between nationalists, regarded as traitors in Unionist dogma, and the Unionists themselves. And, worst of all, when Thatcher returned to London in late February 1985, new talks began between high-level Irish and British diplomats. The Unionists regarded the Republic of Ireland not only as a foreign nation, but as a hostile government that gave refuge to IRA terrorists. And yet the British, under Margaret Thatcher no less, were talking with Dublin politicians about Protestant Ulster's future. The Unionists' nightmares came true in November 1985, when the Dublin-London talks led to the signing of an Anglo-Irish Agreement almost a year to the day after Thatcher's rebuff of Fitzgerald. In exchange for greater cooperation from the Irish in patrolling the border, London offered Dublin a role in overseeing government efforts to relieve anti-Catholic discrimination in the North. A British-Irish Intergovernmental Council would assist with complaints against the police, and in investigating human rights violations and other matters, including cross-border security. The specific concessions were less important than the general principle, which conceded that the Irish Republic did, after all, have an interest in governing the six counties of Northern Ireland. In the jargon of diplomats, the agreement added an "Irish dimension" to the governing of Northern Ireland. The British also agreed that "if in the future a majority of the people of Northern Ireland clearly wish for and formally consent to the establishment of a united Ireland," legislation would be prepared accordingly. At a time when the Catholic population of Northern Ireland had grown to nearly 45 percent from 33 percent at the state's founding, this concession was more than academic.

Militant Loyalists were outraged, and they charged that Margaret Thatcher had sold out Unionism and the North's claim to be British. Days after the agreement was signed, the rabble-rousing Reverend Ian Paisley addressed a crowd of at least 100,000 outside Belfast City Hall, which was draped with a banner reading "Ulster Says No!" To which Paisley added his own phrase: "Never! Never! Never!" Through the first few months of 1986, Paisley-fueled mobs turned their anger on the Royal Ulster Constabulary, which was nearly all-Protestant and had been regarded as the Loyalists' shield from nationalists and the IRA. The homes of dozens of constables were fire-bombed, and many fled their old neighborhoods rather than face Loyalist terror. The spectacle was designed to recall memories of 1974, when a Loyalist general strike aborted the effort made in the Sunningdale Agreement to build a power-sharing local government in Northern Ireland. But it was no longer 1974. More than 2,500 people had died since 1969 and tens of thousands were scarred and maimed. The province was exhausted. The paramilitaries were fighting an urban equivalent of trench warfare. And the British were tiring of the expense of keeping an army of more than ten thousand soldiers in Northern Ireland. Margaret Thatcher refused to give in to the outraged Loyalists.

The Anglo-Irish Agreement was the beginning of a tortuous, clumsy, and unpredictable effort to find a way to end the violence. The Loyalists who listened to Ian Paisley still resisted the idea of sharing political power with Catholics, and some began importing arms from South Africa to demonstrate their resistance. But others, equally adamant about preserving the link with Great Britain, were questioning exactly why Ulster seemed to be forever saying no, why, indeed, old-line Protestant Unionists presumed that they were speaking for all of Ulster.

One of the "other" Loyalists was Gusty Spence, who emerged from prison in 1984 after serving eighteen years of his twenty-year sentence. He was fifty-one years old, a grandfather, suffering the effects of two heart attacks and gallbladder problems. He had gone to prison as a young man with no education but a heart full of grievance. Prison had been his university, and his studies had led him to reject what he saw as the triumphal sectarianism of traditional Unionism. Reunited with his wife and children in the Shankill neighborhood he loved, he turned his energies to community work, counseling the unemployed and helping the Shankill's schoolchildren avoid the mistakes he had made. He became a prominent member of a political organization called the Progressive Unionist Party, and with everpresent pipe in hand, he was the party's elder statesman and moral authority. Spence and his wife frequently traveled south to Armagh to visit their friend, Cardinal O Fiaich. "We had many a pipe and whiskey together," Spence said.

Although the PUP had ties to Spence's old paramilitary organization, the Ulster Volunteer Force, the party rejected the kneejerk obstruction of Paisley and his apostles, offering instead a working-class sensibility that regarded old-line Unionism as an empty, cruel promise. Among the party's leaders were two men who had come under Spence's influence in prison, David Ervine and Billy Hutchinson. Spence had converted both to nonviolence, and now they took their message to the Shankill Road. The three men became known in Loyalist circles as the "kitchen cabinet," meeting with clergy and community leaders to move the Protestant community away from violence and toward a society where Protestant and Catholic alike had a stake in the province's government and economy.

A larger Loyalist organization with a deserved reputation for murderous attacks on Catholics, the Ulster Defense Association, also seemed to be inching toward some sort of political resolution. In early 1987, the UDA released a surprisingly textured and well-argued pamphlet making the case for power sharing with Catholics in a new local government body that would govern the North in accordance with a new bill of rights that would protect the province's minority community. Even more remarkably, the document asserted that majority rule "in deeply divided societies is likely to be profoundly undemocratic." It argued instead for genuine coalition politics that included members of the minority community.

The UDA entitled its proposal "Common Sense." Its commander, Andy Tyrie, presented a copy to an American reporter visiting the UDA headquarters in Belfast in January 1987. "Make sure Paul O'Dwyer sees this," Tyrie said, referring to the legendary Irish-American civil rights attorney and New York politician. O'Dwyer was a fierce republican, and his law firm defended IRA sympathizers in New York charged with running guns to Ireland. Nevertheless, O'Dwyer had won the respect of the Loyalists in part by arguing that their prisoners, like the IRA's, should be treated as political prisoners. And O'Dwyer, Tyrie explained, had introduced the UDA's leadership to the writings of Thomas Paine, author of the original *Common Sense*, the man who had inspired the Protestants of Belfast to become Irish nationalists in the 1790s.

The slow ascendance of politics was taking place in the republican movement as well. Sinn Féin's electoral successes since 1981 had thus far provided publicity but little power. Sinn Féin candidates refused to take the local government or parliamentary seats they won, for in doing so they would be recognizing British authority in Northern Ireland. The party so guarded its purity that it likewise abstained from taking seats it won in the Irish Republic, which it also regarded as an illegitimate government.

Hints that the Provisional IRA was looking for a way out came even as Prime Minister Thatcher was making conciliatory sounds in front of the American Congress in early 1985. The IRA's ruling body, its Army Council, released a statement inviting John Hume to talk with its members about the issues that divided physical force republicanism and Hume's constitutional nationalism. Hume accepted. He had proved before, and would prove again, that there would never be a conversation he would refuse if he thought it might advance the cause of peace. The meeting took place on February 23, 1985, after Hume was blindfolded and taken to a secret location, but it broke almost immediately when IRA members insisted on videotaping the discussions. Hume objected, and the meeting ended.

Late that summer, however, Sinn Féin president Gerry Adams made a startling admission during an interview on British television. He said that "Sinn Fein . . . made a mistake in not contesting elec-

Gerry Adams

tions and in not being involved in electoral politics. . . . There needs to be a united Nationalist approach to the whole question of the British involvement in this country." In choosing to call for a united "nationalist" approach, Adams was signaling that Sinn Féin and its allies in the IRA were looking for a way to do business with the moderates of the SDLP.

Sinn Féin assembled for a dramatic convention on November 1,

1986, in Dublin's Mansion House, the site of previous Sinn Féin gatherings before and during the War of Independence. Adams put forward his proposal knowing that it would face fierce opposition from hard-liners and purists, who rejected the 1921 Anglo-Irish Treaty and the 1922 general election that essentially ratified the treaty. "I can understand that some comrades view a change in the abstention policy as a betrayal of republican principle," he said. "Some of you may feel that a republican organization making such a change can no longer call itself 'republican.' If there are delegates here who feel like this, I would remind you that another republican organization has already done what you fear we are going to do."

The other republican organization to which Adams referred ever so carefully was the Irish Republican Army. The IRA's Army Council already had given its approval to Adams's change of direction.

Adams won, and dissidents did what dissidents have done for centuries in Ireland: they created their own faction, called Republican Sinn Féin. Like the Fenian hard-liners of old, they would remain on the sidelines while historic events unfolded.

Gerry Adams was from a generation that reached young adulthood just as the civil rights campaign began its historic challenge of one-party sectarian rule in the North. The old guard he replaced in Sinn Féin was from the Irish Republic. Adams was from the Ballymurphy section of Belfast, born in 1948 to a working-class family with a tradition of republican politics. His paternal grandfather had been in the Irish Republican Brotherhood earlier in the century, and his father and his father's brothers were active in the IRA during the 1940s. Gerry Adams Sr. served five years in prison for the attempted murder of a Royal Ulster Constabulary man during civil disturbances in 1942. The senior Adams was sixteen at the time, and was slightly wounded himself in the incident.

Republican blood ran in his mother's family, too. A maternal great-grandfather was a Fenian, and his maternal grandfather served as an election agent for Eamon de Valera in the famous Sinn Féin triumph of 1918.

Adams spent his childhood in a culturally, economically, and politically segregated ghetto. He went to Catholic schools, followed Gaelic sports, studied the Irish language, and learned to regard Dublin, not London, as his capital. More practically, he also learned that if the police stopped him, he should give his first name as John, not Gerry. Catholics had names like Gerry. Protestants had names like John. Conveniently, the surname Adams could be Protestant or Catholic, so only one lie was required.

One day when he was in his mid-teens, he was filling out some paperwork related to his school until he stopped at what seemed like a simple question. He was asked to fill in his nationality. He asked his mother how he should answer.

"Well, some people might put down British," she said.

"Why would they put down British? This is Ireland," Adams replied.

He joined Sinn Féin while he was still in his teens, and he was working as a barman in 1966 when word made its way around Belfast that four barmen had been shot on a June evening in 1966 and one, Peter Ward, was dead. It was for that crime that Gusty Spence was sent to prison for eighteen years.

As the civil rights campaign began, Adams was a familiar figure in Belfast's republican circles and in campaigns for better housing and an end to job discrimination. Though from a family that was hardly wealthy, the poverty he witnessed in Belfast shocked him. When the city exploded after the Battle of the Bogside in Derry in 1968, Adams was in the streets, witnessing the end of the old order in the North. Although he has never admitted to joining the IRA, it is widely believed that he did so at around this time. In a careful memoir published in 1996, Adams is silent on the subject of his exact relationship with the IRA, although he makes clear where his sympathies lie and indeed that he was in close contact with people who were in the guerrilla organization.

He served two short stints in prison, the first after the British introduced internment, allowing troops to arrest suspected republicans without due process. The respect he inspired was obvious early on, when he was taken out of his cell and flown to London for secret talks with British officials in the mid-1970s.

In taking over as president of Sinn Féin in 1986, he was assuming the public face of the IRA's campaign, a job that would become very difficult very quickly. Although he insisted that Sinn Féin was independent of the IRA, few believed him, and besides, Sinn Féin policy enthusiastically supported what it called the IRA's "armed struggle" to rid Northern Ireland of British rule. He started his tenure from a position of unenviable weakness, for not only had the SDLP successfully cut into Sinn Féin's support in several elections after the 1985 Anglo-Irish Agreement, but the IRA committed a series of horrendous, murderous blunders in the late 1980s.

Armed with Armalite rifles and a plastic explosive, Semtex, purchased from Libya, the IRA's four hundred or so active members carried out a disastrous bombing campaign that not only took the lives of innocent civilians, but, from a public relations standpoint, destroyed the respect the hunger strikers had earned for their sacrifice and dedication. The worst attack came in November 1987, when an IRA bomb went off in the town of Enniskillen during a ceremony honoring the dead of World War I. Eleven Protestant civilians were killed. One of them was Marie Wilson, twenty years old, who was awaiting the ceremony with her father, Gordon Wilson. The blast buried them under a pile of rubble. As they awaited rescue workers, Marie gripped her father's hand and said, "Daddy, I love you very much." She died in a hospital hours later. That night, Gordon Wilson spoke to a reporter from the BBC. "I have lost my daughter, and we shall miss her," he said. "But I bear no ill will. I bear no grudge. Dirty sort of talk is not going to bring her back to life. She was a great wee lassie. . . . It's part of a greater plan, and God is good. And we shall meet again." Wilson's words showed that not everybody in Northern Ireland was caught up in old grievances, that, in fact, people there were capable of forgiveness and reconciliation.

The IRA apologized for the attack, but its words of regret could not match Gordon Wilson's.

Gordon Wilson was not to be the last grieving parent of Northern Ireland's violence. A Protestant family was killed when an IRA bomb team mistook its car for that of a judge who was on the IRA's hit list. Two boys were killed in Warrington, England, when an IRA bomb in a letter box went off on a busy commercial street. And so it went. With each horror, the press descended on Gerry Adams for a ritualistic explanation of the inexplicable. His status as a pariah was solidified, even though he had said after Enniskillen that there could be no military solution in the North. The American government, following the wishes of the British government, forbade Adams from visiting the United States. He applied for a visa several times during the Reagan and Bush administrations, but Washington said no. Irish-American leaders, too, wanted to keep him in Belfast.

There was plenty of blame to be passed around for Northern Ireland's sorry state. Protestant paramilitaries became more deadly than the IRA, eventually topping their blood enemies in annual body count. And the British criminal justice system was called to account by a special police investigator from Manchester, England, John Stalker. Stalker was demoted and smeared in the mid-1980s when he found evidence that the Royal Ulster Constabulary covered up premeditated police murders of Catholics. He eventually was vindicated.

When the ten Irishmen arrested in the early 1970s for the bomb attacks in Birmingham and Guildford were released from prison after serving more than fifteen years, press reports indicated that the British government knew they were innocent at least several years before an international campaign on their behalf led to their freedom.

Despite the Anglo-Irish Agreement of 1985 and the hopes it engendered among moderate nationalists like Hume, Northern Ireland in the late 1980s seemed no closer to a political resolution than it had in 1968, when the civil unrest known as the Troubles began. Republican and Loyalist paramilitaries alike made some gestures, but the killing continued.

On January 11, 1988, John Hume and Gerry Adams met for a face-to-face talk. Throughout the 1980s, Hume and the SDLP had been criticized by Sinn Féin for being too middle-class and too willing to cooperate in accepting reforms rather than working for revolution to win a united Ireland.

But one horrible murder after another finally brought the two parties together. In a series of meetings, Hume and Adams and their allies thrashed out their differences. Did the British have strategic interests to defend in Northern Ireland? Sinn Féin said yes; the SDLP disagreed, saying that the British were looking for some sort of permanent settlement. The point was critical, for if Sinn Féin was right, the British would be dislodged only through force. But if the SDLP were right, politics and persuasion might yet prevail. What was the cause of the North's troubles? The British, argued Sinn Féin. The SDLP asserted that the problems were more complex. The meetings lasted off and on until September 1988, when they ended in an exchange of pointed, but not scathing, criticisms.

Behind the scenes, however, Hume and Adams continued to meet in secret.

In October 1990, a representative of the British government contacted Gerry Adams's chief deputy, Martin McGuinness, to explain that the British wished to open covert communication with Sinn Féin and, therefore, with the IRA. McGuinness met with the official, who explained that he was about to retire from his government post and would serve as the contact between Sinn Féin and the government. His identity was secret. Sinn Féin referred to him simply as "Contact."

Days after McGuinness and Contact met, Sinn Féin was sent an advance copy of a speech to be delivered on November 9 by Peter Brooke, the Secretary of State for Northern Ireland. To those fluent in the nuanced language of Northern Irish diplomacy, the speech was astonishing. In it, Brooke—Margaret Thatcher's man in Ireland—offered a gesture and an assurance to nationalists.

"An Irish Republicanism seen to have finally renounced violence would be able, like other parties, to seek a role in the peaceful political life of the community," Brooke said. "In Northern Ireland, it is not the aspiration to a sovereign, united Ireland against which we set our face, but its violent expression." Traditional Unionism by definition opposed not simply violent expressions of Irish republicanism, but the aspiration itself, no matter how gently and politely it might be expressed.

Furthermore, Brooke asserted that the British government had "no selfish or strategic or economic interest in Northern Ireland: our role is to help, enable and encourage." These were exactly the words John Hume wished to hear. In the delicate political ballet underway, a gesture from the republican side was in order. The IRA declared a three-day cease-fire over the Christmas holidays of 1990.

Only a year before Brooke's speech, in November 1989, Cardinal Tomas O Fiaich had created a furious political controversy when he told an Irish radio interviewer that the British ought to declare that they would eventually leave Northern Ireland. Unionist politicians and even high-ranking Protestant clerics denounced the Cardinal's statement, saying that it encouraged IRA terrorism. The president of the Methodist Church said that O Fiaich's "careless talk" was like "handing kilos of Semtex and cargoes of armalites to those whose business is consigning people to the cemetery."

Cardinal O Fiaich did not live to hear Peter Brooke's careful speech. He died, at age sixty-six, during a pilgrimage to Lourdes, the French shrine. The Reverend Ian Paisley could barely contain his glee. He issued a statement saying: "Is it not strange . . . that the Roman Catholic authorities, when the RC Primate of All Ireland was taken ill at the very centre of their Healing Mecca, rushed the Cardinal away from Lourdes to a hospital . . . where he died." The statement bore a heading that said "Even Lourdes Could Not Heal Cardinal Thomas O'Fee." (Reverend Paisley declined to recognize the Cardinal's Gaelicized name.) Several years after the Cardinal's death his friends raised money to build a library in Armagh dedicated to his memory. Gusty Spence sent a contribution.

John Major, the son of working-class parents who had known poverty, succeeded Margaret Thatcher as Prime Minister in 1991. Highly secret communications between London and Sinn Féin continued, even after an IRA mortar team in London fired several rounds at 10 Downing Street while the new Prime Minister conducted a Cabinet meeting on February 7, 1991. Nobody was killed or wounded, but the sheer audacity of the attack was stunning, as if the IRA were reminding John Major that he, like his predecessor, would have to be "lucky always."

Before becoming Prime Minister, Major had been Britain's Chancellor of the Exchequer, in American terms, a combination of Budget Director and Secretary of the Treasury. His counterpart in Ireland

Albert Reynolds

was the Republic's Finance Minister, Albert Reynolds, a fan of American country music who had made a fortune as the owner of dance halls and a pet food empire. The two ministers met often in Brussels as the nations of Western Europe prepared for the next phase of European integration, a single monetary union. Major and Reynolds, in their own disparate ways, were highly unlikely politicians, never mind Cabinet ministers. Major's working-class background was the subject of private scorn among traditional Conservatives, who snickered over that most telling of class distinctions, his accent. Reynolds was a better fit in his party, Fianna Fáil, the populist, nationalist organization Eamon de Valera had founded in 1926, but he, too, was an outsider of sorts. Both men had climbed the proverbial greasy pole without the benefit of the family connections that were important in both parties, and both were from real-life backgrounds that emphasized pragmatism and problem solving. In a sign that an intriguing partnership was being born in Brussels, Reynolds and Major often voted together on the losing side on a variety of European Union issues. "Instead of losing 11 to 1 in votes, it was 10 to 2," Reynolds recalled. Choosing sides with the British, who were skeptical of the emerging European mega-state, against the rest of Europe earned Reynolds few favors at home, where European Union money was attempting to rebuild the Irish economy, but "I was prepared to build up confidence [with Major]," Reynolds said. "We found we could do business together."

A year after his friend John Major succeeded Thatcher, sixty-one-year-old Albert Reynolds became the Republic's Taoiseach (Irish for "leader"), or Prime Minister. In his maiden speech as the Republic's head of government, Reynolds named as his top two priorities the island's most intractable problems: peace in the North, and prosperity in the Republic.

Talks between the two old friends and their representatives went on for the next fifteen months. And, in a dramatic but secret break from traditional Dublin policy, Reynolds eventually established a line of communication with Unionist politicians who had influence with the Loyalist paramilitary armies. Just as Major was trying to lure Sinn Féin away from violence, Reynolds was sending signals to the Unionist parties that the time had come to talk. And all the while, John Hume continued to meet in secret with Gerry Adams in an attempt to forge a nationalist consensus on the North's future. The risks for all concerned were enormous, for if word leaked out of their surreptitious negotiations with the political leaders of armed movements, the uproar might have set back the common cause of peace for years.

Neither the IRA nor the Loyalist paramilitaries had put aside violence. The IRA set off a bomb in the center of London's financial district in April 1992, causing damage estimated at $1.2 billion. And Loyalist gunmen continued to target Catholics considered sympathetic to either the IRA or Sinn Féin.

Newly elected American President Bill Clinton appointed as U.S. ambassador to Ireland Jean Kennedy Smith, sister of Senator Ted Kennedy, in 1993. Smith was new to diplomacy, but was no stranger to Ireland and its modern troubles. She and her husband, Steve Smith, and three of their children visited Derry in 1974, and never forgot the

Jean Kennedy Smith

sight of the city's bombed-out buildings. John Hume, who had been in touch with Senator Kennedy, invited the Smiths to his home, where another memorable sight greeted them: the windows of Hume's house were covered with grating to protect against one of the North's favorite weapons, the petrol bomb. Smith and Hume developed a close friendship, complemented by Hume's already close relationship with her brother.

Smith would visit Ireland nearly every year to promote a program for the disabled called A Very Special Arts. During her travels in the early 1990s, she heard talk at dinner parties of progress in the North. But she brought no specific agenda for peacemaking as U.S. ambassador. She was, after all, the envoy to the Republic, not to the North. Northern Ireland was part of the portfolio of the ambassador to Great Britain, who traditionally accepted the viewpoint of the British government on Irish matters.

Whatever the professionals thought of Ambassador Smith, Albert Reynolds was delighted. The Kennedy name still meant a great deal in a country where pictures of her brother John, the assassinated President, still adorned the mantels over many an Irish hearth. And the new ambassador quickly showed that she had something in common with those, like Reynolds, who were rewriting the rules in Northern Ireland. During a visit over the border to Belfast in August 1993, Smith met the mother of one of seven teenage boys accused of serving the IRA as lookouts. The boys already had been in jail for two years, and only now were being brought to trial. The ambassador agreed to observe the trial, and showed up in court the next day. The British were furious, but President Clinton stood by his rules-breaking ambassador.

Word of the secret talks between John Hume and Gerry Adams was made public in June 1993. The Unionists and the British bitterly condemned Hume for consorting with a pariah, but he insisted that the talks would continue. Behind the scenes, a delegation of Irish-Americans led by publisher Niall O'Dowd was talking with Sinn Féin, Dublin, and the White House. Hume and Adams released a statement in September saying that they had made "considerable progress" toward "the creation of a peace process which would involve all parties." Adams later told a newspaper reporter that Sinn Féin might have to change. Britain's Secretary for Northern Ireland, Sir Patrick Mayhew, replied haughtily that "we have made it clear that we do not negotiate with people who support the use of violence for political ends." But in November, word of Britain's back-channel talks with Sinn Féin broke in a London newspaper, *The Observer*. In the House of Commons, Ian Paisley said that Mayhew no longer had "any trust with the Northern Ireland people," by which he meant *his* Northern Ireland people.

The series of revelations made a tense business all the more brittle. Reynolds met with his friend Major in Brussels on December 10, 1993. "There are some very difficult issues to be put to bed," Reynolds said.

But those issues were more exhausted than Reynolds realized. Five days later, Reynolds and Major were together on Downing Street to announce the signing of a joint agreement that became known as the Downing Street Declaration. The document repeated Peter Brooke's assertion in 1990 that Britain had no "selfish, strategic or economic interest" in Northern Ireland, and, therefore, "it is for the people of the island of Ireland alone" to decide what their future was to be. Britain would not stand in the way of a united Ireland "if that is their wish." The Irish Republic, in turn, recognized that a united Ireland could come about only through the "consent of a majority of the people of Northern Ireland" and that Irish history showed the futility of imposing solutions that were "rejected on grounds of identity by a significant minority of those governed under it." Reynolds conceded Unionist misgivings about a united Ireland, and agreed to support the abolition of clauses in the Republic's constitution that claimed sovereignty over the entire island.

The declaration set up no structures to implement the principles it enunciated. That would come later, through the foundation of "institutions and structures" that would recognize "the special links that exist between the peoples of Britain and Ireland." Those institutions would come about through talks with all parties committed to peace. In its coded language, the declaration invited Sinn Féin as a participant, if Gerry Adams could show that he and his party were ready to put the past aside.

In its careful wording, the declaration was what Reynolds called "a charter for peace" in Ireland. "For the first time, the British government recognized the sins and failures of the past, and I on behalf of the Irish people said there were many aspects of life here [in Dublin] that were not conducive to a settlement," he said.

After the announcement, Ian Paisley circulated an open letter to Prime Minister Major: "You have sold Ulster to buy off the fiendish republican scum." But the Ulster Volunteer Force, the Loyalist paramilitary organization with direct ties to Gusty Spence and the tradition-shattering Progressive Unionist Party, announced that it would have nothing to do with Paisley. It said that the Downing Street Declaration was no threat to the Unionist people.

In a speech in Dublin on January, 10, 1994, a triumphant Albert Reynolds uttered words that no Irish leader dared say before him: "British imperialist interest in Ireland is dead." He added, however, that "we still have to resolve some of its legacy."

With the Downing Street Declaration, it was clear that a breakthrough was close, and that Sinn Féin president Gerry Adams was the key player. If he could persuade the IRA to put aside its weapons and deliver Sinn Féin to the bargaining table, the end of Northern Ireland's troubles might well be near. No Irish leader had attempted what Adams seemed prepared to do since Michael Collins had persuaded most, but not all, of the IRA to accept the Anglo-Irish Treaty in 1921. And Collins's courage had cost him his life.

It was time to send Adams, his allies, and his would-be enemies the strongest possible signal. Just after Christmas 1993, a foreign policy think tank in New York extended an invitation to Adams and other Northern Irish political leaders to address the organization on February 1, 1994. Adams applied for a visa. Three weeks of furious backroom negotiations followed. Access to the American media, the battleground for public opinion, was critical to Adams and Sinn Féin, which is why the British urged Washington to keep Adams out of the United States.

Ambassador Jean Kennedy Smith's opinion was critical in these discussions, for reasons that were uniquely Irish. Because the Republic's constitution claimed sovereignty over the whole of Ireland, citizens of Northern Ireland were considered citizens of the Irish Republic as well. Under British law, Adams was a subject of the Crown. In his past attempts to visit America, he had applied for a visa in Belfast, and it was reviewed by American diplomats attached to the embassy in London. This time, however, Adams applied for a visa at the American embassy in Dublin, where Jean Kennedy Smith forwarded it with her recommendation to the State Department in Washington.

To the outrage of John Major and his government, President Clinton approved the visa application on January 30, 1994. And so Gerry Adams came to America. Years of British-imposed isolation of Sinn Féin were over. And, for the first time, the United States was charting a course on Ireland that was independent of London's.

After his whirlwind American tour, Adams met with the Provisional IRA's Military Council in late August. IRA leaders wanted to send an aging republican activist named Joe Cahill to America, which had twice deported him on suspicion of arms smuggling. Cahill would explain the IRA's thinking about a possible cease-fire to republican activists in America, many of whom knew Cahill personally and trusted him.

The IRA's request, really a demand, was forwarded to Reynolds, who called President Clinton. The President was extremely skeptical.

"I gave Adams a visa, and there's no peace," Clinton told Reynolds. "Now you're asking me to break every rule in the book. Even if I let him in, how do I know there will be a cease-fire? We didn't get it the first time."

"This will deliver it," Reynolds replied, relying on assurances he'd received through intermediaries.

Clinton said that if the IRA leaders were so close to a cease-fire, they must have a statement prepared. "Come back to me with at least one paragraph of it," Clinton said.

Reynolds called Clinton back and read him the words of the proposed IRA statement, which called for a complete cease-fire. Clinton approved Cahill's visa on August 29 after getting further encouragement from Jean Kennedy Smith, who also had been in touch with Reynolds. Cahill flew to New York on August 30. The next day, the IRA released a statement announcing that "there will be a complete cessation of military operations. All our units have been instructed accordingly." Clinton, who had taken a bigger chance with Cahill than he did with Adams, called a jubiliant Reynolds. The Cahill visa, Reynolds assured him, sealed the deal.

Reynolds told the Irish people, and the world, that "as far as we are concerned, the long nightmare is over." On September 6, John Hume and Gerry Adams traveled to Dublin and joined in a very public three-way handshake with Reynolds. For the first time since partition, the three representatives of Irish nationalism, the Irish Taoiseach, the moderate constitutionalist, and the hard-line republican, were united. The strategy that John Hume had laid out years before reached fruition: Sinn Féin had been lured away from the violence of the past and would now be escorted into a future in which the European Union was likely to be more important to the young Irish than either London or Dublin. At 10 Downing Street, Ian Paisley met with John Major and accused him of cutting a secret deal with the IRA. Major told Paisley and his allies to leave his office immediately.

The IRA's cease-fire did not bring an end to the North's sporadic violence. The Loyalist paramilitaries had not reciprocated, a point the

Ulster Volunteer Force made as bluntly as it could with a car bomb attack on a Sinn Féin office in west Belfast on September 4. Behind the scenes, however, the Loyalist paramilitaries were preparing for an announcement of their own. Reynolds once again broke with protocol to make contact with those he considered critical to a Loyalist peace process—Gusty Spence and his fellow former prisoners David Ervine and Billy Hutchinson. He made arrangements to meet them personally in a Dublin hotel. Reynolds believed they were "prepared to break the mold." Spence, for his part, found Reynolds to be "a good, warm man." All were aware, Spence said, of "the historical significance of the meeting."

On October 13, 1994, members of an umbrella organization called the Combined Loyalist Military Command called a press conference in Belfast's Fernhill House. More than eighty years before, Edward Carson had watched as members of his Ulster Volunteer Force paraded by in defiance of Home Rule. Now, the founder of the modern-day UVF, Gusty Spence, read the announcement of a Loyalist cease-fire with a battery of microphones in front of him and a Union Jack to his right. Spence's statement contained grace notes that were notably absent from the IRA's matter-of-fact announcement. "In all sincerity," Spence said, "we offer to the loved ones of all innocent victims over the past twenty-five years abject and true remorse. . . . Let us firmly resolve to respect our differing views of freedom, culture and aspiration and never again permit our political circumstances to degenerate into bloody warfare."

Reynolds told his colleagues in the Dáil that "this decision effectively signifies the end of twenty-five years of violence, and the closure of a tragic chapter in our history."

More than three thousand people had died since 1968. But at last something like peace descended on Northern Ireland. President Clinton celebrated the cease-fires during a trip to Belfast in 1995, and he dispatched former Senator George Mitchell to the North to serve as a mediator in talks intended to reach a political settlement and a permanent peace.

The post–cease-fire talks in Belfast in 1998 were yet another sign that once again in Ireland all had changed, and changed utterly. Loyalists were participating with, if not necessarily talking directly to, republicans, and Great Britain and the Irish Republic, antagonists for most of the millennium, were allied as partners in peacemaking. The talks ended on Good Friday 1998 with an agreement on a new Northern Ireland legislature that would share power with all parties pledged to nonviolence. The accord incorporated the principles of the

Downing Street Declaration and set up institutions designed to end overt discrimination against Catholics. At the same time, the agreement ensured that Northern Ireland would remain within the United Kingdom until a majority of its people decided otherwise. In accepting the agreement, Gerry Adams and Sinn Féin recognized British sovereignty in Northern Ireland for the first time, while the Unionists surrendered their long-held policy of treating Catholics as second-class citizens.

The Good Friday accord was presented to the people of Northern Ireland for their approval, while voters in the Irish Republic were asked to support the agreement by abolishing sections of the Irish constitution that claimed sovereignty over the six counties of the North. An all-Ireland election was scheduled for May 22, 1998. Though a coincidence, the timing was poetic, for the next day marked the bicentennial of the United Irish rebellion, which sought to replace the labels of Protestant and Catholic with the common name of Irishman.

From the beginning, it seemed clear that nationalist voters on both sides of the border supported the agreement. The real contest was for the Unionist-Loyalist vote. Although the referendum in the North could have passed with an overwhelming Catholic vote and minority Protestant approval, such an outcome would have been tantamount to defeat. David Trimble, the leader of the largest Unionist party, led the campaign for a yes vote in the Protestant community. And, in the spirit of the United Irish ideal, the Progressive Unionist Party sent Billy Hutchinson, former gunman, convicted murderer, and one of Gusty Spence's disciples, to a Catholic school to preach the party's message of reconciliation. To a class of thirty girls in Saint Joseph's grammar school in Dungannon, Hutchinson said: "These agreements don't mean anything unless people on the ground create their own bonds of trust."

Ulster said yes on May 22. More than 70 percent of the province's voters—including just over 50 percent of Northern Ireland's Protestants—approved the peace agreement. In the Republic, more than 95 percent approved the changes to the Irish constitution conceding that Northern Ireland was a separate entity. It was the first time all of Ireland went to the polls on the same day since 1918. The verdict of the Irish people was clear, and no group advocating violence could claim any longer to speak on their behalf. For their efforts in leading their communities along the path of peace and reconciliation, David Trimble and John Hume were awarded the Nobel Peace Prize for 1998.

• • •

Three of the key players in the peace process watched from the sidelines as the victors made their speeches. Albert Reynolds had resigned in late 1994, after his Attorney General was accused of delaying the extradition of a pedophile priest (a charge both Reynolds and the Attorney General denied). Reynolds's friend John Major lost a general election on May 1, 1997, and was replaced by Tony Blair, who gave the talks leading to Good Friday an important boost. And Jean Kennedy Smith had returned home to New York after winning praise as the best Ambassador America had ever sent to Ireland. Reynolds spoke for all three when he said that he was immensely satisfied to have been a part of history.

The killing and dying in Northern Ireland did not end on May 22, 1998, though. A dissident republican faction set off a bomb in Omagh, County Tyrone, that killed twenty-nine people in August 1998. In that blast, one man lost his wife, his eighteen-month-old daughter, and his mother-in-law, leaving him to raise three children who had lost their mother, sister, and grandmother in a single act of savagery. Other murders followed.

But the bombers and gunmen did not destroy the peace, nor did they disturb dreams of prosperity. A young generation in the Irish Republic was rewriting the narrative of the previous thousand years. They eagerly embraced the European Union, the global marketplace, and secular politics. They regarded those who killed for the sake of a border, those who even paid attention to borders, as part of an old and outdated order.

In keeping with the ideal of a new Europe, the young Irish eagerly described themselves as post-nationalist, as Europeans, and, for the first time, as global entrepreneurs presiding over one of the world's most robust economies. The mystics of a hundred years earlier may have found cultural riches in the boggy lands of Ireland's west; the young Irish people of the 1990s found other kinds of riches in high technology. The Republic's economy was one of the most astonishing stories of the 1990s, achieving double-digit annual growth, and outpacing Britain and even Germany. Unemployment sank to the low single digits for the first time in generations, and for the first time ever, Irish immigrants in America packed up and returned home. Investments in education and a shrewd use of European Union money in the dreary 1980s paid off in the 1990s with an economy that was the envy of the West.

Ireland in the 1990s also became post-Catholic, thanks in part to a series of clerical sexual scandals that hastened the Church's weakening power and prestige in a country of well-educated young people.

Though still devout, Irish Catholics paid less attention to Church dictates than at any time since the days of Henry II and Pope Adrian. The Irish Prime Minister who helped negotiate the Good Friday Accord, Bertie Ahern, was a married man who lived and traveled openly with his female companion, which was something even the proudly non-judgmental French couldn't brag about. Freed from the Church's strictures, Irish writers and artists inspired a second Gaelic cultural revival that found an audience from Sydney to Frankfurt to San Francisco.

There surely are puzzled warriors in Ireland who will try to bring back the past with a bomb or a bullet. And the political framework which the Irish people north and south approved in 1998 could fall apart. But the men and women who took such risks for peace in the 1990s will take them again, if necessary, to keep Ireland moving forward, toward a future that has never looked brighter.

When during the summer of 1999 the new Northern Ireland legislature broke up after its first meeting amid bitter recriminations over demands that the IRA give up its weapons immediately, a guard watching the politicians leave in frustration assumed that all was lost. "It's over, is it?" he asked.

It may have seemed that way for a moment, but during a tumultuous few weeks in the last autumn of the century, representatives of Ireland's two traditions—Catholic nationalist and Protestant Unionist—put aside their suspicions and bitterness and joined together to create a new, inclusive legislature to govern the province's internal affairs. The Unionist leader, David Trimble, prevailed on his colleagues to end the siege that so defined the old Northern Ireland. And Sinn Féin swore off violence for a chance to participate in building a peaceful and more just society.

An era of bloodshed ended on November 30, 1999, when Gerry Adams rose from his chair in Stormont—the very symbol of monolithic Unionist rule, now the unlikely home of an all-party assembly—and nominated his ally Martin McGuinness to be Northern Ireland's Minister for Education. McGuinness, who was once a ranking commander in the Provisional IRA, took his seat in the new Cabinet and posed for pictures. But he was in the wrong chair: he was sitting in a place reserved for one of the Unionist colleagues.

All was changed. Old walls that for so many years separated Irish from British, Catholic from Protestant, had been torn down. Replacing them with something new and untested will require determination and courage from men and women who would rather live in peace than fight the wars of the old millennium. History offers hope, for it shows that Ireland has never lacked for heroes.

NOTES

CHAPTER ONE
CONQUEST

Page 10: *"You have expressed to us":* Paul Johnson, *Ireland* (Chicago: Academy Chicago Publishers, 1984), 16.

Page 11: *"The Irish live like beasts":* Robert Kee, *Ireland: A History* (London: Weidenfeld & Nicolson, 1980), 32.

Page 11: *One observer remarked:* Jonathan Bardon, *A History of Ulster* (Belfast: Blackstaff Press, 1992), 64.

Page 11: *He wrote to Henry II:* Johnson, *Ireland,* 18.

Page 13: *In addition, Irish "babblers":* Ibid., 25.

Page 14: *Conflicts between settlers and natives:* T. W. Moody and F. X. Martin, *The Course of Irish History* (Cork: Mercier Press, 1984), 159.

Page 15: *Ireland, Parliament said:* Robert Kee, *The Most Distressful Country* (London: Penguin, 1972), 11.

Page 15: *Elizabeth said she wished:* Kee, *Ireland,* 32.

Page 17: *"My ancestors were Kings":* Bardon, *A History of Ulster,* 79.

Page 18: *He delivered a long:* Richard Berleth, *The Twilight Lords* (New York: Barnes and Noble, 1978), 255.

Page 18: *In a letter to the Queen:* Sean O Faolain, *The Great O'Neill* (Cork: Mercier Press, 1997), 127.

Page 19: *"He is worthily reputed":* James Lydon, *The Making of Modern Ireland* (London: Routledge, 1996), 155.

Page 19: *Privately, she spoke bitterly:* Berleth, *The Twilight Lords,* 246.

Page 19: *In a letter to the son:* O Faolain, *The Great O'Neill,* 185.

Page 20: *"You do not know the North":* Ibid., 193.

Page 21: *Hugh O'Neill wrote to the King of Spain:* G. A. Hayes-McCoy, *Irish Battles: A Military History of Ireland* (New York: Barnes and Noble, 1997), 150.

Page 21: *O'Neill demanded that the Catholic religion:* O Faolain, *The Great O'Neill,* 222.

Page 21: *"He means to be head":* Ibid.

Page 21: *"This island of Ireland shall be":* Hayes-McCoy, *Irish Battles,* 146.

Page 22: *"If the Spaniards should prevail":* O Faolain, *The Great O'Neill,* 245.

Page 23: *"No man can yield reasons":* Ibid., 265.

Page 23: *He noted that "the help":* Micheline Kerney Walsh, *Hugh O'Neill: Prince of Ulster* (Dublin: Four Courts Press, 1996), 24.

Page 24: *One English official wrote:* Bardon, *A History of Ulster,* 13.

Page 26: *A Protestant clergyman said:* Kee, *Ireland,* 43.

Page 26: *"I am killing myself":* Hayes-McCoy, *Irish Battles,* 180.

Page 27: *He surely was the man:* R. M. Foster, *Modern Ireland* (New York: Penguin, 1989), 101.

Page 27: *"You, unprovoked, put the English":* Peter Berresford Ellis, *Hell or Connaught!* (Belfast: Blackstaff Press, 1975), 20.

Page 27: *He attacked again:* Kee, *Ireland,* 46.

Page 27: *"It is right that God alone":* Ibid., 46.

Page 28: *Sarsfield estimated that that the land:* Piers Wauchope, *Patrick Sarsfield and the Williamite War* (Blackrock, Ireland: Irish Academic Press, 1992), 7.

Page 28: *An English administrator:* Ellis, *Hell or Connaught!,* 8.

Page 32: *"Sarsfield is the word":* Ibid., 134.

Page 32: *One of William's aides noted:* Ibid., 153.

Page 32: *Before the war was over:* Hayes-McCoy, *Irish Battles,* 242.

Page 33: *"They are beaten":* Wauchope, *Patrick Sarsfield,* 230.

Page 33: *An English observer noted:* Ibid., 232.

Page 33: *"As low as we are now":* Ibid., 268.

Page 34: *"Would it were for Ireland!":* Kee, *The Most Distressful Country,* 18.

CHAPTER TWO
PROTESTANT NATION

Page 35: *"It will no doubt be":* Bernard Acworth, *Swift* (London, Eire and Spottiswoode, 1939), 154.

Page 36: *"I thought a Dean could do less":* Edith Mary Johnson, *Ireland in the Eighteenth Century* (Dublin: Gill and Macmillan, 1972), 70.

Page 36: *Ireland's highest-ranking judge:* Kee, *The Most Distressful Country,* 19.

Page 37: *A landlord's agent complained:* L. M. Cullen, *Life in Ireland* (London: B. T. Batsford, 1968), 97.

Page 37: *A Protestant clergyman:* Ibid., 99.

Page 38: *The Anglo-Irish statesman:* Bardon, *A History of Ulster,* 170.

Page 41: *Referring to the native Irish:* Foster, *Modern Ireland,* 161.

Page 41: *"You are to understand":* Acworth, *Swift,* 167.

Page 41: *There, in the second decade:* Stephen Gwynn, *The Life and Friendships of Dean Swift* (New York: Henry Holt, 1933), 239.

Page 41: *In outlining a case:* Foster, *Modern Ireland,* 162.

Page 42: *"It is wonderful to observe":* Seamus Deane, ed., *The Field Day Anthology of Irish Writing,* vol. 1 (Derry: Field Day Publications, 1991), 341–42.

Page 42: *Swift charged that their:* Ibid., 344.

Page 42: *What followed, in seven letters:* Acworth, *Swift,* 175.

Page 42: *"For in reason"*: Carl Van Doren, ed., *The Portable Swift* (New York: Penguin, 1948), 193.

Page 43: *The British Prime Minister:* Gwynn, *The Life and Friendships*, 261.

Page 43: *"He became the idol of the people"*: Acworth, *Swift*, 177.

Page 43: *In the mid-1720s:* Gwynn, *The Life and Friendships*, 266.

Page 43: *"It is a melancholly Object"*: Deane, *The Field Day Anthology*, 386.

Page 44: *In one of his last letters:* Acworth, *Swift*, 191.

Page 44: *A British administrator:* Kee, *The Most Distressful Country*, 22.

Page 46: *Eventually, the Dubliners were persuaded:* James Kelly, *Henry Flood* (South Bend: University of Notre Dame Press, 1998), 73.

Page 46: *Warden Flood's coach was attacked:* Ibid., 74.

Page 47: *He shocked his colleagues:* Ibid., 90.

Page 47: *If it continued, he said:* Ibid.

Page 47: *"We have heard of the freemen"*: Ibid., 102.

Page 47: *He referred to his class:* Kee, *The Most Distressful Country*, 30.

Page 48: *"Can you call the country free"*: Kelly, *Henry Flood*, 100.

Page 48: *"Flood, the champion of his country"*: Ibid., 218.

Page 48: *Ireland, Lucas had asserted:* Roger J. McHugh, *Henry Grattan* (New York: Sheed and Ward, 1937), 32.

Page 48: *The Chief Justice denounced him:* Ibid.

Page 50: *The soldiers, he said:* Ibid., 51.

Page 52: *"Peace!" Burgh thundered:* Ibid., 55.

Page 52: *"I will never be satisfied"*: Ibid., 65.

Page 52: *The claims of Britain's Parliament:* Ibid., 68.

Page 53: *"I am now to address"*: Ibid., 73.

Page 53: *"Ireland is now a nation"*: Deane, *The Field Day Anthology*, 91.

Page 53: *"If the Catholic is given power"*: Kelly, *Henry Flood*, 305.

Page 53: *"The question is now"*: Kee, *The Most Distressful Country*, 25.

Page 54: *Grattan, in a sweeping condemnation:* Kelly, *Henry Flood*, 352.

Page 54: *Flood, with magnificent disdain:* Ibid.

Page 54: *"The people of this country"*: McHugh, *Henry Grattan*, 134.

Page 55: *Theobald Wolfe Tone made his way:* Marianne Elliott, *Wolfe Tone: Prophet of Irish Independence* (New Haven: Yale University Press, 1989), 134.

Page 56: *Mary Ann, twenty years old:* Mary McNeill, *The Life and Times of Mary Ann McCracken* (Belfast: Blackstaff Press, 1960), 73.

Page 58: *An observer of the scene:* Oliver Knox, *Rebels and Informers* (New York: St. Martin's, 1997), 60.

Page 58: *The rejection stung Tone:* Elliot, *Wolfe Tone*, 126.

Page 58: *"I soon formed my theory"*: Ibid.

Page 59: *"My argument is simply this"*: John Killen, ed., *The Decade of the United Irishmen* (Belfast: Blackstaff Press, 1997), 19–20.

Page 59: *There was much political discussion:* Elliot, *Wolfe Tone,* 139.

Page 59: *A worried Tone noted:* Ibid., 143.

Page 59: *The group unanimously passed resolutions:* Killen, *The Decade of the United Irishmen,* 21.

CHAPTER THREE
THE COMMON NAME OF IRISHMAN

Page 61: *In the fall of 1792:* Stella Tillyard, *Citizen Lord* (New York: Farrar, Straus and Giroux, 1997), 132.

Page 61: *One relative remarked:* Ibid., 152.

Page 61: *"I can compare it to":* Ibid., 136.

Page 61: *"The Revolution of '82":* T. A. Jackson, *Ireland Her Own* (London: Cobbett Press, 1947), 118.

Page 62: *He compared the constitution of 1782:* Edward Fitzgerald Correspondence, Trinity College, Dublin.

Page 63: *Of Fitgerald, a friend complained:* Tillyard, *Citizen Lord,* 158.

Page 64: *"Of what consequence [are] our lives":* Denis Carroll, *The Man from God Knows Where* (Blackrock, Ireland: Gartan, 1995), 101.

Page 65: *He saw as his mission:* McHugh, *Henry Grattan,* 149.

Page 65: *An immensely satisfied Grattan:* Ibid., 153.

Page 65: *"In Ireland, a conquered":* Elliot, *Wolfe Tone,* 239.

Page 66: *Emmet had recently astonished:* Thomas Addis Emmet, *Memoir of Thomas Addis and Robert Emmet* (New York: Emmet Press, 1913), 22.

Page 66: *Tone jokingly pleaded with Emmet:* Henry Boylan, *Wolfe Tone* (Dublin: Gill and Macmillan, 1981), 50.

Page 66: *There, they vowed to each other:* Elliot, *Wolfe Tone,* 258.

Page 68: *Taking a skeptical note:* Daire Keogh and Nicholas Furlong, eds., *The Women of 1798* (Dublin: Four Courts Press, 1998), 14.

Page 69: *Henry Joy asserted:* McNeill, *The Life and Times of Mary Ann McCracken,* 98.

Page 69: *"McCracken is frequently sent":* Ibid., 111.

Page 69: *There, it was said:* Tillyard, *Citizen Lord,* 189.

Page 70: *"Here I am, alone":* Boylan, *Wolfe Tone,* 67–68.

Page 70: *They told Fitzgerald:* Elliot, *Wolfe Tone,* 301.

Page 70: *"We intend, Citizen General":* Ibid., 297.

Page 70: *Some time later, no less an authority:* Boylan, *Wolfe Tone,* 62.

Page 71: *A few days before Fitzgerald's return:* Michael O'Flanagan, *When They Followed Henry Joy* (Dublin: Riposte Books, 1997), 74.

Page 71: *"Put on my regimentals":* Knox, *Rebels and Informers,* 201.

Page 71: *"[S]hould the worst happen":* Elliot, *Wolfe Tone,* 321.

Page 71: *Hoche boarded the* Fraternité: Boylan, *Wolfe Tone,* 85.

Page 72: *"We have been now":* Ibid., 98.

Page 73: *His sister, Lucy, noted:* Tillyard, *Citizen Lord,* 214.

Page 73: *"Went to town for a ball":* Ibid., 221.

Page 73: *"To tell you the truth":* Ibid., 215.

Page 74: *"I hope the present Era":* McNeill, *The Life and Times of Mary Ann McCracken,* 125–26.

Page 74: *"Nothing but terror will keep them":* Bardon, *A History of Ulster,* 231.

Page 74: *"The flame is smothered":* Ibid.

Page 74: *"A visible change took place":* Nicholas Furlong, *John Murphy of Boolavogue* (Dublin: Geography Publications, 1991), 26.

Page 75: *"Loyalty to the gracious good":* Ibid., 12.

Page 75: *John detailed "the barbarities":* R. R. Madden, *The United Irishmen: Their Lives and Times,* vol. 5 (n.p., Dublin, 1843–46), 418–19.

Page 76: *"He is vain beyond all belief":* Elliot, *Wolfe Tone,* 335–36.

Page 76: *"It is terrible to see":* Boylan, *Wolfe Tone,* 118.

Page 76: *"Dearest Love":* Elliot, *Wolfe Tone,* 355.

Page 77: *He presented Bonaparte:* Knox, *Rebels and Informers,* 239.

Page 77: *"But," Bonaparte replied:* Boylan, *Wolfe Tone,* 112.

Page 77: *A local member of the United Irishmen:* Furlong, *John Murphy,* 34.

Page 77: *The curate received an urgent letter:* Ibid., 31.

Page 77: *"I will use every":* Ibid.; 32.

Page 78: *"Yesterday, two men were hanged":* O'Flanagan, *When They Followed Henry Joy,* 78.

Page 78: *"They would rather be":* Madden, *The United Irishmen,* 423.

Page 79: *"We have overwhelming numbers":* O'Flanagan, *When They Followed Henry Joy,* 80.

Page 79: *The British army, he wrote:* Thomas Packenham, *The Year of Liberty* (New York: Random House, 1969), 51.

Page 79: *The cautions of Emmet and McNeven:* O'Flanagan, *When They Followed Henry Joy,* 81.

Page 79: *The British, he wrote:* Daire Keogh and Nicholas Furlong, *The Mighty Wave* (Blackrock, Ireland: Four Courts Press, 1996), 70.

Page 80: *"Be firm, Irishmen":* Tillyard, *Citizen Lord,* 253.

Page 80: *"The insolence of the people":* Packenham, *The Year of Liberty,* 57.

Page 80: *"The pursuit of pleasure":* Ibid., 53.

Page 81: *"You know me, my Lord":* Ibid., 93.

Page 82: *"It would be better for us to die":* Furlong, *John Murphy,* 52.

Page 83: *"Remain firm, together!":* Ibid., 58.

Page 83: *"Rely upon it, there never was":* Ibid., 102.

Page 84: *"Most will find it":* Knox, *Rebels and Informers,* 254.

Page 84: *He issued his orders:* A. T. Q. Stewart, *The Summer Soldiers* (Belfast: Blackstaff Press, 1995), 67.

Page 84: *"If we succeed today":* O'Flanagan, *When They Followed Henry Joy,* 86.

Page 85: *"These are the times":* McCracken Letters, Trinity College Dublin.

Page 86: *"The rebellion in Wexford":* Furlong, *John Murphy,* 116.

Page 86: *"I will never advise anyone":* Ibid., 140.

Page 86: *"We have lost":* Ibid., 153.

Page 87: *"The moment I set my eyes":* McNeill, *The Life and Times,* 181.

Page 87: *"Harry, my dear":* Ibid., 182.

Page 88: *"I wish you to write":* McCracken Letters, Trinity College Dublin.

Page 89: *"Shall it be said of me":* Boylan, *Wolfe Tone,* 128.

Page 89: *"I have attempted to follow":* Elliot, *Wolfe Tone,* 394.

Page 90: *"The hour is at last come":* Boylan, *Wolfe Tone,* 131.

Page 90: *"I can yet find words":* Ibid., 133.

Page 90: *"I would have sewed up his neck":* Packenham, *The Year of Liberty,* 346.

Page 90: *"I despise and hate myself":* Kee, *The Most Distressful Country,* 159.

Page 90: *"The Constitution [of 1782] may":* Ibid., 159.

Page 91: *"I die with a love of liberty":* McHugh, *Henry Grattan,* 207.

Page 92: *"I have but one request":* Kee, *The Most Distressful Country,* 168.

Page 92: *"I have no wish to die":* McNeill, *The Life and Times,* 221.

CHAPTER FOUR
EMANCIPATION AND STARVATION

Page 95: *"I would rather give up my throne":* Sean McMahon, *A Short History of Ireland* (Cork: Mercier Press, 1996), 110.

Page 95: *During a visit to Ireland:* Kee, *The Most Distressful Country,* 170.

Page 96: *"A rich man . . . lets a large tract":* Ibid., 171.

Page 96: *A visitor to the west:* Jackson, *Ireland Her Own,* 207.

Page 97: *"The English people are":* Richard Ned Lebow, *White Britain and Black Ireland* (Philadelphia: Institute for the Study of Human Issues, 1976), 40.

Page 97: *The Irish,* Punch *asserted:* Ibid., 40.

Page 99: *The very idea of French revolutionaries:* Maurice O'Connell, ed., *The Correspondence of Daniel O'Connell,* vol. 1 (Dublin: Irish University Press, 1972), 28.

Page 99: *"Loyalty is not the peculiar prerogative":* Kee, *The Most Distressful Country,* 181.

Page 100: *"If we cannot get rid"*: Denis Gwynn, *Daniel O'Connell* (Cork: Cork University Press, 1947), 151.

Page 100: *"We are beating those bigoted"*: O'Connell, *The Correspondence of Daniel O'Connell*, vol. 1, 253.

Page 100: *"In Ireland, where a little while ago"*: Gwynn, *Daniel O'Connell*, 170.

Page 100: *"While I trust that a Catholic"*: Richard Davis, *Revolutionary Imperialist: William Smith O'Brien* (Dublin: Lilliput Press, 1998), 29.

Page 101: *"From my boyhood"*: Ibid., 21.

Page 101: *"What I now say I wish"*: Gwynn, *Daniel O'Connell*, 177.

Page 102: *The young MP William Smith O'Brien*: Richard Davis, *Revolutionary Imperialist*, 36.

Page 102: *"Property," he said, "has its duties"*: McMahon, *A Short History of Ireland*, 119.

Page 104: *A contemporary once described*: Kee, *The Most Distressful Country*, 195.

Page 104: *"Gentlemen, you have a country"*: Thomas Davis, *Essays and Poems* (Dublin: M. H. Gill and Son, 1945), 5.

Page 104: *"Ask us not to copy"*: Ibid., 147.

Page 104: *"What are the evils"*: Ibid., 155.

Page 105: *"My struggle has begun"*: Gwynn, *Daniel O'Connell*, 219.

Page 105: *"Boys, do you know me now?"*: Raymond Moley, *Daniel O'Connell: Nationalism Without Violence* (New York: Fordham University Press, 1974), 151.

Page 105: *"I want you not to violate"*: Kee, *The Most Distressful Country*, 200.

Page 105: *Davis promised that the paper*: Ibid., 196.

Page 106: *He declared that his audience*: Gwynn, *Daniel O'Connell*, 232.

Page 106: *"They will be all the more dreaded"*: Ibid., 231.

Page 106: *Through it all, however*: Kee, *The Most Distressful Country*, 207.

Page 106: *"Step by step we are approaching"*: Ibid., 209.

Page 107: *"This must be obeyed"*: Gwynn, *Daniel O'Connell*, 233.

Page 107: *Thomas Davis, the intellectual force*: Richard Davis, *Revolutionary Imperialist*, 153.

Page 107: *O'Connell was delighted*: Ibid., 158.

Page 107: *In a letter to her son*: Ibid., 160.

Page 107: *He was older than most*: Kee, *The Most Distressful Country*, 236.

Page 107: *In a letter to* The Nation: Ibid., 216.

Page 108: *"Feud! Feud! Feud!"*: John Neylon Molony, *A Soul Came into Ireland* (Dublin: Geography Publications, 1995), 248–49.

Page 109: *The newspaper charged that*: Charles Gavan Duffy, *Young Ireland* (New York: D. Appleton and Company, 1881), 582.

Page 109: *In a letter to Smith O'Brien:* Ibid., 613.

Page 109: *O'Connell replied:* Ibid., 629.

Page 109: *An ally of O'Connell's:* Molony, *A Soul Came into Ireland*, 307.

Page 109: *Davis spoke next:* Duffy, *Young Ireland*, 702–6.

Page 111: *"My mind is bewildered":* Molony, *A Soul Came into Ireland*, 341–42.

Page 111: *"If you won't educate me":* Horace Wyndham, *Speranza* (London: Boardman, 1951), 14.

Page 111: *"Abject tears, and prayers submissive—":* Duffy, *Young Ireland*, 457.

Page 112: *His sympathy for Ireland's oppressed:* William Dillon, *Life of John Mitchel*, vol. 1 (London: Kegan Paul, Trench & Co., 1888), 49.

Page 113: *"On this subject it will be well":* The Nation, Nov. 1, 1845.

Page 113: *"The air was laden":* Jeremiah O'Donovan Rossa, *Rossa's Recollections* (New York: Mariners Harbor, 1894), 108.

Page 113: *The Duke of Wellington:* Michael Coffey and Terry Golway, *The Irish in America* (New York: Hyperion, 1997), 15.

Page 113: *"The great evil with which":* Cecil Woodham Smith, *The Great Hunger* (New York: Old Town Books, 1989), 156.

Page 114: *"I trust that the time":* Kee, *The Most Distressful Country*, 246.

Page 114: *But he continued to plead:* Richard Davis, *Revolutionary Imperialist*, 201.

Page 114: *With great understatement:* Ibid., 203.

Page 114: *Young Ireland and* The Nation: Kee, *The Most Distressful Country*, 249.

Page 114: *The Repeal Association passed a tame:* Richard Davis, *Revolutionary Imperialist*, 205.

Page 115: *As the voices of dissent:* Kee, *The Most Distressful Country*, 252.

Page 115: *O'Connell told his audience:* T. F. O'Sullivan, *The Young Irelanders* (Tralee, Ireland: Kerryman, 1944), 17.

Page 115: *"I do not condemn the use of arms":* Michael Cavanagh, *Memoirs of Gen. Thomas Francis Meagher* (Worcester, Mass.: Messenger Press, 1892), 63.

Page 116: *In the midst of the dying:* Coffey and Golway, *The Irish in America*, 20.

Page 116: *Referring to the rural heart:* Ibid., 4.

Page 117: *"Weary men, what reap ye?":* O'Sullivan, *The Young Irelanders*, 454.

Page 117: *"Ireland," he said:* Kee, *The Most Distressful Country*, 257.

Page 117: *He saw only:* Terry Golway, *Irish Rebel: John Devoy and America's Fight for Ireland's Freedom* (New York: St. Martin's, 1998), 30.

Page 118: *"I could see, in front":* John Mitchel, *The Last Conquest of Ireland . . . Perhaps* (Glasgow: Cameron, Ferguson, 1861), 148.

Page 118: *"I owe you some gratitude"*: James Fintan Lalor, *Collected Writings* (Dublin: Talbot Press, 1918), xiii.

Page 118: *"The owners of our soil"*: Smith, *The Great Hunger*, 333.

Page 118: *"A new tribune!"*: Ibid., 334.

Page 118: *In one long address*: Lalor, *Collected Writings*, 10.

Page 119: *Its stated goal*: Smith, *The Great Hunger*, 334.

Page 119: *In the first issue*: Dillon, *Life of John Mitchel*, 197.

Page 119: *"These men are honest"*: Mitchel, *The Last Conquest of Ireland*, 159.

Page 119: *To a crowd of cheering Dubliners*: Richard Davis, *Revolutionary Imperialist*, 241.

Page 119: *He suffered the jeers*: Ibid., 246.

Page 120: *"I have acted all through this business"*: Mitchel, *The Last Conquest of Ireland*, 187.

Page 120: *"Ireland! Ireland!"*: Patrick Byrne, *The Wildes of Merrion Square* (London: Staples Press, 1953), 104.

Page 120: *"Oh! For a hundred thousand muskets"*: Wyndham, *Speranza*, 198.

Page 120: *"Do you wish"*: Smith, *The Great Hunger*, 347.

Page 121: *"I am Smith O'Brien"*: Richard Davis, *Revolutionary Imperialist*, 272.

Page 122: *He decided to set sail for Australia*: Kee, *The Most Distressful Country*, 296.

Chapter Five
The Irish Republican Brotherhood

Page 123: *"Mr. Stephens was"*: Desmond Ryan, *The Fenian Chief* (Coral Gables: University of Miami Press, 1967), 40–41.

Page 123: *Echoing the teachings of James Fintan Lalor*: Robert Kee, *The Bold Fenian Men* (London: Quartet Books, 1976), 7.

Page 125: *"Before the Young Ireland revolt"*: Ryan, *The Fenian Chief*, 60.

Page 125: *"The ardour of Young Ireland"*: Kee, *The Bold Fenian Men*, 8.

Page 126: *"I had to give up"*: Ryan, *The Fenian Chief*, 60.

Page 126: *A soldier told him*: Kee, *The Bold Fenian Men*, 8.

Page 126: *"Did Christ ever die"*: Ibid.

Page 126: *He found, perhaps not surprisingly*: Ryan, *The Fenian Chief*, 60.

Page 126: *"You see, Mr. Stephens"*: Ibid., 71.

Page 128: *"Every individual born"*: T. W. Moody, ed., *The Fenian Movement* (Cork: Mercier Press, 1968), 64.

Page 128: *"He had friends who were willing"*: Ibid., 69.

Page 128: *In his letter to Stephens*: Ryan, *The Fenian Chief*, 62.

Page 128: *He recalled that in his journeys*: Ibid., 60.

Page 128: *"My three-thousand mile walk"*: Ibid., 81.

Page 129: *"I . . . in the presence"*: Ibid., 92.

Page 130: *He described himself:* Rossa, *Rossa's Recollections,* 17.

Page 131: *He heard a woman's voice:* Ibid., 127.

Page 131: *He would later write:* Golway, *Irish Rebel,* 25.

Page 131: *"One hundred and thirteen pounds"*: Moody, *The Fenian Movement,* 72.

Page 132: *"It is hard to get the mass"*: Rossa, *Rossa's Recollections,* 304.

Page 132: *But the onetime firebrand:* Ryan, *The Fenian Chief,* 155.

Page 132: *O'Mahony, he wrote:* Moody, *The Fenian Movement,* 63.

Page 132: *"Some of the most learned"*: Golway, *Irish Rebel,* 42.

Page 132: *"The young man . . ."* Ryan, *The Fenian Chief,* 175.

Page 133: *"I am proud to see"*: Kee, *The Bold Fenian Men,* 19.

Page 133: *"He smiled and smoked"*: Ryan, *The Fenian Chief,* 179.

Page 134: *A British periodical sneered:* Patrick Quinlivan and Paul Rose, *The Fenians in England* (New York: Riverrun Press, 1982), 11.

Page 134: *The financial success of the paper:* Marcus Bourke, *John O'Leary* (Tralee, Ireland: Anvil Books, 1967), 47.

Page 134: *O'Leary explained that he:* John O'Leary, *Recollections of Fenians and Fenianism,* vol. 1 (London: Downey and Company, 1896), 122.

Page 135: *After reading Davis's essays:* Bourke, *John O'Leary,* 15.

Page 136: *"My mother . . . actually shed tears"*: R. V. Comerford, *Charles J. Kickham* (Dublin: Wolfhound Press, 1979), 18.

Page 137: *He described America:* Ibid., 63.

Page 137: *"We never, of course"*: O'Leary, *Recollections,* vol. 2, 15.

Page 137: *O'Mahony said that priests:* Rossa, *Rossa's Recollections,* 300.

Page 137: *It was Kickham who developed:* O'Leary, *Recollections,* vol. 2, 33.

Page 137: *Archbishop Cullen charged:* Ibid., 49.

Page 138: *Kickham responded:* Ibid.

Page 138: *Stephens decided that O'Mahony:* Ryan, *The Fenian Chief,* 194.

Page 139: *It declared that the organization:* W. S. Neidhardt, *Fenianism in North America* (University Park: Pennsylvania State University Press, 1975), 13.

Page 139: *The war itself:* Fenian Briefs, 3.713.8, National Archives, Dublin.

Page 139: *"I impressed upon him"*: Neidhardt, *Fenianism in North America,* 15.

Page 140: *"Don't say anymore"*: Kee, *The Bold Fenian Men,* 20.

Page 140: *O'Mahony declared:* Ibid., 21.

Page 140: *She wrote in her diary:* Quinlivan and Rose, *The Fenians in England,* 6.

Page 140: *"I fear the Moffet Mansion"*: Ryan, *The Fenian Chief,* 199.

Page 141: *"Once you hear of my arrest":* Ibid., 210.

Page 142: *"The most reliable accounts":* Thomas Sweeny Papers, New York Public Library.

Page 142: *"In making a plea":* Ryan, *The Fenian Chief,* 215.

Page 143: *"All our work is undone!":* Ibid., 216.

Page 143: *O'Mahony told them:* William D'Arcy, *The Fenian Movement in the United States* (Washington, D.C.: Catholic University of America Press, 1947), 124.

Page 143: *He wrote back to London:* Ibid., 125.

Page 143: *And the plan was hardly: New York Herald,* March 27, 1866.

Page 144: *Thoroughly professional despite:* Sweeny Papers.

Page 146: *Stephens protested that he:* Ryan, *The Fenian Chief,* 249.

Page 146: *Colonel Kelly, whose:* Ibid., 253.

Page 146: *The mayor of the English city:* Public Records Office, Richmond, England: Home Office Papers, HO 45/7799.

Page 146: *In Ireland, a memo:* Ibid.

Page 147: *"I have nothing to regret":* Kee, *The Bold Fenian Men,* 47.

CHAPTER SIX
THE LAND WAR

Page 150: *In the 1870s:* McMahon, *A Short History of Ireland,* 146.

Page 151: *But a reform in 1850:* S. J. Connolly, ed., *The Oxford Companion to Irish History* (Oxford: Oxford University Press, 1988), 206.

Page 151: *A young Irish exile:* Golway, *Irish Rebel,* 92.

Page 153: *In the late 1860s:* Kee, *The Bold Fenian Men,* 58.

Page 154: *Ireland's farmers, although impoverished:* T. W. Moody, *Davitt and the Irish Revolution* (Oxford: Clarendon Press, 1984), 565.

Page 154: *Agricultural output steadily grew:* Foster, *Modern Ireland,* 377.

Page 154: *One disappointed landowner:* Ibid.

Page 154: *The national school system:* Ibid., 385.

Page 154: *The Home Rule Party won:* Kee, *The Bold Fenian Men,* 65.

Page 155: *"Ireland," Parnell replied:* Kee, *Ireland,* 119.

Page 155: *The press and his colleagues:* Robert Kee, *The Laurel and the Ivy* (London: Hamish Hamilton, 1993), 113.

Page 155: *"I think he ought to be supported":* William O'Brien and Desmond Ryan, *Devoy's Post Bag,* vol. 1 (Dublin: Fallon, 1948), 267.

Page 157: *Several of the prisoners:* Sean O Luing, *The Catalpa Rescue* (Tralee, Ireland: Anvil Books, 1965), 57.

Page 158: *He struck one of the politicians:* Moody, *Davitt,* 186.

Page 160: *"They have done their worst:"* Ibid., 183.

Page 160: *"When I was in prison":* Ibid., 186.

Page 160: *"There was the proud resolute bearing:"* Michael Davitt, *The Fall of Feudalism in Ireland* (New York: Harper and Brothers, 1904), 110.

Page 160: *"I would not face it":* Ibid., 111.

Page 161: *In an impromptu speech: Irish World,* Oct. 26, 1878.

Page 161: *In late October 1878:* Golway, *Irish Rebel,* 109.

Page 161: *Devoy later amplified: Gaelic American,* July 14, 1906.

Page 162: *Charles Kickham, the IRB chairman:* Liz Curtis, *The Cause of Ireland* (Belfast: Beyond the Pale Publications, 1994), 92.

Page 163: *Evictions increased:* Moody, *Davitt,* 565.

Page 163: *"You must show the landlords":* Kee, *The Laurel and the Ivy,* 189.

Page 164: *Eventually, the league would have:* Golway, *Irish Rebel,* 130.

Page 165: *An acquaintance described her:* R. M. Foster, *Charles Stewart Parnell: The Man and His Family* (Sussex, England: Humanities Press, 1979), 243.

Page 165: *In private, she was true:* Ibid.

Page 167: *"But God is on the peasants' side":* Ibid., 324.

Page 167: *Michael Davitt described:* Davitt, *The Fall of Feudalism in Ireland,* 292.

Page 167: *"All through history":* Foster, *Charles Stewart Parnell,* 248.

Page 167: *She argued that the Land League:* Ibid., 247.

Page 167: *She did not suffer fools gladly:* Ibid., 104.

Page 168: *Evictions in 1880 more than doubled:* Moody, *Davitt,* 565.

Page 168: *By the closing months of 1880:* Ibid., 458.

Page 168: *Michael Davitt, who returned to Ireland:* William O'Brien, *Devoy's Post Bag,* vol. 2, 22.

Page 168: *"We might pour in thousands":* Moody, *Davitt,* 428.

Page 169: *At a huge meeting outside Limerick:* Kee, *The Laurel and the Ivy,* 277.

Page 170: *"Will we, then, stand idly by":* William O'Brien, *Devoy's Post Bag,* vol. 2, 22–24.

Page 170: *"If your patience becomes exhausted":* Moody, *Davitt,* 449.

Page 171: *"The government land bill":* William O'Brien, *Devoy's Post Bag,* vol. 2, 23.

Page 171: *The Prime Minister took the bait:* Davitt, *The Fall of Feudalism,* 333.

Page 171: *"It is a good sign that":* Kee, *The Laurel and the Ivy,* 389.

Page 172: *Parnell himself opposed the idea:* Davitt, *The Fall of Feudalism,* 340.

Page 172: *"Should this be true":* The Nation, Feb. 26, 1881.

Page 172: *More than sixteen thousand people were evicted:* Moody, *Davitt,* 565.

Page 173: *"The first principle of the Land League":* Anna Parnell, "Tale of a Great Sham," National Library of Ireland, MS 12,144.

Page 173: *For their treatment of women:* Ibid.

Page 173: *Michael Davitt later recalled:* Davitt, *The Fall of Feudalism,* 341.

Page 173: *The work of Anna Parnell:* Foster, *Charles Stewart Parnell,* 268.

Page 173: *"The Irishman has played his cards well":* Davitt, *The Fall of Feudalism,* 342.

Page 174: *He reported to Chamberlain:* William O'Shea Correspondence, National Library of Ireland, MS 5752.

Page 174: *On April 25, Captain O'Shea wrote:* Ibid.

Page 174: *"I have indeed every hope":* Kee, *The Laurel and the Ivy,* 429.

Page 175: *"I am out now":* Curtis, *The Cause of Ireland,* 112.

Page 175: *With his equally stunned colleagues:* Ibid., 111.

Page 175: *She said that Cavendish's predecessor:* Ibid., 112.

Page 176: *Agrarian crimes promptly dropped:* Moody, *Davitt,* 565.

Page 177: *"When writing to me about Irish affairs":* William O'Brien, *Devoy's Post Bag,* vol. 2, 143.

Page 178: *"We cannot see our way":* K. R. M. Short, *The Dynamite War* (Atlantic Highlands, N.J.: Humanities Press, 1979), 155.

Page 178: *Prime Minister Gladstone:* Ibid., 173.

Page 179: *The extent of the discrimination:* Curtis, *The Cause of Ireland,* 133.

Page 179: *Seeing a chance to win support:* Ibid., 129.

Page 179: *And, in a later visit:* Kee, *Ireland,* 379.

Page 180: "You would not confide": Curtis, *The Cause of Ireland,* 140.

Page 180: *He advised his supporters:* Timothy Harrington Papers, National Library of Ireland, MS 8581.

Page 180: *"I cannot allow it to be said":* Curtis, *The Cause of Ireland,* 137.

Page 180: *"Find, if you can":* Ibid., 141.

Page 181: *"Who is to be the mistress":* Kee, *The Laurel and the Ivy,* 595.

Page 182: *"I am not prepared to put":* Dr. Henry George Dixon Papers, Michael Davitt Correspondence, National Library of Ireland, MS 9697.

Page 182: *He became delirious:* Kee, *The Laurel and the Ivy,* 609.

Chapter Seven
To Sweeten Ireland's Wrong

Page 183: *"Irish homes and lives":* Maud Gonne MacBride, *A Servant of the Queen* (Buckinghamshire, England: Colin Smythe, 1994), 158.

Page 183: *"If she said the world was flat":* Margaret Ward, *Maud Gonne: A Life* (London: Pandora, 1990), 25.

Page 185: *"There are some things:"* William Butler Yeats, *The Autobiography of William Butler Yeats* (Garden City: Doubleday, 1958), 143.

Page 186: *He wrote that he "would accounted be":* R. M. Foster, *William Butler Yeats: A Life* (New York: Oxford University Press, 1997), 122.

Page 186: *"She, like myself":* Yeats, *Autobiography,* 41.

Page 186: *"She was plainly very ill":* Ibid., 47.

Page 187: *"I went home asking myself":* William Butler Yeats, *Memoirs* (London: Macmillan 1972), 221.

Page 187: *The tenants could afford housing:* W. E. Vaughn, *Landlords and Tenants in Ireland, 1848–1904* (Dublin: Economic and Social History Society of Ireland, 1984), 4.

Page 188: *The city's infant mortality rate:* Moody and Martin, *The Course of Irish History,* 301.

Page 188: *"Even homelessness is preferable":* Kevin C. Kearns, *Dublin Tenement Life: An Oral History* (Dublin: Gill and Macmillan, 1994), 12.

Page 188: *Dublin's population density:* Ibid.

Page 188: *Officials from charity organizations:* Jacinta Prunty, *Dublin Slums, 1800–1925* (Dublin: Irish Academic Press, 1999), 162.

Page 188: *One landlord told a would-be reformer:* Kearns, *Dublin Tenement Life,* 11.

Page 189: *"Wherever men have tried to imagine":* Donald T. Torchiana, *W. B. Yeats and Georgian Ireland* (Evanston, Ill.: Northwestern University Press, 1966), 5.

Page 190: *"You must never be afraid":* MacBride, *A Servant of the Queen,* 11.

Page 190: *"I had to sit through":* Ibid., 40.

Page 191: *"I want to work for Ireland":* Ibid., 19.

Page 191: *"A big black kettle":* Ibid., 98.

Page 191: *"My head was spinning":* Ward, *Maud Gonne,* 21.

Page 191: *She was, she said:* Mac Bride, *A Servant of the Queen,* 99.

Page 192: *"It was a small two-roomed":* Ibid., 113.

Page 192: *"I wish to show":* Deane, *The Field Day Anthology,* vol. 2, 527.

Page 194: *When the speech was over:* Janet Egleson Dunleavy and Gareth W. Dunleavy, *Douglas Hyde* (Los Angeles: University of California Press, 1991), 183.

Page 195: *The Gaelic League's celebration:* Ann Saddlemyer and Celia Smythe, eds., *Lady Gregory: Fifty Years After* (Gerrards Cross, England: Colin Smythe, 1987), 145.

Page 196: *She was suspicious:* Foster, *William Butler Yeats,* 169.

Page 197: *"Once in childhood":* Saddlemyer and Smythe, *Lady Gregory,* 143.

Page 197: *The two books of folklore:* Lady Augusta Gregory, *Seventy Years* (New York: Macmillan, 1976), 308.

Page 197: *She went to the local workhouse:* Ibid., 309.

Page 198: *He remembered that she:* Yeats, *Autobiography*, 113.

Page 198: *At a meeting of a centenary committee:* Foster, *William Butler Yeats*, 193.

Page 198: *Ireland's freedom, he predicted:* Ibid.

Page 198: *"Whether your kill your enemies":* Ward, *Maud Gonne*, 59.

Page 198: *"Whoever stands by the roadway":* Ibid., 61.

Page 199: *"How many of these children":* Yeats, *Memoirs*, 245.

Page 199: *Lady Gregory delighted in taking:* Lady Gregory, *Seventy Years*, 121.

Page 199: *With her translation and retelling:* Lady Augusta Gregory, *Visions and Beliefs in the West of Ireland* (Gerrards Cross, England: Colin Smythe, 1970), 11.

Page 201: *One reviewer said the performance:* Dunleavy and Dunleavy, *Douglas Hyde*, 220.

Page 201: *"Let Mr. Yeats give us a play":* Foster, *William Butler Yeats*, 249.

Page 201: *"In her, the youth of the country":* Ward, *Mand Gonne*, 74.

Page 201: *"They shall be remembered for ever":* Padraic Colum, *Arthur Griffith* (Dublin: Browne and Nolan, 1959), 69.

Page 202: *"I can still see his face":* Ibid., 70.

Page 202: *"Ireland is truly no longer":* Kee, *The Bold Fenian Men*, 152.

Page 203: *"Since the Almighty forbade us":* Sean T. O'Kelly Papers, National Library of Ireland, MS 8469.

Page 203: *"The Irish Deak":* Colum, *Arthur Griffith*, 82.

Page 204: *Hyde attended to the Gaelic League:* Kee, *The Bold Fenian Men*, 135.

Page 204: *Sinn Féin, Dillon wrote:* Ibid., 159.

Page 205: *"We must be prepared":* Bardon, *A History of Ulster*, 432.

Page 205: *A nationalist newspaper declared:* Kee, *The Bold Fenian Men*, 175.

Page 206: *Speaking at a huge outdoor rally:* Anne Marreco, *The Rebel Countess* (New York: Chilton Books, 1967), 152.

Page 206: *In siding with Irish Protestant militants:* Tim Pat Coogan, *De Valera: Long Fellow, Long Shadow* (London: Hutchinson, 1993), 46.

Page 206: *"We regard the government":* Ibid.

Page 206: *"Think of the consequences":* Sean Cronin, *Irish Nationalism* (New York: Continuum, 1981), 104.

Page 207: *Arthur Griffith, who had not done:* Kee, *The Bold Fenian Men*, 201.

Page 207: *At a time when officials reckoned:* Marreco, *The Rebel Countess*, 98.

Page 208: *"If your policy is to prevail":* Douglas Hyde Papers, National Library of Ireland, MS 18,225.

Page 208: *"The vital work to be done":* Kee, *The Bold Fenian Men*, 206.

CHAPTER EIGHT
BLOODY PROTEST FOR A GLORIOUS THING

Page 210: *"Ten years ago"*: Kee, *The Bold Fenian Men,* 207.

Page 210: *"We are reaching what seems"*: Golway, *Irish Rebel,* 192.

Page 210: *"Rebellion, murder and dynamite"*: Kee, *The Bold Fenian Men,* 174.

Page 212: *"Let them talk!"*: Ruth Dudley Edwards, *Pearse: The Triumph of Failure* (London: Faber and Faber, 1977), 155.

Page 212: *In an essay he entitled:* Ibid., 13.

Page 213: *"I challenge again the Irish psychology"*: Joseph Lee, *The Modernisation of Irish Society* (Dublin: Gill and Macmillan, 1973), 146.

Page 213: *"I care not though I were to live"*: F. S. L. Lyons, *Culture and Anarchy in Ireland* (Oxford: Oxford University Press, 1979), 87.

Page 214: *"It is worth living in Ireland"*: Sean Cronin, *The McGarrity Papers* (Tralee, Ireland, Anvil Books, 1972), 37.

Page 214: *"Harassing morning, noon and night"*: Tom Clarke, *Glimpses of an Irish Felon's Prison Life* (Dublin: Maunsel and Roberts, 1922), 7.

Page 215: *The father of the future rebel:* Louis N. Le Roux, *Tom Clarke and the Irish Freedom Movement* (Dublin: Talbot Press, 1932), 9.

Page 216: *"Now boys," she said:* Kathleen Clarke, *Revolutionary Woman* (Dublin: O'Brien Press, 1991), 51.

Page 216: *In June 1914, Padraig Pearse:* F. X. Martin, ed., *The Irish Volunteers* (Dublin: James Duffy., 1963), ix.

Page 217: *"It could not be controlled"*: Kee, *The Bold Fenian Men,* 204.

Page 217: *"I voted against surrender . . ."*: Bulmer Hobson Papers, National Library of Ireland, MS 13,162.

Page 217: *"It will be an irony of ironies"*: Ibid.

Page 218: *"The army is an object of odium"*: Ibid.

Page 218: *The foreign secretary, Sir Edward Grey:* Max Caufield, *The Easter Rebellion* (New York: Holt, Rinehart and Winston, 1963), 24.

Page 219: *"Thousands of Irishmen are prepared"*: Desmond Ryan, *The Rising* (Dublin: Golden Eagle Books, 1949), 23.

Page 220: *"I never saw anything more pathetic"*: B. L. Reid, *The Lives of Roger Casement* (New Haven: Yale University Press, 1976), 107.

Page 221: *Germany, he decided:* Ibid., 203.

Page 221: *He told Devoy that Casement:* Cronin, *The McGarrity Papers,* 53.

Page 221: *With noticeable disgust:* William Maloney Collection, Joseph McGarrity Correspondence, New York Public Library.

Page 222: *"I am home and in bed"*: O'Brien and Ryan, *Devoy's Post Bag,* vol. 2, 407.

Page 222: *"Rossa dead"*: Kathleen Clarke, *Revolutionary Woman,* 56.

Page 222: *"When are you fellows"*: Ryan, *The Rising,* 57.

Page 222: *"Make it as hot as hell"*: Le Roux, *Tom Clarke and the Irish Freedom Movement,* 168.

Page 223: *"Life springs from death"*: Edwards, *Pearse,* 236–37.

Page 223: *Some six thousand Irishmen a week:* Kee, *The Bold Fenian Men,* 239.

Page 223: *He reported back to London:* Kee, *The Bold Fenian Men,* 239.

Page 224: *"The time for Ireland's battle":* Samuel Levenson, *James Connolly* (London: Quartet Books, 1977), 280.

Page 225: *"The blow darkened my life":* Ibid., 117.

Page 225: *He described himself:* Ibid., 35.

Page 227: *"They all forget":* Ibid., 324.

Page 227: *"The man who is bubbling over":* F. X. Martin, ed., *Leaders and Men of the Easter Rising* (Ithaca, N.Y.: Cornell University Press, 1967), 126.

Page 227: *"You can see the rich men":* Hobson Papers, MS 13,152.

Page 227: *"You cannot teach a starving man Gaelic":* Austen Morgan, *James Connolly: A Political Biography* (Manchester: Manchester University Press, 1988), 31.

Page 227: *"There's no man in Ireland":* Levenson, *James Connolly,* 283.

Page 228: *"We have decided to begin":* *Documents Relative to the Sinn Féin Movement* (London: His Majesty's Stationery Office, 1921), 9.

Page 228: *"I have received an answer":* Maloney Collection, McGarrity Correspondence.

Page 228: *Casement was distraught and paranoid:* Ibid.

Page 229: *"In all due humility and awe":* Kee, *The Bold Fenian Men,* 273.

Page 229: *Pearse indicated exactly:* O Buachalla, *The Literary Writings of Patrick Pearse,* 27.

Page 232: *She also joined:* Jacqueline Van Voris, *Constance de Markievicz* (New York: Feminist Press, 1972), 33.

Page 232: *She fed workers and their families:* Ibid., 65.

Page 232: *As she prepared women:* Ibid., 66.

Page 233: *"I think I know who you are":* Reid, *The Lives of Roger Casement,* 355.

Page 233: *"Now, Pat, above all":* Edwards, *Pearse,* 273.

Page 235: *"Is it for children?":* Levenson, *James Connolly,* 294.

Page 235: *It was, she later wrote:* Van Voris, *Constance de Markievicz,* 203.

Page 237: *"We are going out":* Ibid., 188.

Page 237: *"Left turn! The GPO!":* Ryan, *The Rising,* 125.

Page 237: *"Thanks be to God, Pearse":* Ibid., 127.

Page 237: *"Tom successfully operated today":* Golway, *Irish Rebel,* 229.

Page 237: *"We've done more than Wolfe Tone already":* Van Voris, *Constance de Markievicz,* 196.

Page 238: *The government issued a directive:* 1916 Rebellion Handbook [collection of news accounts from the *Irish Times*] (Dublin: Mourne River Press, 1998), 43.

Page 238: *"The game is up":* Le Roux, *Tom Clarke and the Irish Freedom Movement,* 255.

Page 238: *"I would have followed him":* Edwards, *Pearse,* 281.

Page 238: *"When we are all wiped out":* Ibid., 296.

Page 238: *"Oh, God," he moaned:* Levenson, *James Connolly,* 314.

Page 239: *"We could hold out for days here":* Elizabeth Coxhead, *Daughters of Erin* (Gerrards Cross, England: Colin Smythe, 1979), 96.

Page 239: *As Countess Markievicz marched:* Van Voris, *Constance de Markievicz,* 196.

Page 239: *He told his party leader:* Robert Kee, *Ourselves Alone* (New York: Penguin, 1989), 1.

Page 240: *"I have just done":* Curtis, *The Cause of Ireland,* 280.

Page 240: *"I am to be shot":* Le Roux, *Tom Clarke and the Irish Freedom Movement,* 234.

Page 240: *He told Kathleen:* Kathleen Clarke, *Revolutionary Woman,* 95.

Page 241: *Of the rebels, he said:* Kee, *Ourselves Alone,* 6.

Page 241: *The Easter Rising "is the first":* Curtis, *The Cause of Ireland,* 281.

Page 241: *A prominent New York congressman: Gaelic American,* May 20, 1916.

Page 241: *In Washington, President Wilson's:* Golway, *Irish Rebel,* 236.

Page 241: *"Your life-work destroyed":* Curtis, *The Cause of Ireland,* 283.

Page 241: *"Well, Lillie, I suppose you know":* Levenson, *James Connolly,* 324.

Page 241: *"I will say a prayer":* Ibid., 326.

Page 243: *"I wonder how it will all be":* William Maloney Collection, Casement Correspondence.

CHAPTER NINE
LIBERTY

Page 244: *General John Maxwell declared:* Cronin, *The McGarrity Papers,* 121.

Page 244: *"I regard your action":* Coogan, *De Valera,* 89.

Page 245: *The flag sale, Maxwell wrote:* Kathleen Clarke, *Revolutionary Woman,* 131.

Page 247: *One of those who greeted him:* Ibid., 138.

Page 248: *"I do not think the Rising week":* Edwards, *Pearse,* 296.

Page 249: *By the summer of 1917:* Foster, *Modern Ireland,* 488.

Page 253: *"Nothing additional remains":* Tim Pat Coogan, *The Man Who Made Ireland* (Boulder, Colo.: Roberts Rinehart, 1992), 74.

Page 253: *A British newspaper complained:* Kee, *Ourselves Alone,* 35.

Page 254: *"When the young men of Ireland"*: Ibid., 44.

Page 254: *Secretary of State Robert Lansing:* Golway, *Irish Rebel,* 248.

Page 255: *"Why did they die?"*: Kee, *Ourselves Alone,* 51.

Page 256: *"We are sitting on top"*: Richard Bennett, *The Black and Tans* (London: New English Library, 1970), 5.

Page 256: *The Dáil issued a declaration of independence:* Cronin, *Irish Nationalism,* 124.

Page 257: *"That's good," she said:* Donal O'Donovan, *Kevin Barry and His Times* (Sandycove, Ireland: Glendale, 1989), 48.

Page 257: *"The chapters relating the outbreak"*: Kevin Barry Papers, University College, Dublin, P93/8.

Page 258: *"The British have tried"*: Ibid.

Page 260: *De Valera, he decided:* Daniel Cohalan Papers, American Irish Historical Society, New York.

Page 263: *The effect was transforming:* Maryanne Gialanella Valiulis, *Portrait of a Revolutionary: General Richard Mulcahy* (Blackrock, Ireland: Irish Academic Press, 1992), 4.

Page 264: *A young recruit named Ernie O'Malley:* Ibid., 30.

Page 264: *"We yearn for peace"*: Kee, *Ourselves Alone,* 91.

Page 265: *"I really believe that we shall"*: Ibid., 109.

Page 267: *And so, when a rogue IRA member:* Richard Mulcahy Papers, University College, Dublin, P7/A17.

Page 267: *When a brigade commandant in Limerick:* Ibid.

Page 267: *"This contest on our side"*: Curtis, *The Cause of Ireland,* 324.

Page 267: *When MacSwiney was brought before a court:* Bennett, *The Black and Tans,* 68.

Page 268: *In New York, the rebel government's:* Patrick McCartan, *With De Valera in America* (New York: Brentano, 1932), 199.

Page 268: *Lloyd George refused to back down:* Bennett, *The Black and Tans,* 72.

Page 268: *"I offer my pain for Ireland"*: Terence MacSwiney Papers, University College, Dublin, 48B/437.

Page 268: *"The sergeant was then asked"*: Barry Papers, MS 8043.

Page 269: *A placard was raised:* Curtis, *The Cause of Ireland,* 341.

Page 269: *"They shall be remembered forever"*: O'Donovan, *Kevin Barry and His Times,* 141.

Page 269: *"You are the mother"*: Barry Papers, P93/24.

Page 270: *A little more than a week after:* Coogan, *The Man Who Made Ireland,* 156.

Page 270: *Churchill contended that Britain:* Kee, *Ourselves Alone,* 138.

Page 274: *"What is good enough for you"*: Ibid., 155.

Page 274: *"In my opinion"*: Coogan, *The Man Who Made Ireland,* 301.

Page 274: *"All I ask is that"*: Margery Forester, *Michael Collins: The Lost Leader* (London: Sphere, 1971), 271.

Page 275: *"I'm glad to see you"*: Ulick O'Connor, *Michael Collins: The Troubles* (New York: Norton, 1975), 192.

Page 275: *He talked about wading through:* Coogan, *The Man Who Made Ireland,* 319.

Page 277: *"The only solution of the boundary"*: Gaelic American, Aug. 20, 1924.

CHAPTER TEN
THE ORANGE STATE

Page 280: *"I have always said"*: Michael Farrell, *Northern Ireland: The Orange State* (London: Pluto, 1976), 92.

Page 280: *"The fight is only beginning"*: Oliver P. Rafferty, *Catholicism in Ulster, 1603–1983* (Columbia: University of South Carolina Press, 1994), 232.

Page 280: *More than half of Northern Ireland's labor force:* Bardon, *A History of Ulster,* 517.

Page 281: *There were twenty thousand shipbuilding jobs:* John A. Murphy, *Ireland in the Twentieth Century* (Dublin: Gill and Macmillan, 1975), 158.

Page 281: *Belfast's infant mortality rate:* Bardon, *A History of Ulster,* 531.

Page 282: *In 1937, de Valera sponsored:* Paul Johnson, *Ireland,* 208.

Page 282: *Prime Minister Craig articulated:* Kee, *Ireland,* 228.

Page 283: *"The Celts have done nothing in Ireland"*: Paul Johnson, *Ireland,* 209.

Page 283: *But well-off property owners:* Bardon, *A History of Ulster,* 638.

Page 283: *"I have not one about my place"*: Roger H. Hull, *The Irish Triangle* (Princeton: Princeton University Press, 1976), 220.

Page 284: *He returned to the theme:* Ibid., 220.

Page 284: *As late as 1970:* Bardon, *A History of Ulster,* 641.

Page 284: *But the local government bodies:* Farrell, *Northern Ireland,* 87.

Page 284: *A Unionist Member of Parliament:* Ibid., 89.

Page 284: *Born in 1934:* The Observer (London), Dec. 15, 1996.

Page 284: *He went to work at age fourteen:* Belfast Telegraph, April 3, 1997.

Page 285: *"We were made conscious by politicians"*: The National (Canada) online.

Page 286: *"Everyone was told there was"*: Ibid.

Page 286: *With his limited prospects:* The Observer (London), Dec. 15, 1996.

Page 286: *The first book he read:* Ibid.

Page 286: *He devoted his time to assisting others:* John Hume, *A New Ireland* (Boulder, Colo.: Roberts Rinehart, 1997), 23.

Page 287: *"Son, don't get involved"*: Ibid., 26.

Page 289: *It ended in failure in 1962:* M. L. R. Mith, *Fighting for Ireland?* (London: Routledge, 1997), 72.

Page 289: *From an initial deposit:* Hume, *A New Ireland,* 42.

Page 290: *"Nationalists in opposition":* Barry White, *John Hume: Statesman of the Troubles* (Belfast: Blackstaff Press, 1984), 44.

Page 290: *"Excellent idea":* Bernadette Devlin, *The Price of My Soul* (New York: Vintage, 1969), 92.

Page 292: *She had only scorn:* Ibid., 71.

Page 293: *Ian Paisley held a counterdemonstration:* Bardon, *A History of Ulster,* 658.

Page 294: *Among these was John Hume:* White, *John Hume,* 85.

Page 294: *"I was elected by the oppressed":* G. W. Target, *Bernadette: The Story of Bernadette Devlin* (London: Hodder and Stoughton, 1975), 186.

Page 295: *He declared that it was:* White, *John Hume,* 85.

Page 295: *"I do not with to engage":* Ibid., 87.

Page 297: *"We cried our eyes out":* Bardon, *A History of Ulster,* 686.

Page 297: *"Don't be afraid . . .":* Michael Farrell, ed., *Twenty Years On* (Dingle, Ireland: Brandon Books, 1988), 82.

Page 297: *"That's it," he said:* White, *John Hume,* 120.

Page 297: *The Home Secretary was:* Bardon, *A History of Ulster,* 679.

Page 298: *"Murdering hypocrite!":* *The Times* (London), Feb. 1, 1972.

Page 298: *Afterward, she said her:* Target, *Bernadette,* 352.

Page 298: *A government whip who was standing:* *Daily Mail,* Feb. 1, 1972.

Page 298: *"I say it without reservation":* Bardon, *A History of Ulster,* 688.

Page 298: *"It is suggested that":* Army Reports on Events in Londonderry, Sunday, 30th January, 1972. In author's possession.

Page 298: *At a tense meeting:* Notes of a meeting held at 10 Downing Street, Friday, 4 February, 1972. In author's possession.

Page 304: *"On my knees," he said:* Ibid., 739.

Page 304: *"He knew about the problem":* Ibid., 738.

Page 305: *He issued a statement:* J. Bowyer Bell, *Irish Troubles* (New York: St. Martin's, 1993), 552.

Page 306: *The Cardinal received a letter:* Tom Collins, *The Irish Hunger Strike* (Cork: Mercier Press, 1985), 311–12.

Page 306: *When Spence spotted the Cardinal:* *The Observer* (London), Dec. 15, 1996.

Page 306: *O Fiaich met several other prisoners:* *Irish Press,* Dec. 22, 1980.

Page 307: *"We are living in the most":* Spence statement, Linen Hall Library, Political Collection, Belfast.

Page 307: *He enclosed a line wishing:* *Irish Press,* Dec. 22, 1980.

Page 307: *"Greater love hath no man that this":* White, *John Hume,* 221.

Page 308: *"I am standing on the threshold":* Bobby Sands, *Skylark Sing Your Lonely Song* (Cork: Mercier Press, 1989), 153.

Page 308: *"I am awaiting the lark"*: Ibid., 161.

Page 308: *"We fought the Germans"*: White, *John Hume,* 224.

Page 309: *She said that it was not her practice:* Bell, *Irish Troubles,* 612.

Page 309: *The* Sunday Express *referred to him:* Collins, *The Irish Hunger Strike,* 287.

CHAPTER ELEVEN
THE COMMON CAUSE OF PEACE

Page 312: *Hundreds of factories closed:* Bardon, *A History of Ulster,* 784.

Page 312: *Employment, nevertheless, continued:* Ibid., 785.

Page 314: *"That is a stark reality"*: Ibid., 753.

Page 314: *"I have made it quite clear"*: Bell, *Irish Troubles,* 698.

Page 314: *A mortified Fitzgerald:* Ibid., 690.

Page 314: *"We may yet be driven"*: Gerard Murray, *John Hume and the SDLP* (Dublin: Irish Academic Press, 1998), 140.

Page 315: *"Today we were unlucky"*: Bell, *Irish Troubles,* 687.

Page 315: *She did, telling Congress:* Jack Holland, *The American Connection* (New York: Viking, 1987), 146.

Page 315: *The* Express *headline:* Andrew Wilson, *Irish America and the Ulster Conflict* (Washington, D.C.: Catholic University of America Press, 1995), 195.

Page 316: *The British also agreed that:* Murray, *John Hume and the SDLP,* 169.

Page 316: *"Never! Never! Never!"*: Peter Taylor, *Loyalists* (New York: TV Books, 1999), 182.

Page 317: *"We had many a pipe"*: Author's interview, November, 1999.

Page 318: *Even more remarkably:* UDA pamphlet, *Common Sense.*

Page 318: *"Make sure Paul O'Dwyer sees this"*: Author's interview, January 1987.

Page 319: *He said that:* Murray, *John Hume and the SDLP,* 161.

Page 320: *"I can understand that"*: Bell, *Irish Troubles,* 731.

Page 321: *"Well, some people might"*: Gerry Adams, *Before the Dawn* (New York: William Morrow, 1996), 51.

Page 322: *Marie gripped her father's hand:* Bardon, *A History of Ulster,* 776.

Page 324: *"An Irish Republicanism"*: Peter Taylor, *Behind the Mask: The IRA and Sinn Fein* (New York: TV Books, 1997), 364.

Page 324: *Furthermore, Brooke asserted that:* Ibid., 367.

Page 324: *The president of the Methodist Church:* Irish Times, Nov. 29, 1989.

Page 324: *"Is it not strange . . ."*: Belfast Telegraph, May 15, 1990.

Page 326: *"Instead of losing 11 to 1"*: Author's interview, July 1999.

Page 328: *Hume and Adams released a statement:* Paul Bew and Gordon Gillespie, *The Northern Ireland Peace Process, 1993–1996* (London: Serif, 1996), 18.

Page 328: *Britain's Secretary for Northern Ireland:* Ibid.

Page 329: *In the House of Commons:* Ibid., 30.

Page 329: *"There are some very difficult issues":* Ibid., 32.

Page 329: *In its careful wording:* Author's interview, July 1999.

Page 329: *"For the first time":* Ibid.

Page 329: *"You have sold Ulster":* Bew and Gillespie, *The Northern Ireland Peace Process,* 35.

Page 330: *"British imperialist interest":* Ibid., 41.

Page 331: *"I gave Adams a visa":* Author's interview with Reynolds, July 1999.

Page 331: *The next day, the IRA:* Bew and Gillespie, *The Northern Ireland Peace Process,* 63.

Page 331: *Reynolds told the Irish people:* Ibid.

Page 332: *Reynolds believed they were:* Author's interview, July 1999.

Page 332: *Spence, for his part:* Author's interview, November 1999.

Page 332: *"In all sincerity":* Taylor, *Loyalists,* 223.

Page 332: *Reynolds told his colleagues:* Bew and Gillespie, *The Northern Ireland Peace Process,* 72.

Page 333: *"These agreements don't mean anything":* Wall Street Journal, May 14, 1998.

Page 334: *Reynolds spoke for all three:* Author's interview, July 1999.

Page 335: *"It's over, is it?":* Irish Echo, July 19, 1999.

BIBLIOGRAPHY

Manuscripts and Personal Papers

The National Library of Ireland, Dublin
Kevin Barry
John Devoy
Dr. Henry George Dixon (Michael Davitt Correspondence)
Arthur Griffith
Timothy Harrington (Charles Stewart Parnell Correspondence)
Bulmer Hobson
Douglas Hyde
Joseph McGarrity
Sean T. O'Kelly
William O'Shea
Padraig Pearse

University College, Dublin
Kevin Barry
Terence MacSwiney
Richard Mulcahy

Trinity College, Dublin
Fizgerald Family Correspondence
Madden Papers (McCracken Correspondence)

New York Public Library
William Maloney Collection, including the papers of Roger Casement
and Joseph McGarrity
Thomas Sweeny

American Irish Historical Society, New York
Daniel Cohalan
Friends of Irish Freedom

Catholic University of America, Washington, D.C.
Jeremiah O'Donovan Rossa

Public Documents
Ireland

National Archives, Dublin: Fenian Briefs

Great Britain

Public Records Office, Richmond: Metropolitan Police records; Home Office
correspondence

Her Majesty's Stationery Office: Documents Relative to the Sinn Féin
Movement

UNITED STATES

National Archives, Washington, D.C.: War Department, Division of Military
   Intelligence

MEMOIRS, AUTOBIOGRAPHIES, COLLECTED CORRESPONDENCE

Adams, Gerry. *Before the Dawn.* New York: William Morrow, 1996.

———. *The Politics of Irish Freedom.* Dingle, Ireland: Brandon, 1986.

Clarke, Kathleen. *Revolutionary Woman.* Dublin: O'Brien Press, 1991.

Clarke, Tom. *Glimpses of an Irish Felon's Prison Life.* Dublin: Maunsel and
   Roberts, 1922.

Collins, Michael. *The Path to Freedom.* Boulder, Colo.: Roberts Rinehart,
   1996.

Davis, Thomas. *Essays and Poems.* Dublin: M. H. Gill and Son, 1945.

Davitt, Michael. *The Fall of Feudalism in Ireland.* New York: Harper and
   Brothers, 1904.

Devlin, Bernadette. *The Price of My Soul.* New York: Vintage, 1969.

Devoy, John. *Recollections of an Irish Rebel.* Shannon, Ireland: Irish
   University Press, 1969.

Duffy, Charles Gavan. *Young Ireland.* New York: D. Appleton and
   Company, 1881.

Gregory, Lady Augusta. *Seventy Years.* New York: Macmillan, 1976.

———. *Visions and Beliefs in the West of Ireland.* Gerrards Cross, England:
   Colin Smythe, 1970.

Hume, John. *A New Ireland.* Boulder, Colo.: Roberts Rinehart, 1997.

Lalor, James Fintan. *Collected Writings.* Dublin: Talbot Press, 1918.

MacBride, Maud Gonne. *A Servant of the Queen.* Buckinghamshire,
   England: Colin Smythe, 1994.

McCartan, Patrick. *With De Valera in America.* New York: Brentano, 1932.

Mitchel, John. *Jail Journal.* Shannon, Ireland: University Press of Ireland,
   1982.

———. *The Last Conquest of Ireland . . . Perhaps.* Glasgow: Cameron,
   Ferguson, 1861.

Mitchell, George. *Making Peace.* New York: Alfred A. Knopf, 1999.

O'Brien, William, and Desmond Ryan, eds. *Devoy's Post Bag.* 2 vols.
   Dublin: Fallon, 1948, 1953.

O Buachalla, Seamus, ed. *The Literary Writings of Patrick Pearse.* Cork:
   Mercier Press, 1979.

O'Connell, Maurice, ed. *The Correspondence of Daniel O'Connell.* 8 vols.
   Dublin: Irish University Press, 1972.

O'Leary, John. *Recollections of Fenians and Fenianism.* 2 vols. London: Downey and Company, 1896.

Rosenthal, M. L., ed. *Selected Poems and Two Plays of William Butler Yeats.* New York: Macmillan, 1962.

Rossa, Jeremiah O'Donovan. *Irish Rebels in English Prisons.* Dingle, Ireland: Brandon Books, 1991.

———. *Rossa's Recollections.* New York: Mariners Harbor, 1894.

Sands, Bobby. *One Day in My Life.* Cork: Mercier Press, 1983.

———. *Skylark Sing Your Lonely Song.* Cork: Mercier Press, 1989.

Yeats, W. B. *The Autobiography of William Butler Yeats.* Garden City: Doubleday, 1958.

———. *Memoirs.* London: Macmillan, 1972.

SECONDARY SOURCES

Abels, Jules. *The Parnell Tragedy.* New York: Macmillan, 1966.

Acworth, Bernard. *Swift.* London: Eire and Spottiswoode, 1939.

Amos, Keith. *The Fenians in Australia.* Kensington, Australia: New South Wales University Press, 1988.

Bardon, Jonathan. *A History of Ulster.* Belfast: Blackstaff Press, 1992.

Bell, J. Bowyer. *The IRA.* Cambridge, Mass.: MIT Press, 1970.

———. *Irish Troubles.* New York: St. Martin's, 1993.

Bennett, Richard. *The Black and Tans.* London: New English Library, 1970.

Beresford, David. *Ten Men Dead.* New York: Atlantic Monthly Press, 1987.

Berleth, Richard. *The Twilight Lords.* New York: Barnes and Noble, 1978.

Bew, Paul. *John Redmond.* Dublin: Historical Association of Ireland, 1996.

———. *Land and the National Question in Ireland.* Atlantic Highlands, N.J.: Humanities Press, 1979.

Bew, Paul, and Gordon Gillespie. *The Northern Ireland Peace Process, 1993–1996.* London: Serif, 1996.

Bourke, Marcus. *John O'Leary.* Tralee, Ireland: Anvil Books, 1967.

Boylan, Henry. *Wolfe Tone.* Dublin: Gill and Macmillan, 1981.

Byrne, Patrick. *The Wildes of Merrion Square.* London: Staples Press, 1953.

Carroll, Denis. *The Man from God Knows Where.* Blackrock, Ireland: Gartan, 1995.

Caufield, Max. *The Easter Rebellion.* New York: Holt, Rinehart and Winston, 1963.

Cavanagh, Michael. *Memoirs of Gen. Thomas Francis Meagher.* Worcester, Mass.: Messenger Press, 1892.

Clark, Samuel, and James S. Donnelly, Jr. *Irish Peasants.* Madison: University of Wisconsin Press, 1983.

Coffey, Michael, and Terry Golway. *The Irish in America.* New York: Hyperion, 1997.

Collins, Tom. *The Irish Hunger Strike.* Cork: Mercier Press, 1985.

Colum, Padraic. *Arthur Griffith.* Dublin: Browne and Nolan, 1959.

Comerford, R. V. *Charles J. Kickham.* Dublin: Wolfhound Press, 1979.

Connolly, S. J., ed. *The Oxford Companion to Irish History.* Oxford: Oxford University Press, 1988.

Coogan, Tim Pat. *De Valera: Long Fellow, Long Shadow.* London: Hutchinson, 1993.

———. *The IRA: A History.* Boulder, Colo.: Roberts Rinehart, 1993.

———. *The Man Who Made Ireland.* Boulder, Colo.: Roberts Rinehart, 1992.

———. *On the Blanket.* Boulder, Colo.: Roberts Rinehart, 1997.

Coxhead, Elizabeth. *Daughters of Erin.* Gerrards Cross, England: Colin Smythe, 1979.

Cronin, Sean. *Irish Nationalism.* New York: Continuum, 1981.

———. *The McGarrity Papers.* Tralee, Ireland: Anvil Books, 1972.

Cullen, L. M. *Life in Ireland.* London: Batsford, 1968.

Curtis, Liz. *The Cause of Ireland.* Belfast: Beyond the Pale Publications, 1994.

D'Arcy, William. *The Fenian Movement in the United States.* Washington, D.C.: Catholic University of America Press, 1947.

Davis, Richard. *Arthur Griffith.* Dublin: Dublin Historical Association, 1976.

———. *Revolutionary Imperialist: William Smith O'Brien.* Dublin: Lilliput Press, 1998.

Deane, Seamus, ed. *The Field Day Anthology of Irish Writing.* 3 vols. Derry: Field Day Publications, 1991.

Dillon, William. *Life of John Mitchel.* 2 vols. London: Kegan Paul, Trench & Co., 1888.

Dunleavy, Janet Egleson, and Gareth W. Dunleavy. *Douglas Hyde.* Los Angeles: University of California Press, 1991.

Dwyer, T. Ryle. *Michael Collins and the Treaty.* Cork: Mercier Press, 1981.

Edwards, Ruth Dudley. *Pearse: The Triumph of Failure.* London: Faber and Faber, 1977.

Edwards, Ruth Dudley, and T. Desmond Williams. *The Great Famine.* Dublin: Browne and Nolan, 1956.

Elliott, Marianne. *Wolfe Tone: Prophet of Irish Independence.* New Haven: Yale University Press, 1989.

Ellis, Peter Berresford. *Hell or Connaught!* Belfast: Blackstaff Press, 1975.

Ellis, Steve G. *Tudor Ireland.* London: Longman, 1985.

Emmet, Thomas Addis. *Memoir of Thomas Addis and Robert Emmet.* New York: Emmet Press, 1913.

Falls, Cyril. *Elizabeth's Irish Wars.* Syracuse, N.Y.: Syracuse University Press, 1997.

Farrell, Michael. *Northern Ireland: The Orange State.* London: Pluto, 1976.

———, ed. *Twenty Years On.* Dingle, Ireland: Brandon Books, 1988.

Forester, Margery. *Michael Collins: The Lost Leader.* London: Sphere, 1971.

Foster, R. M. *Charles Stewart Parnell: The Man and His Family.* Sussex, England: Humanities Press, 1979.

———. *Modern Ireland.* New York: Viking, 1988.

———. *William Butler Yeats: A Life.* New York: Oxford University Press, 1997.

Furlong, Nicholas. *John Murphy of Boolavogue.* Dublin: Geography Publications, 1991.

Gahan, Daniel J. *Rebellion!* Dublin: O'Brien Press, 1997.

Goldberg, Gerald Y. *Jonathan Swift and Contemporary Cork.* Cork: Mercier Press, 1967.

Golway, Terry. *Irish Rebel: John Devoy and America's Fight for Ireland's Freedom.* New York: St. Martin's, 1998.

Gwynn, Denis. *Daniel O'Connell.* Cork: Cork University Press, 1947.

Gwynn, Stephen. *The Life and Friendships of Dean Swift.* New York: Henry Holt, 1933.

Harmon, Maurice, ed. *Fenians and Fenianism.* Dublin: Scepter Books, 1968.

Hayes-McCoy, G. A. *Irish Battles: A Military History of Ireland.* New York: Barnes and Noble, 1997.

Holland, Jack. *The American Connection.* New York: Viking, 1987.

———. *Too Long a Sacrifice.* Middlesex, England: Penguin, 1981.

Hull, Roger H. *The Irish Triangle.* Princeton: Princeton University Press, 1976.

Jacob, Rosamond. *The Rise of the United Irishmen.* London: George G. Harrap, 1937.

Jackson, T. A. *Ireland Her Own.* London: Cobbett Press, 1947.

Johnson, Edith Mary. *Ireland in the Eighteenth Century.* Dublin: Gill and Macmillan, 1972.

Johnson, Paul. *Ireland.* Chicago: Academy Chicago, 1984.

Kearns, Kevin C. *Dublin Tenement Life: An Oral History*. Dublin: Gill and Macmillan, 1994.

Kee, Robert. *The Bold Fenian Men*. London: Quartet Books, 1976.

———. *Ireland: A History*. London: Weidenfeld & Nicolson, 1980.

———. *The Laurel and the Ivy*. London: Hamish Hamilton, 1993.

———. *The Most Distressful Country*. London: Penguin, 1972.

———. *Ourselves Alone*. New York: Penguin, 1989.

Kelly, James. *Henry Flood*. South Bend: University of Notre Dame Press, 1998.

Keogh, Daire, and Nicholas Furlong. *The Mighty Wave*. Dublin: Four Courts Press, 1996.

———, eds. *The Women of 1978*. Dublin: Four Courts Press, 1998.

Killen, John, ed. *The Decade of the United Irishmen*. Belfast: Blackstaff Press, 1997.

Knox, Oliver. *Rebels and Informers*. New York: St. Martin's, 1997.

Lebow, Richard Ned. *White Britain and Black Ireland*. Philadelphia: Institute for the Study of Human Issues, 1976.

Lee, Joseph. *The Modernisation of Irish Society, 1848–1918*. Dublin: Gill and Macmillan, 1973.

Lefevre, G. Shaw. *Peel and O'Connell*. London: Kegan Paul, Trench & Co., 1887.

Le Roux, Louis N. *Tom Clarke and the Irish Freedom Movement*. Dublin: Talbot Press, 1932.

Levenson, Samuel. *James Connolly*. London: Quartet Books, 1977.

Lydon, James. *The Making of Modern Ireland*. London: Routledge, 1996.

Lyons, F. S. L. *Charles Stewart Parnell*. London: Fontana/Collins, 1977.

———. *Culture and Anarchy in Ireland*. Oxford: Oxford University Press, 1979.

———. *Ireland Since the Famine*. New York: Charles Scribner's Sons, 1973.

MacCurtain, Margaret. *Tudor and Stuart Ireland*. Dublin: Gill and Macmillan, 1977.

Madden, R. R. *The United Irishmen: Their Lives and Times*. 7 vols. Dublin: 1843–46.

Mahony, Robert. *Jonathan Swift: The Irish Identity*. New Haven: Yale University Press, 1995.

Marreco, Anne. *The Rebel Countess*. New York: Chilton Books, 1967.

Martin, F. X., ed. *The Irish Volunteers*. Dublin: James Duffy, 1963.

———, ed. *Leaders and Men of the Easter Rising*. Ithaca, N.Y.: Cornell University Press, 1967.

McCaffrey, Lawrence J. *The Irish Question.* Lexington: University Press of Kentucky, 1995.

McGee, James. *The Men of '48.* New York: J. A. McGee 1874.

McHugh, Roger J. *Henry Grattan.* New York: Sheed and Ward, 1937.

McHugh, Roger J., and Philip Edwards, eds. *Jonathan Swift: A Dublin Tercentenary Tribute.* Dublin: Dolmen Press, 1967.

McMahon, Sean. *A Short History of Ireland.* Cork: Mercier Press, 1996.

McNeill, Mary. *The Life and Times of Mary Ann McCracken.* Belfast: Blackstaff Press, 1960.

Mith, M. L. R. *Fighting for Ireland?* London: Routledge, 1997.

Moley, Raymond. *Daniel O'Connell: Nationalism Without Violence.* New York: Fordham University Press, 1974.

Molony, John Neylon. *A Soul Came into Ireland.* Dublin: Geography Publications, 1995.

Moody, T. W., ed. *The Fenian Movement.* Cork: Mercier Press, 1968.

Moody, T. W. *Davitt and the Irish Revolution.* Oxford: Clarendon Press, 1984.

Moody, T. W., and F. X. Martin. *The Course of Irish History.* Cork: Mercier Press, 1984.

Morgan, Austen. *James Connolly: A Political Biography.* Manchester: Manchester University Press, 1988.

Murphy, John A. *Ireland in the Twentieth Century.* Dublin: Gill and Macmillan, 1975.

Murray, Gerard. *John Hume and the SDLP.* Dublin: Irish Academic Press, 1998.

Neidhardt, W. S. *Fenianism in North America.* University Park: Pennsylvania State University Press, 1975.

Newsinger, John. *Fenianism in Mid-Victorian Britain.* London: Pluto, 1994.

O'Brien, Conor Cruise. *Parnell and His Party.* Oxford: Oxford University Press, 1957.

O'Casey, Sean. *The Story of the Irish Citizen Army.* London: Journeyman Press, 1980.

O'Clery, Conor. *Daring Diplomacy.* Boulder, Colo.: Roberts Rinehart, 1997.

O'Connor, Ulick. *Michael Collins: The Troubles.* New York: Norton, 1975.

O'Donoghue, D. J. *Life of Robert Emmet.* Dublin: James Duffy and Co., 1902.

O'Donovan, Donal. *Kevin Barry and His Times.* Sandycove, Ireland: Glendale, 1989.

O Faolain, Sean. *The Great O'Neill.* Cork: Mercier Press, 1997.

———. *King of the Beggars.* New York: Viking, 1936.

O'Flanagan, Michael. *When They Followed Henry Joy.* Dublin: Riposte, 1997.

O Luing, Sean. *The Catalpa Rescue.* Tralee, Ireland: Anvil, 1965.

O Mahony, Sean. *Frongoch: University of Revolution.* Killiney, Ireland: FDR Teoranta, 1987.

O'Neill, Thomas P., and the Earl of Longford. *Eamon de Valera.* Boston: Houghton Mifflin, 1971.

O'Sullivan, T. F. *The Young Irelanders.* Tralee, Ireland: Kerryman, 1944.

O Tuathaigh, Gearoid. *Ireland Before the Famine.* Dublin: Gill and Macmillan, 1972.

Packenham, Thomas. *The Year of Liberty.* New York: Random House, 1969.

Poirteir, Cathal, ed. *The Great Irish Famine.* Cork: Mercier Press, 1995.

Prunty, Jacinta. *Dublin Slums, 1800–1925.* Dublin: Irish Academic Press, 1999.

Quinlivan, Patrick, and Paul Rose. *The Fenians in England.* New York: Riverrun Press, 1982.

Rafferty, Oliver P. *Catholicism in Ulster, 1603–1983.* Columbia: University of South Carolina Press, 1994.

Reid, B. L. *The Lives of Roger Casement.* New Haven: Yale University Press, 1976.

Reeve, Carl, and Ann Barton Reeve. *James Connolly in the United States.* Atlantic Highlands, N.J.: Humanities Press, 1978.

Rogers, Patrick. *The Irish Volunteers and Catholic Emancipation.* London: Burns Oates and Washbourne, 1934.

Ryan, Desmond. *The Fenian Chief.* Coral Gables: University of Miami Press, 1967.

———. *The Phoenix Flame.* London: Barder, 1937.

———. *The Rising.* Dublin: Golden Eagle Books, 1949.

Saddlemyer, Ann, and Celia Smythe, eds. *Lady Gregory: Fifty Years After.* Gerrards Cross, England: Colin Smythe, 1987.

Savage, John. *'98 and '48: The Modern Revolutionary History and Literature of Ireland.* Chicago: Belford, Clarke & Co., 1882.

Short, K. R. M. *The Dynamite War.* Atlantic Highlands, N.J.: Humanities Press, 1979.

Simms, J. G. *Jacobite Ireland.* London: Routledge and Kegan Paul, 1969.

Smith, Cecil Woodham. *The Great Hunger.* New York: Old Town Books, 1989.

Stewart, A. T. Q. *The Summer Soldiers.* Belfast: Blackstaff Press, 1995.

Tansill, Charles Callan. *America and the Fight for Irish Freedom.* New York: Devin-Adair, 1957.

Target, G. W. *Bernadette: The Story of Bernadette Devlin.* London: Hodder and Stoughton, 1975.

Taylor, Peter. *Behind the Mask: The IRA and Sinn Fein.* New York: TV Books, 1997.

———. *Loyalists.* New York: TV Books, 1999.

Tillyard, Stella. *Citizen Lord.* New York: Farrar, Straus and Giroux, 1997.

Torchiana, Donald T. *W. B. Yeats and Georgian Ireland.* Evanston, Ill.: Northwestern University Press, 1966.

Valiulis, Maryanne Gialanella. *Portrait of a Revolutionary: General Richard Mulcahy.* Blackrock, Ireland: Irish Academic Press, 1992.

Van Doren, Carl, ed. *The Portable Swift.* New York: Penguin, 1948.

Van Voris, Jacqueline. *Constance de Markievicz.* New York: Feminist Press, 1972.

Vaughn, W. E. *Landlords and Tenants in Ireland, 1848–1904.* Dublin: Economic and Social History Society of Ireland, 1984.

Walsh, Micheline Kerney. *Hugh O'Neill, Prince of Ulster.* Dublin: Four Courts Press, 1996.

Ward, Margaret. *Maud Gonne: A Life.* London: Pandora, 1990.

Wauchope, Piers. *Patrick Sarsfield and the Williamite War.* Blackrock, Ireland: Irish Academic Press, 1992.

White, Barry. *John Hume: Statesman of the Troubles.* Belfast: Blackstaff Press, 1984.

Wilson, Andrew J. *Irish America and the Ulster Conflict.* Washington, D.C.: Catholic University of America Press, 1995.

Wilson, T. G. *Victorian Doctor, Being the Life of Sir William Wilde.* New York: L. B. Fischer, 1946.

Wyndham, Horace. *Speranza.* London: Boardman, 1951.

NEWSPAPERS AND PERIODICALS
IRELAND

Belfast Telegraph, Freeman's Journal, Sunday Independent, The Irish People, The Irish Press, The Irish Times, The Nation

GREAT BRITAIN

Daily Mail, The Observer, The Times

UNITED STATES

Gaelic American, Irish Echo, Irish Nation, Irish Voice, Irish World, New York Herald, New York Times, Wall Street Journal

ACKNOWLEDGMENTS

The generosity and patience of colleagues, friends, and family made this book possible, and I can't thank them enough.

Arthur Carter, publisher of the *New York Observer*, is a journalist's dream: an iconoclastic thinker who is not afraid of afflicting the comfortable. At a time when independent voices are muted, he remains fiercely committed to spirited, provocative writing. His support has been overwhelming.

Peter Kaplan, editor of the *Observer*, has managed to remain decent and kind in a business not known for either attribute. He is a treasured friend. Mary Ann Giordano, the *Observer*'s managing editor, covered for me while I was thinking about 1798 instead of 1999. My thanks to her and my *Observer* colleagues, particularly Devin Leonard, Greg Sargent, Josh Benson, Andrea Bernstein, Joe Conason, Peter Stevenson, Jim Windolf, Lauren Ramsby, Frank DiGiacomo, Nick Paumgarten, and William Berlind, who waited patiently for me to return from the mists of Irish history, and to Caroline Pam and Barry Lewis, who patiently walked me through the mysteries of technology.

The staff at the American Irish Historical Society in New York put the Society's treasures at my disposal. Thanks to Paul Ruppert, Elizabeth Toomey, William Colbert, and Chris Cahill. Claire O'Gara Grimes, Tom Connelly, Ray O'Hanlon, Jack Holland, and Eileen Murphy of the *Irish Echo* offered much-needed advice and encouragement. Thanks to Eamonn Delaney, John Kelly, Peter Quinn, and Kevin Kelly of *World of Hibernia* magazine and Niall O'Dowd of the *Irish Voice* for their encouragement.

The staffs of the National Library of Ireland, the National Museum of Ireland, the National Gallery of Ireland, Trinity College, University College Dublin, the Linen Hall Library in Belfast, the Cardinal Tomas O Fiaich Library in Armagh, Catholic University of America, the New York Public Library, the National Archives in College Park, Maryland, and the Public Record Office in Britain were gracious and generous in their help. Special thanks to Yvonne Murphy of the Linen Hall Library, Angela Carter, Denise O'Meara, Eamon Lynch, Peter Loughran, Amy Siegenthaler, and Maybeth Fenton.

Bob Bender, my editor, managed to hack a path through this manuscript's briars and brambles. Johanna Li, Bob's assistant, was patient and thorough when confronted with panic and disorganization.

Copy editor Fred Chase brought a sharp eye and a wealth of knowledge to this project. And Simon & Schuster's publicity department, particularly Aileen Boyle, was on the job early and often.

John Wright, my agent, was a guide and a muse from beginning to end. I owe him a great debt.

My wife, Eileen Duggan, is patient and loving beyond belief. She makes everything possible.